ZEN AND THE ART OF
POSTMODERN PHILOSOPHY

ZEN AND THE ART OF POSTMODERN PHILOSOPHY

*Two Paths of Liberation
from the Representational
Mode of Thinking*

Carl Olson

STATE UNIVERSITY OF NEW YORK PRESS

Published by
State University of New York Press, Albany

© 2000 State University of New York

For information, address State University of New York Press,
State University Plaza, Albany, N.Y. 12246

Production by Cathleen Collins
Marketing by Michael Campochiaro

Library of Congress Cataloging-in-Publication Data

Olson, Carl.
   Zen and the art of postmodern philosophy : two paths of liberation from the
representational mode of thinking / Carl Olson.
      p. cm.
   Includes bibliographical references and index.
   ISBN 0-7914-4653-0 (alk. paper) — ISBN 0-7914-4654-9 (pbk. : alk. paper)
      1. Zen Buddhism—Philosophy.   2. Postmodernism—Religious aspects—Zen Buddhism.
I. Title.
BQ9268.6 . O46 2000
181'.043—dc21
                                                                    99-058390

10 9 8 7 6 5 4 3 2 1

This work is dedicated to my retired colleagues, Brownie Ketcham and Jim Sheridan, and to the memory of my colleague, Jim Day. Thanks for your support and friendship over the years and for the opportunity to teach at the college on the hill.

Contents

Preface

According to the postmodern philosopher Jacques Derrida, a preface embodies within itself a falsehood because it informs a reader beforehand what is coming by functioning as a preview of the subsequent contents of the book. Derrida equates a preface to semen or a seed that is disseminated in advance of the body of the work that does not really inseminate anything, cannot be retrieved or recovered, and is spread about without any real chance to fertilize anything. It is spilled thus in vain. There is yet a presumptuous quality to the preface because it is bold enough to repeat what is to come in the body of the text. This impertinent quality of the preface is a bit absurd because it previews a book, which is nothing more than a series of repetitions, that does not actually exist. Therefore, a preface gives one a preview of a text without a firm identity due to an endless play of identity and difference with a text.

Not only does the preface suggest a lack of a fixed present identity, it indicates that the text possesses no stable origin (past) or conclusion, a future that becomes a manifest presence. This observation suggests that a preface is subject to time. The preface makes the future present by announcing in a future tense what one will be reading. Since the preface is at the mercy of time, this emphatically suggests that the preface is in a state of flux and can never become fully present. Before one can read the entire preface from beginning to end, the preface cancels itself out, although it does leave a mark of erasure. The remainder is added to the subsequent text. Therefore, a preface possesses inherent limitations for Derrida, due to its subjection to time, a position on the impermanence of the preface with which Zen Buddhists could agree in spirit with the postmodern thinker.

In a Derridean spirit, the body of this book is a comparative study of the philosophies of certain Zen Buddhist and selected postmodern thinkers in order to demonstrate that the latter is moving in the direction of the former with respect to the mutual philosophical attack against and attempt to overcome the perceived shortcomings of the representational mode of thinking that conceives of the mind like a mirror. In order to make this case, we will examine the phiiosophical positions of both sides with respect to the following: language and play; modes of thinking; skepticism and doubt; body; self and other; time and death; nihilism and metaphysics; and the conception of the end of philosophy. Although some postmodern philosophers share the attempt to overcome representational thinking with Zen philosophy, the overall outcome and general perspective of postmodern philosophy is very different than Zen. If postmodern philosophy is, for instance, a search for new paradigms, Zen philosophy undermines all past, present, and future paradigms.

No matter how unstable the nature of this preface or the body of the subsequent text proves to be, this time-bound product was made possible by the free time allowed to me by the senior administrators of Allegheny College—former President Daniel Sullivan and former Provost Andy Ford—for appointing me Holder of the National Endowment for the Humanities Chair. Some fine colleagues on the hill helped to nurture this work, as well as members of my immediate family Peggy, Holly, and Kelly. I also want to thank my student assistant, Christy Repep, for her conscientious work on the bibliography and general research.

CHAPTER 1

Signing In

L ike any author of a book who does not write under a Kierkegaardian
type of pseudonym and desires credit for his/her work for personal
or professional reasons, I have signed in by signing my name on the title
page of this book. Of course, at this point this is a book that I intend to
write. According to Jacques Derrida's theory of signature, signing is not
a conscious or intentional act. It is a continual act because an author is
constantly signing his/her name in the text, even after signing one's name
to the title page or outside of the text. If one's signature is both inside and
outside of the text, the ordinary distinction between the author and a text
is difficult to maintain. Moreover, the signature itself both remains and
disappears at the same time.[1] If we assume for the sake of argument that
Derrida is correct about the impermanent and ambiguous nature of this
activity, these features of signature make it difficult to circumscribe the
boundaries of a text.

By inscribing a signature into the body of a text, one transforms it
into a monument, which makes it a thing: "But in doing so, you also lose
the identity, the title of ownership over the text: you let it become a
moment or a part of the text, as a thing or a common noun."[2] Not only is
the author divorced from the text, but the written signature suggests the
actual nonpresence of the original signer.[3] What Derrida is implying is
that the process of signature is temporal because it leaves a mark of one's
former presence in a past moment now or a present moment that will continue to be a future now or present.

The general nature of signature, or the signature of the signature, is
related to the work of writing which designates, describes, and inscribes
itself as an act. By signing itself in the text before it ends, the activity of
writing gives another the opportunity to read by producing an event that

1

in effect announces "I am writing" or "this is writing." Derrida explains this process further: ". . . when the placement in abyss succeeds, and is thereby decomposed and produces an event, it is the other, the thing as other, that signs."[4] Derrida seems to suggests that the best that a signer can hope for is to leave some accidental or intentional marks in the text. Derrida might not be aware, however, how similar in spirit his reflections on signature are to Zen Buddhism. In order to grasp this commonality in spirit between Zen Buddhism, Derrida, and some other postmodern thinkers, it is essential to bring them into dialogue with each other. At first, it is not even necessary that they speak to each other because it is only essential for them to stand opposite each other and look into each other's eyes.

Eye to Eye

From the existential perspective of Jean-Paul Sartre, the phenomenon of the eye forms the basis for the look or gaze. The continual gaze of the other enables me to be what I am, even though the gaze of the other hides his/her eyes from me.[5] When I look at the other this does not suggest that he/she is presented to me as an object, which would involve the other's collapse of the other's being-as-a-look. Before the gaze of the other, I stand guilty, feel naked before the other's gaze, and experience my alienation. Likewise, I experience guilt when I gaze at the other, "because by the very fact of my own self-assertion I constitute him as an object and as an instrument, and I cause him to experience that same alienation which he must now assume."[6] In his book on the French playwright Jean Genet, Sartre argues that it is the gaze of the other that transforms him into a thief when Genet is observed stealing, and the same gaze forces him into assuming the character of a homosexual.[7] Other French writers have taken Sartre's insights in a different direction.

The influential psychologist Jacques Lacan disagrees with Sartre about the nature of the gaze, which for the former possesses an inside-out structure and not the character of surprise of Sartre's conception. Lacan also disagrees with Sartre's assertions that one does not see the eye when under the gaze of the other, and when I see the eye of the other the gaze disappears, which motivates Lacan to conclude that Sartre did not complete a proper phenomenological analysis. In contrast to Sartre, Lacan states, "It is not true that, when I am under the gaze, when I solicit a gaze, when I obtain it, I do not see it as a gaze."[8] Moreover, the gaze can see itself, although the gaze that one encounters is "not a seen gaze, but a gaze imagined by me in the field of the Other."[9] Thus the gaze is connected to the presence of others, whose gaze reveals the cause of one's desire that is identified with the *objet petita*. By examining the nature of the gaze, Lacan wants to demonstrate the intersubjective nature of desire. What happens in the case of peering through the keyhole of a door like the example provided by Sartre in his work or in voyeurism?

In an example like voyeurism, the individual is not present in the sense of seeing, but is present as a pervert. Lacan identifies the object with the gaze itself or the gaze that is the subject, the completely hidden gaze. In contrast to Sartre, Lacan explains, "The gaze is this object lost and suddenly refound in the conflagration of shame, by the introduction of the other."[10] Lacan exposes here the conflict between the gaze as an object and the actual gaze of the other. Moreover, Lacan testifies to the split between the eye itself and the gaze, its object of desire. With the intention of providing an answer, Lacan raises the following rhetorical question: What is the subject trying to see? And he answers: "What he is trying to see, make no mistake, is the object as absence. What the voyeur is looking for and finds is merely a shadow, a shadow behind the curtain."[11] With the commencement of the gaze, the individual continually attempts to adapt oneself to it, a point of disappearing being. In the final analysis, the gaze is unapprehensible for Lacan within all the possible objects in the sphere of desire.

The postmodern figure Georges Bataille, a novelist, literary critic, philosopher, and religious theorist, conceives of the eye as an erotic entity. The interrelated motifs of human and animal eyes plays a central role in his novel entitled *Story of the Eye*. In the erotic climax of the story, the major female protagonist sits in the stands surrounding a bullfighting rink playing with the gonads of a bull that she inserts into her vagina, an act that distracts the observing bullfighter who is thereby gouged in his own eye by the horn of the charging bull. Bataille erotically connects in this novel the gazing eye with the gonads, anatomical items of the same shape, which can both enable one to see erotic events or blind one, give life or death. Bataille also connects gazing and sexuality with violence in a holy alliance in this work and in other texts.

From a different perspective, Michel Foucault discusses both directly and indirectly in his study of punishment how the gaze objectifies and controls those incarcerated in a penal institution. The best example of this type of control is the architectural design of the Panopticon sketched by Jeremy Bentham, a Utilitarian philosopher. The central tower of the structure, an example of the microphysics of power that is integrated into the macrophysics of a web of power, is surrounded by prison cells. The circular structure gives the guards an opportunity to see the prisoners without themselves being seen in return. The incarcerated person, a visible object, stands metaphorically naked before the prying eyes of the guards, invisible powers, who insure an automatic exercise of power.[12] Those in control can thus objectify and monitor the criminals, but those incarcerated do not have the opportunity to do the same to the guards because they do not know when they are being observed. Since there is no mutual gazing encounter, the person incarcerated is broken down analytically, penetrated, monologically isolated, and controlled by observers. From Foucault's perspective, the eyes can become instruments of power if they are used in the proper context. Moreover, the medical gaze of the clinic establishes the individual.[13] The privileged place of the gaze is also evident in Foucault's study of madness in which such a person is declared to be blind (a metaphor for madness), or if cured to see the daylight, a dazzling light similar to that shared by the person of reason. But the madman sees this brilliant light as void or as nothing.[14]

In contrast to Foucault, Derrida understands that the eyes possess a more ambiguous character because when one catches the gaze of the other one sees the other see as well as no longer simply seen. When the eyes of the other become visible, "one no longer sees them see, one no longer sees them seeing."[15] Within the context of discussing drawings of blind people, Derrida claims that the staring eye resembles an eye of a blind person because it sees itself disappear as it is gazing upon itself. The gazing eye sees the seeing, but it does not see what is visible. Since it sees nothing, the seeing eye perceives itself as blind. Moreover, the blind person does not see oneself exposed to the look of the other, which suggests that the blind person possesses no shame. Derrida also draws an analogy between the eye and sex due to his conviction that the blind person is a figure of castration: "More naked than others, a blindman virtually becomes his own sex, he becomes indistinguishable, from it because he does not see it, and not seeing himself exposed to the other's gaze, it is as if he had lost even his sense of modesty."[16] Derrida takes the gaze of the artist into consideration in his discussion.

From Derrida's perspective, the artist's gaze leads to ruin. Why is this the case? When the artist attempts to draw a self-portrait of himself the image can maintain its appearance for only an instant, the briefly created image becomes a memory. The act of recalling the image or memory is the actual action of drawing. Derrida is affirming that the artist cannot recapture the presence of the original gaze. The time factor of the face—what Derrida calls the ruin of the face—does not indicate aging or the passage of time. This is why he can write: "In the beginning there is ruin. Ruin is that which happens to the image from the moment of the first gaze. Ruin is the self-portrait, this face looked at in the face as the memory of itself, what *remains* or *returns* as a specter from the moment one first looks at oneself and a figuration is eclipsed."[17] Ruin enables one to see, but it does not show you anything. Derrida suggests that the self-portrait is a mere trait that is incomplete and eclipses itself. Does this discussion of the eye and gaze in Derrida's works imply that the eye is without any essence?

Derrida is opposed generally to the notion that something possesses an essence because it smacks of a metaphysical stance. Although it cannot be stated with absolute certainty that the human eyes possess an essence, it is perhaps possible to suggest that their essence is represented by tears, which both obstruct sight and unveil vision. Tears contain an ability to reveal "nothing less than *alētheia*, the *truth* of the eyes, whose ultimate destination they would thereby reveal: to have imploration rather than vision in sight, to address prayer, love, joy, or sadness rather than a look or gaze."[18] Derrida thinks that the sheading of tears goes beyond seeing and knowing.

If we take the views of these various postmodern thinkers and place them eye to eye with some Zen Buddhist thinkers, we will find some remarkable differences and some interesting similarities. The importance of visual metaphors in Zen Buddhist writings cannot be understated. According to the Zen philosopher Dōgen, our eyes are connected with the origin of the divine light within us.[19] The ability to truly see, according to Dōgen, is essential for success: "If we do not see ourselves we are not capable of seeing others—both of these are insufficient. If we cannot see others we cannot see ourselves."[20] Many centuries after the death of Dōgen, Hakuin stresses again the importance of the eye and gaining the ability to genuinely see: "But if you do not have the eye to see into your own nature, you will not have the slightest chance of being responsive to the teaching."[21] The type of seeing with which these two Zen masters are concerned is an intuitive perception and not a subject/object kind of perceptual process. They are also not concerned with the eye as a physical object. Dōgen is, for instance, convinced that there is a unity between the eye, mind, entire body, and enlightenment.[22] If Dōgen is not concerned with the physical eye, what does it mean to properly see?

In order to see things correctly, one must see things as they are by combining the phenomena of seer and seen. Dōgen wants us to accept things as they are and not to let our prejudices or prejudgments influence the way in which we actually see things. We must stop assuming that objects are external to our mind because they are rather the mind itself.[23] The eye and/or vision that Dōgen is discussing is both primordial and directly connected with the body: "'Right vision' is within the enlightened vision of our entire body. That is why we must possess the eye which existed before our body was born. This vision sees all things as they are in their true form—the actualization of enlightenment. We share that vision with the Buddhas and Patriarchs."[24] This primordial eye and its insightful vision forms a unity with the body. Thus Dōgen is not referring to ordinary seeing which is something exercised by a subject upon an object, but he is more concerned with what he calls the Buddha-eye.

What Dōgen means by the Buddha-eye is illustrated by an often repeated apocryphal story about the origin of Zen Buddhism in which the historical Buddha preached before a large gathering on Vulture Peak without speaking a word; he simply held up a flower and winked to which the monk named Mahākāśyapa responded with a smile and accepted from the Buddha the direct transmission of the enlightened being's teachings, a practice that was imitated by all the Ch'an or Zen Patriarchs throughout the ages. Without getting into his entire interpretation, we will focus on Dōgen's comments about the eye. By holding up the flower for all those assembled to see, the Buddha both conceals and reveals himself in the flower, an act that involves more than using the fingers because it involves the vision and mind of the Buddha. By means of this vision, one can understand that: "Mountains, rivers, heaven and earth; the sun, moon and earth; rain and wind; human beings and animals; trees and grasses— all these are nothing but the holding up of an udumbara flower."[25] When the Buddha winks in the narrative all human beings lose their ordinary vision and their Buddha-eye opens. And when the Buddha raises the flower for all to see it, everyone is performing the exact same action unceasingly from a primordial past with their entire bodies. Moreover, concealed within the flower itself is the Buddha-eye.

When our Buddha-eye opens we reflect the eye of the Buddha in our own eye because we now have the "Buddha's vision and original face."[26]

We can now see the Buddha (*kembutsu*) face to face, which enables us to see the unlimited nature of the Buddha and to observe the "sun-faced and moon-faced Buddha."[27] When this occurs the entire world and all its inhabitants and all moments of time are nothing but the practice of seeing Buddha. In other words, to truly see the Buddha we must open our own Buddha eye, which suggests that we see the Buddha by means of the very eye of the Buddha—Buddha eye seeing Buddha eye. This type of seeing is the actualization of the eye of the Buddha, and to attempt to conceal this actualization is impossible because it will eventually emerge by itself.[28] The type of seeing connected with the eye of the Buddha is a not-seeing, which involves a seeing without a subject and without an object that is seen. It is thus nondual seeing because it is both subjectless and objectless.

A similar point about not-seeing is made by Nishitani, a modern Buddhist philosopher associated with the Kyoto school, who thinks that the eye is a physical sense organ when it sees things, but when the eye is grounded in itself, it manifests the nature of not-seeing. He elaborates, "The eye is an eye through that essential not-seeing; and because of that essential not-seeing, seeing is possible."[29] Moreover, it is the unity of seeing and not-seeing that forms the true nature of the eye and gives it a nonobjective mode of being.

This seeing that is a nondual not-seeing is not limited to perception because Dōgen is certain that we can hear sound through our eyes. This means that it is possible to hear the teachings of the Buddha through the eyes, even though this might initially seem absurd. Dōgen pushes his point to the limit: "Further, we can hear the sound throughout our body in every part of our body."[30] A Japanese scholar makes clear that Dōgen is not confused about the different functions of the various sense faculties nor is he espousing some kind of Zen nonsense. This scholar refers to Dōgen's position as a synesthesia, a process that possesses two major implications. The five sense faculties are devoid of fixed and determined functions because they can be modified or interchanged, and the second implication is that it represents the development of a totally new sensory circuit based on the harmonization of the five sense faculties.[31] The radical nature of Dōgen's position distinguishes him from the postmodern thinkers previously considered.

Lacan's gaze, the erotic eye of Bataille, Foucault's gaze that objectifies and controls, and Derrida's ambiguous eyes are all different than the understanding of the eye offered by Dōgen and Nishitani because they are dualistic conceptions. Although this is the major difference between the Zen thinkers and the postmodernists, they do share some common features. Derrida agrees with the Zen thinkers, for instance, that not-seeing makes possible the seeing to be seeing, even though the Zen thinkers attribute this to emptiness and a postmodernist like Derrida discovers not-seeing through a process of deconstruction. Nishitani clarifies what he means by seeing as emptiness: "Emptiness here means that the eye does not see the eye, that seeing is seeing because it is not-seeing."[32] Derrida and Nishitani also agree, although for different reasons, that blindness is simultaneously present in seeing. Nonetheless, perception is connected in western thought with a representational mode of thinking. It is this mode of thinking from which many postmodernists are attempting to free themselves as they attempt to find new paradigms that bare some resemblance to the nonrepresentational mode of thinking of Zen Buddhism, although in the final analysis it is not the same as the Zen way of thinking. This fundamental difference is evident when perceiving a work of art.

A Work of Art

According to Lacan, a picture is a trap for the gaze.[33] This interesting remark gives us reason to pause in order to consider a work of art and its relation to the eye. Due to his profound influence on many postmodern thinkers and the importance that he accorded to art, the thoughts of Nietzsche on the subject also give us reason to consider art. Nietzsche thought that art represented the highest value in contradistinction to knowledge and truth. Since art is closer to life and more akin to what is actual, it is more valuable than truth. Nietzsche was convinced that art possessed the power to transform and transfigure life into higher, as yet unexperienced, possibilities. By considering the nature of a work of art, we will be further able to view some of the differences and commonalities between Zen thinkers and postmodernists.

In his work entitled *Holzwege*, Martin Heidegger devotes an essay to the origin of a work of art. Not only is the artist the origin of a work of art, but the work itself is the origin of the artist.[34] Heidegger wants to get beyond the ordinary view of the origin of a work of art and to call attention to the work of art itself that establishes equally as well the origin of the artist as artist. A work of art possesses a thingly character that can take the form of stone in an architectural work, wood with a carving, color with a painting, and sound with a musical composition. Due to the fact that it can also be a stone, a piece of wood, color or whatever, the work of art is a thing, which does not simply mean that it is an aggregate of traits or a collection of properties, because its thingness is its matter, forming a basis and sphere for the actions of the artist. The arrangement of the matter is determined by its form, although this does not imply that matter and form are the primary determinations of the thingness of a thing.[35]

In order to illustrate his argument, Heidegger examines Van Gogh's painting of a pair of peasant shoes, which simultaneously discloses truth and being. Van Gogh's painting does not simply reproduce a pair of peasant shoes that are present; it rather reproduces the general essence of a thing. The painting of the peasant shoes establishes a world in a nonobjective sense to which we are subject. This painting is also an occurrence of truth, which is creatively preserved by art in the work itself.[36] If the painting of the peasant's shoes involves an occurrence of truth, this must be grasped as truth putting itself into the painting. Thus, art is a way, although not the only path, on which truth can happen.

Instead of the occurrence of truth and the manifestation of being, Lacan and Jean-François Lyotard find alienation of the observer from a work of art, a frustrated wish-fulfillment, a set of traces, and lack of signification by a work of art. By identifying with the object of one's gaze for Lacan, the subject alienates oneself from oneself. A painting is not, for instance, a mere representation of objects perceived in life because it can transform subjects and force them to give up the gaze and that aspect of the ego formed by the gaze.[37] For Lyotard, the goal of art, a set of traces, is to expose the unfulfilled wish.[38] Lyotard analyzes the statement "This is art," and concludes that it is a cognitively inconsistent sentence because to determine an object one must already possess its rule of signification. Without the rule, we cannot possess the object because we are not in "a position to signify or name it."[39]

Similar to Heidegger and Lyotard and their focus on the origin or nature of art, Derrida considers the origin of drawing, which implies the thought of drawing in the form of a memory of a trait. The trait is not invisible and not something sensible.[40] The trait is a tracing, an imperceptible outline. Since a trace represents a limit for Derrida, when we think about drawing it takes us to the limit. Derrida explains further, "This limit is never presently reached, but drawing always signals toward this inaccessibility, toward the threshold where only the surroundings of the *trait* appear—that which the *trait* spaces by delimiting and which thus does not belong to the *trait*. *Nothing belongs to the trait*, and thus, to drawing and to the thought of drawing, not even its own 'trace.'"[41] Drawing, as tracing, separates one thing from another and divides itself by starting from itself and leaving itself, and it also retraces the nonideal borderlines or the unintelligible limits.

Within the context of postmodern art, Mark C. Taylor identifies, for instance, two processes at work: disfiguring and cleaving. These two operations are identified by Taylor in his attempt to grasp the *chora*, a nonexistent that stands behind being and becoming, makes possible all existence, and forms the essential space where both form and copy are inscribed. The operation of disfiguring is connected to activities like marring, destroying, deforming and defacing in a process of negation or deprivation that also includes the negation of the notions of calculating, considering, and comprehending. By enacting denegation in the realm of form, the process of disfiguring interweaves revelation and concealment and presence and absence which allows for "both a re-presentation and a de-presentation."[42] If the artist removes, deforms, or defaces a figure and destroys its beauty, he/she leaves a trace of something that is other, which itself is neither being nor nonbeing, present nor absent, immanent nor transcendent.[43] Associated with the notion of disfiguring is that of cleaving, which suggests both dividing and joining as well as separating and uniting. Cleaving is an operation that allows opposites to emerge and remain suspended in a process that is unthinkable and beyond the distinction of identity and difference.[44] The dual processes of disfiguring and cleaving are indicative that there can be nothing original from the postmodern perspective because such operations render everything secondary due to the tendency of the postmodern artist to disjoin, fragment, distort, and partially destroy a work of art in order to figure what cannot be figured.

In contrast to a postmodern deconstruction of drawing or consideration of the nature of art in the postmodern era, Dōgen quotes a saying by the Ch'an Master Hsing-yen (Japanese: Kyōgen Shikan): "'A painting of a rice cake cannot satisfy hunger.'" Many different kinds of people have diligently studied this saying without arriving at an useful understanding of its meaning. Like a similar saying, it is a mere clever expression and possesses no viable relationship to our real experience. To this puzzling statement, Dōgen offers his own interpretation: "The painting of a rice cake can be said to be everything: [Buddhas, sentient beings, illusion, enlightenment]. A rice cake, made from glutinous rice, represents both transitory and unchanging life. The painting of a rice cake actually symbolizes detachment, and we should not think about coming or going, permanence or impermanence when we look at it."[45] Dōgen offers an nondual interpretation of the saying; he denies the common view that a painting is unreal while the rice cake is real. The painting of the rice cake is not different from the various forms of existence. In other words, an actual rice cake is not different from a painting of a rice cake. Dōgen warns: "Do not try to find a real rice cake outside of the painting, if you do not know what the painting signifies."[46] From Dōgen's perspective, the painting may or may not appear in its true form: "The true meaning of a painting of a rice cake transcends the distinction of past and present, or birth and destruction."[47]

Dōgen further develops his interpretation of the painting of the rice cake by discussing unsatisfied hunger, which symbolizes the illusion of sentient beings for Dōgen. Hunger is used as a metaphor and/or symbol by Dōgen to illustrate the condition of illusion. By becoming detached from the opposites of enlightenment and illusion, a person loses his/her hunger. Dōgen indicates the nondualism of his position in the following way: "In reality there is no hunger of rice cake conflicting with each other, but when you think you are hungry the entire world becomes hungry; conversely, if there is a real rice cake it exists everywhere."[48] From this viewpoint, since an eatable rice cake and a pictorial representation of a consumable rice cake are both empty, either one can satisfy a person's hunger, and are examples of ultimate reality in diverse forms. Moreover, an insightful observer of a painting can see, for instance, both movement and inertia, the way of practice, truth of the Buddha's teaching and of the painting itself, the entire universe is manifested in the painting, and one can find one's true self in the painting. Therefore, viewing a painting possesses the potential to lead one to an awakening, which functions to actualize the painting.[49] Thus a painting, from Dōgen's perspective, can satisfy one's hunger.

In comparison to Taylor's notions of disfiguring and cleaving and his emphasis on the surface of a work of art, Dōgen grasps a depth and mysteriousness (*yūgen*) to a work of art, whereas Taylor seems content with initiating a nonstop dialectic that gives birth to a double negation, a negation of negation. Dōgen and Taylor agree that we exist in a world of flux, although Taylor disagrees with Dōgen that we can catch a glimpse of the eternal in the world of flux. Rather than disfiguring or cleaving a work of art, Dōgen lets it be itself and does not seek to mark or spoil it in any way.

Both thinkers agree, however, that art can express loneliness and sadness, and they tend to agree about the centrality of intuition and its epistemic role. With his emphasis on disfiguring and the splits or cracks that it can initiate, Taylor's postmodern perspective shares a stress on the gap or opening, the space or time between one thing and another. Much like the *chora* stressed by Taylor, Zen artistic theory recognizes the prominence of *ma*, the ground of all existence. It is *ma*, an interval between two or more spatial or temporal things, that makes possible the coexistence of opposites, stands behind, and unites such opposites as being and nonbeing.

Zen Buddhism and Postmodernism

According to D. T. Suzuki, a modern Zen Buddhist apologist and introducer of Zen to a western audience, the nature of Zen is unique within the context of world philosophy. Suzuki identifies several characteristics of Zen that are reflections of its uniqueness; he claims that it is irrational and inconceivable, it emphasizes direct pointing to the essence of human beings, it is the art of seeing into one's own being, it points the way from bondage to freedom, it is nonintellectual and mistrusts reason and words, it stresses what is natural, common and concrete, it is iconoclastic, it is playful and comic, it assumes a nonintentional approach to life, and it rejects conceptual categories.[50] Rather than viewing Zen from an historical perspective like the Zen scholar Hu Shih,[51] Suzuki stresses the nature of its pure experience or *satori* (enlightenment). In fact, there is no Zen without *satori* in the opinion of Suzuki.[52] This is confirmed in his own words: "Satori is thus the whole of Zen. Zen starts with it and ends with it."[53] Suzuki uses this experience, which he identifies as irrational, inexplicable, and incommunicable, as a critique to characterize Zen as a whole or to indicate its essence. Within the confines of a reverse Orientalism directed at the West and founded on dual, strong sectarian and nativistic positions, Suzuki thinks that Zen Buddhism represents the religious and philosophical culmination of all thought: "As I conceive it, Zen is the ultimate fact of all philosophy and religion. Every intellectual effort must culminate in it, or rather must start from it, if it is to bear any practical fruits."[54] Although it has taken some time, Zen Buddhist scholars are now challenging Suzuki's interpretation of the nature of Zen and its tradition.

Suzuki's attempt to demonstrate both the continuity and homogeneity of the Zen Buddhist tradition is considered by Faure to be misleading because it gives a slanted view of the actual tradition in which diverse religious and philosophical trends appear and disappear under different sectarian affiliations. Unlike Suzuki, Faure denies any identifiable essence of Zen.[55] Faure also accuses Suzuki of an excessive, secondary Orientalism that "offers an idealized, 'nativist' image of a Japanese culture deeply influenced by Zen."[56] Faure also claims that Suzuki is a biased sectarian who misconstrued the Sōtō position and favored certain periods of Japanese history that represented a more pure and virile teaching.[57] Suzuki's hidden agenda is to prove in a comparative way the mystical superiority of Zen to Christianity.[58] Faure also criticizes Suzuki for perpetuating a misunderstanding of unconsciousness in the tradition by means of his psychological interpretation of *satori*, for his reliance on categories of nineteenth-century Orientalism, for his denial of historical continuity between Indian religious traditions and Zen, for his teleological fallacy that makes the early Ch'an tradition culminate with modern Japanese Zen, and for his emphasis on the *Lankāvatāra Sūtra* as an original text.[59] Along similar lines, Hseuh-li Cheng criticizes Suzuki for his failure to recognize that *dhyana* (meditation) and *prajna* (wisdom) are interrelated and cannot be separated.[60] Moreover, Suzuki did not understand that the change from northern to southern forms of Ch'an represents a shift from *kuan-ching* (keeping an eye on purity) to *chien-hsing* (looking into the nature), and he did not grasp that they are not incompatible.[61] By means of his writings and promoting of the superior nature of the Rinzai school, Suzuki carries on a sectarian polemic against the Sōtō school. Even though not all the characteristics of Zen identified by Suzuki are entirely accurate, he does capture some of its spirit that connects it in some ways to the spirit of postmodern philosophy.

Postmodernism is difficult to define precisely because there are several opinions about its nature offered by different writers. This opinion is supported by a philosopher on the same subject: "It appears to be more like an assemblage of attitudes and discursive practices."[62] I would disagree, however, with McGowan's connection of postmodernism with romantic dreams of transformation and his claim that it is a romantic vision of a unified world that is experienced as a frightful reality.[63] In the final volume of his study of Nietzsche, Heidegger anticipates the term postmodernism: "Western history has now begun to enter into the completion of that period we call the *modern*, and which is defined by the fact that man becomes the measure and the center of beings."[64] The vision of the end of metaphysics by Heidegger in his latter works serves as a philosophical inspiration for postmodern thinkers, as well as the Dionysian vision of Nietzsche with its call for frivolity, artistic creativity, and playfulness. Some writers trace the term postmodernism to changes in architectural design or history.

Mark C. Taylor gives postmodernism a historical grounding: "Modernity ended and postmodernity began in Hiroshima on 6 August 1945."[65] A closely related spirit is expressed by Jameson who describes postmodernism as the disappearance of the past, which includes the sense of historicity and collective memory.[66] Jameson perceives something ironical in this contemporary form of forgetfulness because the concept of the postmodern is an attempt "to think the present historically in an age that has forgotten how to think historically in the first place."[67] In contrast to historical consciousness of Taylor and Jameson, Lyotard thinks that we are confronted with a crisis of narratives, the quintessential form of knowledge. From Lyotard's perspective, knowledge became altered in the postindustrial age into a commodity to be produced and sold like any other product of industrial production, a process that causes knowledge to loose its utility and value.[68] It is necessary for us to become more sensitive to the heterogeneous character of the rules of language games and to improve our ability to tolerate their incommensurability.[69]

Lyotard does not use the term postmodern to characterize a period of cultural history because the term would exclude consideration of the present moment and any grasp of chronological succession.[70] Lyotard thinks that the term postmodern is always implied in the term modern "because of the fact that modernity, modern temporality, comprises in itself an impulse to exceed itself into a state other than itself."[71] Temporal succession does not then play a major role in the meaning of the term postmodern. The "post" of postmodernity suggests more a matter of tone, style, experimentation, and multiplicity. Beardsworth offers us a lucid statement on this matter:

> The 'post' of 'postmodernity' is not only neither a socio-historical category nor a fanciful, 'post-structuralist' play on the 'signifier'; it is also not a concept which can be thought of in terms of linear time. In this sense it is probably not a *concept* at all, subsuming under itself the unity and stability of a referent (a 'postmodern' case). Rather, the term should be seen as itself an *experiment* which is trying to witness reflectively the difficulty of 'presenting' *events*.[72]

If Lyotard's work and that of other postmodern thinkers represents a series of experiments, postmodernism should not be viewed as a radical departure from modernism. In fact, an interpreter of Lyotard's work views it as not representing a radical break with modernity, but "instead a dialectical intensification of its democratic impulses."[73] This same author sees Lyotard's work as responding to a need for renewal and further development of the modern democratic tradition.

An example of an experiment by Lyotard is his notion of rewriting, which represents a new beginning that is exempt from any prejudice. The second sense of rewriting reflects Freud's term *Durcharbeitung* (working through), which suggests working with a hidden thought obscured by past prejudice and future dimensions.[74] Within Lyotard's philosophical context, postmodernity can be grasped as not a new epoch but rather a rewriting of aspects of modernity. This process of rewriting is writing again and making modernity itself real: "Modernity is written, inscribes itself on itself, in a perpetual rewriting."[75] This rewriting does not result in knowledge of the past because it is more concerned with the anamnesis of the thing. This type of experiment de-emphasizes the importance of grand theories. This type of thinking experiment results in a "postmodern epoch devoid of all truth-claims, all standards of valid argumentation or efforts to separate a notional 'real' from the various forms of superinduced fantasy or mass-media simulation."[76]

If one takes a more economic view of the phenomenon of postmodernism, it represents a cultural reification, which represents an effacement of the traces of production, an objective commodity that is produced. Evolving from a protracted period of ossification, postmodernism represents a renewal of production.[77] For the consumer, this means freedom from the guilt associated with the exploitative aspects of the process of production because the consumer is able to forget the laborious work that is expended in order to produce his/her product. An important consequence of this forgetfulness is that it "generates a radical separation between consumers and producers."[78]

From a more philosophical perspective, postmodernism is a reaction against the philosophy of the Enlightenment and its values like tolerance, individual freedom, reasonableness, and confidence in the inevitable nature of progress due to scientific discoveries and rationality, which served as the criterion of measurement for progress and as a reliable guide in a universe that could be gradually understood. The vision of the Enlightenment period was that of human beings capable of learning the

secrets of nature and the laws that governed the physical world and gaining control over nature in order to improve human life. At an elevated
position in the center of the world stood the rational, self-determined,
autonomous, human being, reflecting an epistemological optimism and
anthropocentrism that is anathema to many postmodernists.

Within the context of postmodern thought, the self disappears to the
margin of the world instead of occupying its center. Although there was a
skeptical spirit in Enlightenment philosophy especially with respect to
metaphysics, postmodernists develop this trend even further by stressing
that meaning and knowledge are uncertain and that one cannot rely on
texts for certainty. For a postmodern thinker like Foucault, knowledge
becomes an act of power. Since there is no longer any truth or certainty
that can be established by a correspondence between the human mind and
objective reality, and since it is impossible to gain any vantage point outside of the world in order to conceive of a unified worldview, not only is
an all-encompassing worldview untenable, but Rorty claims that we
should give up the search for truth and be satisfied with interpretation.

In contrast to the static world envisioned by Kant and Descartes,
postmodernists emphasize becoming, contingency, and chance. Some of
the consequences of such a position are elucidated by Gilles Deleuze:
"To become is never to imitate, nor to 'do like,' nor to conform to a
model, whether it's of justice or of truth. There is no terminus from
which you set out, none which you arrive at or which you ought to
arrive at."[79] Within the world of flux, there are no universal and timeless
truths to be discovered because everything is relative and indeterminate,
which suggests that our knowledge is always incomplete, fragmented,
and historically and culturally conditioned. Therefore, there can be no
foundation for philosophy or any theory, and it is wise to be suspicious
of any universal claims to validity made by reason. Moreover, there is
no center of society, culture, or history. There is instead an emphasis on
pluralism that is, for instance, expressed by artists by deliberately
juxtaposing different styles for diverse sources in the way that the
bricolage reconfigures different objects or images. The use of irony
exemplifies a preference for aesthetic categories and a different style of
writing that Julia Kristeva thinks is an attempt to expand the signifiable,
human realm to the very limit of experience.[80] Instead of irony, a writer
can use humor, an art of pure events, for instance, to undermine "games
of principles or causes in favor of the event and games of individuation
or subjectivation in favor of multiplicities."[81] Another scholar recog-

nizes the shift in sensibility, practices, and discourse formations that represents a transformation in Western culture.[82]

The postmodern era is characterized by discontinuity, irregularity, rupture, decenteredness, and lack of hope for any type of utopia. With respect to utopian nostalgias, Taylor states, "In theological terms, this means that we must let go of the dream of salvation."[83] There is no trans-historical value for many postmodernists because of the death of God, an example of the postmodern iconoclastic spirit. Nonetheless, a person can be a revolutionary because anyone who can write can play such a role. But writing involves a wandering, erring, marginal lifestyle in which one experiments with words and thoughts. Deleuze advocates, for instance, becoming a nomadic thinker with neither past nor future.[84] Where does this wandering, nomadic, erring type of journey lead? According to an acknowledged postmodernist thinker, the future destiny of modernity is decadence, which anticipates an unpredictable postmodernism, "diverting the vague sense of a future into more fantastic forms, all borrowed from the misfits and eccentrics, the perverts and the Others, or aliens, of the present (modern) system."[85]

There is a tendency in postmodern philosophy to prolematize time because it is uncomfortable with the past that tends to embody the roots of logocentrism and other undesirable things like authority, the scientific worldview, hierarchy, hegemony, and grand narratives. There is a desire in postmodernism to be devoid of tradition "to stand outside of all traditions and view the play of heterogeneous discourses with an attitude of neutrality if not outright indifference."[86] There is a tendency to emphasize the present moment in postmodern thought over the past and future. The future offers little hope and makes even fewer demands on the individual. From his perspective on postmodernism, Schrag makes the following observation: "As the past is the residuum of authority, hegemony, and ideology, so the future is viewed principally as a projection of utopian dreams and unrealizable ideals."[87] If postmodernism is a series of experiments within time that emphasizes the present moment, it shares something important with Zen Buddhism, and this will be discussed in a later chapter at greater length.

In a sense, the practice of *zazen* (seated meditation) by Zen practitioners is also an experiment with the body and mind, representing a new path of thinking, which makes it akin in spirit to a goal that some postmodern thinkers are attempting to reach. Zen Buddhism and many postmodern thinkers share a radical skepticism with respect to the powers of reason; they provide a challenge to rationality and even problematize it because neither party accepts any universal claims made by reason. Although they both share a radical skepticism with respect to reason, Zen allows for the possibility of a radical certainty that postmodern philosophy does not. An autobiographical account by Hakuin, the great reformer of the Rinzai branch of Japanese Zen Buddhism in the seventeenth century, gives us an excellent illustration of this from references to three separate enlightenment experiences:

> One day when I was passing through southern Ise I ran into a downpour and the waters reached to my knees. Suddenly I gained an even deeper understanding of the verse on the Roundness of the Lotus Leaf by Ta-hui. I was unable to contain my joy. I lost all awareness of by body, fell headlong into the waters, and forgot completely to get up again. My bundles and clothing were soaked through. Fortunately a passer-by, seeing my predicament, helped me to get up. I roared with laughter and everyone there thought I was mad. That winter, when I was sitting at night in the monk's hall at Shinoda in Izumi, I gained an enlightenment from the sound of snow falling. The next year, while practicing walking meditation at the monk's hall of the Reishō-in in Mino, I suddenly had an enlightenment experience greater than any I had had before, and was overcome by a great surge of joy.[88]

From the Zen Buddhist perspective, there is nothing that can logically refute the enlightenment experience. Zen Buddhist philosophers and most postmodernists agree that there is no substantial self. Both parties also agree that time and history are characterized by a radical contingency. There are numerous other differences and similarities that will become evident as we proceed in future chapters.

Comparative Philosophy and Cross-Cultural Dialogue

In a summary fashion, it can be affirmed that comparative philosophy is inherently about altarity. The other always remains external and mysterious to us, even though his/her thoughts and actions might resemble our patterns. The fact of altarity within comparative philosophy is indicative of the necessity for engaging in it within the context of a life-world that calls into question the world inhabited by each participant, although we are placed into a common milieu by means of language. This encounter with the other refrains from reducing the other to the same, and it summons participants in the dialogue to take responsibility for each other in such a way that each person becomes radically significant for mutual self-understanding.

Comparative philosophy is a promiscuous activity because the participants experience a broadening of cultural horizons, and try out new connections, new directions, new ideas, new thoughts, and different ways of thinking and being human. The comparative thinker must remain intellectually promiscuous because of the possibility of the fusion of divergent horizons. This promiscuity takes place on the margins of philosophy, which is indicative of the uncertainty, riskiness, and dangers associated with comparative philosophy and one's willingness to venture one's self-understanding in the presence of the other. An advantage of being on the margin is that it can offer one a perspective and freedom that one might not have in normal circumstances. The marginal nature of comparative philosophy does not exclude anyone from active engagement in the life of more than one culture. By the nature of its location on the margins of culture, the comparative philosopher is a liminal being, struggling with revealment and concealment on the margins of different philosophical cultures trying to make sense of the hermeneutical dialogue in which one is engaged.

Hermeneutical dialogue is both honest with itself and necessarily incomplete. It is honest because it admits the existence of certain presuppositions, preunderstandings, and prejudgments by the participants under discussion and interpretation. It also admits that there is no definitive interpretation or dialogical exchange because hermeneutical dialogue is always incomplete by nature, which points to the necessity for continued dialogical exchange. Hermeneutical dialogue is also incomplete because there is never a conclusion to the dialogue due to its inner dynamic as a continual process within the context of temporality. Not only is there the normal give and take of an dialogical encounter, but agreeing and disagreeing, correcting and being corrected are also continually taking place. Comparative philosophy can be conceived as an incomplete game that engrosses us, draws us to it, and holds us in its spell in a repetitive pattern that constantly renews itself. If the true spirit of play is without any goal or purpose, hermeneutical dialogue is different than play at this point because its goal is mutual understanding. If we correctly play the game of hermeneutical dialogue and are an integral part of it, we must necessarily interpret what we encounter from within the game.

There are some advantages to this approach that include building cross-cultural bridges of understanding, acknowledging the other, comprehending the value of foreign philosophical insights and positions, enabling participants to transcend spatial and temporal separations, enhancing a search for common ground on which to construct mutual understanding and appreciation, and helping us to share similar concerns and problems common to all human beings. Hermeneutical dialogue also involves the participants in a comparative realm of meaning, regardless of what some postmoderns think about a lack of meaning. It also possesses the potential to set the individual on the path to truth. Moreover, it can provide us with possible insights with which to solve philosophical problems.

A secondary motivation for entering this particular dialogue between postmodern philosophers and representatives of the Zen Buddhist tradition was prompted by the work of some contemporary scholars. Within the same realm of discourse as this work, Magiola argues that Nāgārjuna's middle path follows the Derridean trace, and it even goes beyond the postmodernist in that it approaches the unheard of thought, and allows the reintroduction of the logocentric. Magliola also argues that Nāgārjuna's notion of emptiness (*śūnyatā*) is the equivalent of Derrida's *différance*, and represents the absolute negation which both constitutes and deconstitutes the directional trace.[89] Although one can find some similarities between Derrida's notion of *différance* and emptiness, to claim that they are the same is to miss the more important differences between them. There are also problems with another part of Magliola's discussion of Derrida as a representative of postmodernism and Zen Buddhism. Referring to D. T. Suzuki's work as support for his position, Magliola claims that logocentric Zen is its most popular form, which relies heavily on the *Lankāvatāra Sūtra* of the Yōgācāra School of Mahāyāna Buddhism.[90] By relying on Suzuki, Magliola is necessarily very misinformed about the history of Zen Buddhism and the importance of the *Lankāvatāra Sūtra* because Suzuki claims that Bodhidharma, the legendary founder of the Ch'an tradition brought the text from India, gave it to his first disciple, and the text was studied and commented upon continuously by monks in China for centuries.[91]

More recent scholarship demonstrates the inaccuracies of Suzuki's position. David W. Chappell, for instance, argues that the Ch'an Buddhist dynastic line of transmission of the teaching of Bodhidharma in China was not based on exegetical preoccupation with the *Lankāvatāra Sūtra*.[92] This position contradicts Suzuki's claim of a long tradition of continuous study of and commentary upon the text. Moreover, Philip Yampolsky writes that there is no evidence to support the claim that Bodhidharma used the text or wrote a commentary on it.[93] This is not to imply that the text was unimportant to the Chinese. There is evidence that the text inspired the Chinese about the value of synthesizing Buddhist doctrine.[94]

Besides the problems associated with the work of Magiola, there are also problems connected to the attempt by Newman Robert Glass to rethink the Buddhist notion of emptiness. In his lucidly argued book, Glass attempts to reinterpret emptiness through the postmodern philosophy of Gilles Deleuze. Although he is certainly entitled to do this, the emptiness that he discusses possesses little resemblance to the Buddhist understanding of emptiness. Moreover, during the course of his attempt to re-read and reinterpret emptiness through the perspective of Deleuze, Glass misinterprets the philosophy of the Zen philosopher Dōgen. We will discuss the work of Glass at greater length in the final chapter of this work. Moreover, there is a tendency in these kinds of writings to make some postmodernists more akin to the spirit of Zen Buddhism than they really are in fact.

In addition to the scholarly contributions of Magiola and Glass, I also want to briefly consider the work in comparative philosophy of David Loy and David A. Dilworth. The overall purpose of Loy's book on nonduality is to support the Mahāyāna Buddhist assertion that *saṃsāra* is nirvana. Loy's book includes an interesting criticism of Derrida that should be considered after we have compared the philosophy of the deconstructionist with various Zen philosophers, which will be attempted in the final chapter. Dilworth offers an interesting typology of Eastern and Western philosophy that includes some of the postmodern thinkers like Derrida, Foucualt, and Deleuze who will be considered in subsequent chapters. After considering these postmodern thinkers and others, it will be necessary to return to the typology of Dilworth and test his four major types (perspective, reality, method, and principle) in order to discern if they enhance our understanding of these figures in comparison to Zen philosophy.

In the following chapters we will attempt to correct some of the misperceptions created by the work of these scholars by looking at the similarities as well as the differences between various postmodern thinkers and Zen philosophers. This will be accomplished by comparing the two parties with respect to the following central topics: language; ways of thinking; radical skepticism and doubt; body; self and other; time and death; and nihilism and metaphysics. This study will argue that many postmodern thinkers move in the direction of Zen Buddhism, but they do not make the final leap or transition to the Zen philosophical position or something akin to it, even though both parties perceive shortcomings in the representational mode of thinking, which is a type of thinking that assumes a correspondence between appearance and reality and is supported by a metaphysical edifice. The various topics for the dialogical and comparative encounter that will follow in subsequent chapters have been chosen to illustrate the different attempts and strategies for overcoming representational thinking by Zen thinkers and postmodern philosophers.

CHAPTER 2

Language, Disruption, and Play

In his later works Martin Heidegger examines more closely our relationship to language and finds that it is vague and obscure. Even though our relation to language is problematic, we possess a pre-grasp of it because in order to inquire about its nature we must already have language in our possession. In order to learn what language is or to experience it, we attain it by traveling along a way, a path in which we encounter it, hear its appeal to us, and become transformed by it. And yet it is ever allusive because it is always ahead of us when we refer to it.[1] When we speak about language we demonstrate its essential being, and we listen to it when we speak about it. We do more than just speak about it because we also speak by way of language.[2] The ways of speaking and language are intertwined for Heidegger: "The way to speaking is present within language itself. The way to language (in the sense of speaking) is language as Saying."[3] Heidegger understands saying in the sense of setting beings free to their presence, allowing the openness for an appearance to announce itself, and the gathering together of all appearances.

Much of what Heidegger says about language is an attempt to explain what he means by referring to language as the house of Being. All human beings dwell within this house, and they can never step out of language in order to perceive it from an objective perspective. Heidegger also connects language to presence: "It is the keeper of being present, in that its coming to light remains entrusted to the appropriating show of Saying. Language is the house of being because language, as Saying, is the mode of Appropriation."[4] Appropriation (*Ereignis*) is an event that is experienced as a gift given by Saying; it brings humans and Being together.[5] By calling language the house of Being, Heidegger wants to stress that language is more than a mere signifying process or something with the characteristics of a sign. And if we are to reach Being, it is necessary for us to go through this house.[6] Within this abode, a human being is not the master of the house, according to Heidegger in his later work *Vorträge und Aufsätze*, because language is rather the master of the person.[7] By examining the nature of language, or more appropriately following its path, we come to realize that "language stands in an essential relation to the uniqueness of being."[8] If we can thus grasp the nature of language, we can discern the special nature of Being, a philosophical subject neglected for a long time. But is it possible to discern the essence and the origin of language?

Since Being possesses a meaning that reveals itself through language for Heidegger, it is possible for language to achieve its task which is to name beings in what they are and how they reveal themselves. Thus language becomes manifest along with the revealment of beings and preserves in itself this disclosure. If language comes into presence along with the disclosure of beings, and if its essence represents the arrival of Being into words, then *Dasein* can interrogate Being itself.[9] The origin of language, however, remains a mystery.[10] A human being does not invent language, but one, on the contrary, discovers oneself in and with language, which is Being manifested as word. Although it is possible to say that language is a possession of a person, this does not mean that language is a mere tool that is used by someone, but it is rather an event that gives a person the "possibility of standing in the openness of the existent."[11] Heidegger is also opposed to reducing language to a mere instrument or tool by simply using it to describe or inform because this type of use tends to objectify things. Instead of this objectifying use of language, Heidegger proposes a nonobjectifying use of language in order to demonstrate that which cannot be verbally stated, to indicate without explicit description, or to simply allow something to appear without categorizing it or giving it a name.

The same kind of perspicacious attention given by Heidegger to the nature of language is also offered by Derrida in many of his works. In fact, according to Rorty, Heidegger writes about language in such a way that it becomes transformed into a quasi-divinity in which we live and share Being with others, and with some qualifications we could include additionally Derrida.[12] Within the context of the present study, we want to examine closely some of the features that Derrida finds in language with the Zen Buddhist tradition by returning to a classical period of the Chinese Ch'an tradition. It is not possible to accept Rodolphe Gasché's contention that Derrida's method of deconstruction is an infrastructure that helps to account for the differences in language and various kinds of literature.[13] The last thing that Derrida wants to do philosophically is to create more structures. Instead of seeing these features of Derrida's work as infrastructures, Rorty views "these notions as merely abbreviations for the familiar Peircean-Wittgensteinian anti-Cartesian thesis that meaning is a function of context, and that there is no theoretical barrier to an endless sequence of recontextualizations."[14] We will discover that much of what Derrida writes about language and the way in which Ch'an masters used language share many features in common, even though they approach the problem and nature of language from totally different perspectives. We will discover that Ch'an Buddhist and Derrida share some similar ideas about the nature of words, the disruptive nature of language, the playful quality of language, and the significance of silence. We will also learn that the importance of the performative nature of language for Ch'an teachers is clearly distinct from Derrida's position, although both parties in the ensuing comparative dialogue seek to use language in a nonrepresentational way. We will occasionally introduce Dōgen into the discussion in order to clarify certain aspects of the Zen grasp of language.

Words and No Words

From its inception, Buddhism recognized the limitations of language due to its human origin for the purposes of communication, which suggests that words have no intrinsic worth or metaphysical grounding in a supreme power or entity. Since language is merely conventional in nature, there is no specific word or sequence of words that corresponds to some type of independent reality. Among Mahāyāna philosophers, Nāgārjuna observes that language can only refer to perishable objects of thought, but it cannot directly indicate the truth of things. From within the context of his two-fold theory of truth (conventional truth or *saṃvṛti-satya* and ultimate truth or *paramārtha-satya*), Nāgārjuna suggests that language can never capture the way things really are due to its inherent limitations. In his *Prasannapadā*, Candrakīrti comments on the philosophy of Nāgārjuna to explain that ordinary language loses its effectiveness and validity when it is no longer referring to objects in the realm of higher truth.[15] Therefore, it is absolutely impossible for any metaphysical assertions to be made that are based on facts of language.[16] Such a philosoph-

ical position implies that language possesses no ability to represent ultimate reality, a conviction that is adopted by the Ch'an Buddhist tradition,
although the Ch'an tradition often discovered inventive ways to use language to aid in the search for liberation.

Yün-men Wen-yen (862/4–949) was a Ch'an master famous for his
single word responses to questions. After being asked, "What is the right
Dharma-eye?" The master replied, "All-comprehensive." As a response
to the question: "What is Tao?" He replied, "Go!"[17] These examples of
Yün-men's response to direct questions demonstrate his spontaneous
reactions and not a thought-out, rational, or contrived answer. We use language normally in a habitual sort of way on the basis of our dispositions
at a given moment without really thinking about it. We do not respond
ordinarily in a complete way, insightfully, or sensitively to the existential
situation in which we find ourselves. Rather than allowing one to continue reacting habitually in accordance with one's conventional dispositions, Yün-men wanted to unlock the spiritual condition of the person
asking the question, and he was convinced that a logical response was
inadequate. Moreover, he did not want to entangle the questioner in a
rational response that would only further confuse the person who needed
help. The individual word response to a question is itself empty of any
substantial nature.

These single word answers function as signs that indicate nothing in
particular. Derrida agrees that these words have no intrinsic denotative
power because there is nothing itself to which a sign can point. Human
action supplies the interpretative dimension by which a sign and its signified are always mediated. A sign is also always a supplement of a thing
itself because it represents a prior interpreted formation of knowledge.
And by adding itself, the sign forms a surplus in order to replace or to
insinuate itself in-the-place-of a signified, which suggests that the sign
remains exterior and alien.

This observation about the alien nature of the sign is shared to a
large degree by Ch'an Buddhists, if we consider, for example, a name. A
good example of this is found in the *Blue Cliff Records* where "A monk
asked Tung-shan, 'What is Buddha?' Tung-shan said, 'Three pounds of
hemp.'"[18] A more humorous dialogical examination of the nature of a
name is given in *The Record of Tung-shan*:

The Master asked a monk, "What is your name?" "I,"
answered the monk. "What, then, is the Acarya's host?" asked

the Master. "Just who you see answering," replied the monk.
The Master said, "How sad, how sad. The likes of people
today are all just like this monk. They can only see themselves
as the horse behind the donkey. That is to make the Buddha
Dharma common. They still don't even understand the guest's
view of the host. How could they perceive the host from the
point of view of the host?"[19]

The response of the master possessed no connection to the question or
the name of a person from Derrida's perspective because a name is a
supplement, which suggests being without essentiality. From the Ch'an
perspective, words or names are incapable of expressing ultimate truth,
a position acceptable to Derrida. The Ch'an Buddhists are also convinced that words are useful in ordinary discourse and can express conventional truth.

The Ch'an masters often attempt to overcome the limitations and
supplemental nature of a word or name by advocating the utility of no
words. The *Lin-chi lu* makes this clear:

> When Lin-chi reached Ts'ui-feng, Ts'ui-feng asked:
>
> "Where did you come from?" "I came from Huang-po," said
> Lin-chi.
>
> "What words does Huang-po use to instruct people?" asked
> Ts'ui-feng.
>
> "Huang-po has no words," said Lin-chi.
>
> "Why not?" asked Ts'ui-feng.
>
> "Even if he had any, I wouldn't know how to state them,"
> answered Lin-chi.[20]

The Record of Tung-shan relates a story about Yün-yen addressing an
assembly of monks about a son who can answer any question asked of
him. The master inquired about the size of his library, and Yün-yen
responded, "Not a single word."[21] Due to the limitations inherent in the
nature of words, it is not wise to rely on them too heavily. It does not necessarily follow, however, that words are useless.

In contrast to Derrida, Dōgen asserts that words do have an ultimate
value, even though ordinary words are mere signs. Dōgen thinks that the
words of an enlightenment person are not limited: "The Buddhas and
Patriarchs, who have totally cast off body and mind, use words to pro-

claim the Dharma and turn the wheel of the Law and many benefit from seeing and hearing it."[22] Dōgen believes that language becomes transmuted and vivified by the realization of enlightenment, and he uses the neologism *dōtoku* to mean the ability to speak or voice the way.[23] Although these are not the words of ordinary language, they have a value because they have been vivified by an enlightenment experience.

Ch'an Buddhist made a distinction between live words (*huo-chu*) and dead words (*ssu-chu*). The former type of words were effective at overturning and opening the mind, whereas the latter type included everyday discourse, explanatory, or analytical terms, which accomplished nothing to awaken a person from the bounds of ordinary discourse. The context in which words were spoken was important:

> All words gained their power from the situation in which they were spoken or written. Words do not possess this power in themselves; they are, according to Buddhist theory, 'empty' of inherent meaning. Instead, 'turning words' are words that fit into a context in such a way that they open that context to view in some revealing way. They do so by virtue of their fit with the context and not on account of their own inherent power.[24]

Turning words possess a transformative power. Another distinction made between words was identification of nondual words, which reflects an intimate union between speaker and situation, whereas dualistic terms point to the previous intentions of the speaker and a desire to maintain control of the situation. The speaker of nondual words surrenders control and in a sense flows with the words in whatever direction they take, and remains open to the possibility of awakening.[25] Besides its hermeneutical function, the distinction between live and dead words suggests a distinction between performative and communicative aspects of language and eventually created a departure from hermeneutics.[26]

The letters, words, and sentences that convey the teachings of enlightened masters often eventually evolve into texts. When the teachings of a master becomes a text it also becomes an independent entity that possesses a textuality of its own from the perspective of Derrida. In other words, the teachings of a master contained in a text becomes independent of the historical figure. Derrida thinks that a given text is constituted tenuously by a series of signs that have different relations to each other and react against each other. This suggests to Derrida that a text does not have a stable meaning, although it is possible for a reader of a text to create meanings in it by discovering a range of meanings within the text. Moreover, the reader becomes the author of the work and an instrument in the development of the myriad possible meanings of a text.

Derrida develops his ideas about the text using the interrelationship between teacher, reader, and text itself. In contrast to this dualist grasp of a text, Dōgen perceives a text in a more nondualistic way. The text is not to be distinguished from the teacher: "When a teacher washes his face or drinks tea, it is an ancient sūtra."[27] Zen Buddhist texts are used as instruments to instruct others and lead them to liberation, and they are constituted by any activity of a teacher. The scope of these activities is made clear by Dōgen: "When we learn the ultimate criteria, even inhaling and exhaling is a sūtra, and moving the feet is a function of the sūtras. All actions are functions of the sūtras—even before our parents were born, before the universe was created."[28] Dōgen is not content with these kinds of implications, and he pushes his insights to an even more radical position.

In his essay entitled *Sansuikyo* in the *Shōbōgenzō*, Dōgen suggests that mountains and rivers are *sūtras* or texts and students should study them like texts.[29] Dōgen wants to suggest that the entire world can become a sacred text. If it is possible for the world and elements within the world to become texts, it is not beyond the realm of possibility for mountains and rivers (nonsentient beings, *mujō seppō*) to become preachers of these sacred texts. Such an unusual type of preaching cannot be expected to be heard in the ordinary way. This type of wordless preaching and its soundless sound cannot be heard with one's ears, but it must be heard rather with one's eyes. And just as the mountains and rivers learn about themselves as mountains and rivers, so must we listen and learn about them as mountains and rivers.[30]

Dōgen's nondualistic grasp of the nature of a text includes the element of time, a feature that his understanding of a text shares with Derrida. For Dōgen, one does not obtain and read the text in the past or in the present because both moments of time are "the occasion to obtain the sūtras."[31] In fact, the text compresses all time because: "Within the sūtras there are the letters of all the awakened Buddhas, the letters of all the Buddhas of the present world, and the letters of all the Buddhas in Parinirvana."[32] Dōgen and Derrida agree that language and a text are impermanent, a feature that the latter understands as a form of play. This necessarily implies for both that language possesses no lasting structure, although Dōgen gives language a provisional value as a form of *upāya* (skillful means), a pedagogical method of communication and instruction.

The lack of structure for language can be discerned within its very nature for Derrida because it embodies a supplementary aspect, neither a presence nor an absence, that moves it toward disorientation.[33] By moving away from a unified structure toward disunity, language makes additions to itself only to be replaced in its supplemental aspect and remaining alien and exterior to what it in fact replaces. A consequence of this supplemental nature of language upsets the traditional hierarchy between language and truth. Moreover, Dōgen and Derrida agree that their grasp of language disrupts the preestablished hierarchy between reality and representation. By stating that a painting of a rice cake can satisfy hunger just as well as an actual rice cake, Dōgen disrupts traditional philosophical hierarchies in a manner that is different than Derrida, although the results are similar. Language assumes an ancillary position to experience for Dōgen, whereas language is primary for Derrida.

Disruption

The Blue Cliff Records record a dramatic story about the master Nan Ch'uan's encounter with some monks who were arguing about the ownership of a cat. The master seized the cat, held it up, and said, "'If you can speak, then I will not kill it.'" When no one was able to respond, Nan Ch'uan cut the cat in half.[34] On the surface, this action by the ancient Chinese master seems to have been arbitrary, cruel, vicious, and a violation of the basic Buddhist tenet not to harm any living creature (*ahiṃsā*). From the Ch'an Buddhist perspective, it was intended to disrupt or sever the ignorant monk's attachment to the feline. Dōgen speculates about what he might have said in response to Nan-ch'uan's question: "You know how to cut the cat in two with one sword, but you don't know how to cut the cat in one with one sword."[35] In other words, Dōgen offers an opinion about a possible nondual way to cut the cat.

Not withstanding the human or clever responses that one might find associated with such an incident, this narrative about the cat is an excellent example of the Ch'an use of language to disrupt a person or persons in order to disorient their experience, shock them out of their ordinary way of doing or viewing things, and to reorient them to a totally new perspective. The scope of this reorientation is made lucid by Wright: "The language of Ch'an throws into question the self/world relation that supports the reader's position as the one who grasps and acts on the world. The text acts to evoke a disorientation and then reorientation of the reader's subjectivity."[36] The same kind of disruption takes place because of the features that Derrida finds and stresses within language. And we can find many of the same Derridean features in Ch'an Buddhist literature.

The Ch'an master can at times use his words in a dialogical encounter with another person to disrupt that individual. A good illustration of this is the encounter between the master Ma-tsu (709–88) and a hunter who passed near the master's cottage hunting deer. After getting the hunter to identify himself, the master asked him how many deer he could shoot with a single arrow. Responding that a hunter can only shoot one deer with one arrow, the master replied that it is obvious that the hunter did not know how to truly shoot an arrow. The hunter asked the master how many he could shoot with one arrow, and Ma-tsu replied that he could shoot an entire herd with a single arrow. The incredulous hunter challenged the master about his insensitivity to killing a complete herd of living creatures to which the master responded with his own challenge by suggesting that the hunter shoot himself, but the hunter confessed that he did not know how to shoot himself. Ma-tsu then announced the end of the hunter's ignorance, and the hunter converted to the life of a monk by breaking his bow and arrows, cutting off his hair, and submitting to the master. In this narrative, the hunter's perspective on his way of life became disorientated because he was accustomed to acting in accord with presuppositions, dispositions, and inclinations of the life of a hunter. Ma-tsu calls the hunter to move beyond his ordinary way of acting on the basis of his prior habits and expectations. When the hunter is able to respond sensitively to the context in which he finds himself with Ma-tsu, he proceeded to change his situation forever by making the existential decision to become a monk.

Besides the dialogical exchange that disrupts someone, Ch'an masters sometimes use a much more simple device by availing themselves of the shout. The greatest practitioner of the shout was Lin-chi:

> The Master asked a monk: "Sometimes a shout is like the jeweled sword of the Vajra King; sometimes a shout is like the golden-haired lion crouching on the ground; sometimes a shout is like a weed-tipped fishing pole; sometimes a shout doesn't function as a shout. How do you understand this?" The monk hesitated. The master gave a shout.[37]

In another case Lin-chi reproves a nun who imitates his style of teaching and shouted in response to a question of the master: "'Well-come or ill-come?'" Picking up his stick, the master challenged the nun to speak to which she responded with another shout. Thereupon, the master struck her.[38] These two examples of using the shout or violence in response to false imitation function to erase any possible meaning. The use of violence or the shout are used to cut off words, and represents a call to react spontaneously to this call in whatever situation one is located. The shout itself possesses no meaningful significance, which is nicely illustrated in the following anecdote:

> Mu Chou asked a monk, "Where have you just come from?" The monk immediately shouted. Mu Chou said, "I've been shouted at by you once." Again the monk shouted. Mu Chou said, "After three or four shouts, then what?" The monk had nothing to say. Mu Chou then hit him and said, "What a thieving phoney you are!"[39]

From Derrida's perspective, the Ch'an masters are indicating that the shout, which is devoid of meaningful significance in itself, functions as an erasure of meaning, an obstacle to rationality, and a summons to become aware of the present moment and one's ignorant condition.

The function of erasure in Derrida's view of language can be seen more clearly when we attempt to name some object, a process of distinguishing one thing from another. By naming something, we separate it from other objects, and dispense with image and sensory experience because we have a tendency to think by means of names. The name of something, which represents a relative unity, can not assume a position of privilege.[40] By concentrating on how language functions and not how it represents things, we can realize that by giving an object a name, it installs itself on the object and destroys the purity of the idiom by not acknowledging the other as pure other, a process that suggests a radical dislocation of things. Thus to name an object is simultaneously to erase it.

Ch'an masters agree with the spirit of Derrida's position with respect to naming and erasure. They also demonstrate another way to name something by pointing to its function:

> A monk asked Chao Chou, "For a long time I've heard of the stone bridge of Chao Chou, but now that I've come here I

just see a simple log bridge." Chou said, "You see the log bridge; you don't see the stone bridge." The monk said, "What is the stone bridge?" Chou said, "It lets asses cross, it lets horses cross."[41]

Another Ch'an method of naming something is not to name it. This is evident in the following dialogical exchange: "A monk asked Pa Ling, 'What is the Blown Hair Sword?' Pa Ling said, 'Each branch of coral supports the moon.'"[42] This nonsensical response disrupts any further naming, erases the name of the sword, and the name of an objective weapon.

Another disruptive feature of language that the Ch'an masters manifest in their words and actions that they share with Derrida is repetition. In an incident that combines the use of the shout and violence, Lin-chi responded to a question about the most important principle of the teachings of the Buddha from a monk by raising his whisk, and the monk responded by uttering a shout only to be hit by the master. Another monk asked the same question, and the master responded again by raising his whisk to which this second monk answered with a shout. But this time the master returned the shout, and when the monk faltered in his response he was struck by the master.[43] In another context the master Ma-tsu had been ill for some time, and he was asked by the temple superintendent about his recent health. He responded by saying, "'Sun Face Buddha, Moon Face Buddha.'"[44] These incidents are evidence that the Ch'an masters and Derrida share the opinion that repetition embodies, to use the words of Derrida, "an unlimited power of perversion and subversion."[45] From a Ch'an perspective, the purpose of repetition is to disrupt a person's normal mode of being and thinking. This is evident in the case of the master Yün-men who asked a monk where he came from and what was being said there. The monk responded by extending both of his hands, and the master slapped him once. When the impertinent monk replied that he was still talking the master then extended his hands, and when the monk did not respond he was struck by the master.[46] The unfolding exchange of words and gestures resulted in the disruption of the monk's mind, who thought that he had been making the correct responses until the moment of his failure.

In Derrida's observations of language, repetition is an aspect of iteration, which alters, blurs, undermines and dislocates an utterance: "It blurs the simplicity of the line dividing inside from outside, undermines the order of succession or of dependence among the terms, *prohibits* (prevents and renders illegitimate) the procedure of exclusion. Such is the *law* of iterability."[47] When iteration alters something a new thing takes place. Iteration introduces into an utterance what Derrida refers to as a dehiscence, which "marks emphatically that the divided opening, in the growth of a plant, is also what, in a *positive* sense, makes production, reproduction, development possible. Dehiscence (like iterability) limits what it makes possible, while rendering its rigor and purity impossible."[48] This disruptive feature of language discovered by Derrida is also evident within the language of the Ch'an masters.

Lin-chi blurred the lines dividing an economic activity when he asked the steward of the temple where he had been and what he had been doing there. The steward replied that he had been to the provincial capital in order to sell millet. The steward made a positive response to the master's inquiry as to whether or not he had sold all of it. After drawing a line on the ground with his staff, the master asked the steward if he could sell that. In response the steward shouted, and the master hit him in return.[49] In another episode Lin-chi undermined the honor, distinction, and symbolic significance of a high seat. After being told to assume a high seat by the prefectural governor, a monk asked him a question to which he simply repeated the same question to the original questioner, who then proceeded to pull the master down from the seat and sat on it himself. When the monk hesitated to respond to a question raised by Lin-chi he was in turn pulled from the high seat and left the room. When this happened the master stepped down from the seat of honor.[50] In this episode, Lin-chi subverts the symbolic significance of the chair and any dependence upon what it might mean to others. The subverting of normal assumptions is evident in the following statements: "Master Shogen said, "'Why is it that a man of great strength cannot lift his leg?'" Again he said, "'It is not with his tongue that he speaks.'"[51] This unanswerable question and enigmatic statement is designed to disrupt the mind of the hearer and to subvert itself in the first place. Moreover, these kinds of statements are intended to leave one with nothing substantial on which to stand and with nothing upon which to intellectually or audibly grasp. The subsequent mental insecurity created by the perplexing statement of a master underminds the representational mode of thinking. And yet it forces one to respond spontaneously.

Ludic Encounters and Dialogues

While Ma-tsu sat across a path with his legs stretched out, a monk named Feng was pushing a wheelbarrow on the path until he came to the legs of Ma-tsu, and he asked the master to withdraw this obstacle in his path. After Ma-tsu refused to withdraw his legs, Feng pushed the wheelbarrow forward and over the outstretched legs of the master hurting Ma-tsu, who returned to the dharma-hall with an axe in his hand and commanded: "'Let the one who has just hurt this old monk's legs come forward.'" Thereupon, the undaunted Feng stepped forward with his neck stretched out in front of the master. Ma-tsu responded to the fearlessness of the monk by putting his axe away.[52] This narrative is an excellent example of a deadly serious language game. There is, however, a playful quality to the encounter between Ma-tsu and Feng. When many encounters between Ch'an monks and others are grasped as ludic activities within the context of a language game, this represents another example of a common thread running through Ch'an literature and Derrida's understanding of language.

Even though Ma-tsu was famous for his use of violence as a teaching device, his violent methods were often within a playful context. In response to the perennial question about why the first Patriarch came from the West, Ma-tsu asked the monk to be quiet and to come closer to him. When the monk moved close enough to the master Ma-tsu boxed him on the ear and said: "Among six ears one does not scheme plots."[53] In another incident, a different monk asked the master the same question, and Ma-tsu asked him to bow down. While the monk was bowing, Ma-tsu gave him a kick which caused the monk to have a great awakening and to respond with laughter and profuse joy.[54] In the first episode, Ma-tsu hit the monk on the ear in order to sever his attachment to words, and the playful kick administered to the questioner while in an exposed position was intended to accomplish the same thing as the first episode. In the second instance the unsuspecting victim was able to join into the spirit of play due to his awakening experience because emptiness makes the possibilities for play limitless.

If the Ch'an dialogical encounters possess a ludic quality, a similar spirit of playfulness is evident in the philosophy of Derrida, who does philosophy in the spirit of play, due in large part to the play element that is embodied within language, which represents a play of differences.

Because play represents the alternation of presence and absence and manifests the disruption of presence, Derrida thinks that it is necessary to conceive of play "before the alternative of presence and absence."[55] For Derrida, play is limitless, infinite, and indefinite; it is purposeless, meaningless, frivolous, useless, and nonserious. Even though it is not necessary for a participant to have goals, play involves risk and insecurity. Play also possesses the potential to challenge traditional values, subvert established hierarchies, invert accepted meaning, and become a form of perversion that is subversive. Embodied within Derrida's neologism *différance*, which is more primordial than the ontological difference or Being itself, is the play of traces.[56]

Although it does not indicate anything in particular, the Derridean trace is a presence-absence, denoting its play, that represents a reserve, implying that it is an indeterminate medium that reveals the world.[57] According to Derrida, the best paradigm for the trace is the cinder because "If a place is itself surrounded by fire (falls finally to ash, into a cinder tomb), it no longer is. Cinder remains, cinder there is, which we can translate: the cinder is not, is not what is."[58] Derrida wants to make clear that the trace, an interplay of identity and difference, is not simply a presence "but is rather the simulacrum of a presence that dislocates, displaces, and refers beyond itself."[59] It operates in this manner because effacement belongs to its structure, which suggests that a trace neither exists itself nor becomes present because it is always being effaced and disappearing. The trace is also supplementary by nature, continually overflowing and supplementing itself. It is possible to find examples of the Derridean trace within the Ch'an Buddhist use of language.

In *The Record of Tung-shan* a master announced, "'There is a person who, in the midst of a thousand or even ten thousand people, neither turns his back on nor faces a single person. Now you tell me, what face does this person have?'" A monk came forward to say, "'I am going to the Monk's Hall.'"[60] On the one hand, it is obvious that the monk's response to the paradox of the master had no relationship to the question. On the other hand, it is a genuine Ch'an response because he is indicating by his words that such a person possesses only a trace of a face, which effaces itself as soon as it appears from a Derridean perspective, whereas the Ch'an Buddhist would call it no-face. A dialogue that captures the to-and-fro spirit of play is the following exchange between two monks:

A monk said, "The Master normally tells us to follow the bird path. I wonder what the bird path is?"

"One does not encounter a single person," replied the Master. "How does one follow such a path?" asked the monk.

"One should go without hemp sandals on one's feet," replied the Master.

"If one follows the bird path, isn't that seeing one's original face?" said the monk. "Why do you turn things upside down so?" asked the Master. "But where have I turned things upside down?" asked the monk. "If you haven't turned things upside down, then why do you regard the slave as master?" said the Master.

"What is one's original face?" asked the monk.

"Not to follow the bird path," responded the Master.[61]

From the perspective of Derrida, the bird path is merely a trace of a path because as soon as it reveals itself as a path it disappears. There is no need for sandals to travel on a no-path because the traveler cannot leave any track or trace on the bird path, which itself is without any marks. By following the non-path, one finds without a face one's true face—the no-face. The master is instructing the inquiring monk that his original face is never a face that he can find traveling down some designated path. The master is implying that there is no path and nothing to find because it is all—path and face—right here now at this present moment.

Other important aspects of play indicate that it also reflects spontaneity and a lack of meaning according to Derrida. We can find the same spirit of play in Ch'an dialogues: "A monk asked Chih Men, 'What is the body of wisdom?' Chih Men said, 'An oyster swallowing the bright moon.' The monk asked, 'What is the function of wisdom?' Chih Men said, 'A rabbit getting pregnant.'"[62] These spontaneous and meaningless responses paradoxically embody the wisdom of the master. The playful spontaneity of three monks on their way to pay their respects to the national teacher Chung is evident in the following story: "When they got halfway there, Nan Ch'uan drew a circle on the ground and said, 'If you can speak, then let's go on.' Kuei Tsung sat down inside the circle; Ma Ku curtseyed. Nan Ch'uan said, 'Then let's not go on.'"[63] Having invented a game on the spot, Nan Ch'uan did not see the need to proceed because his companions played spontaneously and successfully. The following coarse dialogue embodies a playful spirit:

A monk asked T'ou Tzu, "All sounds are the sounds of Buddha—right or wrong?" T'ou Tzu said, "Right." The monk said, "Teacher, doesn't your asshole make farting sounds?" T'ou Tzu then hit him. Again the monk asked, "Coarse words or subtle talk, all returns to the primary meaning—right or wrong?" T'ou Tzu said, "Right." The monk said, "Can I call you an ass, Teacher?" T'ou Tzu then hit him.[64]

This humorous exchange suggests that farting, an involuntary expelling of bodily gases (a debatable point among experts), is the primordial sound of the Buddha. And since all words—whether beautiful or coarse—are empty, it does not really matter if the monk calls the master an ass. Of course, it also does not matter whether the master lovingly embraces the monk or hits him because a fond embrace or a violent strike are both equally empty methods of teaching. Finally, in the spontaneous spirit of play, the Ch'an master Tan-hsia went into the monk's hall and climbed onto the head of a statue of the bodhisattva Mañjuśri and sat on it to the amazement of the other monks. When Ma-tsu saw the feat of this monk, he renamed him spontaneous.[65] Spontaneity appears to exclude truly meaningful dialogue.

From Derrida's perspective, meaning is something that cannot be discovered because nothing precedes it and nothing controls it. We can begin to grasp meaning as the space between terms, their relations and interrelations. But it is best understood as a function of play.[66] The spontaneous nature of the play in the following episode illustrates Derrida's understanding of meaning as a function of play:

A monk asked Yao Shan, "On a level field, in the shallow grass, the elk and deer form a herd: how can one shoot the elk of elks?" Shan said, "Look—an arrow!" The monk let himself fall down. Shan said, "Attendant, drag this dead fellow out." The monk then ran out. Shan said, "This fellow playing with a mud ball—what end will there be to it?"[67]

The message of this episode is look no elk, look no arrow, look no dead person. Yao-shan's final question suggests that the game never ends.

These often ludic dialogical encounters are examples of what Dōgen refers to as *kattō* (entanglement), a term that ordinarily refers to an ignorant person's entanglement in language. Within the context of the dialogical encounter between a student and master, Dōgen gives *kattō* a positive connotation by attaching the nuance of intertwining and demonstrating how it is possible to sever the entanglement with words.[68] Even though the master utilizes words to entangle both himself and his disciple in the web of language, they also function as a team to use language to break free from any entanglement in it. Moreover, they learn together that the words of the patriarchs and disciples transcend the distinction between universals and particulars. From Dōgen's perspective, entanglement within language possesses the possibility to liberate us.[69]

Performative Language

As J. L. Austin demonstrates in his classic work on performative language entitled *How To Do Things with Words*, such language involves the uttering of a sentence that is directly connected to the doing of an action.[70] There are certain conditions that are necessary for a performative utterance that include an accepted conventional procedure and result within a certain context. The persons and circumstances must be "appropriate for the invocation of the particular procedure invoked."[71] A final criteria involves the complete and correct execution of the procedure by all participants.[72] Derrida is opposed to Austin's theory of performative utterances because the latter does not consider—before illocutory or perlocutory determinations are made—a preexisting system of predicates that Derrida calls graphematics. Austin also blurs all the differences that follow.[73] According to Derrida, one must not be concerned with a difference between original event-utterances and citational utterances, because we are rather confronted with different kinds of iterable marks that introduce a split into the utterance, which suggests that it can never be present to itself and its content. Moreover, the context of the utterance can never be completely determinable because it is necessary for conscious intention to be present and immediately apparent to itself and the other.[74] The most crucial objection made by Derrida to the theory of Austin is that metaphysics reigns over his philosophical heritage.[75]

Even though Derrida and Austin are at odds with each other, there are numerous examples of performative utterances in Ch'an literature, which serves as a major distinction between its use of language and Derrida's understanding of how it operates. A typical attempt to execute a performative utterance occurs in *The Record of Tung-shan* when the monk Tung-shan asks the master Kuei-shan for more understanding and lucidity about an abstruse element of the Buddhist teachings, and the master responded by raising his fly whisk and asking the inquiring monk if he understood.[76] The shouts uttered by Lin-chi can be construed as performative utterances because they are expressed by a master trying to shock a student into enlightenment or make something happen. Lin-chi was also famous for his use of violence to bring about an awakening experience. While encountering an old woman on the road on his way to visit another monk, Lin-chi was told that his friend was away by the woman. When Lin-chi asked her where his friend had gone, she turned and walked away. Lin-chi responded by calling to her. When she turned her head he hit her.[77] In another episode, after an exchange of physical blows between Lin-chi and Huang-po near a garden, the latter called for the monastery personnel supervisor to help him get up from the ground. While helping him to his feet, the supervisor asked Huang-po how he could let such a lunatic get away with such rudeness. Thereupon, Huang-po hit the supervisor after getting to his feet and hearing his words. Resuming his hoeing of the ground, Lin-chi summarized the situation: "'Everywhere else the dead are cremated, but here I bury them alive at once.'"[78]

Besides shouts, raising a whisk, or violence, masters have also taught by raising a finger. *The Blue Cliff Record* testifies that Chu-ti was famous for his one finger Ch'an. Whenever Chu-ti was asked anything, he would just raise one finger.[79] While away from Chu-ti's hermitage, a servant related to another that his master taught by simply raising one finger. Recounting this episode to the master upon his return, Chu-ti took a knife and cut off the youth's finger; as he ran out screaming, Chu-ti called to him. When the servant looked back, the master raised his finger; the servant attained understanding at that moment.[80] In this case the servant realized the truth of no-finger by means of the gesture of the master. The gesture of raising a finger made something happen; it triggered the awakening of the young man. When Chu-ti was nearing death, he said to the assembled monks, "'I attained T'ien-lung's one-finger Ch'an and have used it all my life without exhausting it. Do you want to understand?'"[81] Raising his finger, he then died. Chu-ti's pedagogical method of finger raising can be construed as a form of direct pointing to that which is not normally accessible to an individual. Like performative words that make something happen, actions can also cause something to occur and become events of signification. Spoken words and physical gestures function as mediators. Mediation eventuates because pointing is indirection.[82]

Shouts, beatings, and raising a fly whisk or a finger are intended to make something happen, which includes shocking someone and awakening them.[83] Leaving the uninitiated no chance to reason, these kinds of performative actions help one to avoid rational entanglements and subsequent confusion. A shout is, for instance, a manifestation of what is in one's mind.[84] The shout seems like a meaningless utterance because the Buddhist think that truth cannot be captured in words. Beatings, shouting, and finger or whisk raising are all designed to make enlightenment happen. This is why one should not view them as the sadism of the teacher or the masochism of the student.[85] Although they may appear to be crude or a form of punishment, they are intended as an incentive and practical means for comprehending reality.[86] The Ch'an literature testifies to the success of these unusual pedagogical methods, which are forms of skill-in-means (*upāya*). The various shock tactics used by Ch'an masters do not allow the unenlightened person an opportunity to remain aloof or disengaged. Not only is the unenlightened person pulled ineluctably into the encounter in which shouts, beatings, and finger raising are used by the master, but the uninitiated person is forced to drop any hope of security, safety, and pretense in an interpersonal encounter that leads to the realization of unimpeded intimacy.[87]

In this vein, Dōgen draws a distinction between the true man without rank (*mui shinnin*) and the true man with a rank (*ui shinnin*). Dōgen advocates the latter type of person because he gains awakening by means of language and within its context, whereas the former awakens without the use of language.[88] According to Dōgen, the performative types of dialogues are indicative of a departure from ontology. In other words, performative dialogical encounters are a departure from the notion of an already present truth that simply must be discovered toward another conception of truth as a dynamic process that emerges in continual realization.[89] This is an enacted form of truth that is contextual in relation to time and place.

In contrast to beatings, shouting, and gesturing, a more verbal form of performative utterance is the kōan, an illocutionary and perlocutionary form of language to use Austin's terminology. It is illocutionary in the sense that it creates an event and necessitates some kind of social ceremonial. The perlocutionary act produces often unseen effects.[90] The changes that are caused by the language of the kōan involves an ontological shift from a perspective that views truth as already present to a more dynamic process of emergence and continual actualization.[91] By presenting before the mind of a novice an enigmatic and unsolvable statement or problem, like the sound of one hand clapping or the reason for the Patriarch coming from the West, the master enables the novice to fix his/her concentration on a single point in order to check the intellect and to motivate the mind to move in a new direction. Much like other Ch'an forms of performative language, the kōan is intended to shock the student. If the kōan works to help a novice attain enlightenment, it functions like a performative utterance because it makes something happen, even though it may be paradoxical.

The paradoxical characteristic of many kōans indicates that to use language in an assertive manner is to create an endless cycle of questions and answers. Kōans seem paradoxical to the unenlightened because they are unconnected to an ordinary ontological structure. Chung-ying Cheng thinks that the paradoxical nature of kōans reveals a dialectical process that is capable of exposing a deeper ontological structure within a person. Cheng explains how this process works: "The process and method of resolving the paradoxicality of a Zen puzzle or paradox in terms of forbidding any ontological commitment to any semantic structure of language may be called *the principle of ontic noncommitment*."[92] Therefore, the principle of ontic noncommitment possesses the potential to resolve or dissolve the paradoxical nature of kōans. According to Heine, Cheng's comments on paradox works with the *watō* method, which indicates the inner contradictions of all forms of speech, and it reinforces the view that kōans lead to an insurmountable doubt that blocks the mind. Heine perceives problems with Cheng's methodology and his grasp of the *watō* tradition, which does not try to solve the paradox as much as recognize the futility of attempts to discover solutions to it.[93] Heine states that it would be more appropriate to investigate the parallactical nature of Ch'an discourse in which contexts change depending on how they are perceived.[94] Heine's suggestion might be fine for scholars, but it does not address the student grappling with the absurdity of a kōan and what it can help perform for the student.

Although Derrida is critical of the performative theory of language, his work suggests that he would appreciate the ability of the kōan to decenter a person struggling with it. Instead of the power inherent within the kōan to decenter a person, Derrida looks to the word center itself, and finds that it is a contradictory concept. If we assume that the center is at the hub of a totality, it does not belong to the totality as its center because the true center is elsewhere. A concept like the center is constituted, for

Derrida, by its differences from other concepts and its relations to a plethora of other concepts, which embody within themselves traces of that to which they stand in opposition.[95] Moreover, Derrida's many essays devoted to the topic of language suggests that he appreciates the boundless openness of the Zen use of language that is devoid of any fixed metaphysical center. However, Derrida would disagree with the unstated premise of the kōan that there is a deeper meaning to be discerned underneath the apparent nonsense of the dialogues. From Derrida's perspective, there is no further insight to be gained by the nonsensical words.

Silence

According to the *Blue Cliff Records*, the Emperor Wu of the Liang Dynasty requested Mahasattva Fu to explain the *Diamond Sūtra* to him, and the master responded to the request by shaking the desk once and getting off his seat to the astonishment of the emperor.[96] In another Ch'an episode, Yang-shan asked Kuei-shan: "'When the great action is taking place, how do you determine it?'" Kuei-shan responded by leaving his seat and proceeding to his room. Yang-shan followed the master to his room where Kuei-shan asked the monk: "'What was it you asked me?'" After repeating the question, Kuei-shan replied: "'Don't you remember my answer.'" Yang-shan replied affirmatively, but he was pressed further by the master to make the proper response. Thereupon, he retired immediately from the room without uttering a sound.[97] These examples of silence in the Ch'an tradition are good illustrations of how silence can either disrupt discussion or put a stop to further dialogue. These two episodes demonstrate how unnerving silence can make someone, who is expecting a reply to his/her question and continuation of the dialogue.

By ending in silence, the previous dialogues stress that their climax is reached by the expression of silence. The significance of silence is insightfully summarized by Chang Chung-yuan:

> When a Ch'an Buddhist abides in silence his inner nature is in harmony with the Ultimate Reality. His silence expresses the power of living nothingness. Silences in ordinary converse are silences in the relative sense; they are a dead stillness, which is quite the opposite of what silence is in Ch'an. Unless one's silence transcends both words and stillness, one's answer will

not be correct at all. All of the leading Ch'an masters who answered questions with silence had in common this highest level of inner awareness.[98]

From another perspective, Ch'an rhetoric shaped the use of silence and its experience. By shaping it in either way, it has transformed silence into a sign.[99]

As expressed throughout his works, the postmodern writer Edmond Jabès attaches profound significance to silence because "Silence envelops life."[100] Much like the Zen Buddhists, Jabès thinks that words can lead us astray from the goal of truth, and he suggests that we are wise to become silent ourselves and to listen for the silence that formed the word.[101] It is important for us not to construe silence as a weakness or lack of language because it is rather the strength of language.[102] The Zen Buddhists and Jabès share a common conviction that silence can express something profound (although they may not agree about what it might be), that it might upset others, and that it might be able to disrupt discussion.

In a way similar to Ch'an masters, Derrida suggests that he is interested in the silence that is manifested in the spaces between words, which represent a pause, a break, a blank, an interval that forms the origin of signification. The space between words, which is unseen, nonpresent, and nonconscious, is engaged in a process of flux because it is subject to space and time, which are continually becoming in the sense of the becoming-space of time and the becoming-time of space.[103] The silence of the space in between the words takes one to the limits of philosophy. It also places us in a sphere of strangeness with the potential to liberate us from ordinary discourse. The strangeness of silence "yet remains a modality of speech: a memory of promise and a promise of memory."[104]

Concluding Remarks

Both Derrida and Zen thinkers have attempted to find inventive and creative ways to communicate with language. Although we have called attention to several features in Zen Buddhist language and its uses that are similar to aspects of language isolated by Derrida, a major difference between Derrida and Zen is the latter's grasp of language as nondualistic. We can find evidence of this in Dōgen's works and in a discussion about the nature of a thing.

Dōgen relates, for instance, the episode of Seidō Ezō (Ch. Hsi-t'ang, 735–814), who pulled his student's nose after the student responded to the master's question about comprehending universal emptiness by grasping a handful of air. Dōgen offers his own interpretation of this story. The student wants to know the true state of reality, to demonstrate the suchness of universal emptiness. When the student grabs a handful of air, it demonstrates that he does not truly know the full truth because he thinks that emptiness exists outside of himself. When the pain caused by the pull of the teacher on his nose prompts the student to touch it himself, it is as if he hides in Seidō's nostril, which suggests universal emptiness in the forms of both teacher and student united in one nostril.[105] If one grants that the teacher's pulling of the nose of the student is a performative type of language, Dōgen is attempting to convey in his interpretation of this episode the nondual nature of language and ways in which it can function in a nonrepresentational way. We have called attention to the way that Zen masters refused to use common modes of discourse to discuss everyday sorts of things. By evading normal or everyday modes of rhetoric, they were avoiding the use of philosophical propositions and representational discourse.[106]

The *Mumonkan* collection of kōans preserves an encounter related to the topic of the nature of the thing. The master instructed a monk: "'Keichu made a cart whose wheels had a hundred spokes. Take both front and rear parts away and remove the axle: then what will it be?'"[107] In other words, what is the essence of a thing? Can it be called an object or a subject? If we make Derrida the monk, he would respond that a thing is neither an object nor a subject.[108] It represents the other that addresses one and makes a demand on a person. The thing addresses one as singular and different.[109] Therefore, it is wrong to use a word to describe a thing because both represent "referential limits that only the supplementary structure can produce and mark."[110] The thing of Derrida's conception always remains an other, whereas this is not true for Dōgen because he neither wants us to abandon words nor cling to them. He does, however, want us to use words as a means to follow the way, although Dōgen does share with Derrida a sense of the otherness of rhetoric.

The otherness of language for both Zen Buddhist and Derrida possesses important implications for ontology and subjectivity. The strong otherness of Zen language and Derrida's emphasis on the otherness of language are both intended to undermine ordinary subjectivity. This is especially true of subjectivity associated with representational modes of thinking. With respect to Derrida's attack on subjectivity, Charles Taylor finds something paradoxical because "Paradoxically, for all the talk of the 'end of subjectivity,' one of the strong attractions of this kind of position is precisely the license it offers to subjectivity, unfettered by anything in the nature of a correct interpretation or an irrecusable meaning of either life or text, to effect its own transformations, to invent meaning."[111] Moreover, from a Zen perspective, Derrida uses language ontologically, whereas language is not ontologically bound for a Zen philosopher like Dōgen.

According to Dōgen, words are not only not different from things, events, or beings, but they can also convey ultimate truth because of their nondual nature. Kim confirms that "Dōgen clearly recognizes the possibility that language, despite its aspects as a tool of duality, can partake of nonduality; only thus does language become 'expression' (*dōtoku*)."[112] From another perspective, Dōgen argues that words are valuable "not because of their capacity to represent reality (mimesis), but because of their power to produce it. Truth has no essence; it exists only through its effects and in particular through speech: such is the 'enacted' or 'realized' kōan (*genjōkōan*)."[113] Derrida would agree with Dōgen that words cannot represent reality, but the former would not consent with the Zen Buddhist that words can produce reality because it is impossible to designate it or reach it from our limited and everchanging situation. Since the intimate link between a sign and a given reality is broken, this necessitates an alternation in the nature of language and allows it greater independence with respect to a given reality. Instead of operating to designate reality, the detaching of words from a specific reality or a variety of things within the world allows language to develop more freely and creatively in a nonrepresentational way.

Erasure, repetition, iteration, play, and trace are all aspects of language that play an essential role in Derrida's understanding of the nature of language. And we noticed that they also can be discovered functioning in some sense in the Ch'an Buddhist use of language. Within the context of his theory, Derrida claims that a speaking subject, representing an irreducible secondary status, is no longer the person who speaks because his/her origin is elusive in an already established field of speech. From this, Derrida concludes, "Speech is stolen: since it is stolen from language it is, thus, stolen from itself, that is, from the thief who has always already lost speech as property and initiative."[114] An episode from the Ch'an tradition illustrates a similar attitude toward the stolen nature of speech. A monk asked, for instance, the hermit T'ung-feng what he would do if he encountered a tiger. After the hermit responded by roaring like a tiger, the monk acted frighten. When the hermit ceased laughing, the monk replied, "'You old thief!'"[115] By means of his gesture, the hermit is adroitly able to steal the speech of the monk.

CHAPTER 3

Ways of Thinking

In the *Mumonkan* collection of kōans, an interesting question is raised: "Master Sekiso said, 'From the top of a pole one hundred feet high, how do you step forward?' An ancient Master also said that one sitting at the top cf a pole one hundred feet high, even if he has attained 'it', has not yet been truly enlightened. He must step forward from the top of the pole one hundred feet high and manifest his whole body in the ten directions."[1] Dōgen uses this kōan to illustrate that the thinking characteristic of enlightenment entails a leap. Although Heidegger is not concerned with enlightenment in the same sense of Dōgen, he also conceives of correct thinking as a leap. Even though it is necessary to take a few practice leaps, the final leap, for Heidegger, takes one into the neighborhood of thinking. This neighborhood, where everything is different, appears as strange and will confound the leaper.[2] In his work *Satz von Grund*, Heidegger discusses thinking as a recollective forethinking that is the leaping of the leap (*Sprung*), a movement (*Satz*) to which thinking submits.[3] The leap to this new form of thinking, for both thinkers, is abrupt and opens one to an entirely new way of thinking, a path that is also sought by other postmodern thinkers influenced by the thought of Heidegger.

If thoughts are metaphorically clouds for Lyotard, a person perceives the shape of clouds differently depending on one's standpoint. Like the differently shaped clouds in the sky, thoughts cannot be possessed by a person, even though one might try to enter into them or attempt to belong to them in some way. It is also not possible to construct by the power of thinking a "system of total knowledge about clouds of thoughts by passing from one site to another and accumulating the views it produces at each site—such an idea constitutes *par excellence* the sin, the arrogance of the mind."[4] Sharing a similar attitude toward thinking with Lyotard, Derrida views thinking as a way of deconstruction, play, and *désistance*, a neologism that will be explained later in this chapter. Following the lead of Derrida, Taylor wants to think the not, an unthinking suggested by all thinking, which is a position not far removed from the spirit of Dōgen's philosophy, whereas Deleuze wants to continuously create concepts in order to think difference. The four postmodernists agree with Heidegger that thinking, as they view its usefulness, is not concerned with logic. Deleuze views logic, for instance, as interesting only when it is silent.[5] Deleuze sees logic as a rival of philosophy that is attempting to supplant it. In a similar vein, Heidegger did not believe that taking a course in logic is the best way to learn to think or to practice thinking. Heidegger is concerned with original thinking, and he elaborates:

> But we do not learn to think originally when someone shows us how to think, in an inferior and long-since impossible manner, 'about' thinking. Rather, we learn to think only when we try to attain an essential and genuine relation to what above all else is thought-*worthy*.[6]

And what is thought-worthy for Heidegger will become clear later. Thus this chapter is devoted to a consideration of the philosophical notion of thinking. The center of our attention will be focused on a comparison of the philosophical positions of the later Heidegger and Dōgen. Consideration will also be given to Lyotard, Derrida, Taylor, and Deleuze on the topic of thinking.

Withdrawal

A human being, for Heidegger, is an animal involved in thinking, although this is not necessarily the case. He asserts, "Being a rational animal, man must be capable of thinking if he really wants to."[7] Even though a person possesses the ability to cogitate, this is no guarantee that such a person does think, and before he/she thinks he/she must learn. Heidegger elaborates, "Man learns when he disposes everything he does so that it answers to whatever essentials are addressed to him at any given moment. We learn to think by giving our mind to what there is to think about."[8] What is given to us to think is thought-provoking, and what is at the beginning of all else and is always thought about is referred to as most thought-provoking. What is most thought-provoking to a philosopher is that which one is still not thinking.

For Dōgen, it is not a matter of learning but of unlearning. One must unlearn what one has previously gained so that one possesses no preconceptions. He explains that, "Students cannot gain enlightenment simply because they retain their preconceptions."[9] Heidegger disagrees that one can be free of one's preconceptions.[10] Whether or not one overcomes one's preconceptions, what is most thought-provoking and most worthy of thought for Heidegger is Being, whereas what is most worthy of thought and most thought-provoking for Dōgen is the Buddha-nature, although it is necessary to understand in what sense this is true. This will be discussed at greater length later in this chapter.

It is not true, for Heidegger, that a person is not thinking because he does not turn to that which wants to be thought: "Rather, that we are still not thinking stems from the fact that the thing itself that must be thought about turns away from man, has turned away long ago."[11] This does not mean that this event happened at a given historical time. Rather, what must be thought has turned away from human beings since the beginning. Dōgen would reply that it is the individual who has turned away from his/her true nature. It is not possible for the Buddha-nature which is always arriving to turn away.[12]

In contrast to Heidegger and Dōgen, Mark C. Taylor wants to think the not, an unthinking aspect suggested by all thinking. Not only is the question of the not extremely ancient, it is also chronologically prior to "thought itself, for it is impossible to think without already having thought not. To think not is not, however, to think not as such."[13] Moreover, it is not something that we can neither think nor not think because we are always thinking it. The not for Taylor is not equivalent to nonbeing. By falling between being and nonbeing, the not involves a radical alterity. Unlike the binary opposites of Kierkegaard's either/or or Hegel's synthesizing both/and, Taylor's grasp of the not is more difficult to convey adequately in language due to its elusive nature. If the not that Taylor wants to think falls between being and nonbeing, this distinguishes his position from that of Heidegger, who thinks that by thinking Being we are also thinking the nothing within it.[14]

Taylor follows a path already begun by Heidegger and later by Derrida, who also wants to think the unthought that suggests its possibility, its necessity, or its structure. Derrida wants to think prior to the ground of the unthought. In order to help himself think prior to the unthought, Derrida develops what he calls *désistance*, a neologism designed to examine the structure of subjectivity within a double movement of negation. The term *désistance* is basically untranslatable, although it conveys the sense of renouncing a suit or some legal action or a responsibility. *Désistance* is something that happens before the subject can reflect on anything, it happens before a decision is made about some action, it is prior to a decision about what one should do in a given situation, and it occurs before one's passions are aroused about some matter of consequence.[15] The kind of thinking that Derrida wants to avoid is the type that leads to representational knowledge, which is shaped by the postulation of presence. In this respect, Derrida is following Heidegger and his polemic against representational thinking in his earlier philosophy that viewed things as objectively present at hand (*vorhanden*), and did not perceive the usefulness and/or contexuality of things. And prior to Heidegger's thoughts on the subject, Nietzsche argued that the goal of thinking is not simply to know in the sense of creating a mirror of reality, but it is to create as much regularity and form as needed upon the chaos of the world, a realm that is always in a state of flux.[16] This continual state of flux renders our basic concepts fictitious because they reify the world and transform what is everchanging into something static.[17]

Along similar lines of thinking, Lyotard undermines representational epistemology and hermeneutical theories of meaning, which from his perspective are grand narratives that are unstable and lack certain self-identity. Lyotard is especially critical of the rational critique because it tends from his viewpoint to create unity and totalization, which tends to make it immune from self-criticism due to a failure to maintain a distance from itself.[18] Rational critique is unable to think the altarity of an object because it is a captive of its own vacuous space and can only think its object as represented in language. What Lyotard refers to as the differend is defined in part as "the unstable state and instant of language."[19] Part of the background of Lyotard's position is his conviction that there is no adequate means of judgment between heterogeneous genres. Rational theory is blind from Lyotard's perspective of the inherent connection between power and knowledge, a point made even more emphatically by Michel Foucault in his later works,[20] reflecting a view that any knowledge relationship embodies power and a drive for domination. Therefore, Lyotard perceives the need for a paradigm or metaphor shift, which is somewhat akin to the metaphor shift advocated by Richard Rorty in his discussion of the mirror of knowledge.[21]

Another type of paradigm shift is offered by Deleuze with respect to thinking, which for him represents the art of creating, inventing, and even fabricating concepts. Philosophical thinking is not concerned with contemplation, reflection, or communication because "The object of philosophy is to create concepts that are always new."[22] Furthermore, the concepts that one creates are always singular because the basic principle of Deleuze's thought is that universal concepts are useless for explaining anything due to the fact that they need to be explained themselves. The singularity of a concept reflects, moreover, its nature to relate to other concepts, made of components that can themselves be grasped as concepts, each concept is a point of accumulation of its own components, and its distinctive feature is "that it renders components inseparable *within itself.*"[23] This means that Deleuze rejects Kant's coherence theory of concepts, which is literally a "thinking together," according to Kant, that gives one an awareness of various sensations that become a concept when thought through the understanding (*Verstand*).[24] For Deleuze, a concept, which is both relative and absolute, is much different than that conceived by Kant because, even though it is a whole, it is a fragmentary whole that is always becoming, composed of heterogeneous components, possesses "intensive ordinates," and gives utterance to the pure event, a hecceity.[25] These characteristics suggest that concepts do not cohere or correspond with each other, which is the reason that it is best to grasp them as centers of vibrations that resonate with each other.

If philosophical thinking is about creating concepts for Deleuze, it is less about articulation or demonstration, and is best grasped as a practice of creating concepts, which is its normative task, and must be evaluated by its results. The entire purpose of Deleuze's approach to philosophy is to think difference, which is both positive and disruptive. By thinking difference, one affirms surfaces or planes not as something derivative or secondary, but one must rather grasp surfaces as constitutions of a fluxuating series that forms them. Deleuze wants us to conceive of concepts as a series of waves that lack depth: "Concepts are like multiple waves, rising and falling, but the plane of immanence is the single wave that rolls them up and unrolls them."[26] According to Deleuze, concepts are concrete, whereas the plane is abstract and a horizon of events. The plane, an indivisible milieu, is populated by concepts that it continuously links together. There are no pure concepts for Deleuze as there are for Kant that are without any empirical content and universally express a formal and objective conditioning of human experience. This emphasis on concepts upon planes indicates that Deleuze wants to stress immanence without any ground beneath it, and he also wants to reject all forms of transcendence, a position that places him at odds with both Dōgen and Heidegger. If Dōgen thinks in terms of both immanence and transcendence, and if Heidegger thinks in terms of the ground of being, Deleuze thinks from the surface in order to think difference, which necessarily involves thinking on and affirming the surface, which now becomes a primary rather than secondary mode of focus for the philosopher, instead of the depths or transcendence.

Unlike Lyotard and Deleuze, since what must be thought withdraws from the person for Heidegger, it refuses to arrive. This withdrawal must not be conceived as nothing: "Withdrawal is an event."[27] That which withdraws from us draws us along. In other words, that which withdraws attracts us by its withdrawal. Consequently, a person is a pointer to that which withdraws. Being a pointer is part of a person's essential nature by which one becomes a kind of sign: "As he draws toward what withdraws, man is a sign."[28] By a person's ability to become a sign, this calls attention not so much to that which draws away but to the event of the withdrawal itself. Since that to which a person points has not yet been transposed into language, a person is a sign that is not read.[29] In summary, what Heidegger means by withdrawal is that Being moves away from a person. In the withdrawal of Being, an individual is drawn along with it. The relation between Being and a person is, for example, like a magnetic field. As the magnet (Being) draws away, a person is drawn towards it. In its withdrawal, Being gives itself to thinking as language.[30] Furthermore, a person, functioning as a sign, points to Being which a person allows to hold sway over him/her, and thus a person is held together in his/her essence.[31] Being, even in its withdrawal, gives a person the possibility to be.

Dōgen might ask Heidegger: To where would Buddha-nature withdraw? Dōgen uses in one of his works the image of a bright pearl to represent the unity of world, self, and Buddha or all that is.

> One bright pearl is able to express Reality without naming it, and we can recognize this pearl as its name. One bright pearl communicates directly through all time; being through all the past exhausted, it arrives through all the present. Where there is a body now, arrived now, they are the bright pearl. That stalk

of grass, this tree, is not a stalk of grass, is not a tree; the mountains and rivers of this world are not the mountains and rivers of this world. They are the bright pearl.[32]

This passage reminds one of the famous golden lion of Fa-tsang (643–712) of the Hua-yen school of Chinese Buddhism, which exercised such a profound influence on Neo-Confucian philosophy. Not unlike Dōgen's pearl, the many hairs of Fa-tsang's lion are the lion, the one hair is the lion, and the lion is many and one hair, symbolic of the interrelationship of the noumenon (e.g., gold or principle of *li*) and phenomenon (e.g., lion). The figure of the golden lion is an attempt to suggest the interdependence of all things, the harmonization of all things, the interwovenness and mutual identity of all things.

Since there is an intimate relationship between Being and thinking, Heidegger asserts that thinking has withdrawn from people. To discern what thinking is, one must radically unlearn what thinking has been traditionally, a position to which Dōgen would readily agree. One cannot know what thinking is by constructing a definition of it. For example, one does not learn the art of swimming by reading a treatise on it: "Only the leap into the river tells us what is called swimming."[33] What Heidegger intends to do is to refrain from the type of reflection which makes thinking its object. In other words, it is not his intention to think about what thinking is because this would be to engage in logic. Lyotard, Derrida, and Taylor would be inclined to accept Heidegger's line of argument. Lyotard, for instance, wants to rethink the nature of thinking in which no presentation of its nature becomes primary. The process of rethinking is necessary because "Every emergence of something reiterates something else, every occurrence is a recurrence, not at all in the same thing or that it could repeat the same thing or be the rehearsal of the same play. . . ."[34]

There is in Heidegger's philosophical task and in the works of the four other postmodernists being considered in this chapter a sense of urgency which is also present in Dōgen's thought. Dōgen writes, "Think only of this very moment, and waste no time in turning your minds to the study of the Way."[35] A person's allotted time is brief and to waste it is foolish, because one could be struck with death or an incapacitating disease. Dōgen is convinced that "Our life is like a dream, and time passes swiftly. This dewlike existence easily fades away. Because time waits for no one, you should, during this short lifetime, vow to follow the Buddha's will

and help others in every way possible, no matter how small."³⁶ Since the
time is short, one must marshall all one's energies for the arduous task
ahead of oneself.

The major task stressed by Dōgen is the realization of the Buddha-
nature. But is the Buddha-nature something that has withdrawn from
human beings, as Being and thinking have for Heidegger? The Buddha-
nature is openly manifest and at the same time concealed. As such, it
evades the grip of knowledge. The Buddha-nature is all inclusive; it
includes both sentient and insentient beings: "Thus, these mountains,
rivers, and earth are all the Buddha-nature Sea."³⁷ Thus it is manifest to
one who can see it. However, since no one, unless he/she is enlightened,
sees the all, the Buddha-nature is also concealed. Dōgen might rightfully
ask: To where could it withdraw? Although the Buddha-nature does not
withdraw from a person, in Heidegger's sense of withdrawal, it can be
obstructed by a person's egoism for Dōgen because "If you want to see
the Buddha-nature, you must first eliminate your self-egoism."³⁸ With the
destruction of egoism, the obstacle blocking insight into the Buddha-
nature is removed.

The Way

For Heidegger, thinking is essentially a way: "Thinking itself is a way.
We respond to the way only by remaining underway."³⁹ To be on the
way of thinking is meant in a double sense: (1) a person must open oneself to the emerging prospect and direction of the way itself; (2) a person must also take steps by which alone the way becomes a way.
Heidegger explicates this path: "Thinking clears its way only by its own
questioning advance."⁴⁰ This suggests that thought is interrogative, and
the clearing (*Lichtung*) is the unthought location of philosophical thinking, which is incapable of thinking the clearing. An individual must
travel the way of thinking, if he/she is to understand what it is. To travel
on the road of thinking is to realize that Being gives itself as thought-
worthy. Since the giving proceeds from a want in Being itself, it possesses the connotation of an appeal that calls thought forth. This giving
under the guise of an appeal is what Heidegger means by the "e-voking"
of thought.⁴¹

Likewise, for Dōgen, the path to enlightenment is a way. However,
one cannot arrive at one's goal by ordinary thinking, as Heidegger

would agree. To enter the way entails ceasing discriminating between one thing and another.[42] The way to enlightenment is not a procedure for moving forward, as Heidegger seems to imply, but rather a radical, backward movement. Dōgen advises an aspiring student, "You should therefore cease from practice based on intellectual understanding, pursuing words and following after speech, and learn the backward step that turns your light inwardly to illuminate yourself."[43] Dōgen agrees with Heidegger that one must question everything that one has been previously exposed to and to cast off completely all thought and concepts. For Dōgen, the way is through *zazen* (seated meditation) alone. What is it that one learns?

Both Dōgen and Heidegger agree that one discovers the ground of one's own self, however differently this may be conceived. Dōgen states, "To learn one's self is to forget one's self. To forget one's self is to be confirmed by all dharmas. To be confirmed by all dharmas is to effect the casting off one's own body and mind and the bodies and mind of others as well."[44] Not only is there no trace of mind and body, but there is also no trace of enlightenment. And just as thinking clears the way for Heidegger, *zazen* clears the way to enlightenment, although it must be noted that there is no difference between enlightenment and *zazen*.

In contrast to Heidegger and Dōgen, Lyotard understands the way of thinking as a process of removing clouds or thoughts by recognizing them as enigmatic examples because one cannot know their intrinsic nature when they are occurring in time.[45] This journey to grasp the unthought for Lyotard is painful because we feel safe and comfortable with what is already common or thought. Lyotard argues that we must accept this discomfort in order to conquer it.[46]

Following Derrida, Taylor perceives the way that he follows as a wandering path that inevitably leads one astray from the direction that one intended to pursue. Necessarily, Taylor equates this going astray with erring, a directionless roaming about, deviating from the right course, or missing one's mark.[47] Taylor elaborates the serpentine nature of the wandering of erring: "To saunter is to wander or travel about aimlessly and unprofitably. The wanderer moves to and fro, hither and thither, with neither fixed course nor certain end. Such wandering is erring—erring in which one not only roams, moves, and rambles but also strays, and errs."[48] The end of this errant wandering comes with its own erasure, a crossing out of a word and a reprinting of both the crossed-out word and its deletion. When one wanders one is rootless, groundless, and without a center, which enhances the possibility for exorbitant erring and the one's inability to identify with certainty the origin, middle point or goal of the wandering. In comparison, Dōgen is convinced that human beings and everything else in the world are firmly grounded in the Buddha-nature, even though it embodies permanence and impermanence.

A major problem with Taylor's errant thinking from the perspective of Dōgen is that it corresponds in its errant way with objective reality within which it is located and against which it negatively reacts. Moreover, the errant thinking of Taylor manifests certain postmodern dispositions that hinder one from relinquishing the view of errancy. From within the context of the emptiness of non-thinking, Dōgen suggests that a person must give up all philosophical or conventional views and not merely this or that particular view. From the perspective of Dōgen, Taylor must be ready to relinquish the view of errant thinking, a requirement for a genuine transformation of thinking that also applies to the philosophy of Derrida.

Within his notion of *désistance*, Derrida identifies a rhythm that constitutes and deconstitutes us. This rhythm of *désistance* is described as having the ability of collecting and dividing us which results in the following: "There is no subject without the signature of this rhythm, in us and before us, before any image, any discourse, before music itself."[49] Therefore, the rhythm with which Derrida is concerned represents a separated idiom within us of *désistance*. From Derrida's perspective, his way of doing philosophy does not involve assuming a position and defending it because there is no place that one can stand and take a philosophical position. It is sufficient to be playful.

Not only is there a different rhythm to be discovered in the philosophy of Deleuze in contrast to that of Derrida, but the notion of thinking in Deleuze's thought is unlike that of Dōgen because Deleuze does not view thinking as an expression of a deep interior process; it is rather a way of creating connections among a multiplicity of impersonal forces. According to Deleuze, thinking is about change and transformation, becoming, and the coexistence of planes.[50] Thinking is also an infinite movement devoid of spatiotemporal coordinates; it is best to understand movement as a horizon that is in motion, which recedes as the subject advances to it. This infinite movement is a coming and going that does not advance to some definite destination without already turning back on itself.[51] In sharp contrast to Deleuze, Zen thinking avoids the creation of concepts and other forms of intellectualization because these ways of thinking are inadequate for expressing in language what we actually experience as it is directly experienced.

It is common practice in the Buddhist philosophical tradition from its early inception to connect the creation of concepts with ignorance and to presuppose that ignorance is often expressed in concepts. This does not mean that concepts are completely useless. If concepts are flexible and heuristic, we can use them judiciously to attain some practical result. We must, however, avoid losing sight of the conventional and dependent nature of concepts and not allow them to become habitual, intellectual proclivities or fixed forms of cognition that rigidly determine in advance the ways that we distinguish consciously or pre-consciously one thing or notion from another. Zen philosophers want to get rid of preconceptions, concepts, and other mental stuff that interfere with our direct experience of reality. Although Deleuze almost suggests the importance of spontaneity in his thinking, Zen thinkers are convinced that the efficaciousness of thought is connected to its arising spontaneously from a problematic situation. This pattern of thinking is elucidated by Kasulis' explanation that "When thought arises as a spontaneous response to a break in immediacy, however, it serves as an intermediary stage in the return to spontaneity."[52] This type of centrality accorded to spontaneity by Zen thinkers is absent in the philosophy of Deleuze.

If Heidegger's conception of the way is orientated towards the future, and if Dōgen's way is a backward movement, Deleuze's grasp of the way of thinking is repetitive because he is attempting to think difference and repetition itself appears as difference. Deleuze explains, "Repetition thus appears as a difference, but a difference absolutely without concept; in this sense, an indifferent difference."[53] But this is a repetition that disguises itself in its appearance, and a difference that appears by means of disguise. Deleuze wants to suggest that difference without a concept is equivalent to the essence of repetition. Moreover, Deleuze does not intend to inscribe difference within the concept in general because "In reality, so long as we inscribe difference in the concept in general we have no singular Idea of difference, we remain only with a difference already mediated by representation."[54] Thus, because repetition differs in kind from representation, that which is repeated cannot be represented, although it can be signified in a process that masks it. It is possible to imagine Dōgen asking Deleuze the following: How can difference maintain its own concept and its own reality?

The Call

Being, for Heidegger, gives itself as a gift by calling the thinker unto Being. This gift, which is sustained by Being, constitutes the essence of the thinker. The call possesses an assonance of helpfulness and complaisance because it means not so much a command as a letting-reach: "To call means: to call to arrival and presence: to address commendingly."[55] Therefore, Being, by calling, helps the thinker into presence (Being).

Unlike Heidegger, Dōgen informs us that his call to attain enlightenment was aroused by an awareness of the impermanence of existence.[56] The Buddha-nature bids all human beings forth on a quest to discover the teachings of the Buddha. Dōgen expresses this almost poetically:

> Wind and fire undispersed is Buddha preaching the Dharma.
> Undispersed wind and fire is the Dharma preaching Buddha.
> That is to say, it is the arrival of the time when one sound preaches the Dharma. One sound preaching the Dharma is the arrival of the time. The Dharma is one sound, because it is the one-sound Dharma.[57]

This lone sound is prior to the time of creation. It is the primordial and undifferentiated sound which is the source of all that is.

Heidegger argues that to call implies an approach which contains the possibility of giving a name. A person calls, for instance, a guest in one's home welcome. One does not name him/her welcome. However, one names a guest by calling him/her a friend in the sense that one is glad to see him/her. Calling is not a call that possesses anything, but it is still calling and inviting even if it is not heard or makes no sound.[58] Thus Being calls and appeals to us to think. In fact, Being gives us food for thought which Heidegger identifies with Being itself. And the response to the call of Being is foundational thought.

Dōgen agrees that the call to realize one's Buddha-nature is never ending. Even if one gains enlightenment, one should not stop practicing. One must continue to practice because *zazen* is practice in enlightenment, and enlightenment must be continually confirmed in *zazen*. And since the Buddha way is endless, once one is enlightened one must practice even more.[59] Dōgen also agrees that the sound makes no noise: ". . . the sound that issues from the striking of emptiness is an endless and wondrous voice that resounds before and after the fall of the hammer."[60] What is it that the Buddha-nature says and what can a person say in response? The Buddha-nature which is emptiness "is the power articulating no."[61] If emptiness is expressing no, can a person respond with an affirmative answer? Dōgen's answer is: "One does not say emptiness, because it is emptiness. One does not say no, because it is no. One says no because it is Buddha-nature-emptiness."[62] Thus emptiness can only be adequately expressed by no. The response to the call must be *zazen* which for Dōgen is the foundation for all other activities and response to the call of emptiness.

Even though Lyotard does not react to a call of Being or a call of emptiness, as Heidegger and Dōgen do respectively, he does refer to a call of thinking for which one must remain sensitive and responsive.[63] In fact, Lyotard refers favorably to Dōgen's *Shōbōgenzō* that he read in French translation. And he translates a passage about the trouble caused by saying many things and the little force generated by saying few things into his own idiom. The translation into Lyotard's idiom goes as follows: "'Place oneself in the flood of clouds, disappoint the call of knowledge, disavow the desire to grasp and appropriate thoughts.'" Lyotard helps us to recognize that cross-cultural borrowings can be very productive, and he resembles Dōgen's call to avoid adopting a set of fixed dispositions or pattern of thinking.

In comparison to Dōgen's notion of *zazen* (seated meditation) and its unity with enlightenment, Derrida describes *désistance* as ineluctable. If one compares Dōgen's understanding of *zazen* with Derrida's notion of *désistance*, the latter thinker's position seems to suggest something that has "already happened, to have happened before happening, to be forever in a past, prior to the event,"[64] whereas Dōgen emphasizes the present moment with respect to the practice of *zazen*. According to Derrida, a subject can appropriate *désistance* only as a preinscribed mark made in advance by the imprint of *désistance* itself, which constitutes the subject but is not intrinsic to it. Derrida's notion of *désistance* does not mean that the subject attains a state of neither perception nor nonperception as non-thinking does for Dōgen. From the Zen viewpoint, Derrida's philosophy gives birth to *désistance*, which possesses the danger of leading a person to making distinctions, whereas Dōgen's non-thinking does not seek anything, does not find anything, and does not have to reject necessarily anything.

In sharp contrast to the call of Being in Heidegger's philosophy that helps the thinker to presence, Deleuze argues that Being, which is univocal, is simultaneously nomadic and anarchical.[65] Since Being is univocal for Deleuze, this suggests that it cannot be identical because univocity implies difference, which can only arise in relationship to surfaces or planes. The univocal nature of Being also makes it impossible for there to be unifying forces or enduring structures in Deleuze's thought. Thus there is nothing like the Buddha-nature of Dōgen's philosophy that serves as a unifying or guiding principle in the philosophy of Deleuze, and it is impossible for difference to assume the role as an underlying principle because it is forever in a state of flux and only located precariously on surfaces. Moreover, it is impossible for Being to call a thinker to presence like it does for Heidegger because repetition does not call back the same: "Returning is the becoming-identical of becoming itself."[66] This means that the only real identity is returning itself in the sense of a secondary power, which implies that it is only possible to think of the same on the basis of difference.

Waiting

If one were to ask Heidegger what one should do in relation to thought, he would reply that one must do nothing but wait. Prior to waiting, a person possesses a pre-understanding of Being which places one from the very beginning within the hermeneutic circle.[67] One can wait "for" or "upon" something. In the process of waiting for something, one waits for that which can fulfill one's needs. When waiting upon something one does not know exactly for what one is waiting. Heidegger explains, "In waiting we leave open what we are waiting for."[68] Waiting can be understood as an attitude of attentiveness to Being, which lets Being come into presence as itself.[69] The notion of waiting for Dōgen assumes a very different connotation.

An objective observer of someone doing *zazen* might conclude that the practitioner is simply waiting. Dōgen seems to affirm waiting rather than an active seeking of enlightenment. He writes, "The very moment one begins to seek the Dharma he becomes far removed from its environs."[70] Again, "If your mind does not seek anything, then you will gain a great peace."[71] However, the superior seeking is no-seeking and the best form of waiting is no-waiting. To await for Buddha-nature is not related to one who waits. There is no correct or incorrect way to wait. There is no-seeking and no-waiting. In other words, there is no duality of someone seeking or waiting.

There is only arrival for Dōgen. To affirm that it might arrive is the same as stating that it is already here. It is unnecessary and impossible for the Buddha-nature to come out of the past into the present moment:

"There has never yet been a time not arrived. There can be no Buddha-nature that is not Buddha-nature manifested right here."[72] Since the present is already here, its arrival implies the immediate manifestation of the Buddha-nature.

In reply to Heidegger and Dōgen, Lyotard makes several critical points. Lyotard does not think that Heidegger's linkage between thinking and time, a criticism that he could also level at Dōgen, can be sustained because Heidegger does not give an adequate account of the synthesis between imagination and sensitivity like that located in the third critique of Kant.[73] The idea of presence that can be construed from the philosophies of Heidegger and Dōgen is extremely problematic for Lyotard because presence cannot be conceived or experienced according to the sensibilities of the self, since the subject can never refer to itself within the course of time.[74] More radical than Heidegger and yet more akin to Dōgen, Lyotard wants to develop a mode of thinking that is more in accord with the essence of time. If it is time that blows away the cloud or the unthought for Lyotard, actively forgets former modes of thinking, and motivates thinking to begin anew, this forms a description of thinking coming to grips with the demands of the principle of relativity.[75]

In comparison to the waiting advocated by Heidegger and Dōgen, waiting is too passive for Deleuze because thinking demands movement. If waiting is being attentive to Being and its coming into presence for Heidegger, and if waiting represents no waiting for Dōgen in a situation in which there is only arrival, Deleuze argues instead for movement on a plane of immanence that is akin to chaos, which is characterized by infinite speed and dismantling of any consistency or structure, that inscribes contours on the surfaces of the planes of immanence. These planes of immanence must be multiple because no single plane is capable of encompassing all of chaos without collapsing into it.[76] From Dōgen's perspective, thinking for Deleuze walks a thin line between creativity and collapse, insight and benightedness. Dōgen might also wonder when, if ever, thinking arrives at anything, at any point, or at any time for Deleuze, if thinking is always becoming.

Releasement

A human being, for Heidegger, is an openness to that which is given, and what is given is an awareness of a horizon, which is defined as an openness that surrounds us,[77] without limits of the consciousness of things. Thus consciousness is set in a horizon of openness which is called a region: "That-which-regions is an abiding expanse which, gathering all, opens itself, so that in it openness is halted and held, letting everything merge in its own resting."[78] Thus thinking commences with an awareness of the horizon within which objects are given. Thinking, as an opening, refers beyond the human and beyond the horizon. At this point, Heidegger's thought is remarkably similar to that of Dōgen. Both philosophers are opposed to a representational type of thinking so common to scientific thinking, an observation that can also be accurately applied to Lyotard, Taylor, Deleuze, and Derrida. Heidegger and Dōgen both attempt to transcend the subject-object dichotomy. For Dōgen, mind, a totality of psychophysical being identified with the Buddha-nature, does not exist in a vacuum. Everything in the world is an expression of mind which includes the conscious and nonconscious. Applying Heidegger's terminology to Dōgen, it can be stated that the mind exists within a region, an identification that is not made by Heidegger. In other words, Heidegger does not end with a nondualistic position, although he appears to be on the way to such a position.

Heidegger asserts that to wait upon the opening is releasement (*Gelassenheit*); it is beyond the distinction between activity and passivity. Releasement is let-in, and it is not something that a person awakens in oneself.[79] Dōgen agrees with Heidegger, by affirming that the practice of *zazen* is not the cause of releasement (enlightenment) because practice and realization are identical. Thus there is no distinction between acquired and original enlightenment. True releasement excludes the working of the conscious mind. Dōgen elaborates, "When buddhas are genuinely buddhas there is no need for them to be conscious that they are buddhas. Yet they are realized buddhas, and they continue to realize buddha."[80] Thus true releasement is beyond the consciousness of being released.

Heidegger and Dōgen agree that releasement is a path and a movement. An individual can be released from something or to something. Authentic releasement, for Heidegger, is being released to something,[81] although this distinction does not apply for Dōgen because enlightenment is always present. At the moment of one's own enlightenment, there is a simultaneous attainment of the way (*dōji-jōdo*). This means that with one's own enlightenment everything in the universe attains enlightenment simultaneously.[82] However, both thinkers agree that the path never ends.

Even with the attainment of enlightenment, Dōgen stresses that *zazen* must continue because *zazen* is practice in enlightenment and enlightenment must continually be confirmed in practice.[83]

Releasement, for Heidegger, situates a person within a region to what is prior to thought. What happens to thinking in releasement? From a representational type of thought, thinking changes "to waiting upon that-which-regions."[84] A person is situated within a region and towards the approach of things. In a sense, a person waits in a "between" which joins thinking and releasement. In other words, a person forms the conjunction between thinking and releasement. Thinking becomes, according to Heidegger's position, a matter of not willing as it is transformed into a matter of letting-be. If a person dwells in releasement to that which regions, to what is one released for Heidegger? A person is released to the unfolding of truth.[85] However, a person possesses no power over truth, and it remains independent of a person. In this sense, a person is given over to truth.[86]

In contrast to Heidegger, Derrida's notion of *désistance* destablizes truth internally by introducing instability into it, all the while resembling it yet displacing it and giving one a feeling of unease or uncanniness.[87] According to Derrida, truth is actually destablized in advance by *désistance* in the form of mimesis, a redoubling process that is related to an essence without essence. The fact that it is not must not be construed in a negative manner because it simply *désists* by itself.

Due to the context of flux and movement within which one creates concepts for Deleuze, there is a certain amount of unstableness associated with the creation of concepts, which themselves are a form or a force and never a function. Nonetheless, concepts are events and a plane represents a horizon of events. Deleuze defines events as the consistency of concepts.[88] The event, which exists between two instants, belongs to the process of becoming and is actualized in a body or state of affairs, but it possesses a secret part that is constantly subtracted from or added to its actualization because it retains its infinite movement. Deleuze further defines the event as pure immanence that is immaterial, incorporeal, and a pure reserve.[89] Although the event is part of becoming, Deleuze oddly claims that it is not part of the eternal nor of time. He explains further:

> The meanwhile, the event, is always a dead time; it is there where nothing takes place, an infinite awaiting that is already infinitely past, awaiting and reserve. This dead time does not

come after what happens; it coexists with the instant or time of
the accident, but as the immensity of the empty time in which
we see it as still to come and as having already happened, in
the strange indifference of an intellectual intuition.[90]

This means for thinking that one must wait for forces that can make
thought something active. Thinking is not the exercise of some mental
faculty, but it is rather "an extraordinary event *in* thought itself, *for*
thought itself."[91] Deleuze's emphasis on impermanence and immanence
with respect to the process of thinking is remarkably similar to Dōgen,
but his notion of thinking is ultimately very different than the Zen Buddhist philosopher because of Dōgen's emphasis on the essential relationship between thinking and Being, lack of an intentional attitude for
non-thinking, and its claim to be able to think the unthinkable. Heidegger
and the other postmodernists discussed in this chapter appear to have
more in common with Dōgen in terms of the direction of their philosophy
than does Deleuze.

     According to Heidegger, a person is released to that which from the
very beginning he/she belonged to, which Heidegger identifies as Being.
"Thinking does not arise," according to Heidegger, "It exists insofar as
Being becomes present."[92] Thus thinking and Being are essentially
related, although they are not identical, a position unacceptable to Dōgen.
Thinking is other than being and dependent upon it for Heidegger.
According to Derrida, Being is not a genre or a category: "Like the Other,
Being is not at all the accomplice of the totality. . . ."[93] Derrida does not
want to emphasize sameness because he wants to stress the importance of
difference. But what happens to thinking in Dōgen's philosophy?

     Dōgen advises one practicing *zazen* to "Think of not-thinking. How
do you think of not-thinking? Non-thinking. This in itself is the essential art
of *zazen*."[94] Therefore, enlightenment is to be discovered in thinking and
non-thinking. Dōgen is making a distinction between thinking (*shiryō*), not-
thinking (*fushiryō*), and non-thinking (*hishiryō*). By thinking, Dōgen suggests ordinary mental activity in which one might, for instance, consider
one idea against a competing idea or a kind of mental activity that objectifies. The act of thinking is negated by not-thinking, which possesses for its
intentionality thinking itself; it negates and objectifies the process of thinking. Accepting the presence of ideas without either affirming or denying
them, non-thinking, a more fundamental mode of consciousness than either
thinking or not-thinking, assumes no intentional attitude. The following

response of Dōgen is instructive: "An ancient Buddha said, 'Think not-thinking.' How? By using 'non-thinking.'" This is right thought. Sitting until the cushion is worn away is also right thought."[95] This suggests that for Dōgen non-thinking both unites and sublates thinking and not-thinking because it is equivalent to emptiness. In short, it is thinking of the unthinkable. Heidegger's later philosophical reflections move in a direction that is similar to those of Dōgen because the former conceives of thinking as a listening (*Erhören*) that brings into view the unheard, which causes ordinary hearing and seeing to pass away from us.[96]

By ceasing involvement in worldly affairs, ceasing all movements of the conscious mind, and ceasing making distinctions, one should simply sit silently and immobile and think of non-thinking which is the essence of *samādhi* (concentration). Non-thinking functions by realizing both thinking and not-thinking.[97] It is also beyond thinking and not-thinking. It is thinking of the unthinkable which is emptiness, which means that it is beyond egocentric thinking.[98] As such, non-thinking is objectless, subjectless, formless, goalless, and purposeless. In this sense, Dōgen's philosophy of thinking moves beyond Heidegger and the other postmodernists, although this does not mean that Dōgen's philosophical position is impractical.

We can witness the pragmatic aspect of non-thinking by examining Dōgen's analysis of the fifth case of the *Mumonkan*, a collection of kōans, in which a man is hanging from a branch of a tree by his mouth, and a person on the ground asks him a standard Zen question: "Why did the first Patriarch come from the west?" According to Dōgen, the best way to grasp this kōan is from the nonperspective of a non-thinking mode of mind. From Dōgen's nondualistic perspective, the man hanging from the tree is not simply suspended in space, but he is rather hanging in emptiness. Moreover, the man asking the question, the tree and the question itself are all the same. The dilemma for the man hanging from the tree is that if he answers the question he will plunge to his death, but if he does not answer the question he will not be performing his duty. Dōgen is convinced that it is important for the man hanging from the tree to answer because it is a matter of life and death. To respond to the question is the only way to help the person standing on the ground: "'If he does not answer he avoids his duty.' You must realize that in this case the answer is not different from the question."[99] This case allows us to understand that non-thinking can help us to gain insight into a complex situation and to find a pragmatic solution.

In addition to Heidegger, the distinctions made between the three modes of thinking by Dōgen also share something in common with Lyotard, Derrida, and Taylor. Lyotard refers, for instance, to the necessity of the emptying of the mind that is necessary in order for the mind to think. What Lyotard suggests by emptying the mind is the suspension of giving the mind rules and instructing it to be receptive instead.[100] Derrida's notion of *désistance* marks a rupture in thinking that departs from normal modes of thinking, similar to non-thinking in Dōgen's philosophy, and is concerned with heterogeneity with respect to essence, which is unlike non-thinking in Dōgen because of its transcendence of all distinctions. According to Derrida, *désistance*, a neologism, gives birth to insanity or the irrational,[101] whereas Dōgen's notion of non-thinking renders insight into emptiness, which encompasses all rationality and irrationality, sanity and insanity. Along lines of thought reminiscent of Dōgen, Taylor argues that "thinking of not is the unthinking implied in all thinking."[102] To think the not that both enables and prevents thought, according to Taylor, is to think the name of God and its inherent *not* signified by the name of God. In contrast to Taylor, the plane of immanence, according to Deleuze, must be thought: "It is the nonthought within thought."[103] Unlike Taylor's attempt to think the not, it is sufficient for Deleuze to not think so much an actual plane of immanence as simply to demonstrate that it is there, which it is fair to claim he attempts to accomplish in his collaborative works with Guattari like *Anti-Oedipus* and *A Thousand Plateaus*. The *not* that Taylor and Deleuze attempt to think and suggest that we do not understand is disputed by Stanley Rosen, who asserts that we do understand the *not* or negation and hence think it "in the simple act of thinking negation."[104] It is Rosen's philosophical point that one cannot construct a concept of nothing because it does not possess a sense or reference.

Even though the thinking of Lyotard, Derrida, and Taylor, move in the direction of Dōgen's philosophical observations about non-thinking, the postmodernists are not quite able to make the transition to an objectless, formless, and subjectless mode of thinking. This is also true of Deleuze whose philosophy possesses some similarities to the other postmodernists, but it moves in a much different direction than the thought of Dōgen and embodies an ethos of repetition, difference, surface, and concept formation. If that which is thought is inevitably influenced and governed to some extent by the specificity of that which forms the foundation, or in some cases a lack of foundation, of thinking, Being shapes thinking for Heidegger, Buddha-nature or emptiness for Dōgen, difference as it is defined by Lyotard, Derrida, and Taylor, and repetition and difference for Deleuze.

Concluding Remarks

To conclude that thinking for Heidegger and the other postmodernists considered in this chapter is not transcendental and that it is transcendental for Dōgen is too simplistic.[105] Heidegger and Dōgen agree that true thinking is egoless, will-less, objectless, and formless. Heidegger's reflections on thinking, as they appear in *Gelassenheit*, are an example of transcendental thinking, although it is not a nondualistic type of thinking. Since thinking is egoless, will-less, and objectless, the relationship between subject and horizon is transcendental thinking.[106] Transcendental knowledge is not concerned with objects as much as it is concerned with one's way of knowing objects.[107] Transcendental and ontological knowledge are identical.[108]

Dōgen's mode of thought, on the other hand, is not transcendental. To think is to take a step beyond the top of a hundred-foot pole. This means to cast away both body and mind.[109] To take the step beyond the top of the pole is to think the unthinkable. Non-thinking is not transcendental thinking; it is rather realizational seeing.[110] In what other way can one characterize thinking in Dōgen's philosophy? It can be termed trans-transcendental. In other words, it cannot in the final analysis even be characterized. To characterize Dōgen's way of understanding thinking as transcendental implies that there is something to transcend. The Buddha-nature, which is being and being itself, emptiness, impermanence, existence and time, cannot be transcended. With the attaining of enlightenment, the universal horizon of Buddha-nature is open to one.[111]

I stated above that Heidegger's way of thinking is not nondualistic. This can be seen most vividly in the following statement by Heidegger: "Truth needs man"[112] Is this not an emerging of Heidegger's humanism? This question is relevant for Heidegger because he thinks that it is possible for a humanism to be either grounded in a metaphysics or transformed into a ground for one.[113] Furthermore, there is still someone who dwells in releasement and gives thanks for the gift given by Being. In the final analysis, the entire process of thought is historical.[114] If the way of thinking for Heidegger moves towards the image of the coming night, as it does in the conclusion of his work *Gelassenheit*, and Dōgen moves towards a leap from the top of a hundred-foot pole, both philosophers follow a path to openness, mystery, emptiness, and unification, whereas Taylor, Lyotard, Deleuze, and Derrida follow a path of thinking that focuses on the importance of difference.

All the philosophers considered at some length in this chapter agree about the necessity of overcoming representational thinking that is common to scientific inquiry. Dōgen's focus on non-thinking reflects an objectless, subjectless, formless, and intentionless kind of thinking that is nondualistic. Heidegger moves in a similar direction in his later philosophy. This is made clear by Sallis: "If clearing first grants thinking, then thinking cannot be a representational activity of a subject that would take the clearing as the object of thinking."[115] Heidegger advocates a kind of thinking (*Besinnung*) that represents a releasement from representational and calculative thinking and involves one's entire body, mind, and being. Taylor advocates thinking the most radical kind of alterity—the not— which is impossible to represent. Taylor follows Derrida and his philosophical desire to think prior to the ground of the unthought by means of *désistance*, which is prior to reflection on something and its presence. This suggests that Derrida wants to push thinking to its limits and to examine what kind of thinking might occur on the margins of philosophy. Lyotard also wants to subvert representational modes of thinking, undermine the grand narratives that accompany such thinking, and call into question the entire process of rationality. Derrida and Lyotard share something in common with an observation made by A. C. Graham, a distinguished scholar of Chinese thought, when he discusses the notion of prelogical thinking, which is a necessary starting point for the beginning of analysis. Graham argues that it is impossible to draw a line between prelogical thinking and that based on perception. The former can be a reliable form of knowledge, and it is not necessarily irrational. The prelogical is only irrational when it is accepted without being tested by logic to confirm its adequacy for solving problems.[116]

Deleuze deserves special recognition because he refers to an orgiastic representation that is connection to a self-recognition by representation to the infinite within itself and discovery of its limits. Deleuze draws a distinction between organic representation, which is characterized by form and finitude, respectively its principle and element, and orgiastic representation represented by the ground for its principle and the infinite for its element. The latter can discover the infinite within itself by allowing the existence of the finite as something vanishing.[117] Deleuze is critical of the infinite representation that one gets with a representational form of thinking because it ultimately represents the principle of identity. With his notion of non-thinking, Dōgen finds, however, another way to avoid the identity pitfall that Deleuze thinks is common with the representational mode of thinking.

CHAPTER 4

Radical Skepticism and Doubt

In probably his most popular and widely read work Nietzsche's prophetic figure in *Thus Spoke Zarathustra* speaks eloquently of knowledge that can purify the body, be used for experiments, elevate a person, transform a person's instincts into something holy, and turn one's soul gay.[1] In a later work Nietzsche denies, however, that knowledge possesses the innate power to know the things-in-themselves, an unconditioned thing that by definition is unknowable.[2] Taking this positive attitude toward knowledge and acknowledgement of its limits, it is not surprising to find in Nietzsche's works negative attitudes expressed towards skepticism. Nietzsche views skepticism as a spiritual expression of exhaustion and sickliness that originates during historical periods of change.[3] But later in his unfinished work *Will to Power* Nietzsche equates the great man with the skeptic, providing that such a person possesses the ability "to *will* something great and the means to it."[4]

Many postmodern thinkers have followed the lead of Nietzsche's attitude toward knowledge and his advocacy of the necessity of skepticism by developing various forms of heterological methodologies. A Zen Buddhist type of methodological skepticism is provided by the use of radical doubt in the philosophy of the Zen master and reformer Hakuin, whose use of doubt and its role in his writings is grounded in his own personal experience. Although it is unusual to find a Zen master giving a personal account of his own spiritual odyssey, Hakuin recounts his experience as a twenty-four-year-old monk:

> Night and day I did not sleep; I forgot both to eat and rest. Suddenly a great doubt manifested itself before me. It was as though I were frozen solid in the midst of an ice sheet extend-

ing tens of thousands of miles. A purity filled my breast and I could neither go forward nor retreat. To all intents and purposes I was out of my mind and the *Mu* alone remained. Although I sat in the Lecture Hall and listened to the Master's lecture, it was as though I were hearing a discussion from a distance outside the hall. At times it felt as though I were floating through the air.[5]

This condition lasted for several days. Then the sound of the temple bell transformed him: "It was as if a sheet of ice had been smashed or a jade tower had fallen with a crash."[6] At this very instant, Hakuin is devoid of ego or self and bell. There is simply the hearing of the bell, a pure state of experience that represents non-thinking. Kasulis elucidates the Zen master's situation: "Hakuin became nothing other than the experience of hearing-the-sound-of-the-bell. This was pure presence, the directly experienced genjōkōan, the state of without-thinking."[7] With this experience, Hakuin's doubt vanished and certainty replaced it.

It is possible to identify three types of doubt: skeptical, methodological, and existential. Hakuin accepts methodological and existential forms of doubt, whereas many of the postmodern thinkers favor a skeptical type of doubt, which is an attitude taken toward all human beliefs, sense experience, and knowledge, leaving one without any certainty. Hakuin's acceptance of a methodological kind of doubt possesses nothing in common with the doubt implicit in the scientific method, which tends to be permanent in the sense that it always calls into question the facts and conclusions of research. Hakuin rather perceives a different possibility for methodological doubt that is directly connected to one's existence and quest for enlightenment. This chapter will examine and compare the radical doubt of Hakuin with the different forms of heterological methods used by various postmodern thinkers. On the postmodern side of the comparison, we will examine the genealogical method of Foucault, deconstruction in the work of Derrida, schizoanalysis developed by Deleuze and Guattari, and joining of a semiotic approach with psychology in the work of Kristeva.

Necessity for Methodological Doubt

According to Hakuin, the root problem of life is ignorance, which prevents a person from seeing into his/her own nature. There is a person, for example, in Chinese Ch'an literature, who witnessed a rabbit collide with a tree stump and die. After taking the rabbit for food, the man waited by the stump hoping that it would obtain another rabbit for him. This is the universal plight of all human beings who ignorantly stand waiting for the tree stump to provide them with a meal. The fact of ignorance can be reduced to a single concept: the self is real. Hakuin elaborates, "Because of this view that the self exists, we have birth and death, Nirvana, the passions, enlightenment."[8] Although a person does not possess a permanent self, he/she is still endowed with the wisdom and form of the Buddha. Therefore, a person lacks nothing because he/she possesses the Buddha-nature, which is eternal and unchanging, like a hidden jewel in one's robe.

Because of the existential fact that a person is sunk in the mire of ignorance, a way must be found to extricate an individual from his/her dilemma. The mechanical wrench used to pull a person out of the muck of ignorance is the kōan, an enigmatic saying of a Zen master, which operates by creating doubt. Hakuin invented one of the most famous kōans: We are all familiar with the sound of two hands clapping, but what is the sound of one hand clapping? In order to solve this kōan, one must discard all emotions, concerns, and thoughts. When working on this kōan with utmost attention the aspirant is trapped in a nonconceptual, nondiscriminating state of consciousness characteristic of not-thinking. Using all one's energies, one must investigate the kōan single-mindedly by meditating on it. As one utilizes all one's energies to investigate this kōan with single-minded purposefulness, a great ball of doubt arises: "It must be understood that this ball of doubt is like a pair of wings that advances you along the way."[9] Doubt may lead one to a feeling of insecurity, anxiety, and despair. The existential crisis encountered by the aspirant is captured by the following description: "On all sides the student is engulfed by nothingness. This is a dark nothingness, the nothingness of complete nihilation, the nothingness of not-thinking rather than without-thinking."[10] However, the risk that one can become totally shipwrecked must be taken if one is to achieve total certainty. The risk involved is like trying to ride a tiger, or like the dangerous chance that one takes by entering a tiger's den; unless one enters the tiger's den, one will never capture the tiger cub. Thus Hakuin uses doubt as a method enabling the successful aspirant to advance to a point beyond existential doubt.

When one hears the sound of a single hand clapping, one has arrived at the place where reason is exhausted and words are terminated. Hakuin explains, "At this time the basis of mind, consciousness, and emotion is suddenly shattered; the realm of illusion with its endless sinking in the cycle of birth and death is overturned."[11] What occurs at this point is that doubt blocks any form of conceptualization from entering one's consciousness because Hakuin was trapped in not-thinking, an unsatisfactory and incomplete situation. This process is explained in the following way: "To detach oneself willfully from all thinking, one has to *objectify* one's own thought processes, and in so doing one takes an intentional attitude toward thought."[12] Thus the resolution of doubt, which was created by the kōan, leads to awakening, although the Great Doubt itself must not be confused with enlightenment. This implies that ignorance is overcome, and the karmic root of the cycle of birth and death is stopped. When the sound of a single hand enters one's ear: "All is vast perfection, all is vast emptiness."[13] This type of experience represents the non-thinking mode, which is the source of thinking and not-thinking and prior to them. At this point, there is nothing more to deny, nothing more to doubt.

It can be affirmed that the Zen Buddhism of Hakuin is simply the resolution of the ball of doubt. As Hakuin affirms, "At the bottom of great doubt lies great awakening. If you doubt fully you will awaken fully."[14] Once one is awakened, no fears arise, no thoughts creep in, and one is spiritually reborn. However, before one can be reborn one must die to one's former condition. The ball of doubt which is raised by the kōan leads to the Great Death (*Daishi*): "If you take one kōan and investigate it unceasingly your mind will die and your will will be destroyed."[15] Like a phoenix that frees itself of the net which binds it, one returns to life but without body and mind, which are cast off.[16] Freedom from body and mind implies union with the kōan. And being reborn entails truly seeing into one's own nature, devoid of any trace of existential doubt.

Genealogy and Difference

The old method of grasping what is occurring within historical time and place is inadequate for a postmodern scholar like Michel Foucault, much like it was for Nietzsche before him, because it is impossible to reach a total picture of history. The history passed down to us is not a body of facts, but it is rather a collection of interpretations of various kinds of data, which continues into the future. By means of scientific or research tools, it is impossible to reach primal, untainted material because even the most primary historical data is a product of interpretation.[17] The study of history is also difficult because the scholar, along with everyone else, stands within an interconnected web of power relations and cannot find a place outside of this play of relations of power by which to make an accurate analysis. Because the scholar or any other citizen is a direct descendant of the web of power-knowledge, it is impossible for a person to be a creator of history or a bearer of the continuity of history. Moreover, it is not possible for such a person to account adequately for the paradoxical nature of the discontinuity of history. Thus, it is essential for the historian to find a way of making sense of what is happening.

In his work *The Archaeology of Knowledge*, Foucault turns to what he calls the method of archaeology, a purely descriptive approach, that takes into consideration the discontinuity of history, its temporal ruptures and factual gaps. Focusing one's attention on the discontinuities of history and integrating them into one's discourse, the historian no longer finds them problematic and refrains from themes of convergence and culmination and creation of totalities, which tend to be misleading because they neglect discontinuity and differences.[18] Foucault's emphasis on identifying differences, dividing, increasing diversity, blurring lines of established communication by finding multiple layers of events within discourse, all suggest eliminating meaning from the concerns of the historian. And since history represents a series of reinterpretations in narrative form, it is only possible in the final analysis for the historian to compose fiction. If the great man of Nietzsche's later writings is the skeptic, Foucault's skeptical historian or archaeologist is in the final analysis a creator of fictive history.

Although the general spirit of Foucault's approach to history remains the same, he turns again to Nietzsche and his notion of genealogy to complement his earlier archaeological method in order to develop a new theory of discourse in order to find a more adequate method for his purposes.The difference between archaeology and genealogy for Foucault can be summarized as follows:

> Archaeology attempts to isolate the level of discursive practices and formulate the rules of production and transformation for these practices. Genealogy, on the other hand, concentrates on the forces and relations of power connected to discursive practices; it does not insist on a separation of rules for production of discourse and relations of power. But genealogy does not so much displace archaeology as widen the kind of analysis to be pursued.[19]

Foucault agrees in spirit with Nietzsche's work entitled *The Gay Science*, wherein Nietzsche thinks that a purely descriptive history is useless because of the limited perspective of so-called scientific history, a disciple of dates and facts. For Nietzsche, we need rather to explore patterns and trace developments which can be accomplished by means of the method of genealogy, an historical sketch that elucidates values in transition. In an important essay, Nietzsche writes about the need for a discipline of history that will benefit people in the present: "The knowledge of the past is desired only for the service of the future and the present, not to weaken the present or undermine a living future."[20] It is important for history to serve the forces of life. In other words, history needs to be put to a practical use, which is the reason it can never become a pure science like mathematics.[21]

The descriptive role of the archaeologist is complemented by the diagnostic approach of the genealogist for Foucault by focusing on the interrelations of power, knowledge and the human body. The mutually creative relationship between power and knowledge is made clear in the following statement: "It is not possible for power to be exercised without knowledge, it is impossible for knowledge not to engender power."[22] Although this statement does not mean that they are identical, there is an intimate interconnection between them, and they are joined together in discourse. Foucualt is still concerned, however, with discontinuity, differentiation, dispersion, and mutations, which are the neglected and forgotten aspects of history. Foucault's book on madness, for instance, is not actually about mentally ill people as such, but it is concerned with the madness of society and how it alienated certain people, classified them, isolated them, and designated them as outsiders unfit to be members of society. Among the different phenomena to be discovered, Foucault wants to reconstruct the generative processes that are at work and to elucidate invisible relations among the various phenomena.[23] The genealogist concentrates on scientific statements, philosophy, moral propositions, architecture, institutions, laws, and administrative practices and decisions.

This heterogeneous ensemble helps the genealogist to discern the punctuating gaps of history and to attempt to compose a history of the present, which is a history of the basic duality of Western consciousness.[24] This can only be accomplished by being located within the web of power in the present moment and not outside of historical time and place and the interconnecting web of power relations.[25] This effective history (*wirkliche Historie*) is not connected with metaphysics, acknowledges no absolutes, does not claim to be objective, and is without constants.[26] This radical type of history asserts no truth claims and recognizes that all knowledge is relative.[27] According to Neville, Foucault's position does not represent an attempt to rethink the nature of thinking at its foundations. Neville thinks that it is unnecessary to assume that thinking is grounded in reason or that reason is somehow faulty and to thus conclude that reason is without a solid foundation because it is possible to offer the hypothesis that "thinking is founded in valuation."[28] Nonetheless, Foucault appears to question the foundations of thinking in order to undermine the solidity of its starting point. Since notions of method, starting-point, and theory are anathema to Foucault, a dilemma in his work is seen by Rorty: "On the one hand, he wants to give up all the traditional notions which made up the "system of possibilities" of a theory of knowledge. On the other hand, he is not content simply to give a genealogy of epistemology, to show us how this genre came into being."[29] The Nietzschean spirit in Foucault's work wants to abandon objectivity and any unitive vision of truth.

By acknowledging the limits of knowledge and attempting to write a history of the present for Foucault, the geneologist finds oneself in a non-place between conflicting forces, a location where new ideas and values can be discovered, and within the dualities of Western consciousness. Foucault's nonlocation possesses certain advantages because it allows one to study the dispersions of descent, which reveals differences, discontinuities and divisions, in contrast to the origins of accidental events, and it enables one to study the recurrence of events.[30] Hakuin, a Zen master who thinks that the truth can be self-evident for an enlightened person, would conclude that Foucault's method calls the present moment into question by rendering its apparent truths problematic and developing a counter-history. Hakuin agrees with Foucault about finding oneself within a context of dualities, and he would correctly observe that Foucault did little to extricate himself from these western dualities because he wants to be a political revolutionary, which suggests further involvement in western cultural dualities and not less entanglement in them. By playing the role of the political revolutionary, Foucault wants to accelerate the process of destruction of western culture in order to create new values much like his intellectual hero Nietzsche.

Deconstruction

Due to its adoption by literary critics in the United States and other countries, the method of deconstruction developed by Derrida is probably the most widely known postmodern method applied to texts. But Derrida ironically denies that it is a method at all, and it cannot be transformed into a method.[31] If this is the case, what then is deconstruction? Like so many of Derrida's terms, deconstruction is elusive and difficult to define with absolute precision.

Although he admits being influenced by the term *Abbau* (dismantling), a nonreflective procedure that makes it possible to regress to something that cannot in principle be given by the pregiven world, from Edmund Husserl and Heidegger's use of the notion of *Destruktion*, deconstruction is an ambiguous term for Derrida. In Heidegger's work *Being and Time*, he writes about the necessity of destroying the old philosophical traditions, and the reason for this call for destruction is: "The question of Being does not achieve its true concreteness until we have carried through the process of destroying the ontological tradition."[32] Heidegger thinks that by following this path he will be able to show that we cannot avoid the question of Being, and we will be able to show the significance of retrieving this problem for philosophy. By destroying the ontological tradition and recapturing that to which one returns, Heidegger advocates using a nonreflective movement of thought (*Besinnung*) with that with which it comes into contact. This is a nonobjective involvement with something, a calm surrender to it.[33] The term *Besinnung* is opposed to representational thinking and does not represent ordinary consciousness because it involves one's entire body and mind.

By referring to Heidegger's later work, Derrida indicates, even though he pursues a different agenda than Heidegger, that he is continuing a trend begun by the German philosopher: "And if Heidegger's later work deconstructed the domination of metaphysics by the *present*, he has done so in order to lead us to think the presence of the present. But the thinking of this presence can only metaphorize, by means of a profound necessity from which one cannot simply decide to escape, the language that it deconstructs."[34] Implied in Derrida's statement is his desire to not only continue the work begun by Heidegger but to also bring it to completion by deconstructing the presence of the present. In comparison to Heidegger, deconstruction is an even more radical form of a nonreflective approach.[35] When analyzing the term Derrida explains that "the 'de' of *de*construction signifies not the demolition of what is constructing itself, but rather what remains to be thought beyond the constructivist or destructionist scheme."[36] Deconstruction should not be confused with a type of philosophical analysis that presupposes a reduction of entities to their simple or essential elements. It is also not an act that is created by a subject or an operation executed by a subject upon a text. Moreover, deconstruction is not to be confused with an entity or a thing, and it is not universal or unitary.[37] Emerging through the ambiguity of the term, there is the suggestion of disarranging the construction of terms in a sentence and disassembling the parts of a whole.[38] Thus deconstruction is about the deconstruction of texts that attempts to exceed the sphere of its conceptual totality. If Derrida denies that deconstruction is a particular event, a human act, or an operation, what is the goal of deconstruction? Its goal is to locate an instance of otherness within a text that reflects a logocentric conceptuality and then to deconstruct this conceptuality from the standpoint of alterity, a procedure that suggests obtaining a position of exteriority with respect to that which one is deconstructing. This position of alterity is a form of writing that is accomplished on the margin of the text. Without waiting for any conscious deliberation by a person, deconstruction does occur as an event that enables it to deconstruct itself.[39] Derrida is suggesting that deconstruction is not a method because it is not reductive like an ordinary method, whether it is primary or derived, and it is not a nonmethod because it does not advocate uncontrollable free play.

Since deconstruction is nothing and not everything, what value can it have for Derrida? The term deconstruction is like an *exergue*, an inscription on the face of a coin or at the beginning of a book, suggesting the functions making something evident, bringing forth, or displaying. Like an inscription, deconstruction possesses value only within a context or in a series of possible substitutions of inscriptions.[40] A philosophical concept, for instance, is likewise inscribed within a chain that is related to a plurality of other concepts, which are constituted by their difference or interval from each other. This external difference between concepts is also part of an internal process in which the interval divides the concept within itself. Derrida thus finds that concepts are cracked and fissured by differences and contradictions, and deconstruction does not attempt to overcome these internal differences. In fact, it works to maintain these heterogeneities. Deconstruction is not a philosophical position or an encompassing perspective from which one can analyze something finite. Moreover, deconstruction is not singular, homogenous, determinable, self-identical, and pure; its nature is identified by what "it does and what is done with it, there where it takes place."[41] We find it functioning in Derrida's works in a parasitic manner because it preys on other readings or interpretations in an endless process. Derrida's use of deconstruction suggests that he subordinates rationality to spontaneity and attacks subjectivity because there is no central point of reference for his philosophy in the sense that no stance can become permanent. As philosophical positions become established, they are immediately erased. Deconstruction is antidialectical in the sense that it destroys any progress of the dialectic. The subordinate place of rationality in Derrida's work and his use of deconstruction suggests that conceptual wholes are impossible because conceptual constructs are always falling apart into a multiplicity of parts. Deconstruction does not destroy preexisting structures from the outside, but it rather subverts them from the inside, which is another way of overturning hierarchies.[42]

Derrida's notion of deconstruction and the philosophical attitude that it embodies has been the subject of extensive criticism by other western philosophers. Schrag suggests, for instance, that there is a blind spot in Derrida's approach when he writes, "But the sad irony in the Derridean project of deconstructing structuralism is that his project unwittingly buys into the structuralist definition of meaning as signification (which in the end is simply a linguistic version of epistemological representationalism)."[43] Within the context of his call for a renewal of western philosophy, Putnam accuses postmodernists of playing skeptical games and refusing to recognize the common world that we all share in order to construct a better world.[44] Postmodernists also place an exaggerated importance upon metaphysics and falsely assume that it forms the basis of the entire western culture, figuring that its destruction would cause the collapse of western culture.[45] From a different perspective, Charles Taylor indicates the dangers of deconstruction and its obliteration of old hierarchies that not only upsets traditional distinctions between such subjects as philosophy and literature but also possesses the potential to disrupt such distinctions as equal/unequal, community/discord, uncoerced/coerced and other such distinctions whose undermining would create a fluid cultural situation. Taylor's criticism of Derrida's philosophical approach is lucidly stated: "Nothing emerges from his flux worth affirming, and so what in fact comes to be celebrated is the deconstruction power itself, the prodigious power of subjectivity to undo all the potential allegiances which might bind it; pure untrammelled freedom."[46] Echoing similar criticisms of Derrida, Richard Rorty, who is frequently categorized as a postmodern thinker himself, adds to the criticism by lamenting the lack of an agreement about the criteria for intelligibility and rationality in the writings of Derrida.[47] Another critic does not think that Derrida's critique is radical enough because his deconstruction is incomplete due to its failure to deconstruct itself and transform our experience of the world.[48] For such a critic, Derrida replies, "Ça se déconstruit" ("It deconstructs itself").[49] Derrida means that it deconstructs itself whenever something takes place.

In spite of such criticisms, different applications of deconstruction can be readily witnessed in Derrida's studies of the gift and the spirit. The study of the phenomenon of gift relates it to time, which renders the gift impossible because of its predominance. The gift is only possible at a paradoxical moment when time is torn apart because the present instant is related to temporal synthesis.[50] Furthermore, the conditions of the gift—donor, gift itself, and donee—also indicate the impossibility of the gift because they produce the destruction of the gift.[51] Derrida is attempting to think of gift in its original state in which it is devoid of exchange, reciprocity, or debt. Derrida is also examining the limit of the gift: "At the limit, the gift as gift ought not appear as gift: either to the donee or to the donor."[52] In the final analysis, it is time that destroys the gift, and it is time that operates as the deconstructive agent.

Reflecting on Heidegger's use of the term spirit, Derrida states that it is not Christian or Platonic, is not a figure or a metaphor, and is not a thing or a body; it is something that will not allow itself to be thingified. As part of his deconstructive strategy, Derrida considers the spatial and temporal aspects of spirit, and decides that its spatiality is original with it and "If spirit 'falls' into a time itself determined as negation of the negation, it must also present *itself* as negation of the negation."[53] Derrida then claims that its essence is the concept, which is a "difference of difference." Much like the continual return of metaphysics, spirit also surprises us by its constant return, which represents spirit haunting itself.[54] The nonbodily spirit possesses the power to awaken us, yet it is also destitute in the sense that it loses its power. This difference within itself is expressed as follows: "That spirit is a force and is not a force, that it has and has not power."[55] By deconstructing it to its smallest element, Derrida affirms that spirit is flame, fire, burning, or conflagration: "Spirit is flame. A flame which inflames, or which inflames itself: both at once, the one and the other, the one the other."[56] Taking into consideration the connection of spirit to flame and Heidegger's association with the Nazi Party in Germany in the 1930s, it is not easy to miss Derrida's irony in the following paragraph when he connects the spirit (flame) with a furnace, which evokes images of the Holocaust. Thus, embodied in Derrida's little book on the spirit in the work of Heidegger is a deconstruction of the concept of spirit, a warning about a return of metaphysics, the *différance* embodied in the concept, and an ironical allusion to the greatest systematic conflagration of all time—the Holocaust.

Derrida shares some characteristics with Zen Buddhism because both subordinate rationality to spontaneity. Both are critical of a subjectively based philosophy because both are convinced of the impermanence of the subject. Moreover, both parties agree that conceptual categories are impossible due to their lack of permanence. Deconstruction is akin in spirit to non-thinking in Zen in the sense that they both displace human constructs that have themselves displaced an originating unity, and they both do not attempt to deal with other things or events in an objective way. Furthermore, Derrida's use of such terms as hymen and invagination are intended to explore gaps in sentences or paragraphs, blank spaces between words, or the mystery at an opening. In a similar vein, Dōgen's monumental work *Shōbōgenzō* can be understood, for instance, to be an example of *yūgen* (profundity, mysterious depth).[57] This religio-aesthetic term is also concerned with gaps, pauses, and blank spaces, and expresses their profound suggestiveness and mysterious depth. Within the world of ceaseless change, this term suggests a sudden insight into something strange and possibly a glimpse of things eternal within the continual flux of existence.

Another Japanese religio-aesthetic term also possesses something in common with what Derrida is trying to convey to others with his process of deconstruction. The word *ma* can be translated as an interval, gap, or opening between two or more spatial things or events.[58] It is a term that possesses much in common with Heidegger's notion of clearing (*Lichtung*), an unthought location of philosophical thinking. By discussing clearing (*Lichtung*) Heidegger wants to get beyond subjectivism and indicate that anything can appear, which necessarily requires that there be a being to whom a phenomenon appears as an object. Since a phenomenon can appear and disclose itself, it can be experienced and known by a knower.[59] With relation to space, the Japanese term *ma* means to be open, cleared out, and pure; it is an opening that allows the light to shine through it. Deconstruction shares with *ma* a place at the margins of culture where they deconstruct all boundaries and mental constructs and function experientially at the interstices of being.

Schizoanalysis

If deconstruction represents a dismantling or destruction, a different kind of taking apart is evident in the work of a cooperative effort between

Gilles Deleuze and Félix Guattari who advocate a method called schizo-analysis. This method takes apart egos and their presuppositions in both a psychological and mechanical way because their basic presupposition is that everything is a machine. This suggests that there is no individual man or woman because it is a mechanical process that "produces the one within the other and couples the machines together."[60] The process itself and its manufactured products give birth to desiring-machines and schizophrenic machines without any meaning. The method of schizoanalysis is not intended to resolve the Oedipus complex or to deny its existence. What Deleuze and Guattari deny about the Oedipal complex is its origin and production in the unconsciousness.[61] These writers think that psychoanalysts produce an abstract person by using the Oedipus complex to analyze people, which it is their responsibility to dismantle. In order to reach real human problems, the necessary goal of schizoanalysis is to de-oedipalize the unconscious and to reach those areas of the unconscious untouched and untainted by the problem of Oedipus.[62] If we can break down the abstract conceptualization of Oedipus, it will be possible to emancipate desire.

The liberation of desire, which is by its very nature revolutionary, is only possible by means of schizoanalysis. This radical method is destructive: "The task of schizoanalysis goes by way of destruction—a whole scouring of the unconscious, a complete curettage. Destroy Oedipus, the illusion of the ego, the puppet of the superego, guilt, the law, castration."[63] Schizoanalysis is a functional process with the schizoanalyst functioning like a mechanic working on a machine. The initial task of this mechanic is to discover the nature and functioning of the desiring-machine in the subject.[64] The second positive task is to recognize the social machines that form the context for the individual desiring-machines.[65] These various machines are interrelated in a social field constituted by desire. The authors view schizoanalysis as potentially revolutionary.

This revolution is directed at the coercive nature of capitalism and the ideology of psychoanalysis, which are both responsible for repressing life-affirming desire. But what could possibly be wrong for someone who wanted to remain schizophrenic? Would this not be a proper desire? These hypothetical questions are indirectly answered by Deleuze and Guattari when they write about the schizophrenic:

> He is and remains in disjunction: he does not abolish disjunc-
> tion by identifying the contradictory elements by means of

elaboration; instead, he affirms it through a continuous over-flight spanning an indivisible distance. He is not simply bisexual, or between the two, or intersexual. He is transsexual. He is trans-alivedead, trans-parentchild. He does not reduce two contraries to an identity of the same; he affirms their distance as that which relates the two as different.[66]

The schizophrenic is a fragmented, divided, and false person because such a person can only become himself/herself by being someone totally foreign to oneself. Since the schizophrenic is a desiring-machine that is subject to a binary law governing its associations, it is desire that brings the binary machines together with other desiring-machines by means of its continuous flowing.

The lack of a centered and whole subject gives Deleuze and Guattari something in common with Hakuin, although the Zen philosopher thinks that there is something beyond the impermanent, fractured, empirical self. Beyond the flux of the temporally bound self, Hakuin finds the following: "Man is endowed with the wisdom and form of the Buddha. There is nothing that he lacks. Each person is possessed with this treasure jewel that is the Buddha-nature and for all eternity it radiates a great pure luminescence."[67] Within the worldview of Deleuze and Guattari that is shaped by the philosophy of Nietzsche, capitalism, Marxism, psychoanalytic theory, and the centrality of desire, it is impossible for them to accept the possibility of an unchanging Buddha-nature. Deleuze and Guattari think in terms of increase and decrease, whereas the Buddha-nature is devoid of changing in either direction in a sentient being. From one perspective, the Buddha-nature is here and now in the present moment. In this sense, it represents an event upon being realized by the aspirant. For Deleuze, an event is equivalent to what he calls hecceity, which he defines as follows: "Hecceities are simply degrees of power which combine, to which correspond a power to affect and be affected, active, or passive affects, intensities."[68]

Hakuin and the two postmodern thinkers do share an opposition against any philosophy of subjectivity, which tends to search for an individuation principle within a subject. Deleuze and Guattari refer to a body without organs:

The body without organs, the unproductive, the unconsumable, serves as a surface for the recording of the entire process of production of desire, so that desiring-machines seem to emanate from it in the apparent objective movement that establishes a relationship between the machines and the body without organs.[69]

This imageless body possesses an energy that runs through it. When it enters into relationship with desiring-machines it gives birth to the paranoiac machine.[70] This anonymous configuration makes any certain self-identity impossible because the body without organs simply presents a smooth, slippery, and opaque surface that functions as a barrier. Although Hakuin does not agree with the particular points of the philosophy of Deleuze and Guattari, he does agree that a philosophy of subjectivity is not possible because in the final analysis everything is vast emptiness. There is no place from which to take a stand except in emptiness, and one cannot develop a philosophy of subjectivity from emptiness.

In contrast to the anonymous configuration of a body without organs, Hakuin agrees with Lin-chi's emphasis on a person without status whose source of being is the *mu* kōan. By entering into the *mu* kōan, which is neither a concept nor something physical, one arrives at a prereflective non-thinking, a source of all experiences and differentiations, that is totally free of concepts like a body without organs. From Hakuin's perspective, Deleuze and Guattari do not successfully liberate themselves from a dependence on categories that tends to obstruct the directness and immediacy of one's experience. In other words, one's experience is filtered through one's categories. The non-thinking mode involves freedom from fixed dispositions, opinions, or biases that can interfere with direct experience, and it means to be unincumbered and free of patterns of discrimination and unconscious presuppositions.

Semanalysis

Semanalysis is a combination of psychoanalysis and semiology, the theory of signs, in the work of Kristeva in which both disciplines benefit from the other. Kristeva is heavily influenced by the psychoanalytic theory of Jaques Lacan, although she is also critical of certain aspects of it. She thinks, for instance, that Lacan, as well as Freud, neglects the complex nature of the maternal function in the development of the child.

According to Lacan's theory, a human being develops in five stages. From an uncoordinated body with natural capabilities, an infant enters the mirror stage by identifying with a visual image, which marks a spacial identity for the infant. There are two substages of the mirror stage: jubilant identification with the image in the mirror and the orthopaedic, a promise of totality.[71] Lacan calls the infant's ambivalent identification with its mirror image narcissistic. As the infant develops further, it begins to have doubts about its identity because it recognizes a disparity between the apparent unity of the image and the infant's disjointed bodily experience. Any previous jubilation gives way to a feeling of alienation that commences lifelong doubts of one's true identity. These doubts are often referred to as paranoia or dehiscence by Lacan. The primordial form of the ego beginning with the mirror stage becomes more fully formed in relationships with others, a social grounding of one's identity. This means that the child's identity is constituted by accepting the visual identity presented by others.[72] An important consequence of modeling oneself on others is that one is equally imitating the desires of others, a practice that inevitably leads to aggressive behavior by the child for any object desired by the other. At around two years of age, the child reaches the fifth stage and becomes socially determined with the acquisition of language.

Even though Lacan's theory shapes Kristeva's approach, she is not uncritical of aspects of his work. Kristeva, for instance, challenges what Lacan says about the mirror stage and its initiation of the child into subjectivity by arguing that subjectivity begins not with the mirror stage as Lacan argues but with the material body. Another important criticism made against Lacan's theory by Kristeva is that Lacan does not account for the semiotic drive that operates prior to the mirror stage and the oedipal situation.[73] Besides these criticisms of Lacan, Kristeva also challenges his interpretation of the phallus, castration, and sexual difference. Before the mirror stage in Kristeva's reworking of Lacan's psychoanalytic theory, she locates a prior semiotic disposition, which functions as a location where one is both generated and negated.[74] Kristeva calls this location the *chora*, which is devoid of any unity or identity, and its organizing principle is the maternal body due to the fact that the *chora*, even though it is subject to a regulating process, represents the space where oral and anal drives are regulated by the maternal body. And it is the primal mother-child relationship that grounds the semiotic disposition. Therefore, psychoanalytic theory alone is inadequate to grasp the human situation and the functioning of the semiotic *chora*.

Since the semiotic is associated with pre-oedipal drives that are the result of an intimate relationship with the mother's body, the semiotic is not only maternal, but it is also absolutely necessary in order to understand human nature and the human situation. Due to its connection to the signifying units of speech, the discipline of semiology is part of linguistics. Semiology is connected to the development of models, which are spatiotemporal representations, and produces by itself its own theory of model-making. Consequently, semiotics cannot be disconnected from its own self-constituting theory, which distinguishes it from the exact sciences: "Semiotics is therefore a mode of thought where science sees itself as (is conscious of itself as) a theory."[75] This does not suggest that semiotics can become a science. Why is this the case? Kristeva claims that it is an open form of research in the sense that it is continually reflecting back on itself and offering to itself a self-critique. Therefore, semiotics is a place of dispute and self-questioning, a circle that always remains open.[76] This implies that it cannot become a system. According to Kristeva, her conception of semiotics does not imply either a relativism or agnostic skepticism and rejects humanistic and subjectivistic language because it uses the vocabulary of the exact sciences.[77] From the perspective of Hakuin, Kristeva's conception of semiotics is inconsistent because she claims that it is devoid of a teleological vision like a science, but then she claims that it enters into union with the "scientific practice of Marx to the extent that it rejects an absolute system . . . but retains a scientific approach."[78] Kristeva does not elucidate how an alleged nonteleological semiotics can unite with a teleological Marxism and not acquire this precise characteristic of Marxism.

The unconscious, language, and linguistics possess heterogeneous features. Semanalysis studies the heterogeneity in all these areas by concentrating on signs that form a mixture of sign systems in which no single sign can exactly define the meaning of any other one sign, which possesses the characteristics of being irreducible, dualistic, hierarchical, and arbitrary. A sign is irreducible in the sense that it cannot be reduced from a referent to a signifier or from a signified to the signifier. Within its synchronic function, its dualistic and hierarchical characteristics suggest reified universals transformed into objects.[79] The arbitrary character of a sign is a result of its not referring to a single reality and tendency to distance itself from any transcendental support. From a diachronic perspective, a sign represents a metonymic sequence that continually creates metaphors.[80] A particular sign's interaction with other signs within a web of meaning can resolve contradictions due to the nondisjunctive feature of the sign, which stands in contrast to the disjunctive nature of a symbol. Because it possesses the ability to generate and transform new structures, a sign is transformative.[81]

A sign shares many of its characteristics with a symbol. Without delving very deeply into the nature of a symbol in Kristeva's theory, she does define the symbol as being restrictive, suggesting that it does not refer to a single unique reality and is not arbitrary. The restrictive nature of a symbol is intended in a relational sense because it is confined to its symbolized universal. In contrast to Kristeva, judging by the way that he uses symbols in his work, Hakuin does not accept that symbols are restrictive except in a limited contextual sense. Hakuin refers to a saying of an ancient Chinese master equating the practice of meditation in the world of desire to be like a lotus rising from fire that is indestructible. Hakuin understands the lotus to be a symbol of the unstained, indestructible, ever present, eternal Buddha-nature.[82] From Hakuin's perspective, symbols can refer to a single reality, even though it is also indicative of the process of meditation, spiritual progress, and the world of desire. But the lotus symbol is ultimately empty.

Concluding Remarks

In the early Buddhist tradition, doubt (*vicikiccha*) is one of the five hindrances (*nivaranas*) to spiritual progress. Before progress on the path of liberation can be made, it is necessary to rid oneself of doubt, which is accomplished not by blind faith, but rather from the certain conviction based on critical study and evaluation. Hakuin transforms the meaning of doubt from a hindrance to a method for attaining salvation. When doubt becomes totally shipwrecked at the absolute paradox of the kōan, the means of inducing doubt, one discovers the way of getting the goose out of the bottle without injuring the goose or breaking the bottle. The paradox is never solved; it rather serves as a springboard to an intuitive insight into the nature of reality.

Hakuin's work suggests that the objective of the kōan, a process of holding up before the mind a problem unsolvable by rational means, is to stimulate the mind to move in a totally new, uncharted direction, which means toward enlightenment (*satori*). The kōan does not give factual information; it is neither true nor false. Like the sound of one hand clapping, the dog with or without the Buddha-nature, or the appearance of your face before your parents were born, the kōan refers to an ontological absurdity, which cannot be experienced or conceived. The kōan uses language as a tool to unlock ontological secrets. The paradoxical nature of many kōans, which gives rise to Hakuin's ball of doubt, destroys one's ordinary understanding of the world. If one's understanding of the world is based on reason, it is the function of the kōan to call one's rational understanding into question and to point to what is arational. Dumoulin makes this clear, "The essence of the kōan is to be rationally unresolvable and thus to point to what is arational. The kōan urges us to abandon our rational thought structures and step beyond our usual state of consciousness in order to press into new and unknown dimensions."[83] From the perspective of a Zen philosopher like Hakuin, reason can hinder or totally obstruct one's direct experience of reality just as concepts can come between one and reality.

If one does not retreat from the paradoxical nature of the kōan, and if one grapples with it with all one's being and energy, an intuitive understanding of a transcendental realm of reality is unveiled. With this shift to another realm of reality, the paradoxical nature of the kōan is resolved, although it is not truly solved in a rational way or dissolved by explaining its incongruity. In a sense, the resolution occurs by clarifying the paradoxicality of the paradox.[84] This means that an enlightened being intuitively understands why the language of the kōan is paradoxical; it reflects the nature of enlightenment itself. The aspirant is enlightened: "When the (Sound of the) Single Hand enters the ear even to the slightest degree, your mind, another's mind, relatives' minds, the Buddha mind, the minds of gods, the minds of all sentient beings are at one glance seen through without the slightest doubt."[85] From the ball of doubt that challenges all one's abilities, one transcends finite existence to a realm without doubt.

Hakuin's understanding of doubt as a liberating power stands in sharp contrast to the thread of radical skepticism in the works of Foucault, Derrida, Deleuze and Guattari, and Kristeva. Hakuin's use of doubt is intended to lead to an absolute certainty that is self-authenticating and self-verifiable. From Hakuin's perspective, the radical skepticism of the several postmodernists can only lead to further skepticism. The use of letters, words, sentences, paragraphs, chapters, books, or a reliance in general on writing and language by the postmodernists to convey their message is considered dangerous by Hakuin because it resembles "a coast of rocky cliffs washed constantly by vast oceans of poison ready to swallow your wisdom and drown the life from it."[86] Moreover, the skepticism of postmodern thinkers is simply another obstacle, according to Hakuin's position, to the immediate experience of reality. From the perspective of Hakuin, the radical skepticism of postmodern thinkers assumes the place of rationality of other western philosophers, and it does not advance one's unobstructed and immediate experience of reality. The radical skepticism of postmodern thinkers is not an improvement over the representational mode of thinking characteristic of Enlightenment philosophers. Even though the postmodern thinkers espouse a radical skepticism that attempts to undermine representational thinking, they merely substitute one mode of thinking for another from the perspective of Hakuin and his liberating notion of doubt.

CHAPTER 5

The Body

I n the Pali texts of the Theravāda tradition and in many Mahāyāna Buddhist texts, one can find numerous negative references to the human body. There are, of course, exceptions in the Buddhist tradition, especially if one takes into consideration Buddhist tantra and the significance of the body in Buddhist meditation. Western philosophy, on the other hand, is infamous for its mind/body dualism. Dōgen and Merleau-Ponty tend to be exceptions, although not necessarily the only examples, to the prevalent tendencies of their respective philosophical traditions. The human body, for Dōgen, is not a hindrance to the realization of enlightenment; it rather serves as the vehicle through which enlightenment is realized by the aspirant. Dōgen argues that those aspiring to become enlightened strive with their bodies, practice seated meditation (*zazen*) with their bodies, understand with their bodies, and attain enlightenment with their bodies. Thus the body attains a metaphysico-religious status in Dōgen's thought.[1] Using the phenomenological method in his earlier work, Merleau-Ponty wants to deliver a fatal blow to the historical tradition of philosophical dualism and overcome it.

By means of a comparative dialogue, this chapter will bring together Dōgen and Merleau-Ponty because of his influence on some postmodern thinkers on the problem of the human body. The cross-cultural discussion will be broadened by including the views on the human body of such postmodern representatives as Levinas, Lyotard, Foucault, Derrida, and with the bulk of our attention given to the thoughts of Julia Kristeva and Mark C. Taylor on the subject of the human body, and the collaborative efforts of Deleuze and Guattari. The postmodern and Zen interest in the human body is partial evidence of the desire to overcome representational thinking. With relation to Merleau-Ponty, I will concentrate my attention on his earlier work, *The Phenomenology of Perception*, and on his later work, *The Visible and the Invisible*, only to the extent that it throws light on his understanding of the body. Due to Merleau-Ponty's extensive discussion of the human body and the unfinished nature of the later book, a certain amount of selectivity seems appropriate in this chapter.

Body and World

When discussing the body Merleau-Ponty is not referring to an object or a mere physical entity.[2] The body cannot be comprehended by measuring its properties, the causal relations among its parts, or its causal relation to other such entities, nor can it be reduced to an object that is sensitive to certain stimuli. If it is not a thing that can be measured, is it a thought? It is neither object nor subject. It is, however, subject and object. Lingis accurately captures the spirit of Merleau-Ponty's explication of the human body when he writes, "Merleau-Ponty's work describes our bodies not as material objects of nature agitated by stimuli, but as organisms capable of perceiving and activating themselves in organized ways—our bodies as structures of perceptual and behavioral competence."[3] From Merleau-Ponty's perspective, the human body is a lived body; it is mine. Since the body is primarily my body, it is personal, subjective, objective, and inhabited by an intentionality that enables it to express meaning, whereas Deleuze and Guattari argue that the body never belongs to a subject and thus can never be yours or mine.

According to postmodern thinkers that have been either influenced by Merleau-Ponty or react against his philosophy, the body is not mine according to Derrida because my relationship to my body does not mean that I am my body or that I possess it in any true sense. My relation to my body is more akin to a deprivation because my body is not merely something that I do not have, but it is actually something that has been stolen from me. Who is responsible for the theft? Derrida identifies the Other as the thief.[4] Emmanuel Levinas, a reader of the work of Merleau-Ponty, views the body differently than Derrida because the former tends to conceive of the lived body as a "cross-roads of physical forces, body effect."[5] Likewise, Deleuze and Guattari view the body as a complex interplay of social and symbolic forces, which excludes its being a substance, an essence, a medium, or a thing. The body is involved in a multiplicity of elements within a number of sign systems. The difference between bodies, which is devoid of an ontological distinction, becomes a semiological question because they can assume chemical, biological, social, or political forms. Nonetheless, all bodies are causes in the sense of being causes in relation to each other and for each other, but the relationship between them is not to be construed as a cause and effect relation.[6]

In contrast to Merleau-Ponty and the postmodernists mentioned, Julia Kristeva views the human body within the context of her theory of abjection, a psychological type that experiences itself as waste. Kristeva focuses necessarily on the borders of the body and the identity of the subject where the refuse of the body is continually expelled in the forms of feces, urine, vomit, tears, spittle, and food. Once these defiling elements are expelled from the body, they are considered unclean, improper, and loathsome. These defiling items and fluids are very instructive, if we bother to reflect upon their significance:

> These body fluids, this defilement, this shit are what life withstands, hardly and with difficulty, one the part of death. There, I am at the border of my condition as a living being, My body extricates itself, as being alive, from that border. Such wastes drop so that I might live, until, from loss to loss, nothing remains in me and my entire body falls beyond the limit— *cadere*, cadaver. If dung signifies the other side of the border, the place where I am not and which permits me to be, the corpse, the most sickening of wastes, is a border that has encroached upon everything.[7]

Kristeva thinks that the various bodily waste products teach one what must be expelled in order for one to live. Moreover, these various forms of filth, which will become sources of defilement, are abominated as abjection, which assumes a variety of forms according to the social and symbolic order with which it is coextensive.

For Dōgen, the body is both subject and object, and more. What does Dōgen mean by more? Dōgen answers, "What we call the body and mind in the Buddha Way is grass, trees, and wall rubble; it is wind, rain, water and fire."[8] Since the mind is all things and vice versa, everything represents a single and total body. There is an important consequence of Dōgen's position: "If your own body and mind are not grass, wood, and so on, then they are not your own body and mind. And if your body and mind do not exist, neither do grass and wood."[9] Therefore, the body and mind represent the entire world. Consequently, human beings are not separated from the world by their bodies, whereas some of the postmod-ernists suggest that we are separated or alienated from the world, although our bodies are within the world. In fact, no one can be absolutely certain where one's body terminates and where precisely the world begins, and vice versa. Due to her concept of abjection, Kristeva would agree with Dōgen that it is difficult, if not impossible, to find clearly marked lines of demarcation between the body and world, pure and impure, proper and improper, order and disorder, but she does not share his nondualist position. In distinction to Dōgen and Kristeva, what Deleuze refers to as the schizophrenic body is more akin to a body-sieve that also includes the primary dimensions of fragmentation and dissocia-tion.[10] In contrast to Deleuze and Kristeva, Merleau-Ponty views the body in a more unitary way.

To have a body means, for Merleau-Ponty, that one is involved in a definite environment, because our body is our vehicle for being in the world.[11] Although the body is to be distinguished from the world, it is our medium for having a world and for interacting with it. If to be a body means to be tied to a certain world, this implies that being a body involves being in the world, a primordial form of existence which is preobjective. The body is not in space in the same sense that water is in a vase, because the body is a point from which space radiates and around which things arrange themselves in an orderly way. Developing some of the insights of Merleau-Ponty, Lingis argues that the body centers things and itself: "There is in the body an immanent knowledge of how to center, how to position itself, how to take hold of things such that they are given and manifest in their intersensorial essence."[12] Although things have their own orientation, the body can center things by taking hold of a field that on which things appear. Since the body is both being-in-itself and being-for-itself for Merleau-Ponty, the spatiality of the body indicates that it is itself the author of space, the low and high, the far and near. If the world pos-sesses spatiality for me, it is because I inhabit it by means of my body, which involves a dynamic, living relationship and not a conceptual rela-tion. The spatiality of the body is not a position; it is rather a situation, because existence includes space and time in this primordial relation to the world.[13]

The situation in which Kristeva finds the body is characterized by abjection, a place where one feels marginal within space. When a social and symbolic system is already established, abjection, a universal phe-nomenon, is encountered by a person as rejection, fear, and aggression, feelings grounded in the pre-oedipal relationship between a child and its mother that gives way to revulsion and horror by the former.[14] The individual tends to repress abjection, but when it is released it shatters the developmental stage of narcissism for the child.

The situation in which the body finds itself is conceived differently by other postmodern thinkers. Levinas thinks, for instance, that the position of the body is revealed by groping.[15] From his genealogical methodological perspective, Foucault examines the relationship between the body, power, and sexuality, focusing on a situation in which the sexual body is embraced by power. By embracing the sexual body, power furthers its control and thus enhances its effectiveness, and it also results in an increase of pleasure and a sensualization of power. "This produced a twofold effect: an impetus was given to power through its very exercise; an emotion rewarded the overseeing control and carried it further; the intensity of the confession renewed the questioner's curiosity; the pleasure discovered fed back to the power that encircled it."[16] The body, which is an element of chance, is a bit more difficult to situate for Deleuze and Guattari because it represents an arbitrary relationship of forces.

Invoking Antonin Artaud's concept of a body without organs, Deleuze and Guattari want to demonstrate its relationship with the constant flows or particles of foreign bodies. The body without organs is nonproductive, although it is produced, imageless, with a smooth, slippery, opaque, taut surface that functions as a barrier.[17] Unlike Merleau-Ponty and Dōgen, the dual authors present a body that is devoid of intellectual fantasy and projection that is also moving toward a disinvestment of any psychical interior. In other words, it lacks depth or internal organization, and it is more akin to a flow of forces on a surface of intensities. The body without organs is similar to an egg, although this does not mean that it rejects or opposes organs. Its egglike appearance and smooth surface represent its exterior prior to its being stratified, organized, regulated and hierarchized by being inscribed by such items as race, culture, and deities.[18] Standing against organization, regulation, and the tendency to hierarchize it, the body without organs forms a boundary or limit that resists such negative tendencies.

Dōgen agrees with Merleau-Ponty and with Deleuze and Guattari that the body includes space and time and occupies a situation. Somewhat analogous to what Merleau-Ponty intends to state in his philosophy is Dōgen's use of the image of a bright pearl to express reality.

> One bright pearl communicates directly through all time;
> being through all the past unexhausted, it arrives through all
> the present. Where there is a body now, a mind now, they are
> the bright pearl. That stalk of grass, this tree, is not a stalk of
> grass, is not a tree; the mountains and rivers of this world are
> not the mountains and rivers of this world. They are the
> bright pearl.[19]

Dōgen, like Merleau-Ponty, states that the human body participates in the external world. In fact, the mind, body, and things of the world interpenetrate one another without the possibility of a lucid demarcation among them. As we will see, this nondualistic position is similar to what Merleau-Ponty calls the flesh. From the perspective of Deleuze and Guattari, the body, a process of intersecting forces, represents spatiotemporal variables that are transitory, mobile, and are constantly changing.

According to Merleau-Ponty, the human body and the perceived world form a single system of intentional relations;[20] they are correlations, which implies that to experience the body is to perceive the world and vice versa. Since the body is the medium of things, its presence to the world enables things to exist.[21] Thus the body and world are an inseparable, internal relation. Instead of a system of intentional relations between the body and world, Taylor finds that the body ultimately betrays us: "The betrayal of the body is disease, which unavoidably involves a certain sickness and illness."[22] For the betrayal of disease to be possible, it is necessary for a person to be incarnate, a material, carnal being. Disease embodies what Taylor identifies as the "not." Taylor elaborates, "This not of disease is the sickness unto death that 'is' before my beginning and after my end."[23] Taylor suggests that the existence of an individual is entangled and encompassed prior to its commencement and even after its final termination. In sharp contrast to Taylor, Levinas tends to agree with Dōgen and Merleau-Ponty in spirit that there is no duality between the lived body and the physical body. In fact, the body allows us by means of our labor to take hold of the world.[24]

If Levinas' point is pushed to an extreme, we arrive in the philosophical vicinity of Deleuze and Guattari where everything is a machine. In fact, the body is constituted by various desiring-machines. The position of Deleuze and Guattari must not be confused with the eighteenth-century notion of *l'homme machine* and its mechanistic model of reality. A student of their work clarifies their position: "They speak of machines to suggest that the unconscious is less a theatre than a factory, and to convey a positive, dynamic sense of the cosmos without falling into religious or anthropomorphic vitalism (since machines have no souls and no personalities)."[25] The parts of this body or desiring-machine are unrelated to the whole. Deleuze and Guattari elucidate further that "The body without organs is in fact produced as a whole, but a whole alongside the parts—a whole that does not unify or totalize them, but that is added to them like a new, really distinct part."[26] Wholes or totalities are always peripheral for Deleuze and Guattari because a whole is a sum of particular parts, but it does not unify them. The whole is something added to the parts.[27]

In contrast to Merleau-Ponty and Taylor, Foucault perceives the interrelations between the body and world much differently because he sees it in more political terms and views the body as forming a subtle and primary relay system for the deployment of sexuality, although he shares more in common with Deleuze and Guattari.[28] From Foucault's geneological perspective, beginning in the seventeenth century in Europe, power developed into two forms: the first centered on the body as a machine: "Its disciplining, the optimization of its capabilities, the extortion of its forces, the parallel increase of its usefulness and its docility, its integration into systems of efficient and economic controls, all this was ensured by the procedures of power that characterized the *disciplines....*"[29] The second form of power focused on the body as a species. What Foucault means is the "body imbued with the mechanics of life and serving as the basis of the biological processes: propagation, births and mortality, the level of health, life expectancy and longevity, with all the conditions that can cause these to vary."[30] Foucault is mostly concerned with how various forms of power were used to bring the body under control. The first form of power represented an anatomopolitics of the human body, and the second form of power is what he calls a biopolitics of the population. By means of diverse techniques of subjugation and control over the human body and population, power was exerted over life during this period of western history by what Foucault calls bio-power. From the perspective of Merleau-Ponty and Dōgen, Foucault's conception of the body tends to be materialistic because as a substance the body can be tortured, punished, and disciplined.

Although not totally unconcerned with political power during his lifetime due to the often fluctuating centers of power in medieval Japan,[31] the focus of attention for Dōgen is on the inseparable interconnection between the body and world. Like everything else, the body is dynamic, a position with which Merleau-Ponty would concur. For Dōgen, life is analogous to riding in a boat in which the voyager uses its sails and tiller to guide and move one to his/her destination. Although the sailor can perform certain tasks to assist him/her in his/her journey, it is the boat that carries him/her. Even though the boat is the sailor's mode of transportation, it is he/she who makes it a boat that becomes a world of the sailor. "It is for this reason that life is what I make to exist, and I is what life makes me. In boarding the boat, one's body and mind and the entire surrounding environment are all the boat's dynamic working; both the entire earth and all space are the boat's dynamic working."[32] Thus the body, mind, and world are nondual and dynamic.

This intuited unity perceived by Dōgen is disputed by Taylor because the body inevitably betrays itself. The location of greatest betrayal is within the immune system of the human body and "the baffling contradictions of autoimmune diseases."[33] The body's betrayal of itself is nothing abnormal; it must rather be grasped as its original condition. If Foucault depicts the human body as being assaulted and subjugated by outside bio-political forces, the picture that Taylor gives us of the body in contrast to that of Foucault, Dōgen, and Merleau-Ponty is of a complex organism at war with itself. A different kind of conflict is perceived by Deleuze and Guattari with respect to the two states of desiring-machines and the body without organs, which constantly oscillate between a functioning multiplicity at one moment and an unextended intensity the next moment. During this continual oscillating process, the desiring-machine traces itself on the smooth surface of the body without organs, forming points of disjunction that enable a new synthesis to be created.[34] By being inscribed on the surface of the body without organs, the desiring-machine can function as a mouth machine, for instance, that speaks, eats, expectorates, or breaths.

When I experience my body, according to Merleau-Ponty, an ambiguous mode of existing is revealed to me because the traditional distinctions between object and subject are called into question. I can, for instance, touch an object with my right hand, and my right hand can be touched by my left hand. Ceasing to be a sensing subject, my right hand becomes a sensed object. Thus the body possesses the ability to turn back on itself and take itself for its own object, manifesting its ability to be for itself (subject) and in itself (object). Thus the body can be both touched and touching. Levinas also perceives an ambiguity associated with the body in two fundamental senses: "The ambiguity of the body is consciousness."[35] The second type of ambiguity connected to the body, a being grasping other beings, and its encounter with the other is produced in labor, an activity that is only possible in an incarnate being in relation to another being.[36]

Since the experience of one's body reveals an ambiguous mode of existing, which is especially true in sexual experience,[37] Merleau-Ponty attempts to overcome this ambiguity of the body by turning to ontology in his later work. *The Visible and the Invisible* represents an attempt, although it is an incomplete work, to discern the metaphysical structure of the body. What Merleau-Ponty calls the flesh, an opening of being or wild being, is not a fact or a collection of facts; it is neither matter nor spirit. The flesh represents an element,[38] an essential element, which enters into the composition of everything and thus appears in everything; it makes everything be what it is. As an element, flesh is the style of all things and appears in everything and everywhere, but it does not itself appear. Thus there is an underlying unity between an individual, a lived body, and the world because both are flesh.[39] In other words, beneath the apparent duality of consciousness and object lies "wild being," which entails that humans are mixed in with being and gathered up with things into a fabric of being.

Body and Consciousness

The body and consciousness, for Merleau-Ponty, are interrelated because the latter is dependent on the body, although consciousness is not reducible to the body. Thus consciousness is incarnate for Merleau-Ponty, a position to which Dōgen agrees because he affirms that the body participates in an individual's inner world. Merleau-Ponty refers to the tacit *cogito*, a prereflective, silent consciousness, and an intentional operative, which supports reflective consciousness, forming the basis of all evidence and certainty that originates in the act of perception and not the prior correspondence of consciousness with itself.[40] In other words, the certainty of perception is the certainty of being present to the world, to be conscious that something appears to me. This beginning consciousness represents a primitive self-consciousness which is simultaneous with the consciousness of the world. Consciousness, an opening upon the world, mutually implies the world because its ultimate correlate is the world and vice versa.[41] Due to the fact that consciousness is conscious of something other than itself, it is able to be conscious of itself. Thus consciousness can possess itself only by belonging to the world.[42]

The influential postmodern philosopher Lyotard agrees with Merleau-Ponty that consciousness is incarnate and that we need the body in order to think. Lyotard thinks that the body and mind share an analogizing power in which each is analogous to the other within the relationship of their respective realms, which is sensible in the case of the body and symbolic with respect to the mind.[43] Lyotard distinguishes himself from Merleau-Ponty by discussing gender differences that mark the body with transcendence and cause infinite thought because "This difference makes thought go on endlessly and won't allow itself to be thought. Thought is inseparable from the phenomenological body; although gendered body is separated from thought, and launches thought."[44] Therefore, it is possible from Lyotard's perspective to have a thought that continues to exist after the death of the body.

These lines of argument by Merleau-Ponty and Lyotard are a trap or a dead end for Dōgen. Rather than a consciousness of the world, and rather than an intentional consciousness which originates in perception, Dōgen wants to go beyond intentional thinking to non-thinking (*hishiryō*), a simple acceptance of ideas or things without affirming or denying them. Non-thinking is more fundamental than the prereflective, silent consciousness of Merleau-Ponty. It unites thinking, an intentional weighing of ideas, and not-thinking, a negation of mental acts, and possesses no purpose, form, object, or subject. Non-thinking, the pure presence of things as they are, is realized in *zazen* (seated meditation)[45] and is a "thinking" of the unthinkable or emptiness. There is importantly, however, no bifurcation of the body and mind in the state of non-thinking.

There are two postmodern thinkers, whose thinking demonstrates the influence of Jacques Lacan, that especially perceive the relationship between the body and consciousness differently than Merleau-Ponty and Dōgen. Following Lacan's analysis of the unconscious, Taylor thinks that "it is possible to argue that not only the unconscious but the body is structured like a language."[46] Kristeva tends to agree with this line of thinking, although she traces the trail of the signifier (which is already present in some form) through the body in the form of presymbolic imagery with the intention of reinscribing the body in language. Kristeva and Taylor pursue their lines of inquiry in different ways. Since semiotic activity can represent dreams that derive from the body, Kristeva traces what she calls the semiotic body, an autoerotic, preoedipal body.[47] In contrast, Taylor traces what he refers to as the architecture of the body that manifests itself most dramatically when the body breaks down, which leads Taylor to conclude the following: "The body is no more stable than the diseases that inhabit it."[48] More importantly, Taylor refines his earlier position that the body is structured like a language because of a consideration of DNA and a conviction that all language presupposes a system of communication. Thus Taylor now claims that the body is structured like a communications system, although he does not want to assert that there is any major difference between communication and language.[49] In sharp contrast to Taylor and Kristeva, the collaborative work of Deleuze and Guattari is an attack on the theories of Lacan, which they interpret as a fabrication and form of bondage for the individual.

Communication between consciousness and the world is possible, according to Merleau-Ponty, due to the body, the third aspect of the dialectic of existence. The body functions as the mediator of consciousness and world; it opens them up to each other in the sense that the body forms the immediacy of the world by placing consciousness in direct and immediate contact with the world.[50] Thus there is a dependency of consciousness on the body and expression in speech, a means by which consciousness stabilizes itself. If thought, the product of consciousness, is independent of perceptible expression grounded in a lived body, then it is fundamentally temporal and historically conditioned.[51] In contrast to Merleau-Ponty, Dōgen views the relation between the body and consciousness in a nondualistic way.

Dōgen argues that the human body is the ground from which consciousness evolves. Since the body and consciousness penetrate each other and are inextricably interwoven, they are nondual: "You should know that the Buddha Dharma from the first preaches that body and mind are not two, that substance and form are not two."[52] Although the mind ultimately transcends them, it is both subject and object; it is consciousness and nonconsciousness. In sharp contrast to Dōgen's claim that the body forms the ground for the arising of consciousness, Deleuze and Guattari argue that the notion of grounding forms rather a surface for desire: "The body without organs, the unproductive, the unconsumable, serves as a surface for the recording of the entire process of production of desire, so that desiring-machines seem to emanate from it in the apparent objective movement that establishes a relationship between the machines and the body without organs."[53] From the perspective of Deleuze in his earlier published work, when Dōgen refers to grounding something he is determining something in accord with the logos, which suggests that it becomes the similar, same, or identical to the ground.[54] If the non-thinking mode of consciousness for Dōgen is prereflective and nonconceptual, Deleuze's connection between grounding and a representational mode of thinking and his criticism of this type of thinking does not apply to the Zen philosopher. Dōgen agrees, however, with the ultimate outcome of the third sense in which Deleuze uses the term ground, meaning to bend towards the forms of representation. After it bends towards what it grounds in the form of representation, the ground "turns and plunges into a groundless beyond the ground which resists all forms and cannot be represented."[55]

Body and Perception

A theory of the body presupposes, for Merleau-Ponty, a theory of perception. If one presupposes that to see the world means to be situated so that objects can show themselves, and that to perceive the world one must dwell within it, then one perceives an object when one inhabits it. "My body is the fabric into which all objects are woven, and it is, at least in relation to the perceived world, the general instrument of my 'comprehension.'"[56] Human perception of the world and its objects is contingent upon the lived body. Therefore, perception is embodied for Merleau-Ponty and also for Dōgen, who writes about seeing forms and hearing sounds with the body and mind.[57] Merleau-Ponty states that one perceives with one's body, which implies that the position and movement of one's body not only allows one to see, but also determines what is accessible to one's view, since one can see no more than what one's perspective grants.[58] If one loses an arm or a leg, not only is one's world altered, but one's perception of the world is changed due to the contingency of one's perception upon one's body.

In contrast to Merleau-Ponty, what is important to perceive for Dōgen is not simply objects that appear, but rather Buddha-nature, which represents both beings and being itself. The individual does not necessarily have to do anything special to perceive Buddha-nature because he should simply be attentive to ordinary temporal conditions. However, what is to be perceived does not refer to the perceiver or that which is to be perceived. There is neither a correct nor an incorrect way to see. It is just *see*. This type of perceiving refers neither to my own seeing nor to the seeing of another. "It is 'Look! temporal condition!' It is transcendence of condition."[59] It is simply seeing Buddha-nature in a flash without conditions, without intention, and without duality.

As a perceiving being, one finds oneself, according to Merleau-Ponty, in a particular situation, which entails being intertwined with a body, an object, and other individuals within a general milieu. A given situation refers to a sedimented situation, "which enables us to rely on our concepts and acquired judgments as we might on things there in front of us, presented globally, without there being any need for us to resynthesize them."[60] The result enables situations to become immediately familiar to us, which means that sediments are closely interrelated in the form of a schema of sedimented structures.[61] This fact possesses three important implications: 1) since a sensation can be sensed only by means of a structure, a sensation is only possible if it is of a certain type; 2) every type of sensation is closely related to every other type of sensation to form a unified schema of sensory structures; 3) if sensations are structural, they are meaningful.[62] Deleuze and Guattari perceive a similar process of sedimentation taking place with the body without organs, which represents the body prior to and in excess of the uniting of its intensities and their sedimentations. Not all that different than Deleuze and Guattari, other postmodernists have a tendency to view the situation of human beings as ambiguous and marked by difference. Food, bodily waste, and signs of sexual difference are broad categories of abjects, for instance, that cause visceral reactions by subjects that can often be disgusting. Other postmodernists emphasize other forms of difference.

In his later work, Merleau-Ponty argues that the body can prevent perception, even though one needs it to perceive. It is not entirely one's body that perceives because it is built around a perception that dawns through the body. Thus perception emerges in the recess of a body.[63] The body is a perceptible reality that can perceive itself, become visible for itself, and become tangible to itself because it can touch itself. For the body to actualize the possibility of becoming a perceiving perceptible is to realize a potentiality which is inherent in the being of the world.[64] Beneath the perceiver and perceived or toucher and touched—a criss-crossing—is a shared, preestablished harmony, which takes place within the individual forming an underlying unity of perception.

If we consider the abject body along with Kristeva, the perceptual reality of the body becomes more complicated because the abject is not an object that one can directly face, give a name, or imagine; it is also not a fleeing otherness or a correlative support that enhances my autonomy. The objective character of the abject is simply something that is opposed to me.[65] If a corpse, or the utmost form of abjection, can be construed as an object of perception for the sake of argument, it can serve as a good example of an abject object that stands opposed to me because it is something that disturbs me in the sense that it disrupts my sense of identity, system, and order. The dead body creates in us uncanny feelings that threaten us because it violates well-defined borders, social positions, and accepted rules of encounter and interreaction.[66]

In sharp contrast to Kristeva, the body actualizes itself and achieves a preestablished harmony for Dōgen in the process of *zazen*, which is not entering into realization, but is already realization even when one begins to sit.[67] *Zazen*, a fundamental form of spiritual life, represents the non-thinking mode of consciousness where body and mind are cast off[68] and one takes a leap to enlightenment. By casting off body and mind, one severs one's defiled thoughts, which originate on one's discriminating consciousness.[69] Dōgen understands this process as dynamic and not something static, taking place in the present moment: "'Body and mind drop off' represents universal truth, real existence in the present, that neither reverts to the past, nor jumps ahead to the future."[70] To advocate casting off body and mind, Dōgen does not mean that one should reject one's body. He wants to affirm that one should not be attached to the body, although he still recognizes that the path to realization is through the body.

An assertion that Merleau-Ponty does not make because he adheres to his phenomenological convictions,[71] even though he recognizes that the body is material and spiritual, is that the body can manifest the absolute. While Dōgen acknowledges the impermanent nature of the body and the necessity of the aspirant for enlightenment to become detached from his body, he asserts that the body manifests Buddha-nature, beings and being itself. Dōgen writes, "The Buddha-body is the manifesting body, and there is always a body manifesting Buddha-nature."[72] This revealing is at the same time a concealing because Buddha-nature eludes the grasp of knowledge. By the power of the Buddha-nature to subsume and transcend existence and nonexistence, the manifesting of Buddha-nature by the body negates the body and transcends it. Thus, to grasp the essence of the body truly is intuitively to grasp emptiness, the dynamic and creative aspect of Buddha-nature. Even though the body without organs resembles the immanent substance of Spinoza's philosophy, Deleuze and Guattari do not equate this body with God, but they do think that the energy that runs through the body without organs is divine. This is, however, a divine energy that inscribes disjunctions on the surface of the body without organs.[73]

Time and Body

Just as the body inhabits space, it also dwells in time for Merleau-Ponty. Like a work of art that is indistinguishable from the existence that expresses it, the body inhabits time, and its temporality is indistinguishable from it.[74] In a sense, within my body I am time: "My body takes possession of time; it brings into existence a past and a future for a present; it is not a thing, but creates time instead of submitting to it."[75] The primordial significance of the body is to be discovered on the preobjective level of experience—not as a mere object among other objects, but rather as radically temporal. Thus the essential intentionality of the body is its temporality, which is also its being.[76]

Dōgen's position on this point is remarkably similar to that of Merleau-Ponty. Our body and mind are time, for Dōgen, just as all *dharmas* (things) are manifestations of being-time (*uji*). "Entire being, the entire world, exists in the time of each and every now."[77] Thus the mind, body, being, world, and time form a unity. Not only are entities time, and not only is time in me, but activities are time: "As self and other are both times, practice and realization are times; entering the mud, entering the water, is equally time."[78] Moreover, Deleuze and Guattari agree with Dōgen in the sense that the body without organs is a field of becomings.

The unity of time is manifested most lucidly for Dōgen when applied to Buddha-nature, whose being is time itself, a position diametrically opposed to that of Merleau-Ponty. "As the time right now is all there ever is, each being-time is without exception entire time."[79] Within the Buddha-nature, both future and past signify the present. Dōgen emphasizes the now moment because there is never a time that has not been or a time that is coming. Dōgen writes, ". . . all is the immediate presencing here and now of being-time."[80] Thus time is a continuous occurrence of "nows." This position has important consequences for Dōgen's philosophy because the Buddha-nature is not a potentiality to be actualized in the future, but it is a present actuality. In other words, every moment of illusion and enlightenment contains all reality.[81] Therefore, Buddha-nature is both illusion and enlightenment.

Time, a transitional synthesis of the world, is literally, for Merleau-Ponty, the presence of the world in which the multiple ways of being in the world are gathered together and dispersed. The present moment contains both past and future; although they are never wholly present, past and future spring forth when one reaches out toward them. In fact, the body unites time. Merleau-Ponty writes, "In every focusing movement my body unites present, past and future, it secretes time, or rather it becomes that location in nature where, for the first time, events, instead of pushing each other into the realm of being, project round the present a double horizon of past and future and acquire a historical orientation."[82] Just as space enables one to be present to others, time makes it possible to be mutually present to other beings. In contrast to Merleau-Ponty's position, Dōgen denies the continuity of time because each instant of time is independent and distinct of every other moment of time.[83] The discontinuity of time means, for Dōgen, that each point of time is independent of each other moment of time.[84] Present time, for example, cannot be conceived as a linear, evolutionary process. Each moment of time—past, present, or future—is distinct from every other, whereas Merleau-Ponty argues that past and future are supported by an objective present. Since each moment of time constitutes a discrete reality for Dōgen, all moments are lived times. Dōgen asserts that time does not pass because in one moment all time is viewed simultaneously.[85] Consequently, the past is retrievable, the future is not beyond grasp, and the present is not merely transient. Rather than being a form of bondage, time becomes an opportunity for human creativity and transformation. Merleau-Ponty agrees with Dōgen by referring to the ecstatic character of temporality, which implies that one can reach out beyond the present into past and future time.

To inhabit space and time, according to Merleau-Ponty, is to encounter other bodies in a common world. My body and other bodies form a system of competing or cooperative intersubjective beings. My body perceives the body of another person and recognizes that it possesses the same structure as my body. "Henceforth, as the parts of my body together comprise a system, so my body and the other person's are one whole, two sides of one and the same phenomenon, and the anonymous existence of which my body is the ever-renewed trace henceforth inhabits both bodies simultaneously."[86] Dōgen is sympathetic to Merleau-

Ponty's position to a certain extent. Just as there is no separation between body and mind for Dōgen, there is no division between oneself and others in the state of non-thinking, since isolation from others only arises upon reflection.[87] Dōgen expresses the unity of being and time as follows: "The *time* has to *be* in me. Inasmuch as I am there, it cannot be that time passes away."[88] Again, "'Time being' means time, just as it is, is being, and being is all time."[89] The common denominator of being and time is impermanence,[90] which is characteristic of all existence. Dōgen argues that Buddha-nature is impermanent; it is that aspect that eternally comes into being and passes out of being. Dōgen's nondualistic equation of being and time results in a radical temporalization of existence and a radical existentialization of time.[91]

In contrast to Merleau-Ponty and Dōgen, the various postmodern thinkers view the encounter with other bodies in rather different terms because Derrida views the body as stolen, Foucault perceives it in terms of his notion of bio-politics, and Kristeva views the body through her understanding of abjection, which are all related in some way to altarity. This pattern is especially lucid in Taylor's work because "disease is the inscription that brands the other as other, thereby creating the space and distance necessary for my identity."[92] Taylor views disease, a form of stigma, as one of the ways in which altarity, which both ambivalently attracts and terrifies us, encounters a person. By dreading and simultaneously desiring disease, we demonstrate how uneasy we feel when disease approaches us. Instead of bodily wholeness, we experience a body that is torn apart. Taylor elaborates further:

> If our initial relation to ourselves is autoimmunity, our body is not originally an integrated whole governed by the principle of inner teleology but is inherently torn, rent, sundered, and fragmented. The body is *always* betraying itself. Otherness is not only a threat from without but is a danger lurking within. Though it seems impossible, *the body is simultaneously itself and other than itself.* Never simply itself, the body is haunted by an altarity with which it cannot identity and yet with which it cannot avoid identifying. This altarity is the *not* of the body—the not that the body 'is' as well as the not that the body cannot be.[93]

Thus Taylor indicates that the body is not whole because it is originally divided within itself and betrays us. The phantom of altarity lurks within

and outside of the body, rendering bodily identity problematic, an omi-
nous specter that does not disturb Merleau-Ponty or Dōgen.[94]

Although time is immeasurable, intangible, and elusive for Merleau-Ponty and Dōgen, both thinkers radically temporalize being, oppose
a quantitative view of time, see time as a lived reality, and propose a
nondualistic equation of being and time and body and time. Merleau-
Ponty disagrees, however, with Dōgen's contention that things and
events of the universe are time. This position leads Dōgen to a nondualistic assertion that mountains, oceans, pine trees, and everything else are
time.[95] The universe, for Dōgen, is not something fixed and motionless;
it is a being in time.

In summary, the various postmodern thinkers discussed in this
chapter contradict any assertion about how postmodern thought is moving in the direction of Zen Buddhism, even though Merleau-Ponty can
be viewed as moving toward a philosophical position much like that of
Dōgen on the phenomenon of the body. A partial reason for this divergence is embodied in contrary metaphors of the body. For Merleau-
Ponty and Dōgen, a metaphor of bodily wholeness seems to be
operative for them. With Derrida's discussion of the stolen character of
the body, Levinas' emphasis on the body as a crossroads of physical
forces and its inherent ambiguity due to consciousness and labor,
Lyotard's stress upon gender differences, Foucualt's focus on the subjugation of the body by bio-political forces, Kristeva's observations
about the borders of the body and its defiling elements, and Taylor's
insights into the betraying nature of the body and its being torn apart by
disease, all these thoughts on the body suggest a metaphor of marginality with respect to the human body. Deleuze and Guattari depict the
body without organs as a surface on which intensities flow and circulate
within a field of becomings, and these bodies without organs are always
becoming something. Thereby, they are always dynamic never static,
always particular and never generic, representing a field of production
in which occurs the intensification of desire. Deleuze and Guattari also
claim that the body without organs represents a model of death, which
is given to it by a catatonic schizophrenia. This does not mean that there
is a death wish because "there is only death that desires, by virtue of the
body without organs or the immobile motor, and there is also life that
desires, by virtue of the working organs."[96] Such evidence strongly suggests that the emphasis on difference, borders, instability, betrayal, divi-

sion, and disease by various thinkers tends to reflect various forms of marginality verses the wholeness suggested in general by Merleau-Ponty and Dōgen.

Body, Limitation, and Boundary Symbol

In conclusion one can ask: What does the philosophical dialogue on the body by the thinkers considered teach us? These thinkers help us understand that the individual is capable of expressing himself/herself in language, exercising freedom, intuiting, and thinking; none of these activities of the individual are possible without a body. Therefore, to be a human being is to be embodied, which entails being pretheoretically and precognitively "with" things and others or in the midst of objects and other embodied beings. Even though we may experience the body as a biological and physical organism, it is fundamentally the locus for one's life and experience. Without reviewing the significant differences of their respective positions, the thinkers surveyed in this chapter arrive at very similar positions at several points, using, oddly enough, very different methodologies: phenomenology for Merleau-Ponty and Levinas, seated meditation for Dōgen, semiotics for Kristeva, deconstruction for Derrida and Taylor, and schizoanalysis for Deleuze and Guattari. Although their methods are different, these thinkers have placed us in a comparative realm of meaning concerning the human body.

In order to avoid a static result for our dialogue, I briefly want to take the problem of the body in a slightly different direction without claiming that any of the thinkers considered in this chapter would agree with the following comments. I not only experience the body as mine, but, just as fundamentally, I recognize my body as radically other than me.[97] If I can recognize that I am both my body and that I am also not my body, this realization expresses that I am radically limited by my body, which irrevocably determines my life by its limitations. In the sense of potential frustration, anguish, disease, pain, fear, dread, and death, I am at the mercy of my body.[98] One does not have to be a medical student to know that there are bodily processes over which I have no control, which indicates that the body possesses a biological life of its own. Since my body is a temporal and biological process, it can proceed without my being aware of it, although Merleau-Ponty and the other philosophers considered want to make us aware of our bodies and their philosophical significance.

Dōgen agrees to some extent with Merleau-Ponty when he states, "The body can symbolize existence because it brings it into being and actualizes it."[99] The body, although it is observable, is the hidden form of our being. As an expression of total existence, the body expresses a unity. Bodily actions are gestures of humans which are not mere signs; they are symbols of themselves and express significance and meaning beyond themselves.

Besides its symbolic significance, the body is closely associated with movement and utility. Lingis summarizes this aspect of the body in the following way:

> Our bodies are sensory-motor systems that generate the excess force which makes them able to move themselves, systems that move toward objectives they perceive, that thus code their own movements. Our bodies are also substances that can be moved and that can be coded. Subjected to regulated operations of force, our bodies become subjects of capacities, skills, and inclinations; they can be made use of.[100]

As previously stated, the body can also be abused in the sense of receiving punishment, torture, or discipline as well as used for good purposes by ourselves or by others who might employ one's skills.

Even though human beings are rooted in time and the world, their bodies symbolize transcendence of biological and natural existence. To be in the world and to be at the mercy of unseen biological forces of the body represents a human limitation. Although humans experience their incarnation as a limitation, this experience is already an overcoming of this limitation.[101] Thus the body restricts our freedom and affirms it.

Just as the dialogue between various figures takes place on the boundary of Eastern and Western philosophy, our body is a boundary symbol, which expresses that we are on the border of freedom and bondage. Our incarnation points to our ambiguous situation. As embodied beings, we are neither totally free nor are we entirely bound. Our embodiment affords us the possibility of freedom, an absence of inhibiting coercion, and a capacity for continual creativity. A person on the boundary eludes normal classification and structure. Such a person overcomes, at least potentially, sexual distinctions, the cosmic rhythms of life and death, the spatial polarities of here and there, the temporal polarities of past and future, the ethical opposition between good and evil, the dichotomy of human relationships, and the ordinary distinction between body and self. Such a boundary person seems to be an ideal candidate for an intercultural, philosophical dialogue. A person's "between-ness" affords one the freedom to listen to both sides and decide for oneself.

CHAPTER 6

The Self and Other

According to Immanuel Kant, if objects are to be thought by means of categories, this epistemological procedure is only possible with a unified perceiving and thinking subject, which suggests that the synthesizing work of understanding is not possible except within the unity of consciousness. Kant explains that "It must be possible for the 'I think' to accompany all my representations; for otherwise something would be represented in me which could not be thought at all, and that is equivalent to saying that the representation would be impossible, or at least would be nothing to me."[1] This suggests that the self, a pure and original unity that precedes all experiences, is the sole source of all conceptual unity because of its synthetic activities, and, by reflection upon the constancy of these activities, it becomes conscious of its own identity. Since consciousness of objects involves consciousness of self and self-consciousness is the form of all consciousness, the consciousness of self and consciousness of objects mutually condition each other. Thus the self that is known to us possesses the character of appearance, which implies that the self is the same as other objects of knowledge.

The Kantian self of pure apperception is not located in time or space: "I am conscious of myself, not as I appear to myself, nor as I am in myself, but only that I am."[2] Therefore, the empirical self is knowable and known, whereas the self of pure apperception is thinkable but cannot possibly be known.[3] At this point, Kant agrees essentially with David Hume when he writes the following: "Consciousness of self according to the determinations of our state in inner perceptions is merely empirical, and always changing. No fixed and abiding self can present itself in this flux of inner appearances."[4] Since Kant is claiming that there is no single empirical state of the self that is constant throughout experience, the self cannot be dealt with as a separate entity. This empirical and conditional ego tends to be synthesized by reason, which synthesizes the inner life by passing from the ego to an unconditional thinking noumenal self. This does not mean that Kant is referring to two distinct selves, but he is rather talking about the self from different points of view with the knowing self functioning as the reality in which the self as known is grounded. Although the knowing self is a pure activity of synthesis in accordance with certain necessary principles, Kant insists that we cannot indubitably know or prove the existence of the transcendental self as a substance because it would involve a misuse of categories such as existence, substance, or unity. Thus the self, which is beyond the range of intuition, is a limiting concept. Subsequent philosophers were directly and indirectly critical of Kant's understanding of the self.

In contrast to the Enlightenment era philosophy of Kant, Hegel seeks to grasp a reality that lives in the particulars by means of a way of thought which passes through and encompasses them. Hegel views the epoch of the Enlightenment as resulting in a person's disinclination to recognize the absolute because its thinkers concentrated on man/woman and humankind, which obscured its vision of the uniqueness of the self. According to Hegel, what makes the self unique is the absolute spirit (*Geist*), which is both otherness or externality and is still internally united with itself, within a historical process.[5]

The Hegelian self is a self-constituting process that includes the recognition of its freedom and the production of that freedom, a process that is illustrated by the master-slave relationship. If the development from consciousness to self-consciousness arises only when the self recognizes selfhood in itself and others, the presence of the other is essential to self-consciousness, even though the initial reaction of a self confronted with another self is to assert its own existence. This process manifests itself in a desire to annihilate the other self as a means of asserting its own selfhood. Due to the fact that the complete destruction of the other would defeat its own purpose, there arises the master-slave relationship by the master imposing him/herself as the value of the other and thus obtaining recognition from the other. The master's self is reflected in his/her dependence and domination of the slave and his/her enjoyment of nature, a double dependence on nature that results in the bondage of the self. On the other hand, the slave sees his/her own true self in the master. An important consequence of this situation is that the master's nonrecognition of the slave as a true self results in depriving the slave of the recognition of his/her own originally demanded freedom. Unable to develop self-consciousness, the slave debases him/herself to a mere living thing. The adherence to the master's will, however, enables the slave to objectify him/herself through labor which transforms material things, allowing the products of the slave to reflect him/herself and in that measure giving him/her a free self-consciousness. By losing his/her bondage through labor, the slave forms him/herself and rises to the level of true existence.

Søren Kierkegaard reacts vigorously to Hegel's philosophy because he thinks in part that the self is swallowed by the Spirit and loses its individuality. According to Kierkegaard, the self is spirit that is a relationship related to itself. This established relation must have been established by itself or another.[6] The self is also a synthesis of the finite and infinite, temporal and eternal, necessity and freedom, which implies that one cannot become an authentic self as long as one remains a synthesis between two such antitheses. A third element is necessary to place the opposites in a relationship; this third element is the self in which the relationship is related to itself, which suggests that the self is a derived relationship. This means that the self is in its relationship to itself also related to something else, and it is established by something else and not self-established. And the basic paradox of the self is that it wants to be a self that it is not. The self also despairs, a sickness unto death because of one's estrangement from God, over itself because it cannot stand to be itself.[7] Besides despair, the self is afflicted by anxiety (*angst*), guilt, and sin, which places humans in a precarious situation from which they cannot escape. The direness of this predicament is evident in Kierkegaard's definition of anxiety as "the dizziness of freedom, which emerges when the spirit wants to posit the synthesis, and freedom looks down into its own possibility, laying hold of finiteness to support itself. Freedom succumbs in this dizziness."[8] It is faith, a deep passion and uncertainty in the Absolute Paradox, which itself forces the self to make a decision that is of eternal significance for the individual and realize authentic selfhood.

Before or after reaching this type of realization, the self can become absorbed in the crowd and become transformed into a mass person.[9] The crowd strives toward totalness, transforms everyone into the same person, and swallows up the single one by destroying one's relationship to God, a relation that gives meaning to a person. As the power of the crowd grows, the individual becomes inessential or accidental. It is necessary for the individual to turn away from the crowd and to exist as a single one in relationship to God. For Kierkegaard, authentic selfhood represents standing before God as a single one and in opposition to the other. Thus the self must take a risk to venture forth without support in order to become actual, a unity of possibility and necessity, which means to submit to one's limitations and to become aware of oneself.[10]

If Kierkegaard's work represents a reaction to Hegel, Nietzsche's philosophy is a critical reaction in part to Kant. Nietzsche appears to have a philosopher like Kant in mind when he criticizes those who think of a person as a thing-in-itself "as something that remains constant in the midst of all flux, as a sure measure of things."[11] According to Nietzsche, not enough philosophers possess a historical sense that would allow them to perceive the flux to which human beings are subject. In several of his works, Nietzsche expresses a very negative view of human beings because "relatively speaking, man is the most bungled of all the animals, the sickliest, and not one has strayed more dangerously from its instincts. But for all that, he is of course the most *interesting*."[12] Nietzsche does not think that humans are naturally equal, do not innately love one another, and are not naturally free. He also thinks that the vast majority of human beings are animals without dignity: "Man is a rope, fastened between animal and Superman—a rope over an abyss."[13] The metaphor of the rope suggests that human beings live between two worlds and grasp for ideas they cannot attain. In his latest and incomplete work *Will to Power*, Nietzsche continues to refer to human beings as manifesting no progress over ordinary animals and equating them with worms.[14] Humans can, however, rise above the beasts because we have concrete examples in the artist, saint, and philosopher, all representatives of true humanity and culture.

Through the voice of his prophet Zarathustra, Nietzsche announces that "Man is something that should be overcome."[15] The prophet also states that he arrives to teach the *Übermensch*, overman. The individual who overcomes him/herself (although Nietzsche would exclude women from this possibility due to his misogynist attitude toward them) is an *Übermensch* because such a person gains self-mastery and transfigures his/her nature. The arrival of the *Übermensch* is impeded by society with its demands for conformity and thus it must be censured for creating obstacles to the advent of this mysterious figure. The *Übermensch* is yet to come according to Zarathustra: "Never yet has there been an *Übermensch*. Naked I saw both the greatest and the smallest man. They are still all-too-similar to each other. Verily even the greatest I found all-too-human."[16] It is best to conceive of the *Übermensch* as a goal rather than a current reality, although Nietzsche does not understand the progress toward this goal as an inevitable process. Similar to Hegel's world historical heroes that are used by the Absolute Spirit for its ends, the advent of Nietzsche's *Übermensch* depends on superior individuals who have the courage to transvalue all values, which will give a direction and a goal to the *Übermensch*, a master of his/her desires, joyous, guiltless, free, and in possession of instinctual drives.

Jean-Paul Sartre is much less concerned than Nietzsche with heroic figures, although he is rather concerned with the implications for existing in the world. Sartre criticizes the early Heidegger's analysis of *Dasein* (there-being) because it lacks consciousness and the *cogito* is where one must begin or human reality will become a mere thing.[17] The reflective consciousness objectifies the prereflective consciousness, an egoless consciousness that is always aware of itself as consciousness, for Sartre that allows for the emergence of the ego, a permanent, present, and enduring self that is coextensive with the totality of one's psyche and not a part of the psyche like that in Freudian theory. Consciousness does not exhaust or cause the self to come into existence because the self is given before consciousness.[18] Moreover, this self is always in the world not simply with others like in the early phenomenology of Heidegger but more significantly for others.

We have noted that both Nietzsche and Kierkegaard stress the danger that the other is to the individual and the necessity for the individual to extricate oneself from the crowd. These thinkers emphatically indicate that the other is an obstacle to the achievement of genuine selfhood. This denigration of the other is corrected in the philosophical works of Sartre and Heidegger, who both share a conviction that philosophy necessarily combines ontology and altarity because human beings live within a world with other beings, although they still recognize the dangers associated with the other and becoming absorbed in the crowd. The importance of the other is stressed even more by a variety of postmodern thinkers. The remainder of this chapter will be devoted to a dialogue between postmodernists like Derrida, Levinas, Lacan, Kristeva, and Taylor on the self and other with Dōgen and Nishitani representing Zen Buddhism. Due to the topics of this chapter, we will examine them with respect to the following themes: presence and absence; decentering; kenosis and *zazen*; and altarity. From one perspective, the philosophical efforts of both Zen and non-Zen camps can be viewed as attempts to overcome essentialism.

Presence and Absence

There is almost complete agreement among the selected postmodernists that the self possesses no enduring presence, a traditionally privileged position in previous western philosophy that is challenged by postmodern thinking. Heidegger establishes the discussion of presence when he acknowledges that Being is presencing, but he does not mean this in the sense of becoming something permanent because becoming present suggests rather emerging or opening up.[19] Heidegger also understands presencing as a transition. Heidegger clarifies his position in *Holzwege* by affirming that being "in being" does signify presence in the sense of an unconcealedness that lets beings happen. But what is truly present is presence itself.[20]

In contrast to Heidegger, Derrida gives a radical twist to the problem of presence by denying its privileged position in western philosophy because presence, a determination and effect, occurs within a system of difference.[21] Thus the self cannot represent presence for Derrida because presence itself is problematic within a system of difference and the self cannot be present as itself and cannot render itself present to itself.[22] Within the system of difference, the self is nothing more than a trace, which represents an erasure of the self and its presence.[23] With the ability of the trace to inscribe itself as a difference into the gaps that it creates in space, it is impossible for a self, an unerasable trace, to attain presence.

The position on the presence of the self initiated by Derrida is followed by Taylor, who thinks that we create a difference between ourselves and others when we assume a proper name that appears to give us presence. But this self-presence is only possible in the quickly passing present moment with its three related modalities of time.[24] The complexity of the present moment compromises the presence of the self because the self-conscious self becomes self-present to itself by means of a process of self-presentation.[25] Since the self is radically temporal and an inseparable modality of each moment of time, it possesses a synthetic and not an enduring identity because difference is always associated with the identity of the self, representing a union of identity and difference and presence and absence. The interplay of identity and difference and presence and absence causes a disruption in the presence of the self and dislocation in its present modality of time, which suggests that the present is merely a trace and that time is forever a transition of moments.[26] Once the self becomes aware of its condition, it discovers to its horror that its proper name is without meaning, its possesses no enduring identity, and is without a definite presence. This scenario results in the absence of a permanent self, a mere trace, and the realization that the self is shattered by the mark of death in the form of a burial marker—a cross.[27] In short, the self disappears for Taylor to be replaced by markings of itself.

In contrast to the lack of identity associated with the self in the work of Derrida and Taylor, Levinas isolates the identity of the self with what he calls ipseity, a nonpresence before itself and in itself. This unusual identity is clarified by Levinas: "There is no ipseity common to me and the others; 'me' is the exclusion from this possibility of comparison, as soon as comparison is set up. The ipseity is then a privilege or an unjustifiable election that chooses me and not the ego."[28] The self is thus both chosen and unique. The self cannot, however, be observed or intuited because its identity is given in an affective experience that is both pleasurable and beyond its being. The self is otherwise than being because Levinas wants to stress its subjective nature.

Lacan and Kristeva agree generally with Derrida and Taylor that the self lacks presence. Lacan and Kristeva concur that a human being is not an autonomous thinking and knowing unified subject, unlike such philosophers as Descartes, Husserl, and Sartre who understand the individual as being completely present to its own consciousness. Lacan perceives a tension between the ego (*moi*) and subject (*je*): "Consciousness in man is by essence a polar tension between an ego alienated from the subject and a perception which fundamentally escapes it, a pure *percipi*."[29] Within this more complex and problematic view of consciousness, the ego, alienating and alienated, plays the role of the protagonist by preventing the subject from becoming identical to this perception. For Lacan, the ego discovers itself in a hostile world surrounded by uncontrollable forces. The inherently feeble ego also represents an illusory identity, a process that commences with what Lacan calls the mirror stage in a child's very early psychological development. The constitution of the illusory identity of the ego in the mirror stage located in the life of a child between six and eighteen months of age when it recognizes its image in a mirror, an image of wholeness that conflicts with the child's own experience of its uncontrollable and fragmented bodily existence, is identified by Lacan as misrecognition (*méconnaissance*). The illusory nature of the ego is continually denied by the subject, which suggests that an individual exists within a lie to itself.

Due to the ego's illusory identity in Lacan's theory and the denial of its condition by the subject, Lacan is able to criticize the foundation of Sartrean existential philosophy for its false basis on the autonomy of the self. From Lacan's perspective, Sartre's autonomous self is an excellent example of the ego's misrecognized identity.[30] For Lacan, the ego's misrecognized identity makes it very difficult for one to truly see one's genuine identity because it gets lost in the unconscious. The fundamental split between the subject and ego manifests a basic alienation within a person without any hope of attaining wholeness. We find something similar in the work of Kristeva due to the strong influence of Lacan on her theory of the self.

Kristeva agrees with Lacan that the self lacks fundamental permanence, presence, or identity. The self, a continual series of fluctuating signifiers, is always splitting apart, resulting in a self that is heterogenous and decentered.[31] In the mirror stage a child develops, for instance, a spatial intuition of an image of itself and a realization that it must remain separate from its unified image. Another important phase of the child's development is castration, representing a completion of the process of separation by detaching the child from its dependence on its mother.[32] These examples suggest that the self is continuously changing and splitting apart for Kristeva.

The ever-changing nature of the self is also to be witnessed in the philosophy of Deleuze where the self represents a series of energies, movements, flows, and serial fragments. It is possible for these different fragments to be linked together in such a way that it does not create a coherent identity for the self, a figure of differentiation, because of their fragmentary and temporary nature. Deleuze conceives of a difference between the self and the I, which actually begins with differences, with the former representing the psychic organization and the latter being the determination of species. Even though the self and I begin with differences, these are differences that are distributed in such a manner that they become cancelled: "The I therefore appears at the end as the universal form of psychic life, just as the self is the universal matter of that form."[33] The background of this philosophical position is formed by Deleuze's conviction that not all differences are individual, but all differences are borne by individuals. This suggests that individuating factors have neither the form of the I nor the matter of the self because the I cannot be separated from identity and the self is inseparable from the different fragments that constitute it.

From Dōgen's perspective, Lacan and Kristeva superimpose on the self psychological categories that do not bring us any closer to grasping its true nature because it is transformed into something abstract. Likewise, Taylor, Derrida, and Deleuze superimpose patterns of thinking that are alien to the true nature of the self. Dōgen views the postmodernists as engaged in a practice of manipulating experience. Dōgen does agree, however, with these postmodernists that the self possesses no permanence or enduring presence.[34] Somewhat like Lacan's rejection of the reality principle because the ego does not have much to do with it, Dōgen states that the self possesses no enduring or intrinsic reality because it is continually changing. The genuine self, for Dōgen, is concrete because it represents the immediacy of experience. Thus there is no transcendental self that is prior to any division between subject and object, and there is no self that is permanent and unchanging for Dōgen.

The self is not something that we can possess for Dōgen; it is also not something that an other can possess: "That is, when our 'self' is the true Self then our self is not ours and not 'others'—it is the four elements and the five *skandhas*."[35] In traditional Pali Buddhism, the four elements and the five *skandhas* (aggregates) constitute what people ordinarily might falsely conceive to be the nature of the self. Due to the fact that these features of the self are in a constant state of flux, there is no such thing as a permanent self. Dōgen is affirming that our genuine self is forever changing just like the four elements and five aggregates, and this is the reason that it is impossible for us or another person to possess it.

Like Dōgen's grasp of the self, Nishitani rejects categories like presence and absence because he identifies the self with *śūnyatā* (emptiness). He explains further: "'Emptiness is self' means that, at bottom and in its own home-ground, the self has its being as such a field."[36] This suggests that the field of *śūnyatā* creates a foundation for the self as a self, an original self in itself. Moreover, the self is truly itself when it rests in emptiness, its own home-ground. By using a term like "ground," Nishitani sets off an alarm from the perspective of Deleuze because such a term suggests the same, identical, and a representational mode of thinking. According to Deleuze, the ground is undermined by the simulacra, systems of difference, which affirms divergence and decentering of that which the term "ground" attempts to exclude in the first place. The simulacrum draws in the ground only to fragment it, leaving in its place a unity that is represented by chaos.[37] By using the term home-ground in contrast to Deleuze's criticism, Nishitani means our true self-awareness, which is not a self-consciousness, a self-knowledge, a reflective knowing, or an intuition. This self-awareness is a nexus at which the self and knowledge are emptied.[38] Thus, Nishitani refers to self-awareness as not-knowing, or knowing of nonknowing, which represents the self as an absolutely non-objective selfness that is only possible on the field of emptiness.[39] After breaking through the field of consciousness and discovering oneself within the field of emptiness, one realizes the "in itself" (*jitai*), which is neither a substance nor a subject. This realization of the self-identity of things indicates directly the thing itself in its original mode of being. From within emptiness, one can grasp a thing in its original mode of being, which is neither a subjective nor substantial mode of grasping.[40] The realization of the "in itself" (*jitai*) is a nonobjective process that is entirely devoid of representation of any kind.

Nishitani disagrees with the postmodernists when they claim that the self cannot know itself. The self grounded in emptiness cannot only know itself, but can also know objects in the world, which is possible because the self is a not-knowing. Nishitani summarizes his position thus far: "Thus we can say in general that the self in itself makes the existence of the self as a subject possible, and that this not-knowing constitutes the essential possibility of knowing."[41] The self is able to confirm itself by the successful search for what Nishitani calls *anjin*, which suggests a pacified mind or assurance about the existence of the self itself. This entire search includes both an absolute affirmation and an equally absolute negation: "Thus in addition to *anjin* signifying absolute affirmation it also incorporates an aspect of absolute negation represented by the Great Death— dying to the self and to the world."[42] This type of certainty with regard to the existence of the self and the overcoming of doubt is lacking in the thought of most of the postmodernists. Even though there are some disagreements between the various thinkers, the postmodernists discussed thus far, Nishitani, and Dōgen reject the metaphysics of presence, or what Derrida calls logocentrism.

But this rejection of the western sense of presence does not mean for Dōgen that there is no sense of presence for a person because he allows for an internal and prereflective act of self-authentication by means of the practice of *zazen* (seated meditation). In general there are three phases of this process: acceptance; check for self-delusions; being grounded in *zazen*. The initial phase is examining the nature of the presence of oneself and accepting oneself as one appears to oneself. It is possible to check for self-delusions by comparing what one discovers with prereflective appearances in *zazen*, a practice devoid of delusion because there is no reflection. Within the context of *zazen* and nonthinking, one encounters each life situation directly as it occurs without making additions to the immediacy of the experience by personal reflection.[43] Moreover, the term *shō* sheds light on this entire process because it means "proving" and "authenticating," which suggests that enlightenment involves a process of self-authentication.[44]

Decentered

The tone for the postmodern thinkers is set by Derrida when he calls into question the entire notion of the center without referring to the self. Since the center of a structure normally allows for the play of its elements within itself, it is impossible to think of a structure that lacks a center. And yet the play permitted by the center of a structure is also confined by the center. Derrida deconstructs the center in the following statement:

> The center is at the center of the totality, and yet, since the center does not belong to the totality (is not part of the totality), the totality has *its center elsewhere*. The center is not the center. The concept of centered structure—although it represents coherence itself, the condition of the epistēmē as philosophy or science—is contradictorily coherent.[45]

Derrida decenters the notion of a permanent center. Thus his statement amounts to pronouncing the absence of a permanent center. A similar scenario is evident in the philosophy of Deleuze with his emphasis on difference, fragmentation, flowing energy, lack of durable identity and repetition.

The path started by Derrida with respect to the notion of the center is followed by Taylor, who argues that the self is not independent because it represents the locus of several relationships. Taylor calls into question the prevailing tradition of western thought and its conception of a self-identical self by investigating the tendency to give priority to the subject at the expense of the predicate with the philosophical result of making the subject independent. Due to the identical content of subjects and predicates and the additional relational nature of predicates, it is only possible to identify the self by means of predicates. Therefore, the self is discovered within the context of a fluctuating network of relations, a kind of linguistic web, and lacks independence and the power of knowing in any comprehensive sense.[46] Taylor's deconstruction of the self, a mere transitory intersection for a plethora of relationships, undermines the integrity of its autonomous nature. This co-relative, codependent, decentered self, a mere image of an image, lacks identity and can be defined as empty. But this does not seem to be sufficient and powerful enough to decenter the self. Is there a more immediate cause for the decentering of the self? Taylor's answer to this rhetorical question revolves around the death of God.

If God forms the basis for the traditional western understanding of selfhood by providing a stable center, the death of God marks the disappearance of the self and the devaluation of the highest values, echoing Nietzsche's proclamation, because there is no absolute, transcendent self to function as the ground of the human self. After realizing the death of God, Taylor is convinced that humanistic atheism is hesitant to take the next logical step which is to recognize that the traditional God's death also involves the death of the self.[47] In Taylor's opinion, humanistic atheism, representing murders of God and deifiers of humans, is irrevocably narcissistic, a tendency to turn the entire world into a mirror in which to see one's face reflected. Besides the disappearance of the self, another important consequence of the death of God is the unleashing of free play, a mode of aberrant levity that does not conform to the normal rules of logic or common sense.[48] This kind of carnivalesque play disrupts traditional hierarchies, inverts and perverts inherited values and accepted meanings.

If Taylor means that the transcendental ego disappears and leaves a person with an immanent self devoid of any transcendental reference, there is a measure of affinity between his position and Nishitani because the Zen philosopher thinks that the self is at play after it becomes detached to itself, the world, actions, and time. As time loses its sequential nature, it and the self are simply united for Nishitani. Time presents itself as world-time or as a whole in the present, opening up a field of transcendence, which is something that Taylor fails or refuses to acknowledge is possible, whereas Nishitani thinks that each moment opens itself to eternity and the self opens itself to the fullness of time or eternity. The self of Nishitani is engaged in complete spontaneity and play. Unlike the disappearing self of Taylor, Nishitani envisions a self that is unattached and yet is active and completely real, although Taylor's notion of wandering and erring appear to suggest also some kind of activity. Once an individual overcomes the false notion of "self" from the Zen viewpoint, the individual's conduct and actions become effortless, and he/she is able to recapture his/her spontaneity and creativity. The active and aimless wandering suggested by Taylor stands opposed to the Zen preference to wait on all things because the individual is not trying to go anywhere, is not striving for anything, and is not attempting to avoid anything. The individual conducts himself/herself according to the spirit of nonaction, which implies that one moves without being moved and acts without acting.

After deconstructing the traditional western philosophical view of the self, Taylor attempts to reformulate it into postmodern terms. The decentered, disappearing, and marginal self is a mark, a form of trace, that signifies the death of authentic selfhood—its proximity, immediacy, and presence. The nonidentical self, a mere trace, is simultaneously present and absent, trapped in an interconnecting web of relations, and caught in temporal becoming. The trace/self is never merely itself because it is always also other than itself, and it can never reach any point of finality. Having become inscribed as a trace, this implies that "the trace simultaneously erases every notion of the self that is based on the principles of propriety, property, and possession and discloses the impropriety, expropriation, and dispossession of the subject."[49] Moreover, the liminality of the trace disrupts distinctions between inside and outside, which renders the self/trace marginal, stained and wounded: "This stain cannot be cleansed, and this wound cannot be healed."[50] This trace/self is a marginal, faceless, and liminal being that becomes eccentric and errant and thus a trickster and a thief. Taylor interprets the decentering and death of the self as the completion of nihilism.

Although his conceptualization of it is different than that of Taylor, Lacan also views the self as decentered. Lacan perceives a basic split between the subject and the ego, which is other than the subject, because it is difficult for a subject to see its genuine identity due to the fact that one is not truly seeing oneself when one views oneself in terms of the ego, an imaginary construction. The subject's real identity gets lost in the unconscious. The fundamental split between the subject and the ego represents a basic alienation within a person. Lacan traces this alienation back to the mirror stage of a child's development because the child takes itself to be something that it is not by identifying with the mirror image. In other words, the child's inner experience of its body and the wholeness perceived in the mirror image creates a split in the child's identity. With disintegration bordering it on one side and delusion on the other, the ego is trapped in an imaginary function.[51] Since the real self cannot be the ego for Lacan, he does not foresee any chance that the self will attain wholeness. In fact, the ego prevents the subject from becoming identical with its perception because the former is alienated from the latter.[52]

Although she formulates it differently, Kristeva agrees with Lacan that the self is decentered. Directly involved in the decentering of the self is rejection, a signifying process that is disposed toward death. As another aspect of the development of the self, rejection is an excessive renewal that destroys presence, which results in the disappearance of both the self and object, dividing the other from the self in a mutually shared experience of splitting apart.[53] Even though the self may disappear along with the object, this does not mean that the process is concluded because the self is continually generated and negated by the *chora*, a nonverbal semiotic articulation of the process that is borrowed from Plato's *Timaeus* to indicate an essentially mobile and provisional articulation constituted by movements and their ephemeral states.[54] The *chora* is not a sign or a signifier and not a model or a copy; it is analogous to "vocal or kinetic rhythm."[55] The *chora* is a repetitive process that creates discontinuities and ruptures and precedes evidence, space, time, and verisimilitude.[56] From the moment this repetitive process commences, the *chora* creates a separation of the self from an object and eventual absence of the self. The self, a mere signifying procedure, is a captive of this repetitive process, which emphatically suggests that it can never become fully present.

In contrast to Kristeva, Levinas does not agree that the self cannot attain presence, although his position is in accord with Kristeva over the decentering of the self. Levinas understands the ego as a mode of existing itself, an existent that breaks out of itself and projects itself forth. Levinas wants to affirm vigorously that the ego literally "ex-ists" by transcending itself and dwells outside the oppositions between permanent and impermanent and the categories of being and nothingness.[57] Being both for itself and with itself, the ego, a substance endowed with thought, forms an identification and bond with itself.[58] Moreover, the ego is attracted to and withdraws from things within the world. This suggests that the ego possesses an inside and an outside dimension.[59]

In a relationship that Levinas refers to as inwardness, the ego is reflected in a self. Unlike the previous postmodern figures, Levinas thinks that the self represents a person's primary identity, becomes present, and endures over a course of time, even though it might be subject to and experience change. Not only does the self remain the same over time, it is also an other, which suggests that it is not autonomous and does not constitute itself.[60] The self dwells within the world with others, and we realize our identity as an existent that dwells with others and interacts with them through dialogical encounter, which makes dwelling a fundamental mode of maintaining oneself. Levinas' position presupposes that the self can only be genuinely related to itself by means of its relation to an other. The double movement of encountering and relating to the other and getting the other to return to the self causes the self to become decentered.[61] Even though the self dwells with others and needs them, it is constantly disrupted and decentered by the other.

In sharp contrast to the various postmodernist, Nishitani views the problem of the center and self very differently because he perceives the issue from the standpoint of the field of *śūnyatā* (emptiness), an infinite space devoid of limitations or orientation. Nishitani also views this field of emptiness as the source of the existence of things. Within the field of *śūnyatā*, the center is everywhere: "Each thing in its own selfness shows the mode of being of the center of all things. Each and every thing becomes the center of all things and, in that sense, becomes an absolute center. This is the absolute uniqueness of things, their reality."[62] It is only in this field of emptiness that each thing is unique, each possesses an absolute center, and all things are gathered into a unity.

Nishitani's position suggests that the self is also centered within the field of *śūnyatā*, whose center is everywhere and its circumference is nowhere. Nishitani clarifies for us that "As a being in unison with emptiness, then, the self is one absolute center, and, to that extent, all things are in the home-ground of the self."[63] Nishitani is discussing the selfless self, not being self in being self, because its being is grounded in the field of *śūnyatā*. This becomes possible through a process in which the self is negated by means of a conversion from the field of nihility to that of emptiness, from a realm of egotistic action to a field of non-ego, and from a self to a selflessness with an absolute center.[64] Thus selfness, authentic selfhood, and the notion of a center are equated for Nishitani. Moreover, the being of a self or a thing is constituted at the center, a point at which the self establishes itself and gains a presence or position.

Nishitani and Derrida agree that the true center is not a center, but it is not a center for Nishitani because it is everywhere and not confined to a particular location in space. From the Zen Buddhist perspective, Derrida is blind to any other possibility when he announces the absence of a permanent center because he cannot apparently entertain the possibility

that a center can be present and absent within a field of emptiness. Nishitani and Dōgen agree with Taylor that the self is part of a web of relations,
but they disagree that this undermines the autonomy of the self. And
when Taylor defines the self as empty he is not implying the same thing
that Dōgen and Nishitani understand by emptiness. Taylor's discussion of
the trace/self, markings that are always other than itself, is much too
vague and abstract for Dōgen because he views the true self as concrete,
which suggests for him that the self is constituted by immediate experience.[65] Nishitani disagrees with Taylor that the death of God unleashes
free play that disrupts, inverts, and perverts. Without aim or reason,
doing, being, and becoming assume the nature of play within the realm of
emptiness for Nishitani. It is not necessary to assume, anticipate, wait for,
or experience the death of God to usher in the free flow of play because,
according to Nishitani, "To the extent that they become manifest at that
point of their elemental source, existence, behavior, and life assume the
character of play."[66] This is all made possible by the field of emptiness in
which all activity manifests the character of playfulness. Nishitani and
Dōgen have a difficult time explaining how the self/trace notion of Taylor can become marginal when it encompasses the totality of events that
comprise experience. Moreover, it is impossible to become marginal in
Taylor's sense within a field of emptiness that is limitless, directionless,
and without a circumference because there is nothing with which to measure one's marginality.

Although the theoretical reasons are distinctive, Lacan and Kristeva
agree that the self represents a split between the ego and subject. The self
never attains wholeness, and there is no hope that it ever will gain integral wholeness. From the Zen Buddhist perspective, this represents a condition of unenlightenment for the individual. Dōgen thinks, for instance,
that genuine selfhood involves the restoration of an original unity lost in
the split between subject and object in unenlightened consciousness.
From Dōgen's perspective, Lacan and Kristeva impose a subjective theoretical structure on the experience of the subject that results in the false
split between subject and object in the individual's consciousness.

Nishitani and Dōgen agree with Levinas that the self does represent
one's primary identity, although they would define this self in terms of
emptiness or Buddha-nature. They cannot, however, agree that the self
remains the same or that the other is responsible for decentering the self,
a possibility that is not plausible within the field of emptiness. With
regard to the possibility that the self remains essentially the same, even

though it might experience change, Nishitani and Dōgen understand the self as impermanent, an understanding of the self that they share with some of the other postmodernists.

Kenosis and *Zazen*

From Dōgen's perspective, it is possible to authenticate the self by means of *zazen* (motionless sitting in meditation). This method possesses some common features with kenosis in the work of Taylor, although he is not attempting to authenticate the self in any way similar to Dōgen's use of seated meditation. Lacan compares favorably his conception of an analytic psychological technique to some of the methods common in Zen Buddhism, which he thinks does not present a danger of making worse the subject's basic alienation. Lacan views the Zen technique as providing a language barrier that puts the analyst and the patient on an equal basis "that we shall try to respond to the echo of his speech."[67] But in this section of the chapter, we will concentrate only on kenosis and *zazen*.

According to Dōgen, the practice of *zazen* is one's passport to freedom: "Sitting in the full lotus posture is a direct transcending of the entire world; it is the most precious and sublime state of the Buddhas and Patriarchs."[68] Thus *zazen* is not a practice prior to enlightenment; it is rather practice based on enlightenment: "It is entering into realization."[69] Since there is no distinction between acquired and original enlightenment, and since practice and realization are identical, *zazen* is not the cause of enlightenment. *Zazen* enables one to cast off body and mind. Thereby, one is able to sever disordered thoughts emanating from one's discriminating consciousness.[70] Egoism is overcome, and all is emptiness, whereas kenosis is not a nondualistic method for Taylor.

Kenosis is a process, according to Taylor, that empties the self of any intrinsic particularity, and is actualized "in the crucifixion of independent individuals."[71] This process renders the self faceless, without identity, nonpresent, acentric, and anonymous, whereas Dōgen's method of *zazen* helps one to find one's center of being. While kenosis represents the disappearance of the self, *zazen* is the realization and authentication of authentic selfhood and the disappearance of egoism. If one's normal worldview is constructed by a subject and the objects that it encounters because a subject and its objects form the ordinary foundation of our empirical experiences, Dōgen wants to overcome this dichotomy of reality, and to reduce, for instance, the act of personal perception from "I see the tree" to just the simple and pure act of perception devoid of the empirical ego.

It does not necessarily follow, for Dōgen, that an aspirant should cease practicing *zazen* upon gaining enlightenment. On the contrary, *zazen* must be continued because awakening must continually be confirmed in seated meditation.[72] Taylor also conceives of kenosis as a continual process of the individual. According to Dōgen, when the moment of enlightenment dawns for the aspirant there is a simultaneous attainment of the way (*doji-jōdo*), whereas Taylor perceives a new faceless subject who is characterized by death, desire, and delight. Acting as a parasite with the subject, death lives within the subject and does not simply negate it. Desire does not have anything to do with fulfillment or satisfaction, but it rather manifests a constant disruption of self-identity. Delight is an inverse of satisfaction that is nonpossessive.[73] In contrast to Taylor, an important implication for Dōgen's position is that once one gains enlightenment everything in the universe attains enlightenment simultaneously.[74]

The essential art of *zazen* consists of thinking of not-thinking, which is accomplished by non-thinking.[75] One must cease the following: involvement in worldly affairs; all movements of the conscious mind; and making distinctions. The aspirant must simply sit silently and immobile and think of non-thinking, which is the essence of *sammai* (Sanskrit, *samādhi*: concentration). Non-thinking, a mode beyond thinking and not-thinking, functions by realizing both thinking and not-thinking.[76] It is thinking of emptiness, a thinking of the unthinkable, which implies that non-thinking is objectless, subjectless, formless, goalless, and purposeless. There is nothing comparable to Dōgen's position in Taylor's thought because for the latter the new subject, a manifestation of death, desire, and delight, represents both a self-negation and an affirmation. This new subject produced by the process of kenosis is a marginal or liminal being.

A major difference between kenosis and *zazen* is intention. Taylor seems to suggest that kenosis is an intentional activity performed by a subject, whereas Dōgen thinks that a genuine method is intentionless in the sense that it is not thought out or contrived.[77] In his work entitled *Shōbōgenzō Zuimonki*, Dōgen refers to the advice of a Zen Master who instructs a student to take a step beyond the top of a hundred-foot pole, if he plans to practice the path of Zen. According to Dōgen's interpretation of the old Master, this involves casting away one's body and mind without intention: "Those who just throw their bodies and minds into Buddhism and practice without even thinking of gaining enlightenment can be called unstained practicers."[78] But this does not represent the full story for the Zen Buddhist master. Dōgen cites Zen Master Daijaku Kōsei to the effect that practicing *zazen* is the intention of becoming Buddha. Dōgen asks a rhetorical question: "'What part does intention play in becoming Buddha?'" And he gives the following answer:

> It is continually involved right from the start. At this time, each thing completely becomes Buddha, involvement directly exhausts becoming Buddha, and all things have this intention. Do not reject a single intention. When we reject even one intention, our life is lost. Yet, when our life is lost, we are involved with that intention.[79]

Dōgen is affirming at this point that the best intention directly relates to becoming enlightened. This does not mean that we must be concerned with achieving enlightenment. What is really important is not what occurs to me or you specifically, but what happens between myself and others and the genuineness of any relationship with others. As we will see from the Zen perspective, the individual is constituted by a complex of relationships.

Altarity

For the vast majority of the philosophers mentioned in this chapter, the topic of altarity is directly linked to the problem of the self. Many of the postmodernists tend to understand altarity, a heterogeneity of the other, in radical ways. We will see that Levinas is concerned with ethical responsibility toward the other, Lacan's notion of the self cannot be fully grasped without examining its relation to the other, Derrida discusses a double altarity, and Kristeva concentrates her attention on the stranger. We have excluded Taylor at this point in the chapter because his notion of a disappearing self does not appear to need the other, and he does not develop his own philosophical or theological consideration of the topic in any depth, although he considers the topic at length in other postmodern figures in his work entitled *Altarity*. The status of the other is also not without significance to Dōgen and Nishitani.

Levinas thinks that exposure to the other helps the self over its egoistic tendencies by acknowledging our resemblance to the other, even though this similarity is exterior to us and our relationship to the other is mysterious. The exteriority of the other, which constitutes its entire being, does not exclude the possibility that the other is our relative or neighbor. It is even possible for me to substitute myself for the other, although "the substitution of the one for the other does not signify the substitution of the other for the one."[80] The possibility of substitution indicates that the self can overcome its own selfish self-absorption, and can become more concerned with the other. As the self stands before the other, it is infinitely responsible, an attitude that is impossible to escape for the self. By responsibility, Levinas means a process that is akin to kenosis, an emptying, of the egotistical aspects of the self and a confirmation of its uniqueness.[81] The necessity of responsibility is connected to the basic relationship between the self and the other because the former exists through and for the latter.[82] The responsibility of the self for the other extends to the requirement of becoming a substitute, a submissive and passive stance, or a hostage for the other. By becoming a substitute for the other, the self is practicing the self-emptying of its being and becoming "otherwise than being."[83] The self arrives at a greater comprehension of compassion, pardon, and proximity when it assumes the role of a hostage, an increase in the degree of responsibility for the other, liberation from self-absorption, and becoming truly oneself. Our relationship to the other fuses together our understanding and addressing the other because "to understand a person is already to speak to him."[84] Moreover, the excessive nature of the encounter with the other also suggests that we meet the other as a face, which signifies the "otherwise" nature of the other and our inability to kill the face that we encounter.[85]

Derrida takes exception to several of the points affirmed by Levinas because he is convinced that the other never loses its exteriority with respect to you and can never become interiorized. It is not possible to unequivocally state that the other, a perpetual outsider, is either interior or exterior in relationship to oneself. By assuming the guise of the inconceivable wholly other, the other is located on the margin, which is maintained in a relationship with you by *différance*, a neologism that signifies the alternation of presence and absence, rendering both possible and impossible our relationship to the presence or sameness of the other. Derrida perceives a double moment operating in this case: a present moment that is exceeded by the relation to the other because it induces the other to return to the same and a second moment that is no longer and the exact opposite of the initial moment.[86] This entire scenario suggests that the self and the other cannot be made into a conceptual totality.

Derrida is also critical of Levinas' emphasis on responsibility and the obligations that accompany it. Derrida criticizes Levinas with an ironical play on the latter's words by stating that one must read Levinas' philosophy otherwise. Derrida ironically and not without a touch of humor suggests that one must read the works of Levinas otherwise than obligation and otherwise than otherwise.[87] Moreover, the call of the other to the self to become responsible in Levinas' theory is problematic for Derrida because the other is never initially truly present. Thus Levinas' call is more like a recall that announces itself in advance.[88]

In comparison to Levinas and Derrida, the work of Kristeva on the stranger, a person of no importance located outside of the predominant group, sheds a different light on the topic of the other. By encountering the other, we are confronted by the possibility of not being an other for someone else. It is not enough that we be able to accept the other, but we must be able to put ourselves in the place of the other, and "this means to imagine and make oneself other for oneself."[89] The other challenges the established group not simply because he/she is not part of the group, but the stranger—the rejected one—calls into question his/her own identity and that of the group. The other states to the group that he/she is different than members of the group. Besides the challenge and intrusion of the established group, the stranger/other calls for love, which Kristeva seems to grasp as a plea for recognition.[90] Again, we notice the emphasis on the difference between the self and the other in Kristeva's concept of the stranger/other that is also evident in the work of Levinas and Derrida, but Kristeva shares Levinas' stress on the importance of an ethical encounter with the other that is missing in Derrida's work.

In contrast to the postmodern thinkers mentioned thus far, Deleuze perceives differently the problem of the other because it functions as a representative of the individuating factors of the I-self, although the other cannot be reduced to these factors. For the psychic system of the I, this means that the other is the I in the sense of a fractured I. Since they are constituted structures, neither the self nor other are primordial with the other being a possibility in the interstices between selves. Unlike the implications in the position of Levinas, the other is not within a field of perception, but it rather forms the conditions in a spacial and temporal sense for such a field of perception, which thereby "ensures individuation

within the perceptual world."[91] Thus the I and self need this structure created by the other in order for them to be perceived as individualities.

Dōgen and Nishitani view the other and the problem of responsibility much differently than Derrida, Levinas, Deleuze, and Kristeva. Within
the context of discussing the four ways that a Bodhisattva, an enlightened
being on the path to becoming a fully liberated being after his/her vow to
save all beings is fulfilled, acts to benefit human beings, Dōgen, for
instance, mentions almsgiving (*fuse*), loving words (*aigo*), beneficial
actions (*rigyō*), and most importantly for the purpose of this discussion
dōji, an identification with those beings to be helped. Dōgen defines it as
follows: "*Dōji* means not to differentiate self from others. . . ."[92] Even
though all these virtues are interdependent, *dōji* is the virtue that represents the foundation for the other three. When one genuinely practices
dōji one is in harmony and unity with others and oneself.[93] The virtue of
dōji is based on a conviction grounded in an intuitive insight by Dōgen
that all things are interrelated: "Each particle of the phenomenal world is
interrelated; but still each particle exists of itself."[94] Dōgen's position suggests that the individual is a complex web of relationships. Moreover, the
relationality between the self and others is a reciprocal and horizontal
type of relationship, a position shared by the postmodern philosophers
mentioned in this chapter because they are also opposed to relationships
that tend to be hierarchical or vertical. Since all things that are interrelated
are ultimately empty from the Zen viewpoint, this insight possesses epistemological implications for Dōgen because "If we can understand a
speck of dust we can know the entire world; one who truly knows one
dharma can understand all dharmas."[95] Moreover, each self is necessarily
interrelated with every other self within a mutual web of responsibility for
the welfare of each other. To be an authentic self for Dōgen necessarily
involves being a self for others.

Although he expresses himself differently, Nishitani agrees essentially with Dōgen, who in turn finds himself in agreement with the
emphasis by Levinas and Kristeva on interpersonal relationships and
responsibility for others. For Nishitani, all things are linked together, but
his emphasis on nothingness accounts for the difference of expression
from that of Dōgen: "In this system, each thing *is* itself in not being itself,
and is not itself in being itself. Its being is illusion in its truth and truth in
its illusion."[96] Nishitani is stating that each thing supports every other
thing and maintains it to be what it is. Thus each thing or other is interconnected, fundamentally united, unique, and shares the same basis as

everything else. What makes it possible for each thing or other to be itself with each other is its grounding in the field of *śūnyatā* (emptiness).

In response to postmodern philosophers who establish or undermine the self by its relationship to the other, Nishitani says, "As long as the existence of self is established by means of protection by some kind of 'other,' in other words, as long as the certainty of the self is based on a relationship with an 'other,' that certainty exists essentially within a significant degree of doubt."[97] But to completely break all conceivable relationships with the other is equivalent to the Great Death. Nishitani's position means that the self-centeredness realized within emptiness is a selfless self-centeredness. A major implication of this realization is that the self and other are entirely nondual. Since they mutually interpenetrate each other, "self-centeredness and other-centeredness are dynamically one."[98]

According to Levinas, the other plays an instrumental role in helping the self gain self-understanding, a position not unlike that of Dōgen if one takes into consideration the relationship between the student and the Zen Master. Levinas' position suggests that the self achieves authentic selfhood through its encounter with the other, whereas genuine selfhood is achieved by non-thinking or the intuitive realization of emptiness for Dōgen. From Lacan's perspective, it is impossible to gain self-understanding by meeting the other because we encounter a lack in the other,[99] whereas Kristeva views the stranger/other as a psychological symptom that indicates our difficulty of existing as an other ourselves and living with others.[100] In comparison to Dōgen, Levinas attempts to protect the exteriority of the other against the kind of unitive experience advocated and thought possible by the Zen Buddhist. Due to the nature of emptiness for Dōgen, it is impossible and unnecessary to guard the exteriority of the other, and whatever lack we can find in the other is a deficiency that we can also find in ourselves.

Since Dōgen traces the origin of altarity to ignorance, Levinas disagrees by looking for its origin in the *illeity* (*il y a*, there is), which lacks presence or absence akin to a pure trace that is irreducibly nonphenomenal.[101] Even though it might be fleetingly brief, the other is already there, according to Lacan in essential agreement with Levinas, when something arises from the unconscious.[102] Within this philosophical context, Levinas criticizes Derrida because his method of deconstruction is defective because it continues to make use of the present tense of the verb "to be."[103] For Dōgen and Nishitani, the "there is" originates in emptiness, which itself is empty, as Dōgen states: "This emptiness is that of emptiness is emptiness. Within this emptiness a solid rock is emptiness."[104] Even though the field of emptiness represents absolute transcendence for Nishitani, it is still an absolute immanence.[105] If we attempt to isolate the origin of the other for Kristeva, we find it expressed in hatred directed at the stranger, which provides the other with consistency: "Hatred makes him real, authentic so to speak, solid, or simply existing."[106]

We previously stated that the other is mysterious for Levinas. Does he mean something more definite by the term mysterious? The other as other is what the self is not by its very nature; it even possesses priority over the self for Levinas. Its mysterious aspect is connected to the fact that it cannot become an object that we can possess, it cannot become us, and it withdraws from us as we approach it.[107] This suggests that its mysterious aspect is directly related to its altarity, constituting the essence of the other. In contrast to Levinas, Lacan traces the mysterious nature of the other to a tension between consciousness and unconsciousness in which the unconscious other is forever hiding within a person. This ever-lurking unconscious other is a phantom because it is pre-ontological, being neither being nor nonbeing.[108] Although he does not use the term mysterious like Levinas to discuss the relationship between the self and other, Derrida does indicate something similar to the mystery of Levinas because they represent both the possibility and impossibility of self-identity, an ambiguity that one could not find in the work of Dōgen and Nishitani, due to the insuperable gap between them, since their fundamental difference both combines and separates identity and difference.[109] In contrast to Levinas and Derrida, the stranger of Kristeva possesses no self, is considered a nothing, and belongs nowhere, which renders the other a mystery to members of the predominant group.[110] Again, we notice a thinker associating mystery with altarity.

According to Levinas, the most radical sense of the other is what he calls the infinite, the absolutely other. By thinking more than one can think, this means to think of infinity, an excess and a desire, but without extinguishing or exhausting it with one's thought.[111] When we encounter the other we also discover infinity. Derrida perceives a danger in Levinas' position at this point, and he criticizes him: "If one thinks, as Levinas does, that positive Infinity tolerates, or even requires, infinite altarity, then one must renounce all language, and first of all the words of *infinite* and *other*."[112] The overall purpose of Levinas is not the destruction of language, but he seeks rather to affirm the altarity of the other and to stress that language possesses no limits. Moreover, Derrida asserts that Levinas cannot speak of the infinitely other without also affirming the Same.[113] For Levinas, this is not a valid criticism because it is conceptually possible to discuss the infinite without necessarily affirming it. Levinas is also very cognizant of not compromising the altarity of the other by thematizing or interiorizing it. Instead, he stresses the absolute altarity of the other, by affirming that it is beyond totality, possesses no place, and cannot be grasped as a relation because it cannot be reduced to some kind of relationship. This indubitably asserts that the other is completely exterior to any totalizing intention of thought and suggests that it overflows language, leaving only a trace of its altarity within language. In contrast to Levinas and Derrida, Lacan disagrees by claiming that the beyond aspect of the other is located in the unconscious as the discourse of the other.[114]

Due in part to Levinas' emphasis on the infinite, he misses the significance of double altarity from the perspective of Derrida, who defines it in the following way: "The altarity of the transcendent thing, although irreducible, is such only by means of the indefinite incompleteness of my original perceptions. Thus it is incomparable to the altarity of Others, which is also irreducible, and adds to the dimension of incompleteness. . . . But without the first altarity, the altarity of bodies (and the Other is also a body, from the beginning), the second altarity could never emerge."[115] It is necessary to think of this double altarity as a whole because the second altarity is inscribed in the first altarity, causing a dual indefiniteness and ambiguity within which Derrida tends to revel in his playful way of doing philosophy.

Derrida's double altarity might cause a problem for Levinas, but it does not present an obstacle for Dōgen. In a playful spirit that is not unlike that of Derrida, the Zen Master cites an incident involving another Master, a layman, and an earthworm that is cut in half. Since both sides of the severed worm move, is it possible to determine which part contains the Buddha-nature? Dōgen comments on this episode in Zen lore: "'An earthworm that is cut in two' implies that originally there was one worm; is this Shosho's understanding? Everyday life of Buddhas and Patriarchs is not like this. Originally the worm was not one; it was not cuttable into two. Think deeply about one and two."[116] Dōgen does not perceive any distinction between the two halves or any double altarity for two reasons. The moving halves of the worm represent the simultaneous action of *samādhi* (meditative concentration) and *prajñā* (wisdom). Moreover, the words of the Master indicate the function of

Buddha-nature, which Dōgen defines as "Buddha-nature and no Buddha-nature exist both in life and in death."[117] In other words, there are no distinctions within Buddha-nature between one and two, right and left, initial and secondary altarity. This kind of possibility is beyond the philosophical realm of Derrida to entertain except to attempt to criticize or deconstruct it. At this point, Kristeva is closer in spirit to Dōgen than the other postmodern figures because she asserts that we are strangers within ourselves due to our divided interior natures. Instead of the intuitive realization of Buddha-nature advocated by Dōgen, Kristeva conceives of psychoanalysis as a journey "into the strangeness of the other and of oneself, toward an ethics of respect for the irreconcilable."[118]

From Levinas' perspective, Lacan and Derrida miss the significance of the face of the other, a means by which the other reveals him/herself with a nonconceptualized nature. When we encounter the other, we meet its face, an ethical epiphany that identifies a being, and calls upon us to react to its questions.[119] We are able to encounter this face due to our pregiven proximity, which is prior to any experience or encounter with the other. The face of the other that we encounter comes from the beyond and is without a specific origin; it is nearby us, but it never completely arrives because it signifies a trace and a withdrawal from us, which makes it impossible to fully grasp its nature.[120] Levinas' position leads to Derrida's charge that the face represents presence.[121] In response to such criticism, Levinas counters against Derrida: "The defection from presence led up to the defection from the true, to significations which do not have to comply with the summation of knowledge. Truth is no longer at the level of an eternal or omnitemporal truth—but this is a relativity that no historicism would ever have been able to suspect."[122] According to Kristeva, we simply stare into the face of the other and do not see a unique individual. If the stranger lives within us as Kristeva claims, the other represents the hidden face within our own identity.[123] Nishitani differs from these thinkers by equating the face with absolute nothingness.[124] This does not imply that the person is unreal or simply an illusion because within and without, reality and illusion form a unity with absolute nothingness.

Within the context of discussing the significance of the face-to-face transmission of the Zen teaching between novice and teacher, Dōgen elaborates on the importance of the face by claiming that the face of the teacher is really the same face as the historical Buddha. Dōgen explains: "In each generation, every face has been the face of Buddha, and this original face is direct, face-to-face transmission."[125] Dōgen is saying that the face of the Buddha and one's own face are nondual, which makes it possible for direct transmission of his teachings from Buddha to teacher to student in a single tradition of giving and receiving of the face. Unlike the face espoused by Levinas, this face is grounded in emptiness, which means that it is actually no-face. With his/her no-face, the Zen person is without status, whereas a secular Japanese person is defined by his/her status and situation before one is able to act. In contrast to the importance of context for a secular person who is defined by this organic reality in Japanese society, Dōgen's person is not defined by context, which assumes priority over an individual in a secular situation. Kasulis elucidates Dōgen's convictions about how the Zen Buddhist is to function within any situation: "The Zen ideal is to act spontaneously in the situation without first objectifying it in order to define one's role."[126] From Dōgen's perspective, the various postmodernists appear to fail with respect to the other by objectifying it and failing to respond spontaneously, even though some of them tend to emphasize spontaneity. Since the meditating Zen person is grounded in non-thinking, this person is not limited by either the variety or scope of his/her experience.

Concluding Remarks

Nishitani and Dōgen share with Kant a conviction in the unity of the self and its ability to become aware of its own identity, whereas the postmodernists tend to view the self as disunified or split in some way and unable to find its identity. None of the postmodernists and Zen Buddhists seem all that interested in following Kierkegaard's project of protecting the individuality of the self. The Zen thinkers and postmodernists agree that the self is subject to change much like Nietzsche emphasizes in his philosophy. And we have seen that the Zen philosophers, Levinas, Lacan, and Kristeva remain interested in the consciousness of the self much like Sartre does in his work.

The Hegelian emphasis on the presence of the other to the self-consciousness of the self, Kierkegaard's focus on the self's relation to the other and the danger of the crowd, and Sartre's attention to being for the other are also aspects of the nature of the self that are also interesting to the postmodernists and the Zen thinkers. All the postmodern thinkers agree that the other is extremely important to the self and its development, as well as representing a danger to the self. In fact, the postmodern emphasis on the other suggests an eclipse of the self, which looses its centrality to philosophical thinking and discourse. Dōgen and Nishitani do not share this drift away from the importance of the self to the other because the other shares the same Buddha-nature, a position that is too metaphysical for most postmodernists.

The eclipse of the self can be witnessed in the work of Derrida and Taylor and their stress on the lack of an enduring presence and identity for the self. Embodied within Levinas' philosophy is a potential for the eclipse of the self with his emphasis on locating its identity in a nonpresence and a conviction that it cannot be intuited because its identity is associated with an affective experience. Agreeing with Derrida, Taylor, and Deleuze, Lacan and Kristeva affirm that the self lacks presence. For Lacan, the self possesses an illusory identity, whereas Kristeva claims that the self, a series of fluctuating signifiers, lacks identity because it is perpetually changing and splitting apart. These postmodern thinkers agree that the self is decentered. Following Derrida's deconstruction of the concept of the center, Taylor finds a self that is corelative, codependent, and decentered in part because of the death of God that marks the disappearance of the self and the successful conclusion of humanistic nihilism. The internal split between the subject and the ego convinces Lacan that the self is decentered. For Kristeva, rejection destroys the possibility of presence for the self that is captive to the repetitive process of the *chora* that creates discontinuity and ruptures within the self. In contrast, Levinas views the decentering of the self differently than the other postmodernists because it is due to the ability of the self to project itself forth and the double movement of encountering and relating to the other and getting the other to return to the self, which causes it to become decentered, whereas Deleuze envisions a flowing of energy, fragmenting, and individuating taking place that disallows any prospect for the self to become centered.

From the perspective of Dōgen and Nishitani, the self is saved from eclipse by its grounding in the field of emptiness. In response to Derrida and Taylor, Dōgen thinks that they superimpose alien modes of thinking on the self, whereas Lacan and Kristeva superimpose psychological categories on the self that transform it into something abstract rather than something concrete and make it impossible to experience directly and immediately the self. Although Dōgen agrees with the postmodern thinkers that the self possesses no permanence or enduring presence, he also thinks that they manipulate personal experience to the detriment of one's gaining an understanding of the genuine self. Nishitani agrees with Dōgen that authentic self-awareness is possible, and he rejects all conceptualizations of the self because of its basis in emptiness. If the self is viewed from the field of *śūnyatā* for Nishitani, the self is never without a center because the center is not confined to a single location in space, but is spread everywhere in sharp contrast to the shared position of the postmodern thinkers. The differences between the Zen Buddhist and postmodernists are also evident in the method of kenosis advocated by Taylor and its producing of a marginal being that manifests the disappearance of the self and the method of *zazen* for Dōgen that enables one to realize and authenticate the self.

Even with Levinas' emphasis on how the other can help the self gain understanding of itself and his stress on the importance of responsibility, Dōgen and Nishitani help us to see in contrast to the other postmodernists discussed in this chapter that the self and other are intimately interrelated both ethically and ontologically within a field of emptiness. For these Zen thinkers, the other is not there standing against the self, representing some mysterious threat that may serve to help decenter the self. The other for these Zen philosophers is myself, and the self is a complex of relationships. Even though Kristeva says that the stranger/other is really myself, she does not mean exactly the same thing as the Buddhist thinkers because she does not share the presuppositions of their worldview and the self-validating factor of their existential experiences.

This comparison of the self and other represents a good example of how both dialogical parties stand opposed to essentialism, which can be defined as accepting the objective and subjective dichotomy and conceiving each aspect of the dichotomy as self-subsistent substances that are inalterably shaped by its essence.[127] The postmodernists tend to agree that an essentialist position is a direct product of representational thinking. With their emphasis on impermanence, the path of philosophy for Dōgen and Nishitani negates essences. Since there are no self-contained essences, and emptiness represents the nonbeing of essences, there is nothing that arises from essences. Therefore, with respect to the topic of this chapter, there is no true "I-ness," if we conceive of it as representing the essence of the self.

Beside these many differences between the dialogical parties of this chapter, the overall postmodern emphasis on the contingency of the self suggests the de-divinizing of the self and the world. An insightful observation is offered at this point by Rorty: "To say that both are de-divinized is to say that one no longer thinks of either as speaking to us, as having a language of its own, as a rival poet."[128] Along with this process of de-divinization, it might be added that the other fills the void created by the disappearance of the self. Levinas' emphasis on the other in the radical sense of the infinite and its mysterious aspect suggests, for instance, a movement toward the divinization of the other. And the importance of the other in the development of the self for Lacan and Kristeva moves in a similar direction. Dōgen and Nishitani demonstrate another and more balanced approach to the relationship between the self and the other without transforming the other into something divine or quasi-divine.

CHAPTER 7

Time and Death

H uman beings of many diverse cultures have long recognized that the seasons follow one another, dynasties and governments fall, people are born, mature, grow old, and eventually die, and buildings and walls made of durable materials eventually crumble to the ground. The earth itself grows old during the course of a year and periodic rituals of renewal punctuate the annual calendars of many cultures. All of these things are related to time. But how does one account for time? Different cultures have attempted to measure time by using sun dials or mechanical clocks. Although cultures have been able to measure the passage of time, their thinkers have had a more difficult task of trying to account philosophically for the actual nature of time, which remains something mysterious to everyone.

The mysterious nature of time did not intimidate Immanuel Kant from attempting to account for it in his philosophical system in his work entitled the *Critique of Pure Reason.* Kant thinks that it is not possible to derive an understanding of time from empirical experience by abstracting from sense perception because time is an *a priori* particular, although it is not a property or relation between particulars. When we assume the existence of something at one instant or over a course of time, we tend to presuppose the existence of time, a representation that supports all our intuitions and is thus *a priori.*[1] Time allows for the possibility of appearances, but it does not vanish when the appearances are removed or disappear. It is impossible for us to imagine an act of perception that would not be located in time, even though it might be possible to construe empty time. Thus time is prior to the existence of objects.

Another important feature of time for Kant is that it possesses one dimension. This implies that past, present, and future moments of time are successive and not simultaneous.[2] Since time cannot be thought away or given to us from outside of ourselves by an object, Kant argues that it is a subjective necessity from which follows its objective necessity. This suggests that time is an immediate intuition, which excludes the possibility that time determines appearances. If time is a purely subjective aspect of human intuition, it is nothing apart from a subject, does not absolutely belong to things, and cannot be absolutely real.[3] Kant wants to claim that time is both empirically real in relation to sense objects and transcendentally ideal because it belongs to things in themselves and cannot be given by means of the senses.

Even though alterations are possible in time, Kant states that time is something real: "Certainly time is something real, namely, the real form of inner intuition. It has therefore subjective reality in respect of inner experience; that is, I really have the representation of time and of my determinations in it."[4] Because time conditions our experiences, it possesses empirical reality, although it does not have absolute reality. Time, a pure form of sensible intuition, possesses logical implications for Kant because it, along with space, serves as a source of knowledge from which can be derived *a priori* synthetic propositions, which are judgments made logically independent of all sense impression and experience.

From the philosophical perspective of Hegel, the conclusions drawn by Kant neglect the creativity of time—its becoming. And unlike Kant, Hegel also thinks that it is inaccurate to claim that time is a subjective form that is imposed upon the world by perception. Hegel equates time with *Begriff* (notion, concept) in his philosophy: "Time is just the notion definitely existent, and presented to consciousness in the form of empty intuition."[5] This suggests that it is the integration of all notions and not simply a specific notion. Hegel argues that truth is whole, and the notion at its highest level of development represents the absolute idea. The *Begriff* owes its origin to the negative action of negating the given that is identified with time. Not only is time a process for the attainment of completeness, it is real, representing the destiny and necessity of incomplete spirit as well as negativity and creativity.

As the notion in the form of existence, time presupposes a real world, a realm of matter that resists negation, which it negates by transforming each instant into the nothingness of the past. Hegel wants to stress here that time is the being of becoming, which is a necessary human reality without which there would be no time because human beings usher negation into the world. Hegel explains, "Time, as the negative unity of self-externality, is also purely abstract and of an ideal nature. It is the being which, in that it is, is not, and in that it is not, is."⁶ From another perspective for Hegel, time originates in desire, an absence that is present, and assumes the form of an empty intuition to consciousness. And when desire is finally fulfilled time arrives at its end.

Since the *Begriff* always develops toward further realization, the future represents an unfilled demand. The future works to negate the past which enhances the synthesis of the present, a location where the future is realized. These three dimensions of time "constitute the becoming of externality as such, and its dissolution into the differences of being as passing over into nothing, and of nothing passing over into being."⁷ Within the three moments of time, Spirit, a pure form of sensibility, manifests itself and becomes conscious of itself, and Spirit appears in time as long as it does not annul it by grasping its pure notion.⁸ For Hegel, it is incorrect to claim that things and humans originate and pass away in time; it is more accurate to say that time itself is the becoming, the coming to be and passing away.

Besides Hegel, another thinker concerned with becoming is Friedrich Nietzsche. Although Nietzsche does not examine the concept of time systematically, a basic notion of his later philosophy is temporal: eternal recurrence. With this notion of time, Nietzsche wants to radically call into question the ordinary concept of time and eventually subvert and displace it. A good example of this subversion of time is located within a dialogue between the prophet Zarathustra and a dwarf that the prophet encounters in a vision. During the dialogue, they discuss a gateway which is inscribed with the name "moment," representing the juncture of the opposition between past and future that remains a tension and is not reconciled. In response to a question by the prophet, the dwarf, a creature of the earth, replies that whatever is straight is false: "'All truth is crooked; time itself is a circle.'"⁹ Nietzsche wants to question the status and consecutive nature of the now moments by suggesting that time is not only horizontal, but each moment is also vertical, a dimension that reveals the possibility of depth and experiential intensity.

In contrast to the Judaeo-Christian concept of time, the notion of eternal recurrence represents a transvaluation of the earlier concept of time. This notion came to Nietzsche as a nightmare, and this is reflected in his writings:

How, if some day or night a demon were to sneak after you into your loneliest loneliness and say to you, "This life as you

now live it and have lived it, you will have to live once more
and innumerable times more; and there will be nothing new in
it, but every pain and every joy and every thought and sigh
and everything immeasurably small or great in your life must
return to you—all in the same succession and sequence—
even this spider and this moon-light between the trees, and
even this moment and I myself. The eternal hourglass of existence is turned over and over, and you with it, a dust grain of
dust." Would you not throw yourself down and gnash your
teeth and curse the demon who spoke thus? Or did you once
experience a tremendous moment when you would have
answered him, 'You are a god, and never have I heard anything more godly.'[10]

This prophetic vision or nightmare suggests that there is no beginning,
middle, or end. The eternal recurrence is an untestable hypothesis, implying that its veracity cannot be verified objectively, although one scholar
calls it "the only nontranscendental eternal verity."[11] Since this teaching
represents the antithesis of any faith in continual progress, no possibility
of novelty in the universe, and eternal monotony, history is without a
goal, purpose, or meaning. Nietzsche views this as the most extreme form
of nihilism: meaninglessness eternally.[12] Nietzsche views eternal recurrence as a replacement for religion and metaphysics.[13] Although they do
not share his notion of eternal recurrence, Heidegger and Derrida share
with Nietzsche a conviction that ordinary concepts of time embody values that can be described as more ontological than temporal.

In contrast to Kant, Hegel, and Nietzsche, the work of Edmund
Husserl marks a change in the western philosophical approach to the
problem of time because he does not investigate time as a reality. Husserl
is more concerned with how we experience time or the way in which it is
manifest in our consciousness. Since time is connected to objects in time,
Husserl focuses on our knowledge of temporal objects, which are both
transcendent and immanent. These immanent objects, like sensations and
intentions, are constituted in inner time, and their temporal constitution is
more fundamental in comparison to those that form reality, like sense data
and appearances.[14]

Husserl distinguishes between objective time and inner time. The
former type of time embodies real things, is manifest to consciousness
through time appearances, seems to flow independently of our con-

sciousness, and can be measured by clocks and similar mechanical devices, whereas inner time is the sphere of immanent things, is prior to all other appearances, and renders it possible for us to experience them. This inner time manifests a very primitive form of consciousness—the consciousness of things.[15] The constitution of immanent objects occurs through a series of temporal phases, a sequence of nows and retentions, that gives them individuality, a process dissimilar to external objects. Husserl makes a distinction between the past that must be reproduced because an event is completely over and must be recreated and the past held in retention, an ability to capture the immediately lapsed past in the current instant of consciousness, which is not susceptible to the inevitable imperfection of reproduction with its vagueness and possible distortion. Retention of the immediate past is able to avoid the imperfections of reproduction because of the inconsequential lapse of time between the immediate past moment that constitutes retention and the present moment.

According to Husserl, our consciousness experiences time as a now moment, an edge-point of an interval of time, along with it horizons, which implies its retentional (past) and protentional (future) phases, representing an anticipation of the moment to follow the now instant. When we experience the now moment we also experience that which has just elapsed and protention into imminent now moments. When we experience a now instant this does not suggest that the past instant disappears immediately, but it is rather held in retention.[16] By means of protention and retention, the three moments of time are interconnected in a single moment of reflective consciousness.

Husserl thinks that consciousness is temporal within the context of a threefold horizon of memory, expectation, and instantaneous compresence. Self-consciousness expects, for instance, that the present moment will past into a new moment within which one's present self-awareness will continue as in the now moment, which suggests the occurring and repeatable nature of self-consciousness. In fact, time is the unifying agent of all subjective processes, and it renders experience possible. In the fourth of his *Cartesian Meditations*, Husserl refers to time as the universal form of all ego origination.[17]

Within the phenomenological tradition of Husserl, Merleau-Ponty is concerned with accounting for time as it comes into being. Merleau-Ponty is critical of Kant because he thinks that it is necessary to get to the concrete structure of time and not to analyze it through an already established conception of subjectivity.[18] And in criticism of Husserl, Merleau-Ponty claims that an immanent object of consciousness is no longer time for the following reasons:

> It is of the essence of time to be in process of self-production, and not to be; never, that is, to be completely constituted. Constituted time, the series of possible relations in terms of before and after, is not time itself, but the ultimate recording of time, the result of its passage, which objective thinking always presupposes yet never manages to fasten on to.[19]

For Merleau-Ponty, time is not a real process that one can record because it arises from my relation to objects, which embody within themselves the future and past in a preexistent state.

Merleau-Ponty argues that time and its dimensions appear lucidly to one's field of presence, and it exists for someone because one is situated in it, even though one cannot see it just as one cannot perceive one's face. Not only does one have presence, one also exists in the present: "Time exists for me because I have a present."[20] Because being and consciousness coincide for Merleau-Ponty, the present possesses a privileged status. This allows one to be present to oneself, to be present to the world in which one lives, and to hold time in its entirety. This suggests that one is centered in the present. Being centered within the present moment, time flows through a person and is uncreated by any human being. By means of time, being is conceived.[21]

Recalling Husserl's notion of retention, Merleau-Ponty argues that the present represents the passage of future into the present and of the future into the past, moments that are collected in a system of retentions at each instant. What Heidegger calls ek-stase or direction Merleau-Ponty refers to as the general flight out of itself. Since the three moments of time are interconnected, this implies that each present moment "reasserts the presence of the whole past which it supplants, and anticipates that of all that is to come, and that by definition the present is not to shut up within itself, but transcends itself towards a future and a past."[22] Moreover, within the flow of time from present to past, being and passing away are synonymous, which implies that a past event does not cease to be.[23] Due to its continuity, time remains the same, and it can be stated that the person is time.

In contrast to these western views of time, the influential Buddhist philosopher Nāgārjuna in his work the *Mūlamadhyamaka-kārikā* discusses *saṃsāra* (cycle of life and death) in chapter 11, and he states that the time anterior to its beginning cannot be grasped because it possesses no definite commencement or conclusion. Nāgārjuna's point is that priority and posteriority are not absolute and possess merely relative significance in relation to each other. This type of conclusion is also true of the three moments of time, which are relational concepts, and none of them manifests an individual identity in itself.[24] The reason that time is problematic for Nāgārjuna is summarized insightfully by Streng:

> In the context of the *Madhyamakakārikās*, time or some segment of time becomes a problem when it is crystallized into some kind of distinct entity. The problem, then, is not that it is a process of becoming; but that in illusion and craving, man posits an ultimate being-ness in it or in segments of it. From the Mādhyamika point of view there is no 'level of reality' like temporal-existence-as-such; one cannot escape from it because there is no 'it' to escape from.[25]

Even though the three moments of time are germane to this world, these moments of time do not exist from the perspective of higher truth, which implies that there is no absolute time. Moreover, time does not possess *svabhāva* (intrinsic being). Since nothing exists in and of itself for Nāgārjuna, this means that a concept like time also possesses no intrinsic, permanent nature. What then is time? Nāgārjuna states that it is a mental construction with the potential to bind a person to it, if one mistakenly accepts it as something ultimate.[26] We will see that time is not philosophically dismissed as a mental construct by Dōgen and Nishitani.

Based on their philosophical treatments of time, Kant, Hegel, Husserl, and Merleau-Ponty each exert either a positive or negative influence upon postmodern thought with respect to the problem of time. The remainder of this chapter will examine the grasp of time in Heidegger, Levinas, Derrida, Deleuze, and more briefly Lyotard. We will also compare their understanding of time with Dōgen and Nishitani. Finally, we will compare the postmodernists with Dōgen on the problem of death.

The Nature of Time

Time does not have anything to do with its measurement in the form of a wristwatch, clock, sun dial, or a larger mechanical device for all the figures that we will be discussing. Time is also not an indefinite series of nows in which the future represents nows that have not yet come but will arrive some day, the past does not consist of nows that once were but are no longer, and the present does not manifest itself as the now which at this very moment is. According to Heidegger, these inadequate conceptions of time are partly due to our absorption in the way we handle things. Moreover, all the philosophers in this chapter will agree that time is not a thing. Lyotard thinks, for instance, that placing all moments of time on a single diachronic line objectifies time and transforms time from presenting time to presented time, from time as now to time as this time.[27]

Within the context of his analysis of *Dasein* (there being), Heidegger stresses that it is not a mere entity, but it is rather an anticipatory drive-towards-being, representing its own potentiality or constant coming to itself. Finding itself within the midst of other beings, *Dasein* is constantly coming to Being or to itself as having-already-been-thrown or its future (*Zukunft*). The past (*Gewesenheit*) of *Dasein* is it as-having-been and still is, an existential sense of the past, in contrast to the past (*Vergangenheit*) that once was but is no longer, a past time of mere entities.[28] The past is not something distinct from *Dasein* because it is what it has been and what it remains. Thus the authentic sense of the past is still present as having been, a moment that is gone but still here. The "having been" nature of the past arises from the future in such a way that the future which "has already been" releases the present from itself. The future, a genuine completion of the "having been," is a moment that will be real at sometime, and represents the coming (*kunft*) in which *Dasein*, a transcendence, comes toward (*zu*) itself.[29] It is possible to notice a reciprocity between the past and future because the latter presupposes the former by reason of the fact that the past cannot manifest itself unless there is a future. If there is a reciprocal relationship between the past and future, the three phases of time coexist in the present.

According to Heidegger, to begin to speak of the present is already to think of the past, the earlier, and the future, the later. The significance and meaning of the present is manifested in its ability to make present (*Gegenwärtigen*). With respect to *Dasein* as a temporalizing agent, it renders beings present, which presupposes the anticipation of *Dasein's* possibilities in the future and its return to what has been. We can notice here that the present is a result of the two other ecstases of time. This unified phenomenon of temporality reveals itself in authentic concern.[30]

Concern (*Sorge*) consists of the following: an anticipatory drive-toward-Being that corresponds to the future; facticity of *Dasein* that is already-thrown-forth-and-still-to-be-achieved that is associated with the past; and fallenness that is referentially dependent on and pulled toward other beings that represents the present. These three features of concern correspond to the three ecstases or directions of temporality, which are: a direction toward Being (existence); a direction of return toward what-is-as-having-been (facticity), and a direction toward other beings (fallenness).[31] This scenario suggests a few observations. Temporality, a primordial time, is outside of itself due to its three ecstases, each direction possesses its proper horizon, the unity of the three ecstases makes possible the unity of concern, the present is united with the past and future, and their reciprocity signifies the unity of temporality. By excluding the possibility that temporality is an entity, Heidegger wants to emphasize that it is a process that is intrinsically ecstatic, which temporalizes itself in its different modes with an emphasize on the future. This overall structure of time and Heidegger's stress upon the importance of the future motivates Otto Pöggeler, an early interpreter of Heidegger, to be impressed by the way in which "the present is swallowed up by the future (as having been) and thus receives no positive determination. While the temporal ecstasis of the future is richly determined by existence, projection, anticipating death, resoluteness, and that of the past by facticity, throwness, guilt, repetition, the present remains—at least in its authenticity as the insightful moment—empty. . . ."[32]

It was previously stated that an essential feature of the present is that it makes present. In a lecture entitled *On Time and Being* delivered in 1962, Heidegger elucidates what he means by presence: "Presence determines Being in a unified way as presencing and allowing-to-presence, that is, as unconcealing."[33] Although presence conveys the meaning of lasting, Heidegger does not mean this in the sense of mere duration, a representation of time as a sequence of now moments, but he rather wants to stress abiding with respect to lasting in present being. The event of presencing reveals time-space, but this does not convey the sense of a distance between two now-points. Heidegger explains, "Time-space now is the name for the openness which opens up in the mutual self-extending of futural approach, past and present. This openness exclusively and primarily provides the space in which space as we usually know it can unfold."[34]

Similar to Heidegger, the Zen philosopher Dōgen begins his discussion of time with a consideration of how it is ordinarily conceived by people. Dōgen illustrates the everyday view of time by relating a commonplace story about a person who lives in a valley and decides to climb to the summit of a distant mountain. This person must travel across the valley, traverse a river, climb the mountain, and finally achieve the pinnacle of the natural structure. Once the traveller's goal is attained there is a tendency to relegate the valley, river, and mountain to things encountered in the past, which suggests that these past things have no relation to the present. Why is this the case? According to Dōgen, in the everyday view of time, it is measured by the movement from one point (e.g., the starting point in the valley) to the end point (e.g., the summit of the mountain). By means of this type of thinking, time is thus conceived as a linear series of connected now-points without true unity. Such an inaccurate view of time falsely conceives it as something substantial or objective, as reducible, and as differentiated. Moreover, this everyday view of time conceives of it as anthropocentric in the sense that time is limited to human experience. From this everyday perspective, time seems to fly by us. But this is not only an inaccurate view of time, this type of perspective also separates a person from time as experienced.

Dōgen is very critical of this everyday view of time because he wants to affirm that when a person crosses the valley and river and climbs the mountain such a person is time. In other words, a person cannot be separated from time. Dōgen clarifies his position in the following manner: "This means that because, in reality, there is no coming or going in time, when we cross the river or climb the mountain we exist in the eternal present of time; this time includes all past and present time."[35] Much like Heidegger, Dōgen maintains that the past is experienced in our present moment, the passing away of time is only apparent and not real, and the past is contained in the present. Moreover, Dōgen and Heidegger agree that we cannot be truly separated from time, although the former thinker claims that we are time and the latter stresses that we exist in time. As one might expect, Nishitani agrees with Dōgen that "We do not simply live in time: we live time. From one moment in time to the next we are making time to be time, we are bringing time to the 'fullness of time.'"[36] For both Heidegger and Dōgen, time is also indicative of our interrelationship with others in a common union from Dōgen's perspective and a grounding in finitude from the viewpoint of Heidegger.

At this point, Levinas is very critical of Heidegger's position and by implication that taken by Dōgen. Levinas thinks that any consideration of time that does not include the other is a failure, and he rejects Heidegger's philosophical position on time because it tends to emphasize solitude prior to a relationship with the other. Levinas is convinced that time cannot be grasped by an isolated subject because he thinks that it is a relational phenomenon, a relationship of a subject with the other. Levinas elaborates that "The dialectic of time is the very dialectic of the relationship with the other, that is, a dialogue which in turn has to be studied in terms other than those of the dialectic of the solitary subject."[37] In fact, it is the other that represents the origin of a discontinuous time in which no single event is definitive. When Heidegger connects the finitude of being with the essence of time, Levinas critically alters this emphasis by linking the essence of being with the infinity of time.[38] Levinas also rejects Dōgen's understanding of time as a relationship with others because it is not a face-to-face relationship, and he rejects Heidegger at this point because his conception of relationship is being *with* the other and not face-to-face.[39] For a similar reason, Levinas discards Heidegger's emphasis on the three ecstases because a subject becomes absorbed in the object and recovers unity, but it results in the disappearance of the other.[40] In contrast to Dōgen, Levinas thinks that enjoyment represents an experience of time in which its flow is arrested for a while.

In sharp contrast to the apparent certainty of Heidegger and Dōgen that one can experience the present and remember the past in the present moment, Derrida counters them with his notion of trace, a simultaneous presence and absence, that cannot be conceived on the basis of a simple present because it is an indeterminate medium that reveals the world, but it designates nothing specific.[41] The notion of trace, which effaces itself upon presenting itself, subverts the present and presence because it continuously overflows itself and is by nature a supplement that makes additions to itself. If effacement did not overtake the trace, it would have the nature of presence.[42] Moreover, before a being can gain presence, it is subject to the trace, which tends to undermine presence by displacing it. Derrida thinks that time is essentially a metaphysical concept to which he is opposed, and his notion of trace is a device used to subvert time and other forms of metaphysical concepts.

Criticizing Husserl's concept of time, Derrida does not think that it is possible to claim that one can have a self-identical now moment and self-contained subjectivity because the now must point to other moments beyond itself in order to be itself. In other words, to become conscious of the now moment involves consciousness of the other or not-now. Husserl's moments of retention and protention are called autoaffection by Derrida because it is something that constitutes rather than being constituted.[43] In order for the now moment to become present to consciousness, this process requires that it be juxtaposed with something different, the immediately past now. It is thus impossible for the present moment to fulfill past expectations and future anticipations.

Recalling the eternal recurrence of Nietzsche, Taylor, following the lead of Derrida, claims that it subverts the traditional opposition between time and eternity. Since the present, a ceaseless transition and perpetual motion, includes absence, it can never become fully present, suggesting that it always remains absent. Taylor writes, "The 'being' of this becoming constitutes eternal recurrence."[44] Taylor draws the conclusion that time is always errant and irrevocably liminal.[45] For both Taylor and Derrida, it is impossible for there to be any such thing as a certain self-evident presence of being in the present moment.

According to Derrida, when the trace refers to the past it becomes something that cannot be conceived as a past that becomes present. With apparently Husserl's notion of time in mind, Derrida writes, "The concept of trace is therefore incommensurate with that of retention, that of the becoming-past of what had been present. The trace cannot be conceived—nor, therefore, can difference—on the basis of either the present or the presence of the present."[46] From a slightly different perspective, the past is a repetition of past presence, making it always different from any present moment. Derrida's deconstruction of time extends to the future, which for him is not another time because "It is *present* at the heart of experience. Present not as a total presence but as a *trace*."[47] In response to Derrida and Taylor, Dōgen asserts vigorously that each moment is complete in itself and cannot be subverted because each embodies a multitude of simultaneous perspectives.

Nishitani shares with Derrida and Taylor a conviction in the impermanent nature of time, an ever passing away sequence of nows, that is irreversible. The fleeting nature of an instant emphasizes the perpetual newness of time, an unlimited openness without beginning, that renders it a field of limitless possibility and also makes our existence an endless burden, a position not unlike that of Levinas' stress upon the burden of being, although Nishitani also wants to emphasize the additional burden upon the individual of time.[48] Time becomes a burden because our location within it condemns us to be incessantly active. Thus we recognize the equivocal natures of time and newness: creation, freedom, and infinite possibility on the one hand and infinite burden and inextricable necessity on the other hand.[49]

Instead of the three ecstases of time that we find in Heidegger's work or the identity of the person and time in Dōgen's work, Deleuze conceives of a threefold passive syntheses of time: founding time (present); foundation of time (past); and the unfounding of time (a pure and empty form of time). The present is ever moving and contradictory because it is continually passing away and passing within the time constituted or intratemporal. Deleuze concludes that there must be another time in which the initial synthesis of time happens.[50] This first synthesis is identified as habit, a foundation of time, but embodied within the present is an additional dimension that represents its former instant, which Deleuze identifies with the memory of its former present, forming a fundamental synthesis of time that constitutes the past. Thus, the present and its previous presents are not similar to two consecutive instants on a linear line of time. Deleuze's conception of the nature of the present makes it difficult for representational thinking to successfully work because the present represents the former present instant and itself as a particular, and the past is presupposed by every attempt at representation. For the past and the future, representing dual asymmetrical elements of the present, this means that the past is caught between present moments, and it is futile to attempt to recreate the past from the present moments.[51] In contrast to Dōgen's emphasis on the present moment and Heidegger's orientation towards the future, Deleuze stresses the past as the foundation of time, and he acknowledges a basic paradox: the contemporaneity of the past with the present. A second paradox revolves around the coexistence of the moments of time: "If each past is contemporaneous with the present that it was, then *all* of the past coexists with the new present in relation to which it is now past."[52] Therefore, the past is a synthesis of itself, the present and future, which indicates that the present and future are mere dimensions of the past, a pure, general, *a priori* aspect of time.

Like Taylor, Derrida, and Dōgen with their emphasize on the impermanence of the present, Deleuze stresses the constantly changing nature of the present. But unlike Taylor and Derrida with their notion of the trace and how it subverts the present and its role as a metaphysical concept, Deleuze's conception of the present, even though it also subverts itself and the other dimensions of time, stresses its difference from other moments of time and even itself. In contrast to Derrida and Taylor and their contention about the repetitive nature of the past, Deleuze argues that his three passive syntheses of time reveal themselves as repetition, which is defined as difference in itself, and not simply as past. Deleuze clarifies his position: "The present is the repeater, the past is repetition itself, but the future is that which is repeated."[53] Thus the whole of time is repetition for Deleuze with the third synthesis (future) representing the unfolding of time itself in its pure and empty form, whereas each instant is complete in itself for Dōgen, although Deleuze agrees with Levinas that time is a relational phenomenon.

Being and Time

Dōgen thinks that there is no transition or passing away of time in some linear direction, but it is rather occurring right this instant. In contrast to Dōgen, Heidegger states that time does pass away, although it remains as time and does not disappear, that is, as a certain presence, which is not reducible to any present moment. This means that time is determined by Being, and Being is determined by time in turn by the fact that "Being speaks out of the constancy of time's passing away."[54] Without excluding the past and future, Heidegger calls attention to the difference between the present proper time (*Gegenwart*) and presence (*Anwesenheit*) in which time is determined by its reference to presence. Being is not a thing and therefore nothing temporal: "Yet Being as presencing remains determined as presence by time, by what is temporal."[55] To let something attain presence suggests unconcealing it and bringing it into openness, which implies a giving of Being, a letting into presence. Thus Being, a presencing, is a gift of unconcealing that is retained in the act of giving.[56] In the process of giving the ontological gift, Being itself withdraws and thus the giving of Being becomes more of a sending forth. At this juncture, it is unfair to criticize Heidegger for not adequately disclosing the ontological dimension of time, as Heine does, because Heidegger excludes the soteriological concern from his thinking.[57] Unlike Dōgen, eventual salvation or liberation is not a primary focus of his philosophy.

From the perspective of Deleuze, Dōgen and Heidegger are discussing time as *chronos*, a regulated movement of immense presents in which only the present exists and the past and future are dual dimensions that are relative to the present. Not only are the past and future relative to the present, but the moments that constitute the present are also relative to each other. Moreover, the present is corporeal, and is able to measure bodily actions and causes.[58] In contrast to *chronos*, Deleuze advocates what he refers to as *Aion*, a locus of incorporeal events that is characterized by effects and is unlimited. Rather than the past and future undermining the present, it is subverted by the instant, which endlessly displaces it. Deleuze further defines the *Aion*, a subverted and subverting instant without place, as "the eternal truth of time: *pure empty form of time*, which has freed itself of its present corporeal content and has thereby unwound its own circle, stretching itself out in a straight line."[59] Nonetheless, the straight line of *Aion* makes it possible for *chronos* to return on it. This represents a return of pure events, representing a process of a displacing and subverting instant that continually divides into past and future. The displacing, subverting, and perverting present is far more radical in terms of flux than anything conceived by Dōgen and Heidegger, and Deleuze's notion of *Aion* is purposely defined to lack depth because he is solely interested in what occurs on the surface and not in some imagined depth.

In contrast to Deleuze and Heidegger, the philosophy of Dōgen demonstrates a much different grasp of the relationship between time and being, which is embodied in his notion of *uji* (being-time), a kind of primordial time that represents a union. Dōgen makes this union between being and time absolutely clear: "'Existence'" is time itself. Our real form, in its totality, clarifies the relationship of existence and time. The skin, flesh, bones and marrow which make up our body and mind are related with and emerge through time and causality."[60] Although neither is more fundamental than the other, one can perceive *uji* (being-time) from two perspectives, each an authentic response to one's temporal presence: *nikon* (right-now or now moment) and *kyōryaku* (totalistic passage). Neither of these aspects of time possesses priority over the other because they are interpenetrating aspects of time and are ultimately the same, although it can be stated that *nikon* holds priority over a delusory future.[61]

In response to Dōgen and his notion of a union of being and time, Deleuze discusses repetition in the eternal return, which is unconnected to continuation, perpetuation, or prolongation of something with an enduring identity. Unlike the ontological distinction made by Heidegger in his early phenomenology, Deleuze equates being with difference and Being with repetition, which for him means that being is connected to beginning and Being is the recommencement of being. Deleuze connects his distinction to the ambiguity and deceptive nature of the notion of origin. A consequence of his position is that "origins are assigned only in a world which challenges the original as much as the copy, and an origin assigns a ground only in a world already precipitated into universal *ungrounding*."[62] Unlike Dōgen, there is no union between being and time because everything is radically relative, without ground, depth, identity, or universality.

Instead of Deleuze's emphasis on repetition and the constant displacing and subverting of the present, Dōgen stresses the now-moment (*nikon*), which represents the complete spontaneous presencing of being-time. In its fundamental unitive condition, it extends simultaneously throughout past, present, and future, which necessarily implies that there is a continuity of time in which the past and future exist in the immediate moment. The now-moment neither remains still nor does it flow away, although it is not exempt from the passage of time; it is probably more accurate to say that the now-moment simply dwells.[63] In contrast to Dōgen's grasp of the now moment, Derrida does not think that now moments can coexist within temporal movement.[64] If past moments of time could coexist with the present now, this would mean that events of past centuries would be simultaneous with current events. Since coexistence or simultaneity is impossible, this suggests that the present moment is always different than the past or future. The basis of temporal succession always manifests an absolute lack for Derrida.

According to Dōgen, the non-directional, continuing, and connected aspect of time is referred to as *kyōryaku* (totalistic passage), an experiential continuity that engages all aspects and dimensions of the three moments of time right here and now. This response to presencing accounts for the ever creative and regenerating aspects of being-time. If we return to the previous metaphor of climbing a mountain, it is possible to understand that the distinction between *nikon* and *kyōryaku* is a matter of one's point of view. The right-now refers to the activity of ascending the mountain, whereas *kyōryaku* indicates the complete context of the person, the entire universe and encompasses all aspects of time. Thus, from whatever perspective one views time, each individual moment of time is complete in itself, embodying within itself all possible perspectives and situations. With respect to his understanding of time, these two aspects of being-time allow Dōgen to make a conceptual and existential leap beyond the position of Heidegger and Derrida and their grasp of the relationship between being and time.

This leap embodies Dōgen's conviction that everything, every being, and the entire world is time. Thus he can assert: "Mountain is time, ocean is time. Mountain and ocean exist only in the present. If time is destroyed, mountain and river are also destroyed."[65] Within other rhetorical contexts, Dōgen goes on to equate time with one's body and mind, both enlightened and unenlightened people, and life and death. These kinds of identification between time and the world suggests that space and time are inseparably interconnected and interpenetrate each other. In fact, Faure observes that Dōgen's ontologization of time is simultaneously a spatialization of it.[66] Instead of stating that Heidegger's conception of time is also a spatialization, it would be more accurate to claim that his grasp of time is a presencing. Nonetheless, Dōgen and Heidegger agree that time is both temporal and spatial.

In contrast to Heidegger and Dōgen, there is no ontologization or spatialization of time for Deleuze because the genuine character of being is the simulacrum. Deleuze explains how this occurs:

> When eternal return is the power of (formless) being, the simulacrum is the true character or form—the 'being'—of that which is. When the identity of things dissolves, being escapes to attain univocity, and begins to revolve around the different. That which is or returns has no prior constituted identity: things are reduced to the difference which fragments them, and to all the differences which are implicated in it and through which they pass. In this sense, the simulacrum and the symbol are one; in other words, the simulacrum is the sign in so far as the sign interiorises the conditions of its own repetition.[67]

If everything becomes simulacrum for Deleuze, the privileged position assumed by Dōgen and the ontological model created by Heidegger are challenged and overcome. Against Dōgen and Heidegger, Deleuze wants to emphasize that there is no resemblance of time to ontology or space.

In sharp contrast to Deleuze's conception of time, Heidegger and Dōgen also agree that time represents a unity, which implies that existence and time are not independent of each other and time is non-reductionistic, even though they have different ways of conceiving of this unity of time. Moreover, both agree that time is nonobjective and at the basis of all human activity but without connection to ego or substance. Heidegger cannot, however, agree with Dōgen that temporality is not limited to human experience because the latter philosopher thinks that time includes both human and natural experience. They also differ about the importance of the present and the future because Heidegger stresses the importance of the future over the other two moments of time, and Dōgen teaches "Keep your mind in the present. If we always think about the past, our entire vision will revert to the past and it will be distorted."[68] Since the future represents an aspect of time that is not-yet-arrived (*mitō*) for Dōgen, we cannot understand it because it is not yet here. Thus Dōgen views the future as a conventional view of time that conceives of time as passing-by or flying-by. And Heidegger and Dōgen disagree about the latter's nondualist grasp of time. Heidegger cannot concur, for instance, with the following statement by the Zen Master: "Each instant covers the entire world."[69] This type of statement motivates Heine to claim that "Dōgen deepens the existential and ontological meaning of the present by incorporating the past and future within the totalistic passage of all beings spontaneously appearing as all-times."[70] For the most part, I would concur with Heine's statement, although it needs to be observed that Heidegger's later philosophy does move toward the Zen Buddhist position without fully arriving at it, a point made in chapter 3 with respect to his understanding of thinking in his later published works.

A basic contradiction in Dōgen's understanding of time is noted by Faure when he observes that the Zen philosopher offers a stationary model of time by identifying it with the *dharma*. Faure explains, "The stationary . . . topology of time seems to exclude any prediction because there is no link between what precedes and what follows; each individual awakening (and, more generally, each event) takes place *in illo tempore*, in the atemporal realm of suchness (*tathatā*)."[71] It is difficult to accept this criticism as valid because of Dōgen's emphasis on impermanence and its identification with the Buddha-nature. A criticism by Faure of time in the philosophy of Dōgen that is more on target is the following: "Thus, although Dōgen attached a great importance to causality and karmic retribution, he relied on a conception of time that implicitly denied it."[72] Nishitani seems to anticipate such criticism in his philosophy by calling for a breakthrough to a field of ecstatic trans-descendence, which is inner-worldly, to allow for an awareness of birth and death as transmigration. This ecstatic trans-descendence involves being-in-the-world, being rid of all determinations, and revealing the ultimate form of being in the world.[73] With respect to Dōgen, Faure goes on to stress the unprecedented importance assigned to time by Dōgen within the historical context of Chinese and Japanese Buddhism, but he overstates the role of time in Dōgen's philosophy when he claims that it becomes ultimate reality.[74]

Following the pattern of Dōgen's philosophy on the particular relationship between being and time, Nishitani also thinks that time and space interpenetrate, and he asserts the union of being and time: "There, in true Existenz, true being is one with the truth of time; 'to be' means 'to be as time.'"[75] Not unlike Dōgen's emphasis on impermanence and its relation to being and time, Nishitani thinks that "Time and being display a constant pull to nullification from beneath their very ground. That is impermanence."[76] But unlike Dōgen's treatment of impermanence, Nishitani finds that impermanence embodies an ambiguity of its own. Nishitani means that it manifests the volatility of time due to its fleeting nature and an infinite openness. And similar to Levinas in contrast to Dōgen's view of time, Nishitani views being and time as a mutual burden on a person.

Dōgen's view of the relation of time and space and Heidegger's emphasis on time and presence are referred to as logocentrism, a metaphysics of presence, by Derrida. The basic problem with having a desire for such a metaphysical position is that it is impossible for us to have any access to such a transcendental signified because we are caught in a field of signs that simply refer to other signs.[77] Since the concept of time is connected intimately with metaphysics and its concomitant presence, there is no alternative notion of time possible from the viewpoint of Derrida. If we assume that this is the case for the sake of the discussion, is there any alternative approach to the problem of time?

For Derrida, the answer to the metaphysics of presence is his neologism *différance* that embodies for him spatiotemporal significance because its root meaning and connection to the English "differing" suggests a kind of spacing and its association with "deferring" implies a temporalizing in the sense of a delay or postponement.[78] (Because we will examine *différance* in greater depth in the next chapter, we will only concentrate on its significance for a discussion of time). *Différance*, which is neither present nor absent, does not fit into the category of being. In fact, *différance* calls Being and beings into question because it is not a being in presence and in response to Dōgen it is not everything. Without existence or essence, *différance* is simultaneously spacing and temporalizing.[79] Actually, *différance* precedes time conceived as presence because the nothing of *différance* takes priority over being-time as in Dōgen's thought. In other words, absence precedes the presence of the present moment or being present, which suggests that presence is always deferred. From the perspective of Heidegger, by giving priority to *différance* over presence, Derrida appears to be engaged in an exercise of self-stultification.[80] Dōgen replies to Derrida that being-time represents the complete presencing of Buddha-nature, a leap of thinking that Derrida does not and cannot make with his philosophy.

By thinking from the standpoint of *différance*, Derrida criticizes Dōgen's notion of the unity represented by *uji* (being-time) because it appears to represent sameness, which suggests something static and unchanging. Dōgen is ready with a reply to such criticism: "Every living thing is rooted in pure, original Being. Do not think, however, that being is a stable concept; being encompasses all temporary lapses."[81] Moreover, Being is subject to impermanence as is everything else in the world. Dōgen and Derrida do agree that being-time is not some realm that one can attain beyond this world, even though they agree for different reasons. Dōgen thinks that being-time is here and now, whereas Derrida thinks that there is no realm of *différance* because it subverts every realm.[82] Derrida and Dōgen disagree over the latter's suggestion that space and time are intrinsically interconnected because Derrida asserts that "*Spacing* designates *nothing*, nothing that is, no presence at a distance; it is the index of an irreducible exterior, and at the same time of a *movement*, a displacement that indicates an irreducible alterity."[83] Thus it is impossible for space or spacing to be involved in any kind of identity, whereas Dōgen and Nishitani think that, since everything is empty, identity is necessary and inevitable. Based on their philosophical understandings of time, the thought of Dōgen and Nishitani suggest, even though they do not express it this way, that identity (which is probably not the most accurate term that could be used to express their position) embodies a synchronic aspect (identity in the now moment) and a diachronic element (continuity over a period of time).

Contrary to Derrida, Taylor, and Heidegger, the work of Levinas shares in common with Dōgen an emphasis on the *nikon* (now-moment), which Levinas refers to as the instant, associated with beginning, birth, and initiation into Being. The relation between Being and the instant, a monadic, separate and evanescent aspect of time, is paradoxical because "What begins to be does not exist before having begun, and yet it is what does not exist that must through its beginning give birth to itself, come to itself, without coming from anywhere."[84] Since the instant is without duration for Levinas, this places his notion in direct conflict with Dōgen's other aspect of time that he calls *kyōryaku* (totalistic passage). Levinas wants to emphasize the absolute character of the present: "The absolute character of the present is in the very presence of the present; it gives an appearance of being to the past and defies the future, which cannot reduce it to nothingness."[85] There is an intimate connection between the instant and being for Levinas. In fact, the instant represents the emergence of the existent. Unlike Heidegger and Dōgen, the emphasis on the instant by Levinas rejects the importance of the past and future, represents an escape from subjectivity, an emergence from anonymous existence, and relates time to the alterity of the other. And yet the evanescence of the instant means that the present possesses no absolute character except as the "presence of the present."[86] Lyotard agrees with Levinas about the nature of the instant and its presence because he conceives of it as something that cannot be grasped due to its paradoxical nature of being not yet and no longer present. Lyotard clarifies its paradoxical nature: "It is always too soon or too late to grasp presentation itself and present it."[87] Lyotard finds the emphasis on the now-moment in Dōgen and Nishitani unacceptable due to the paradoxical nature of the present moment.

Experience of Time

If time is the realm of the open for the later Heidegger, what determines the mutual relationship between time and Being? Heidegger calls this *Ereignis*, an event of appropriation, which is not an occurrence itself, but it makes possible any occurrence.[88] Appropriation embodies the notions of giving, sending, extending, an essence of owning (*Eignen*), and also withdrawal, although it is neither possible to state specifically that it is in an ontological sense nor that it is spacially present. We can say that it appropriates, but this is not all that helpful for the novice. Appropriation, a co-belonging of Being and a person, is the tendency to make things reveal themselves in the most resonant way. In a later work entitled *Identity and Difference*, Heidegger views *Ereignis* as a self-vibrating realm: "The event of appropriation is that realm, vibrating within itself, through which man and Being reach each other in their nature, achieve their active nature by losing those qualities with which metaphysics has endowed them."[89] The most significant event that Heidegger can think is the *Ereignis* of Being, a gift of presence, because without this event of appropriation it is not capable of existence.[90] Heidegger refers to the gift of presence as the property of *Ereignis*, but in the process of appropriating

Being withdraws. This suggests that it is not possible to fully experience time or Being. Nonetheless, by means of the event of mutual belonging together and creating an opening within the play space (*Spielraum*) of time, Being offers itself to us as a gift and rids itself and us of metaphysical determinations. Heidegger also uses the term *Austrag* to refer to *Ereignis*, a realm beyond Being, suggesting the dynamic nature of the relation between Being and beings and characterized by an interplay of both a revelation of beings and a concealment of Being.[91]

Dōgen agrees with Heidegger that we experience neither time nor being in themselves, although the Zen thinker proceeds to say that we rather experience temporal existence. This means that one experiences a phenomenon just as it is, which is possible because one overcomes the perception of a thing in terms of the past-present-future sequence. In Dōgen's terms: "Every moment contains total reality and is complete in itself."[92] If I am hitting a tennis ball or listening to the music of Mozart, I am the right-now (*nikon*) of being-time. The exertion (*gyōji*) of swinging a racket and hitting a tennis ball realizes or authenticates being-time, but whether or not I am playing tennis there is still being-time, which makes possible my chance to play the game.

If Dōgen and Heidegger suggest that the event occurs in the present, Deleuze disagrees because an event, which is by nature an ideal, is not an occurrence in the present, but it is rather something that has just happened in the past and something that is about to happen in the present. Deleuze is alluding to the power of difference, which he identifies with repetition and its power to accelerate or decelerate time, although it is not something that can be intellectually grasped by an identity discovered in a concept or something similar in a process of representation.[93] The event, if one insists on using such a term, of repetition disappears even as it happens because repetition lacks an in-itself, even though it does possess the ability to alter the mind that encounters it. Since it disappears as it in fact appears, it is essentially unthinkable, incomplete, and cannot contain total reality as the experience of time does for Dōgen. If exertion or action authenticates being-time, and if being-time makes action possible in the first place for Dōgen, repetition renders possible the condition of action prior to its becoming a concept of reflection, which implies that something new can only be produced by means of repetition.[94] For Deleuze, the event of repetition appears as difference, which suggests that we can never experience a thing as it is or directly, and not as an identity of being-time as it does for Dōgen.

Dōgen also thinks that one not only directly experiences a thing as it is, but one, moreover, encounters a stream of ever-changing phenomena. Change itself cannot be located in either the self or a particular object because everything is impermanent for the Zen Master. It is important to simply accept change and what is given without superimposing our prejudices or personal projections upon what we encounter, which is what Deleuze appears to do when he refers to the tragic and comic dimensions of repetition.[95] If we are able to follow Dōgen's advice, we will experience an unending experience of flux and realize that nothing can be experienced independently of change or time, a position with which Deleuze, Derrida, and Taylor concur. Derrida thinks, for instance, that what he calls iterability reveals the constant change of differences. Derrida means that the intention motivating a particular utterance can never be present to itself and its content, because the meaning of any word cannot be controlled by a speaker due to the fact that others will determine the meaning of a specific word. This suggests that iterability dislocates, subverts, and continually displaces any utterance.[96] Derrida appears to imply that iterability not only reveals constant change, but it also promotes continual change. Dōgen, Deleuze, Derrida, and Taylor also agree that this way of grasping time as an endless flux enables them to reject teleology as an impossible realization. Although these postmodernists agree that the common denominator of being and time is impermanence, they cannot follow Dōgen when he equates impermanence with Buddha-nature, which for the Zen Master is the experiential presence of impermanence.

In contrast to the Zen philosophers and other postmodernists, Levinas discusses an event which enables the existent to gain contact with its existing, or as Heidegger would say beings (*Seindes*) and Being (*Sein*), that he calls hypostasis, conveying the root meaning of "standing under." Levinas asks us to imagine everything returning to nothingness and what might remain after this imaginary devastation. Then, imagine that everything returns and suddenly there is (*il y a*), an existing without existents. Within this experience, the fact of existing, an impersonal and anonymous field, imposes itself most profoundly when there is nothing. As one approaches existing (Being), one finds that it cannot be simply affirmed, but it rather imposes itself due to the fact that one cannot deny it.[97] What Levinas calls the "there is" represents the location where hypostasis is produced, which suggests that it promotes a notion of being without nothingness. Levinas explains how this works: "Consciousness is a rupture of the anonymous vigilance of the *there is*; it is already hypostasis; it refers to a situation where an existent is put in touch with its existing."[98] And the event of hypostasis is the present, which represents a new beginning, a tearing apart, and a joining together. Similar to Sartre's attempt to relate consciousness to Being, Levinas also tries to correct a perceived deficiency in Heidegger's philosophy.

In a way somewhat similar to Levinas, Nishitani refers to a revelation of time, which is ambiguous because it can embody both nihility and emptiness and also possesses an infinite openness. This revelation of time for Nishitani represents an infinite openness at the basis of an actual presence: "Only in that infinite openness does time appear as an infinite regression and an infinite progression, as something without beginning or end."[99] Nishitani is referring to a totality of time, which he conceptualizes as an instant and a monad of eternity. The Zen thinker elaborates, "Each moment of unlimited time without beginning or end is a 'monad of eternity' that projects into the present the totality of infinite time; and the *Dasein* that emerges into its nature as such a time is itself, makes itself be itself, and becomes itself in unhindered 'observance' that shoulders without limit all other things that appear within the unlimited world-nexus."[100] What makes this possible for Nishitani is that each instant simultaneously embodies the past and future in contrast to the conception of the instant by Levinas that is devoid of past and future.

Death Divine

Based on their choice of subject matter, there appears to be a fascination among postmodern writers with the topic of death. Edmond Jabès, an insightful and provocative author that other postmodernists enjoy quoting in their own works, conceives of death, for instance, as a universal power: "All is dead, and you think you are living."[101] Death also possesses a revelatory power for Jabès: "Life contemplates death and sees itself as it will be."[102] Maurice Blanchot, a literary critic and theorist, agrees that death contains the power to reveal knowledge and is necessary for liberation.[103] Bataille connects death with eroticism, an excessive, boundless energy that represents an insane realm of play and anti-social activity, which he envisions as paving the way for death.[104] Along the same path, Deleuze agrees that there is no need to distinguish eros from the death instinct.[105] The cultural critic Jean Baudrillard is opposed to the metaphysics of death or a simple biological understanding of death because of the lack of a subject who dies at a particular moment. Baudrillard perceives an ambiguity associated with the *telos* of both life and death: "Neither life nor death can any longer be assigned a given *end*: there is therefore no punctuality nor any possible *definition* of death."[106] Moreover, Baudrillard accuses western culture of attempting to dissociate life and death, a criticism with which Heidegger, Dōgen, and Nishitani would concur.

The fascination with death among many postmodern thinkers extends to its apparent deification by some writers. Jabès, Blanchot, Derrida, and Taylor strongly suggest, for instance, a deification of death based on provocative statements made in their writings. Jabès connects the immortality of God with the equally immortal nature of death in a sentence.[107] Adhering to Jabès' literary lead, Derrida and Blanchot equate God with death.[108] Following the lead of Derrida, Taylor equates God with death within the context of a discussion about the death of God, and asserts that death is now absolute master.[109] In a more recent book, Taylor develops further exactly what he means by stating that "To embrace the death of God is to affirm 'the deleterious absurdity of time' in which meaning is eternally sacrificed in a potlach that is as pointless as the pyramid on which it is staged. The sacrifice of God is the death of the transcendental signified which marks the closure of the classical regime of re-presentation."[110]

In the remainder of this chapter, we will devote attention to other postmodern thinkers, namely Heidegger and Levinas, although Derrida will continue to play a central role in the discussion, and compare their positions with that of Dōgen. Derrida will play a central role in the discussion because he claims to say what Heidegger cannot say just as Heidegger wants to ironically recapture what was not said by the pre-Socratics. Why does Derrida think that it is necessary to say what Heidegger did not say? It is necessary to recover what is left unsaid because death is a secret.[111] Moreover, Derrida calls into question the conceptual distinctions made by Heidegger because he perceives a limit with respect to the topic of death.

As we noted previously, the complete ontological structure of *Dasein* in *Sein und Zeit* by Heidegger is expressed by the word care (*Sorge*), and it is phenomenologically described as always coming-to-an-end, finding itself thrown into the possibility of death. Since *Dasein* exists ahead-of-itself, it possesses openness for all kinds of possibilities, although these possibilities are not infinite, and it never achieves its wholeness as long as it continues to exist because it is already its "not-yet" or lack of totality. *Dasein*, a being-towards-the-end, attains its wholeness by means of its death because death is nonsubstitutive or my own, which suggests that death is characterized by mineness.[112] The mineness character of death implies that a person can only die his/her own death, and it is not possible for someone else to substitute themselves in one's place and die for a given person. By binding *Dasein* together in a sense, death completes the totality of its existence. Even though it achieves its wholeness by means of its death, *Dasein* still loses its being, and it ceases to be referred to as a being-in-the-world.[113] The writings of Dōgen suggest that he agrees with Heidegger that death is mine, if this is understood in a nonegoistic manner. The way expounded by Dōgen includes the realization of life and death: "When (the great Way) is realized, it is nothing but life's total realization, it is nothing but death's total realization."[114] This is a position with which Heidegger can concur in an existential sense.

In contrast to Heidegger and Dōgen, Derrida agrees that death can be characterized by mineness in the sense that it is irreplaceable. Although it is true that no one can die for another person, Derrida reinterprets "my death" to mean the death of the other in me.[115] Derrida distinguishes his position from that of Heidegger by claiming that one does not aim at death, although he does think that human beings anticipate death and imagine it in a similar chain of significations as the anticipation of death, whereas Levinas claims that one does not anticipate death because one attempts to postpone it. How is it possible to postpone death? By constituting my responsibility, the Other gives one time and helps to delay death. Because of the relationship between death and imagination for Derrida, the latter shares the former's representative and supplementary characteristics.[116] By drawing a distinction between demising (*Ableben*) and dying (*Sterben*), Derrida also disputes Heidegger's contention that *Dasein* can be conceived as being-towards-the-end because he thinks that it is possible to consider that *Dasein* is immortal in the sense of "without end." If one is not immortal as the *Dasein* that one is, one is, then, at least imperishable: "I do not end, I never end, I know that I will not come to an end."[117] Derrida understands "immortal" not in the sense of eternal but rather in the sense of Heidegger's term *verenden* translated as perishing, which retains the sense of a passage of a limit. In response to Derrida's challenge, Heidegger claims that only human beings die, whereas animals perish in contrast to humans.[118] And even though Derrida agrees with Heidegger that the other cannot die in my place and there is a sense of "mineness" associated with my own death, the former differs from the latter thinker by claiming that "I can have this experience of 'my own death' by relating to myself only in the impossible experience, the experience of the impossible mourning at the death of the other."[119]

For Levinas, death represents an unforeseeable character that can be traced to the fact that it does not lie within any horizon that one could possibly encounter. Levinas thinks that "Death threatens me from beyond."[120] Deleuze agrees with Levinas that death is an external power, even though death can be affirmed to be inscribed in the self: "From this point of view, death may well be inevitable, but every death is none the less accidental and violent, and always comes from without."[121] In sharp contrast to Levinas and Deleuze, Heidegger and Dōgen agree that death is not an external power; it is rather co-present with life. In other words, death is not an event that puts an end to one's life, but it is rather a intimate part of one's life. Dōgen makes this clear in the following statement: "It is a mistake to think life changes to death. Life is absolute existence with its own time and already possesses a past and future."[122] Thus, for both thinkers, it is wrong to conceive of death as an event that terminates one's life because it is a part of one's life. In fact, life and death interpenetrate each other. Dōgen writes, "Until you die, imminent death will always be right beneath your feet."[123] Although life and death interpenetrate each other for Dōgen, they are still considered independent: "Life is contained in death and death is contained in life, yet life is life and death is death. That is, these two elements are independent in themselves and stand alone without requiring any outside existence or reference."[124] Even though both thinkers agree that death is inevitable and certain for an individual, they agree that death is not something that necessarily awaits us in the future; it is present in the here and now. Thus Heidegger would agree with Dōgen's statement that, "It is a mistake to think you pass from birth to death."[125] Within the context of their understanding of time and death, both thinkers stress the importance of the process of becoming, although Dōgen wants to emphasize, by means of his concept of *mujō* (impermanence), that it is more than a process of becoming which negates the fullness of time. This means that impermanence does not express a deprivation but rather a plenum of the fullness of time.[126] With respect to the emphasis by Heidegger and Dōgen on the imminence of death, Levinas thinks that time represents an interval that separates me from my death: "To be temporal is both to be for death and to still have time, to be against death."[127] Levinas' position is different from that of Heidegger and Dōgen because he does not think that death is ever a present moment. The future nature of death is evident by the fact that the presence of death means my demise and lack of presence and ability to grasp.[128]

Rather than viewing life and death as intimately related like Heidegger and Dōgen, death is repetitive, although not a repetition of the same because it represents difference for Derrida, in the sense that its potentiality is dependent on the possibility of the absence of the repeated and manifests the potential for self-duplication.[129] Standing at the dawn of life because everything commences with repetition, death repeats itself by redoubling itself, distributing itself, and repeating itself through and in life.[130] By calling attention to the repetitive nature of death, Derrida wants to paradoxically assert it cannot be represented and yet is the condition for all representation. With respect to Heidegger's discussion in *Sein und Zeit* that *Dasein* awaits itself, Derrida explores some of the possibilities of the meaning of the term "await," which presupposes arriving late and not early as one might think ordinarily. Derrida thinks that "awaiting" involves imminence, the anxious anticipation of something, and a triple transitivity that includes expectation, the waiting for something to happen in the future that is other than oneself, and a mutual waiting for each other.[131] There is no sense of waiting for death in Dōgen's thought because death is already here with us. Dōgen makes this clear in the following statement: "Life and death appear in each moment. They appear instantly, naturally, without thought."[132]

Although Dōgen would not fully agree with the gist of his analysis, death is, for Heidegger, *Dasein's* ownmost potentiality-for-being which is nonrelational and not to be outstripped.[133] Levinas disagrees with Heidegger because death is rather the impossibility of all possibilities and not the ultimate possibility of existence. In contrast to Levinas' view of death, Heidegger enhances the significance of his own position when he states that *Dasein* possesses a freedom towards death that releases *Dasein* from the illusions of *das Man* (the impersonal crowd) and enables it to achieve its authenticity by expecting and even anticipating its death rather than inauthentically fleeing in the face of death. Dōgen also refers to anticipating death:

> When one speaks of birth, there is nothing at all apart from birth. When one speaks of death, there is nothing at all apart from death. Therefore, when birth comes, you should just give yourself to birth; when death comes you should give yourself to death. Do not hate them. Do not desire them.[134]

This passage is indicative of Dōgen's desire to stress the natural way to abide in life and death. If one does not struggle against them by attempting to decide for or against one or the other, or if one does not desire either of them, and if one simply abides in death, it becomes a death that is paradoxically nondeath.[135] This takes the dialogue in a direction that Heidegger does not wish to follow. Nonetheless, from the perspective of Heidegger and Dōgen, Levinas is wrong to view death as an alien power that destroys every possibility of wanting anything.

Heidegger does not want to follow Dōgen when the Zen Master suggests the possibility of attaining a condition of non-death because he is convinced that *Dasein* cannot overcome the possibility of its demise, which indubitably suggests that death is an impending reality for *Dasein*, although it is indefinite when it will precisely happen. Heidegger stresses that *Dasein*, existing as thrown towards its end, is dying as long as it exists, which it does by way of an evasive falling, a fleeing from death. When it is disclosed to *Dasein* that it exists as thrown towards death, it responds with anxiety, facing the possible impossibility of its existence or nothingness.[136] At this point, Levinas disagrees because he thinks that one does not fear death by encountering nothingness, but rather one fears violence that extends to the fear of others.[137] The flight from death is an inauthentic way of being related to death for Heidegger and Dōgen because it represents for both of them an inauthentic way to encounter death. From Heidegger's perspective, one needs courage to encounter death, whereas Dōgen emphasizes the necessity of acceptance: "Accept life and death as nirvana, do not hate either one, and do not seek nirvana. Only then can you truly be detached from life and death."[138]

In contrast to Dōgen and Heidegger with their emphasis on the certainty of death, Derrida calls this certainty into question by arguing that the certainty of death is heterogeneous to any other. Derrida recalls Heidegger's statement about death "'as the possibility of the impossibility of any existence at all.'" Derrida deconstructs this statement by Heidegger: "The *als* means that the possibility is both unveiled and penetrated *as* impossibility. It is not only the paradoxical possibility of a possibility of impossibility: it is possibility *as* impossibility."[139] After exposing the internal contradiction in Heidegger's position, Derrida claims that death is the most proper and the least proper because it is respectively both possibility and at the same time impossibility, a position that places Derrida at odds with Levinas. Derrida clarifies his position: "If death, the most proper possibility of *Dasein*, is the possibility of its impossibility, death becomes the most improper possibility and the most ex-pro-priat-ing, the most inauthenticating one."[140] By means of his criticism of Hei-degger, Derrida is attempting to introduce the principle of the possible into an existential analysis of death and to view death as the possibility par excellence. This enables Derrida to argue paradoxically for the impossibility of borders, artificial limits, and conceptual demarcations of the existential analysis of death. Derrida operates by marking and eras-ing the lines of demarcation, which actually erase themselves, and trac-ing the delimitations as still possible while also introducing the principle of their impossibility. Dōgen agrees with Derrida that it is foolish to establish borders between life and death. But implied in Derrida's posi-tion is the assumption that life is relative to death and death to life from Dōgen's viewpoint. In sharp contrast to Derrida, the Zen philosopher does not think that life and death are relative to each other: "Life and death have absolute existence, like the relationship of winter and spring."[141] And yet Derrida states that "life is death"[142] and "the purity of life is death."[143] Unlike Dōgen's understanding of their relationship, Der-rida thinks that life and death are related like a supplement, a position that exposes a lack at the center of life.

There is also a disagreement about the possibility of encountering death between Derrida, Heidegger, and Dōgen. We have noted that Hei-degger and Dōgen express themselves in such a way as to suggest that one does encounter death. Although Derrida disagrees with Heidegger, his criticism can also be directed to Dōgen. When we consider a person as himself or herself or as *Dasein*, it is not possible for such a person to encounter death, if one insists that death is the possibility of the impossi-ble and the possibility of an appearance of the impossibility of appearing. Therefore, no person possesses a relation to death in itself. It is possible, however, to have a relation "only to perishing, to demising, and to the death of the other, who is not the other."[144] Based on his discussion of death, Heidegger replies that Derrida is confusing the death of human beings and animals, whereas Dōgen does not make such a distinction.

Dōgen agrees, however, with Heidegger that to view death as the terminal point of life is an inauthentic way of comprehending it. Nonethe-less, Dōgen proceeds beyond Heidegger and Derrida at this point because the former thinker wants to discuss what lies beyond death, the symbol of the impermanence of existence. Dōgen emphasizes that "'Emancipation' means that life emancipates life, and that death emancipates death. For this reason, there is deliverance from birth and death, and immersion in birth and death."[145] In other words, there is no liberation apart from life and death. Would it help if one chose life rather than death? Dōgen offers the following answer: "Just understand that birth and death itself is nirvana, and you will neither hate one as being birth and death, nor cherish the other as being nirvana. Only then can you be free of birth and death."[146] There is thus no Nirvāna apart from life and death or apart from the cycle of *samsāra* (rebirth).

Finally, Dōgen and Heidegger agree that death is a total dynamism, which means that death does not impede life and vice versa. Death belongs inextricably to the structure of *Dasein* for Heidegger and Buddha-nature for Dōgen. Death is a way to be, a way characterized by facing death and abiding in it, a way unto freedom. From Derrida's critical perspective, Dōgen and Heidegger are making their discussion of death from the side of life, which assumes a privileged place in relation to that of death. Rather than making a theoretical departure from the side of existence when discussing death, Derrida emphasizes that we should be more intellectually honest about our approach to the subject of death: "Rather, it seems to me that one should say the opposite: it is the originary and underivable character of death, as well as the finitude of the temporality in which death is rooted, that decides and forces us to decide to start from here first, from this side here."[147] What Derrida is attempting to convey is that any methodological decision involves certain consequences and assumptions. A basic assumption is, for instance, that a method is better than no method, whereas Derrida wants to opt for a nonmethod. If the nonmethod option is taken, there are a few corollaries that will follow. The initial corollary is that death will have no border; a neutral politics of death will be possible; and a place will be made for mourning, an aspect of death for which the works of Heidegger and Dōgen do not account.

From Derrida's perspective, Dōgen and Heidegger seem to imply that death is an event that isolates an individual. In contrast, Derrida views death as a unifying factor. This occurs near the end of one's life, which helps a person constitute his/her own subjectivity.[148] Levinas thinks that solitude is disrupted by death and not confirmed by it.[149] On the one hand, Heidegger disputes this criticism by Derrida and Levinas because *Dasein* is a being-in-the-world-with-others and all are beings-unto-death. On the other hand, Dōgen responds by indicating that distinctions between isolating and unifying with regards to death are nonsensical because ultimately speaking all words are empty. Dōgen thinks that we must not consider death as either isolating or unifying because life and death together represent the actual appearance of truth.[150] Moreover, Dōgen does not draw the sharp distinction between life and death that is presupposed by the criticism of Derrida.

Because Dōgen thinks that Being is impermanent, Derrida cannot claim that the Zen Master is guilty of asserting a presence for Being, whereas this criticism does apply to Heidegger due to his claim that death, the shrine of nothing, is more than something that merely exists because it accounts for the presencing of Being. In this way, this shrine of nothing or death is the shelter of Being.[151] Heidegger thinks that philosophers like Derrida mistakenly think that a person perishes, whereas it is only human beings that die because animals do not have death ahead of themselves or behind themselves. From another critical perspective with which Heidegger and Dōgen would agree, Derrida needs the philosophy of presence to overcome. If writing leads to more writing for Derrida, he would have nothing to write about without the philosophy of presence.[152] There is an interesting irony embodied in Derrida's notion of the inexorable nature of writing and death because the event of death brings about the end of writing.

Concluding Remarks

Despite the differences among postmodernists, the previous, lengthy and comparative discussion of time and death helps us to see that they express a mode of human existence that is empty, disjointed, and decentered, whereas Merleau-Ponty thinks that it is possible to be centered in the present, a moment of time that possesses a privileged status because being and consciousness coincide. The postmodernists also help us understand some of the challenges we face by indicating that everything is always in a state of flux. And due to this constant change, human beings always exist in a precarious condition because there is no safe refuge or place to stand. Within this continuous flux, there is no certainty, although death appears to be the lone exception. If some postmodernists perceive of time or any of its three moments as subverting or displacing other moments of time or even the present itself, Husserl and Merleau-Ponty conceive of an interconnection between the three moments of time. And in contrast to Kant's claim that time is an *a priori* particular, Hegel's equating of time with concept, Husserl's assertion that consciousness is temporal, and Merleau-Ponty's argument that time is a real process that a person can record due to its origin in one's relation to objects, the postmodernists present us with radical skepticism with respect to time due to its relativity. And in general, some postmodern theories of time ground the radical skepticism of their philosophical positions.

An important consequence of the postmodern positions of Derrida, Taylor, and Deleuze with respect to their conception of time is that their respective positions make personal identity impossible through time. And without any personal identity it is not possible to engage in a representational mode of thinking because it presupposes an established ego. With their emphasis on temporal dissimilarity, constant flux, and difference, the postmodernists undermine any genuine possibility for similarity between moments, things, or persons. Thereby, they subvert any definitive identity. Robert Nozick writes the following about personal identity and time:

> What is special about people, about selves, is that what constitutes their identity through time is partially determined by their own conception of themselves, a conception which may vary, perhaps appropriately does vary, from person to person.[153]

For the sake of argument, let us assume that Nozick is correct. This suggests that it is impossible for a person to conceive of a personal identity from the philosophical perspective of a postmodernist. Moreover, it is also not possible to have reflexive self-knowledge unless one possesses a strong and vivid imagination that can function within such a swirl of impermanence.

In contrast to some of the postmodernists, Dōgen demonstrates how self-knowledge is possible within the flux of impermanence. Kasulis summarizes Dōgen's position in the following way:

> Dōgen argues that since the prereflective basis of experience is impermanence, apprehended in zazen as being-time, Buddha-nature cannot be an immutable essence or potential. Rather, it must be the experiential presence of impermanence itself. Simply stated, impermanence is not a metaphysical, but a phenomenological category for Dōgen: no things are directly experienced as substantial in the sense of having a changeless essence.[154]

From Dōgen's perspective of non-thinking, there is a ceaseless unfolding of directly experienced impermanence, a flow of temporal events, that represents the presence of things as they are without objectifying them and falling into the philosophical trap envisioned by several postmodernists of representational thinking. Thinkers like Deleuze and Derrida are critical of the notion of presence, although Dōgen defeats such criticism by asserting that presence is a letting things be as they are and noting that presence itself contains absence.

We have alluded to the significance of how the continual flux of time for Derrida, Deleuze, and Taylor decenters the individual, which places the individual in a precarious existential situation. Such a process of decentering can become something positive, if it helps one to acquire the ability to also decenter one's grasp of reality away from an egocentric stance and to become aware of things and events from the perspective of the other. This type of personal scenario suggests that the ability to become egocentrically decentered is an important aspect of the moral development of the individual.

If one assumes that the various postmodern positions with respect to time demonstrate the impossibility of a metaphysics of presence, the Zen philosophies of Dōgen and Nishitani offer an alternative to such a metaphysics by finding an alternative way to discuss and include absence and impermanence within one's philosophy. Unlike Derrida's claim that time is a metaphysical concept, Dōgen and Nishitani think that one cannot divorce time from a person and that it is possible to have a self-identical now moment that incorporates the other moments of time. These differences between Zen thinkers and some postmodernists are indicative of the latter's phobia concerning the possibility of identity and their henophobia concerning their grasp of the relationship between the one and the many.[155] From the perspective of Dōgen and Nishitani, the postmodern emphasis on difference represents a unity that is a disunity, whereas the Zen philosophers claim that difference and sameness are included within emptiness.

But what are the implications for a discussion about time for representational thinking? We have noted that Taylor and Derrida think that there is no self-evident presence in the present moment and the notion of the trace subverts the present. Furthermore, Derrida's notion of *différance*, a simultaneous spacing and temporalizing, calls into question the ontological distinction because being is not a being in presence; it is always deferred because absence precedes the presence of the present moment. According to Deleuze, it is difficult for representational thinking to work because the present represents the former present instant that subverts, displaces, and perverts the present moment. It is also futile to try to recreate the past from the present moment because it is caught between present moments and the whole of time is repetition, which appears as difference. This means for Deleuze that we can never experience a thing directly, a possibility that is a sharp departure from Zen thought. If the present moment is paradoxical for Lyotard, it is evanescent and devoid of any absolute character for Levinas. These various postmodern positions on time share in common a subverting and undermining of the present moment, which makes it difficult to assert the validity of representational thinking because one is totally displaced within the flux of time. In contrast to this postmodern tendency, Dōgen frees himself from the representational mode of thinking without subverting time and remaining convinced that each moment is complete in itself and cannot be undermined.

CHAPTER 8

Nihilism and Metaphysics

From his nineteenth-century perspective, Nietzsche envisioned the advent of nihilism, an uncanny guest, that represents the logical conclusion of the ideals and values of western culture.[1] Modern humans find that their values are worthless, their pleasures give them no happiness, and their lives are devoid of purpose because everything lacks meaning. This does not mean that Nietzsche's view of nihilism represents a *Weltanschauung* (worldview) that occurs at a particular time and place.[2] The inevitable advent of nihilism will mean, however, the final overthrow of a decadent Christian civilization, creating a way for a new dawn in the West that will also enhance the emergence of the *Übermensch* (Overman). Even though nihilism represents a major crisis for western civilization, Nietzsche still thinks that its arrival is a positive thing because it is potentially a not insignificant restorative and redemptive event.[3]

In his unfinished work *Will To Power*, Nietzsche asks himself a rhetorical question and immediately supplies an answer: "What does nihilism mean? That the highest values devaluate themselves."[4] By realizing that such concepts as reason, aim, unity, or truth are, for instance, without validity or value, one cannot conclude that the world is true or valuable, but it is rather possible to conclude that the old categories of reason refer to a fictitious world. The self-devaluation of values can be pushed to its limits with the consequence that: "The most extreme form of nihilism would be the view that every belief, every considering-something-true, is necessarily false because there simply is no true world."[5] This process involves a courageous development of consciousness, an internal self-criticism, for instance, of our mendaciousness, hypocrisy, and/or dishonesty, and a discovery that our morality is in fact immoral. In his four volume study of Nietzsche and his philosophy, Heidegger clarifies his position on nihilism at this point:

181

Nihilism thus does not strive for mere nullity. Its proper
essence lies in the affirmative nature of a liberation. Nihilism
is the devaluation of previous values, a devaluation that turns
to a complete reversal of all values.[6]

Moreover, Nietzsche speculates that nihilism, as a recognition of a world
devoid of truth, just could be a divine way of thinking.[7]

Nietzsche identifies two forms of nihilism: passive and active. The
first type, an expression of weakness, represents decline and recession of
the power of the spirit and a pessimistic acquiescence to the absence of
value and the meaninglessness of existence. The second type, a manifestation of strength, represents an increase in the power of the spirit and
destruction of that which one no longer believes.[8] Heidegger elaborates
on the relationship between the two types of nihilism and truth:

Passive nihilism says there is no truth in itself, and lets it go at
that. For passive nihilism there is no truth at all. Active nihilism,
however, sets out to define truth in its essence on the basis of
that which lends all things their determinability and definition.[9]

These two types help to account for the ambiguous nature of nihilism,
which Nietzsche calls the "pathos of the in vain."[10] If we take into consideration Nietzsche's distinction between active and passive nihilism,
we find that it is something connected with the condition of the human
spirit or belief. Nihilism is not the direct result of the will to power or
eternal return, and it is not a gift of Being.[11]

By searching for meaningful events or positing a totality that is
superior to oneself in which one can feel secure, one eventually becomes
discouraged because there is no meaning to be discovered and no complete unity that enables one to believe in one's own worthfulness. At the
point of self-discouragement, a realization dawns: "now one realizes that
becoming aims at nothing and achieves nothing."[12] Without a goal and
devoid of a total unity, one grants becoming the status of the lone reality,
which results in the disbelief in any metaphysical world or theory. Nietzsche connects this process of becoming with eternal recurrence, which is
the most hideous and most frightening form of nihilism. Why is this the
case? Nietzsche answers, "This is the most extreme form of nihilism: the
nothing (the 'meaningless') eternally!"[13] According to Heidegger's interpretation of the philosophy of Nietzsche, the eternal recurrence is not an
ultimate fact, whereas the will to power is such a fact, although it is not a

thought like eternal recurrence, the "thought of thoughts." Heidegger interprets eternal recurrence of the same in Nietzsche's philosophy as an inherently counter-thought that matches the counter-movement of Nietzsche's philosophy.[14] Human existence devoid of meaning, without direction, lacking a goal, and recurring endlessly the same exact way is the most terrible form of the eternal recurrence and the most frightening form of nihilism, representing limitless nothingness and a personal conviction in the untenability of existence.

The advent of nihilism is a manifestation of physiological decadence.[15] This decadence is necessary in Nietzsche's opinion because "Decadence itself is nothing to be fought: it is absolutely necessary and belongs to every age and every people."[16] Nietzsche indicates that there are two significant results of decadence: skepticism and nihilism, which is its logical result and not its cause.[17] Fredric Jameson, an self-acknowledged American adherent of postmodern literary criticism, identifies decadence as a characteristic of postmodernism.[18] A skeptical attitude is also another feature of postmodern thought, along with a lack of logical analysis by some postmodern thinkers. It seems that some postmodern thinkers, such as Derrida and Foucault (not withstanding Foucault's wonderful parody of Cartesianism and his emphasis on a scientific methodology in his work *The Order of Things*), are inclined to follow Nietzsche's characterization that a "nihilist does not believe that one needs to be logical."[19] It does not follow, however, that postmodern philosophers who do not pay much attention to logic are nihilist, even though the critics of Foucault and Derrida have accused them of being nihilist.[20] However, there is common ground between Nietzsche's definition of nihilism and many postmodern thinkers about the impossibility of practicing metaphysics.

This chapter intends to investigate the potential connection between nihilism and metaphysics, which is sometimes envisioned as the end of philosophy by some postmodern philosophers, among selected postmodernists and Zen Buddhists as represented by Nishitani and Dōgen. We are motivated in part by the following comment by Nietzsche: "Buddhism is a weary, passive nihilism, a sign of weakness."[21] Can Zen Buddhism be called a form of nihilism? This is a question that we will have to consider. We will begin, however, with an apology for nihilism, and seek to understand the Zen reaction to the challenge of nihilism by Nishitani. We will, then, view the postmodern antimetaphysical attitude of Heidegger and Derrida. Finally, we will compare the nonmetaphysical approaches to philosophy of Derrida, Deleuze, and Dōgen.

An Apology for Nihilism

Even though it may seem highly unusual in the history of western philosophy, Gianni Vattimo, a postmodern thinker, begins a recent book of
his by offering an apology for nihilism, sharing Nietzsche's conviction
that it is ultimately liberating. This scholar warns us that nihilism continues to develop, and it is premature for us to draw any definitive conclusions about it. Vattimo is motivated to make his apology for nihilism
by the crisis of humanism that he conceptualizes. In order to understand
this crisis, it is necessary for one to get outside of the western tradition
in which it occurs but yet remain part of that tradition. In order to
achieve his perspective, Vattimo utilizes Heidegger's notion of *Verwindung* (overcoming).

Vattimo defines his understanding of *Verwindung* as follows: "an
overcoming which is in reality a recognition of belonging, a healing of an
illness, and an assumption of responsibility."[22] This process of overcoming can only occur after an opening up to the call of what Heidegger calls
Gestell.[23] The term represents for Heidegger the totality of the setting of
technology, which includes its summoning, provoking, and ordering that
constitutes its historical essence. According to Vattimo, *Verwindung* functions as a summons to humanity to cure itself of humanism and yet paradoxically to give itself up to and resign itself to humanism as the destiny
of humanity.[24]

Along with leaving behind an outdated humanism, it is also important to extricate oneself from metaphysics. We notice here an overcoming
of metaphysics and a direct connection to nihilism. With the ending of
humanism and metaphysics, the *Gestell* represents "the first flashing up
of the event (*Ereignis*) of being as its giving-forth beyond the limits of the
forgetfulness of metaphysics."[25] Like Nietzsche, Vattimo views nihilism
as an awakening, a devaluation of the highest values, and a form of liberation from metaphysical thinking.

Although he does not offer an apology for nihilism like Vattimo,
Mark C. Taylor uses many of the major ideas of Nietzsche like the death
of God, eternal recurrence, and includes a vigorous Dionysian element in
his work. Quoting Nietzsche with approval, Taylor thinks that the death
of God results in self-devaluation of the highest values. Nonetheless,
nihilism can be a sign of weakness or strength. The nihilism of the modern humanistic atheist, an irrevocable narcissism that forms a mirror in
which the world functions as a mirror in which one's face is reflected, is

a sign of weakness because it is does not have the ability to accept loss and is anxious about death.[26] Taylor rejects this partial nihilism because it does not embrace the death of the self along with the death of God, an act of murder that is really an act of self-deification. With the death of God, it is death that becomes the absolute master.[27] For human beings, the death of God results in a denial or flight from death.

The death of God, the disappearance of the self, and the overcoming of unhappy consciousness are presupposed by the end of history, a product of imagination devoid of unfiltered facts. Taylor thinks that history represents a form of repression because it represses otherness and denies death, and he connects it with an endless struggle for transcendence and the negation of activity. But what represents the end of history? Taylor answers that history becomes an endgame:

> *Endgame* now appears to be a play about ending endgames. The 'end' of the endgame, however, is at the same time the beginning of an unending game. From the perspective of the end of history, the 'final' plot seems to be 'that there is no plot.'[28]

History is without a center, direction, meaning, or goal. History is equated with an unhappy consciousness that leads to discontent because of unsatisfied needs and inescapable guilt, marking the appearance of sin that leads in turn to a lacerated consciousness. If we concentrate our attention on the present moment, we find that it embodies absence and is thus never completely present, representing ceaseless movement and whose being constitutes eternal recurrence. The perpetual motion and endless transition of eternal recurrence subverts the traditional opposition between time and eternity.[29] Moreover, Taylor claims that when history ends erring, a serpentine wandering, commences and vice versa.

Instead of meaningful history, Taylor affirms useless, purposeless, and meaningless play, an unending game that embodies the free play of erring. This type of play, which upsets traditional hierarchies and inverts common values and meanings, is called carnivalesque by Taylor because its play is irregular and its participants are unlawful due to the lack of conformity of play to rules of common sense and logic.[30] Carnivalesque play is totally transgressive, and it gives us an unusual world: "In this perverse and subversive world, propriety, property, and possession give way to impropriety, expropriation, and dispossession."[31]

A similar kind of carnivalesque is envisioned by Julia Kristeva in her work. Kristeva describes it as a spectacle, a game, a daily happening, a signifier and a signified. As with Taylor's conception of carnival, the self disappears for Kristeva: "A carnival participant is both actor and spectator; he loses his sense of individuality, passes through a zero point of carnivalesque activity and splits into a subject of the spectacle and an object of the game. Within the carnival, the subject is reduced to nothingness, while the structure of the *author* emerges as anonymity that creates and sees itself created as self and other, as man and mask."[32] The carnival also challenges God, authority, and social law because it is inherently rebellious. Finally, it is also rebellious because it is anti-Christian and antirationalist.[33]

Although lacking the notion of carnival in his thought, the postmodern, cultural critic Jean Baudrillard thinks that contemporary nihilism is more radical than any example prior to this time, and he confesses to being a nihilist himself. In comparison to the contemporary type of nihilism, the newer kind of nihilism does a more complete job of destroying appearances. Baudrillard envisions the death of the Hegelian-Marxian dialectic:

> The dialectic stage, the critical stage is empty. There is no more stage. There is no therapy of meaning or therapy through meaning: therapy itself is part of the generalized process of indifferentiation.[34]

Other characteristics of this more radical form of nihilism include inertia, implosion of meaning and its disappearance, the reign of melancholy, and the demise of truth. We are left with a sole resource—theoretical violence. From the perspective of Baudrillard, problems and threats are insoluble. Why is the human situation so hopeless? Baudrillard answers, "Because to this active nihilism of radicality, the system opposes its own, the nihilism of neutralization. The system is itself also nihilistic, in the sense that it has the power to pour everything, including what denies it, into indifference."[35] This observation makes nihilism total by giving it internal and exterior features, which suggests that theories devised to cope with the threat are both meaningless and inconsequential and external events and institutions are without consequence, leaving one without any ray of hope. Whatever internal and external meaning exists for a brief time reveals itself as mortal. There is also no hope waiting for us in the future because the future no longer exists, which implies that there is no end of history. We encounter instead a paradoxical process of reversal and disintegration into simpler elements. With the end of linear time, history becomes indefinitely recyclable by extricating itself from cyclical time.[36]

Within the context of this scenario, Baudrillard envisions us leaving history behind and entering into the uncertain realm of simulation, which is actually a consequence of history itself due to its inherent tendency to embody and function as a prodigious model of simulation.

Reaction of Nishitani to Nihilism

Nietzsche views Buddhism as a passive kind of nihilism, a sign of weakness.[37] Contrary to Nietzsche's opinion of Buddhism, the historical Buddha wanted to "steer clear of notions of permanent existence and nihilistic nonexistence."[38] Within the context of the historically later Mahāyāna Buddhist philosophy, classical Mādhyamika thinkers, for instance, emphatically rejected a nihilistic interpretation of the doctrine of emptiness.[39] In his *Mūlamadhyamakakārikā*, Nāgārjuna writes, for instance, the following:

> In truth, the cessation of a real existing entity is not possible.
> For, indeed, it is not possible to have the nature of both existence and non-existence at the same time.[40]

This type of statement motivated some critical interpreters to label such assertions nihilistic. In response to the charge of being a nihilist (*nāstika*), the influential Mādhyamika philosopher Candrakīrti asserted in his work entitled the *Prasannapadā* that emptiness is a method of affirming neither being nor nonbeing, and nihilists are actually naive realists because they assume that things of this world have self-existent natures,[41] whereas Mādhyamikas view all things as arising dependently within a context of causal conditions. And since everything arises in dependence upon casual factors, there is nothing that possesses a self-existent nature. But such attempts to clarify the Buddhist position failed to reach or impress all critics. Huntington interprets, for instance, the phrase "the emptiness of emptiness" as what he calls a "self-deconstructing concept."[42] From the viewpoint of Nāgārjuna, emptiness can never become a concept, and it does not deconstruct anything because there is nothing permanent to deconstruct.

In response to western critics like Nietzsche and others, Nishitani rejects such erroneous claims, and asserts that nihilism is "the single greatest issue facing philosophy and religion in our times."[43] Within our historical time and place, philosophy has failed to provide an adequate response to nihilism, a historical actuality. The failure of philosophy is

connected with the death of the traditional notion of a transcendent deity
that gave history its meaningful basis in eternity. Devoid of any transcendent foundation, history becomes an errant striving for a viable future and
an unbearable burden upon the individual. Nietzsche's response to the
loss of a transcendent God and ground of historical meaning was to
attempt to transcend history in and through time rather than striving to go
beyond time. Since Nietzsche's notion of eternal return depicts time as
closing in upon itself and overcomes its contingency in the will to power,
Nishitani does not think that Nietzsche's vision is a useful solution
because the "will to power" was conceived as a "thing" referred to as
"will." To remain an entity suggests for Nishitani that it did not lose its
connotation as other for us and something of which could help us become
aware of ourselves at a primary level.[44]

Science is also part of the problem because "Modern science has
completely transformed the old view of nature, resulting in the birth of various forms of atheism and the fomenting of an indifference to religion in
general."[45] Moreover, science rejects the possibility of a personal God or a
teleological view of the world, and conceives of nature as something indifferent and impersonal. According to Nishitani, reality is not something that
can be reduced: "It is *both* life and death, and at the same time is *neither*
life nor death. It is what we have to call the nonduality of life and death."[46]

While discussing the contemporary situation in Japan, Nishitani
says that traditional philosophies like Buddhism and Confucianism
served as protective shields against something like nihilism, but these
forms of thought have lost their power, "leaving a total void and vacuum
in our spiritual ground."[47] Referring to the Meiji Restoration as the greatest change in the history of the Japanese nation, Nishitani says that the
people failed to also recognize that a spiritual crisis was also simultaneously occurring within the island nation. In fact, the Japanese people did
not even know that the crisis they were experiencing was an actual crisis.
This crisis of which the people continue to be unaware also involved the
loss of self and a lack of will. Nishitani explains the crisis further in terms
of a deficiency of will: "Without a will toward the future, the confronta-
tion with the past cannot be properly executed; nor is there a true will
toward the future without responsibility toward the ancestors. For us
Japanese now, the recovery of this primordial will represents our most
fundamental task."[48]

Along with the threat of nihilism, there is also the specter of modern atheism with its three major elements: materialism, scientific ratio-

nalism, and the idea of progress. From Nishitani's perspective, contemporary atheism goes further by adding a sense of the meaninglessness associated with a purely materialistic and mechanistic world and "an accompanying awareness of the nihility that lies concealed just beneath the surface of the world."[49] Within contemporary atheism, there is an awareness of nihility in which the existence of God is denied and replaced by nihility. How is it possible to break out of this fundamental crisis of human existence?

It is possible to deepen our subjectivity and freedom by practicing *zazen* (seated meditation) which will help us to become aware of the reality of *śūnyatā* (emptiness). This awareness makes it possible for us to transcend the nihility of nihilism and atheism. Although it is not a vacuum or some kind of primal negativity, the emptiness of Nishitani's conception is not some thing because it is self-emptying of thingness. Emptiness is also not something other than being, but it is "to be realized as something united to and self-identical with being."[50] Emptiness is absolute negativity in the sense that it represents a stance that negates and transcends nihility, but it is also absolute transcendence of being. It is not something that we can turn to that can become objectively present: "It defies objective representation; no sooner do we assume such an attitude toward it than emptiness withdraws into hiding."[51] This does not mean that emptiness manifests an atheistic standpoint. Nishitani views the standpoint of emptiness as an absolute openness.[52] Moreover, emptiness is something dynamic and not static because it is continuously engaged in a process of emptying itself and everything else.[53] From Nishitani's perspective, Zen Buddhism does not represent an eastern form of nihilism.

The field of emptiness, which forms the basis of the relation of subject and object, is always present and where things cease to be mere objects and appear as something real. Within the field of emptiness, the self is stripped of subjectivity or egocentrism, and is capable of attaining its proper mode of being. Nishitani also indicates that emptiness, which is devoid of even representations of emptiness, is united with being.[54] Emptiness stands in sharp contrast to nihilism, a completely negative void that is groundless, whereas emptiness represents fullness due to its emptying of itself into the world as world. It is only within the context of the openness of emptiness that genuine self-realization can take place because one breaks free of egocentrism and anthropocentrism and empties oneself of self-consciousness in a process of self-negation and entering into the openness of emptiness and real autonomy. Since things and ourself are objectified by consciousness as external realities or as also separated from other things, our field of consciousness hinders any attempt to attain reality as such. Thus one must overcome one's field of consciousness in which one is separated from the reality of things and the reality of the self. Nishitani's notion of emptiness is the exact opposite of the nihility of some postmodernists for its already mentioned characteristics and its affirmation of existence.

Nishitani's position shares something in common with Heidegger at this point because the latter thinks that Being and nothing share emptiness, although this commonality is a bit superficial. In fact, Dallmayr contents that Nishitani misinterprets Heidegger's conception of nothingness as a thing, an incorrect reading of Heidegger that cannot be reconciled with his actual texts. Dallmayr correctly summarizes Heidegger's position: "The relationship of being and nothingness is thus one of mutual implication and intertwining; it is not predicated on antithesis or reciprocal exclusion."[55] Nonetheless, Nishitani refers to the elemental mode of being as possessing an illusory appearance: "That being is only being in unison with emptiness means that being possesses at its ground the character of an 'illusion,' that everything that is, is in essence fleeting, illusory appearance."[56] For Heidegger, Being, common and yet unique, is the most empty and still represents a surplus, and nothing is also the emptiest of the empty and without equivalent.[57] Although nothing is not Being for Heidegger, it presences much like Being. In this sense it is not a mere absence and lack of beings.[58] This is possible for Heidegger because nothing is not different from being because it is being itself, although it can be said that nothing needs Being and not being in order to come into presence.

End of Philosophy

In his work entitled *Human, All Too Human: A Book for Free Spirits*, Nietzsche refers to the overcoming of metaphysics and links it with liberation.[59] In his four-volume study of Nietzsche, Heidegger interprets Nietzsche's call for an end of metaphysics in the following manner: "The end of metaphysics discloses itself as the collapse of the reign of the transcendent and the 'ideal' that sprang from it. But the end of metaphysics does not mean the cessation of history."[60] Heidegger's study of Nietzsche depicts him as the last metaphysician. Rosen disputes this claim because Nietzsche views metaphysics as illusion, and "Metaphysics is rendered impossible by the irrational necessity of the Chaos that lies in the heart of all things."[61] Nonetheless, Nietzsche's call for an end of the western metaphysical tradition creates room for the eventual development and retrieval of an analysis of Being from the perspective of Heidegger. In a lecture from his later period, Heidegger claims that "To think Being without beings means: to think Being without regard to metaphysics."[62] Within the space provided by Nietzsche's termination of metaphysics, Heidegger anoints and appoints himself to be the initial philosopher after the end of metaphysics, which for some postmodern thinkers also means the end of philosophy or the conclusion of philosophy as it has been practiced in the West.

In his early phenomenological work *Sein und Zeit*, Heidegger describes metaphysical thinking as conceiving of Being as being constantly present-at-hand, an attitude that does not do justice to its factuality or temporality. Since its origins in Greek thought, metaphysical thinking tended to conceptualize thinking as a kind of seeing, which is erroneous from Heidegger's viewpoint, and to conceive of Being as a constant presence that is continually there to be perceived by us. In his important essay "Letter on Humanism," Heidegger thinks that all forms of humanism are grounded in metaphysics or are transformed into a foundation for metaphysics, which results in the creation of metaphysical humanism.[63] After devoting considerable attention to the relationship between thinking and Being, Heidegger ends his essay with a vision of a new way of thinking, a path that can transport one into the vicinity of Being, that is to come in the future and that is no longer considered philosophy, "because it thinks more originally than metaphysics—a name identical to philosophy."[64] If presence is understood as visibility, if that which is visible represents a form, and if it is Being that brings beings to their actual abiding presence, this pattern suggests for Heidegger that metaphysics is defective due to its tendency to define Being as presence. But since absence lurks within presence, genuine thinking must orient itself by language or by speech, which functions as a sign of the absent or unsaid. Because Heidegger is concerned with the whole (*das Ganze*), a thinker must be concerned with the interplay of presence and absence that reflects the totality of beings, although it is not itself a being.[65] This line of thinking leads Heidegger to ponder overcoming metaphysics.

Heidegger investigates more specifically the meaning of the overcoming of metaphysics in a collection of essays published under the title of *Vorträge und Aufsätze*. Heidegger uses the term *Überwindung* that can be translated as overcoming, but it refers not only to overcoming something; it also means to incorporate it.[66] When we discuss or consider the overcoming of metaphysics, it is not possible for us to accomplish this by standing outside of it and overcoming it does not suggest that it will totally disappear.[67] Heidegger does not intend to accomplish something negative, a point that is elucidated by a Heideggerian scholar:

> When we now speak of the end of philosophy, we do not take the end of metaphysics in a negative sense. Rather, it means the completion of metaphysics; yet that again does not mean the perfection, either, as if metaphysics would attain the highest perfection at its end.[68]

Overcoming assumes importance for our mode of thinking when we can think also about incorporation, which suggests a regression backward to what has been unthought and simultaneously a path into the future. Heidegger argues that the end of philosophy, or more precisely metaphysics, does not represent the end of thinking. In fact, the end of philosophy marks a transition of thinking to a new beginning.[69] A less radical view of intellectually grasping the overcoming of metaphysics and the role of philosophy is given in his work entitled *Holzwege* where Heidegger says that philosophy becomes anthropology.[70] Overall, Heidegger wants to overcome the metaphysics of representation because it manifests the primordial precondition for an overcoming of a metaphysics of presence in general.[71]

In order for Heidegger to overcome metaphysics, he thinks that he must return to the ground of it because nothing is without a ground, which gives to "is" a grounding character.[72] Since overcoming metaphysics also involves its incorporation, thinking must reject the kind of metaphysics that assumes that Being is constantly presencing and fails to inquire about the truth of Being. What is essential to understand is that the ground avoids, for instance, Being as the ground itself, because the ground itself is an abyss or groundless.[73] The abyss or ground is simultaneously the nonground. Heidegger is attempting to convey to us that there is an inherent drive within metaphysics to ground. By returning to the ground of metaphysics, the thinking of Heidegger suggests that it is in transition and located at the limit of metaphysics.[74]

Postmodernists, who are subsequent to Heidegger and influenced by his work, although using their own approaches, agree generally about the end of philosophy reflecting the termination of the traditional way of conceiving metaphysics. According to one interpreter, we have reached a "historical moment in which *the essential possibilities* of metaphysics are exhausted."[75] Another interpreter of contemporary philosophy thinks that the occidental metaphysical tradition exhausted its usefulness.[76] Rodolphe Gasché, a sympathetic interpreter of the philosophy of Derrida, welcomes the end of philosophy because it "heralds the beginning of a new, more radical philosophy."[77] From the perspective of someone less sympathetic to Derrida's thought, Jürgen Habermas looks at the shattering of metaphysical thinking from an historical perspective as events that have been socially conditioned. Referring to the infusion of historical consciousness in the nineteenth century into the humanities, Habermas thinks, "The intrusion of historical consciousness rendered the *dimension of finiteness* more convincing in comparison to an unsituated reason that had been idealistically apotheosized. A *detranscendentalization* of inherited basic concepts was thereby set in motion."[78] Habermas sees a paradigm shift from a philosophy of consciousness to a philosophy of language within the more general context of the objective self-understanding of science and technology in the nineteenth century. Finally, Habermas sees a collapse of the traditional precedence of theory over practice.[79] An exception to the agreement about the overcoming of metaphysics is given by Rosen, who thinks that it is fundamentally mistaken to speak in this way because "Metaphysics cannot be overcome, because it is the thinking of insoluble problems, as even Kant understood."[80]

Nonetheless, whether it is a matter of its possibilities or usefulness, or a combination of historical reasons, many postmodernists agree that it is necessary to move beyond the confines of traditional metaphysics for a variety of reasons. Deleuze and Guattari think, for instance, that metaphysics is an example of arborescent thinking, which is a model of thought like an erect tree, because it has been shaped by arboreal metaphors from the moment of its origin. They explain, "Arborescent systems are hierarchical systems with centers of significance (sic) and subjectification, central automata like organized memories. In the corresponding models, an element only receives information from a higher unit, and only receives a subjective affection along preestablished paths."[81] Deleuze and Guattari want to reject identity and want to emphasize difference, exteriority, and change. In order to do this, they utilize what they call rhizomatics, a method and an objective, that is a root metaphor in sharp contrast to the tree metaphor that suggests linear movement and an ordered system. Even though it also presupposes a unity, rhizomatic unity is hidden or latent like the roots of a tree, but it represents, moreover, an underground network of a multitude of roots and shoots that lack a central axis, direction of growth, or unified sphere of origin. This decentered web of linkages is based on heterogeneity, multiplicity, connections, breaks, discontinuities, and ruptures. By using this method, Deleuze and Guattari want to be able to enhance their chances to map surfaces, discern the interrelationship between things or events, to measure speed and flows and to generally experiment. Such a method is contrary to hermeneutics, semiotics, and especially psychoanalysis, each discipline being an attempt to connect something objective with something hidden. In contrast to these rejected approaches, rhizomatics is pragmatic in the sense that it is concerned with what one can do, and represents an intertwining of unity and difference that concentrates on the surface and the connections between diverse fragments.

Along somewhat similar lines of argument, Foucault emphasizes differences, discontinuities, and divisions within history and culture by adopting from Nietzsche his method of genealogy, a heterological approach that discovers the weak points of rationalism, separates history from metaphysics and acknowledges no absolutes.[82] By means of his method of genealogy, Foucault focuses on the interrelations of power, knowledge, and the human body by standing within the interconnected web of power relations at the current moment and acknowledging the relative nature of all knowledge.[83] In contrast to Foucault's thought, Lyotard criticizes metaphysics as a metanarratology, whereas Derrida attempts to deconstruct western metaphysics.

Derrida denies that there is any such thing as a metaphysical concept or name: "The 'metaphysical' is a certain determination or direction taken by a sequence or 'chain.'"[84] Derrida calls attention to the connection between visual metaphors and thought in western philosophy that makes it a captive to heliocentric metaphysics. In fact, metaphysical concepts are worn out metaphors, which themselves are metaphysical concepts.[85]

Rorty agrees with Derrida that visual metaphors play a major role in shaping our philosophical viewpoints. A basic presupposition from which Rorty argues his position is the role of the mirror in western philosophy: "It is pictures rather than propositions, metaphors rather than statements, which determine most of our philosophical convictions. The picture which holds traditional philosophy captive is that of the mind as a great mirror. . . . Without the notion of the mind as mirror, the notion of knowledge as accuracy of representation would not have suggested itself."[86] Although metaphors do not have a precise meaning, they can function as a new and useful way of speaking that can potentially produce an effect that steers a safe course between the hazards of realism, idealism, and skepticism.

In contrast to Rorty's philosophy, Derrida sees the western metaphysical tradition as representing what he calls logocentrism, a perspective from which the Greek logos implicitly connects the faculty of speech with the notion of reason. He views logocentrism as supporting "the determination of the being of the entity as presence."[87] Since there is only a closed chain of signifiers that points only to itself for Derrida, it is not possible to have a direct encounter with an object of language. Without anything external to the chain of signifers, presence is always deferred. Logocentrism can be overcome by means of grammatology, a new discipline of writing. Since it is impossible to step outside of metaphysics, this new discipline uses the tools of metaphysics against it when deconstructing it. Although Rorty agrees with Derrida on the significance of metaphors in shaping our philosophical positions, he asserts that Derrida does not offer "rigorous arguments against logocentrism."[88] Moreover, Paul Ricoeur accuses Derrida of engaging in metaphysics, or more precisely, being ignorant of the "simultaneous play of unacknowledged metaphysics and worn-out metaphor."[89] Derrida responds to such criticism by replying that our thinking is necessarily metaphysical, and there is little hope that we will escape metaphysics in the future.[90] It is possible, however, to push philosophy to its limits and write about problems on the margins of the western philosophical tradition.

As part of his argument, Derrida states that not all languages are logocentric because Chinese or Japanese nonphonetic scripts are evidence of cultures developing alternatively to logocentrism.[91] In a critical analysis of Derrida's claims about Chinese or Japanese language, Faure thinks that we cannot just assume, as Derrida does, that Chinese language is free of logocentrism because it lacks the notion of *logos* and cannot become a metaphysics of presence. Faure accuses Derrida of idealizing the Chinese tradition, which results in an instance of reverse ethnocentrism.[92] In order to understand more fully Derrida's nonmetaphysical approach to philosophy, we need to turn to his notion of *différance* and compare it to Dōgen's notion of Buddha-nature in order to continue the dialogue between postmodernist and Zen thinkers. We will also include a discussion of Deleuze's notion of difference in order to enrich the discussion with Derrida and Dōgen.

Différance, Difference, and Buddha-Nature

Dōgen thinks that Buddha-nature (*busshō*)[93] is neither a process nor an entity. It is also not something to be achieved because it already is: "It is not independent existence since it is interrelated, nor is it uncreated, for it occurs simply as it is."[94] The Buddha-nature must not be confused with an eternal self. And it must not be construed as enlightenment or awakening.[95] The Buddha-nature is not an innate potentiality to be realized by a person in the future, but it is rather the essential characteristic of things as experienced by a person. Moreover, a person cannot understand Buddha-nature by means of his/her power of reason or through rigorous philosophical arguments. In order to fully understand Buddha-nature, a person must involve him/herself in practicing (e.g., *zazen*, seated meditation), enlightening (*satori*), clarifying, and ultimately forgetting.[96] What makes the Buddha-nature so difficult to comprehend is its being, which is openly manifest and at the same time concealed. These paradoxical manifestations make the Buddha-nature difficult to grasp with one's intellectual powers.

Derrida's neologism *différance* is also difficult to comprehend because it shares many of the same kinds of elusive, ambiguous, and paradoxical aspects as Buddha-nature, although they are ultimately very different notions. *Différance* is unnameable and unutterable, even though it is possible to write it, a process that implies an inevitable rewriting without beginning or conclusion. Prior to all opposition is the finite movement of *différance* that serves to structure them. This emphatically suggests that it exists prior to all differences and represents the play of differences. Because it is constituted by difference and deferment, *différance* cannot reveal itself or produce presence itself.[97] It is neither active nor passive and neither existence nor essence. Derrida hesitates to admit that *différance* is simply a word or a concept because he wants to stress that it possesses spacing and temporalizing aspects, indicating an interval of space and time.[98]

Derrida's notion of *différance* shares spatial and temporal characteristics with the concept of difference in the philosophy of Deleuze in the sense of sharing the features of differing and deferral. And like Derrida's notion of *différance*, difference is inexplicable due to its paradoxical and intensive nature for Deleuze. Since intensity is an uncancelable element in difference, Deleuze conceives of this as a positive process that affirms difference by making it an object of affirmation.[99] Deleuze and Derrida disagree, however, about the priority of *différance* over difference, although they both agree that their respective notions never become fully present, which Deleuze claims inhabits *Aion*, a past and future with no present. Therefore, difference is always past or about to be future, a position that distinguishes Deleuze from the stress on the present moment in the philosophies of Derrida and Dōgen.

As part of the process of explaining the notion of Buddha-nature, Dōgen modifies a famous passage from the *Mahaparinirvana Sūtra*: "All sentient beings possess the Buddha-nature without exception." This altered passage suggests that the Buddha-nature is not a potentiality possessed by sentient beings, but it is rather all inclusive in the sense that it includes both sentient and insentient beings, whereas the older meaning of sentient beings refers to all living beings that transmigrate in the six realms of life (e.g., worlds of hell, hungry spirits, animals demonic beings, humans, and deities). Dōgen affirms that:

> In Buddhism, a sentient is a being that possesses a mind. That is to say, mind means sentient being. In the sense that mind means sentient being, things without mind are sentient beings. Therefore, mind is sentient being. Sentient beings are Buddha-nature. Grass, trees, and lands are mind; thus they are sentient beings. Because they are sentient beings they are Buddha-nature. Sun, moon, and stars are mind; thus they are sentient beings; thus they are Buddha-nature.[100]

Dōgen's argument equates all existences and sentient beings. Therefore, the Buddha-nature includes plant and animal life, and the inanimate world. This unity of sameness and difference within the Buddha-nature is challenged by the work of Derrida and the silent *a* of the neologism *différance*, which is a secret and is analogous to a tomb, that manifests a sameness that is not identical, although it remains active and productive by forming a generative movement within the play of differences.[101] Dōgen is challenged also by Deleuze's notion of difference because in the relationship between the one and the many there is no unity of Buddha-nature in Dōgen's sense of the term. In contrast to the unity perceived by Dōgen, there is merely a multiplicity of difference for Deleuze.[102] Notions like the one, universal being, the multiple in general are rejected by Deleuze because such terms are too all-encompassing or abstract. In place of these kinds of terms, Deleuze stresses the specific, particular, and singular. Moreover, there are no words, phenomena, or events that do not have a multiple sense for Deleuze. From the Deleuzean perspective, the ultimate unity is difference, which refers to other differences that are incapable of identifying its nature except to differentiate it. From the perspective of Deleuze, and partially using the language of Dōgen, every sentient and insentient being must perceive its identity "swallowed up in difference, each being no more than a difference between differences."[103] Thus the all inclusive nature of Deleuze's philosophy centers around difference, and it excludes any unity between sameness and difference, which Deleuze tends to view as a form of representational thinking and Dōgen as non-thinking. Unlike the *Dasein* of Heidegger's phenomenology that manifests the ontological structure of human beings and is ontologically prior (*ursprünglicher*) to humans, Dōgen's notion of Buddha-nature is all inclusive, including within both sentient and insentient beings. Following a *via negativa* line of argument, Dōgen writes:

> It is not being of original (and timeless) being, because it fills the past right on up through the present. It is not being with a beginning, because there is not a single object to be reflected on it. It is not being as separate entities, because it is an inclusive whole.[104]

Buddha-nature is not, however, the possession of these beings; it is beings and Being itself. The absolute inclusiveness of Buddha-nature does not imply that it is immanent in all existences; rather all existences are immanent in it.[105]

In response to the Zen philosopher, Deleuze rejects Dōgen's contention that beings and Being itself are immanent in it. Not only is there no teleological order of existence for Deleuze, being is also devoid of a preconstituted structure or depth. Denying any hidden foundation for being, Deleuze offers an immanent and materialist ontology, a position with which Dōgen can partially agree. They also agree that being is fully expressed in the world. Deleuze and Dōgen disagree, however, about subordinating being to thought by making thinking the ultimate form of being. Actually, Dōgen emphasizes the importance of the non-thinking mode of consciousness that lets things appear as themselves without objectifying them, subordinating them to anything else, or superimposing any preconceptions upon them. If Buddha-nature represents the ground of being and impermanence its dynamic aspect for Dōgen, difference, a movement that supports and subverts being, represents its dynamic feature for Deleuze. It is a misunderstanding of the philosophy of Deleuze by Hardt to claim that his notion of difference assumes a radically new role: "Difference founds being; it provides being with its necessity, its substantiality."[106] Deleuze is adamantly opposed to foundations of all kinds as we have observed in a previous chapter. Deleuze's philosophy of difference is intended to undermine all foundations even difference itself, which subverts itself in its movement.

From Derrida's perspective, the all inclusive aspect of Buddha-nature obscures any possibility to perceive differences, whereas *différance* represents a pure trace.[107] According to Derrida, before one can think of an insentient being or object, one must think of the trace because the field within which the insentient entity is located is structured according to the various possibilities of the trace.[108] This suggests that *différance*, functioning as a trace, is already there and determines an object as it appears to perception, even though this does not mean that the perceived object depends on the trace for its existence. Derrida's notion of trace is sometimes depicted as the space between the terms of a sentence or the movement of spacing that spaces terms, which is analogous to Deleuze's self-differentiating difference. In part, this means for Deleuze that difference in itself does not allow the relation between two examples of difference to be thought. Consequently, Deleuze notes that "Ceasing to be thought, difference is dissipated in non-being."[109]

In contrast to the philosophical positions of Deleuze and Dōgen, Heidegger distinguishes between the existentiell (ontic) and existential (ontological) dimensions of *Dasein*. Existentiell refers to *Dasein* as a being among others, whereas existential refers to *Dasein* in its own Being. Because of the original ambivalence in the term being, Heidegger makes a distinction between Being (*Sein*) and beings (*Seindes*) which he calls the ontological difference.[110] Dōgen does not establish an ontological difference because he denies that there is a distinction between Being and beings, or because all beings are just all beings according to Abe's interpretation of Dōgen's thought.[111] Through the mediation of nothing, Being is beings: "If sentient beings had the Buddha-nature originally, they would not be sentient beings. Since they are sentient beings, they are, after all, not Buddha-nature."[112] Due to Dōgen's emphasis on the idea of no-Buddha-nature, Being is not ontologically different from beings.[113] If all existences are the Buddha-nature itself, even though there is some distinction between them, they are thus neither identical nor different.

Even though it does not appear because it is not an empirical phenomenon, the notion of *différance* for Derrida is prior to Being in the sense that it is more ancient than any name, while simultaneously not itself a name. *Différance* rather suggests the direction of the differential matrix that generates names and concepts. Based on Derrida's definition of *différance*, it is *différance* that makes it possible for Buddha-nature to exist due to its priority and greater antiquity, whereas Dōgen thinks that there is nothing prior to or older than Buddha-nature, a conviction that can be existentially authenticated by every individual aspirant for liberation. Dōgen and Derrida agree that *différance* is not a notion that establishes an ultimate entity or state, and cannot manifest the nonexistence of a super-ontic entity beyond or within the world. In contrast to Dōgen and Derrida, Deleuze thinks that difference disappears in thought when it is subordinated by a person to the identity of a concept. Deleuze wants to restore difference to thought, but it is first necessary to overcome the tendency to represent "difference through the identity of the concept and the thinking subject."[114] This attempt to retrieve difference is similar to Heidegger's attempt to recover Being.

Since being-in-the-world is the basic state of *Dasein*, it represents *Dasein's* intercourse in the world with entities belonging to the world for Heidegger, although being-in is not a physical relation of being-in-the-world.[115] Heidegger conceives of being-in as an existential relation that characterizes the things with which a person is concerned in the world. Let us assume that a person is lost at sea after a shipwreck and lies unconscious in a lifeboat with no one else present and surrounded completely by water. After suddenly awakening and seeing nothing but the boat surrounded by water, the person asks him/herself where am I? To ask this question implies that one is somewhere, and to be somewhere is to be in a world, which tends to suggest that being-in-the-world is the fundamental characteristic of a person's existence. Using the example of the person lost at sea in a boat, Dōgen's interpretation is much different than that imagined for Heidegger because he views the person's body, mind, and world as the dynamic function of the boat, which suggests that the person makes the boat what it is, hence making life what it is, and life making the person what he/she is.[116] Using this different interpretation of the person lost at sea in contrast to another possible interpretation based on observations grounded in Heidegger's philosophical position, Dōgen thinks that it makes no sense to refer to being in Buddha-nature: "Buddha-nature is always *whole being*, because *whole being* is the Buddha-nature."[117] Dōgen also emphasizes the nonsubstantiality of Buddha-nature which implies that it is immanent in the world and within living beings.[118] Due to the nonsubstantiality of Buddha-nature no particular thing or quality in the world corresponds to it. This suggests that Buddha-nature represents the epitome of difference, which makes it even more different than *différance* or the difference advocated by Deleuze. In fact, for Dōgen, Buddha-nature both embodies and transcends Derrida's notion of *différance* and Deleuze's notion of difference. Derrida counters that Buddha-nature sounds like a realm, and it is *différance* that subverts every realm,[119] whereas difference subverts representational thinking for Deleuze. From Dōgen's viewpoint, it is impossible to subvert Buddha-nature, although it is possible to authenticate it by means of *zazen* (seated meditation). For Dōgen, *différance* becomes problematic when one tries to authenticate it because it loses its status as a nonconcept or nonword by overuse, even before one gets an opportunity to authenticate it in some way.

Within the structure of Buddha-nature for Dōgen, there is the element of nonexistence (*mu-busshō*), which represents the liberating and transcending powers inherent in the inner structure of Buddha-nature, although the term traditionally signified the absence of Buddha-nature that was analogous to the antithetical relation between nonbeing and being.[120] Dōgen does not conceive of nonexistence as antithetical to existence, whereas Derrida thinks that *différance* cannot be categorized as either being or nonbeing, present or absent.[121] Therefore, *différance* cannot represent existence, non-existence, or essence. By subsuming and transcending being and nonbeing, Buddha-nature, an absolute nondual principle, is both being and non-being for Dōgen.[122] Besides negating and transcending concrete entities, *mu-busshō* suggests the liberating and transcending powers inherent in the Buddha-nature by liberating fixation on the particularities of existence, whereas Deleuze views difference with its negative and positive aspects as liberating. Deleuze distinguishes between the affirmative topside of difference and its negative underside, which represents its inverted image or image of intensity. The inversion of difference is due to three major factors: requirements of a representational mode of thinking that subordinates difference to identity; problems created by negation; and problems associated with the explication of intensity.[123] In contrast to the notion of difference in the thought of Deleuze, there is no inversion of the Buddha-nature in part because the Buddha-nature of nonexistence indicates the emptiness of Buddha-nature, whose essence is defined by Dōgen as "This emptiness is that of emptiness is emptiness."[124] This implies for Dōgen that the essence of emptiness resides in the intuitive awareness that in the realization of emptiness there is nothing but emptiness. *Mu-bussho* also represents the dynamic and creative aspect of Buddha-nature.

The dynamic and creative aspects of *différance* can be discerned in the movement of play that produces differences. In fact, Derrida identities *différance* with the systematic play of differences and in turn with traces.[125] Within his published works, we find Derrida engaging in verbal play by using puns and homonyms, etymological forms of play, and self-referential discourse that sometimes takes the form of homophonic or anagrammatic play. These various forms of word-play assume different kinds of associations that confront readers with a radically stylized manner of argumentation that is intended to make readers continually feel the effect of the words.[126] This indirect form of communication also blurs common margins of generic demarcation. Play is in a constant state of flux because when it emerges into being or into language it erases itself. By alternating between absence and presence, *différance*, as play, disrupts presence, a signifying and substitutive reference inscribed within a complex system of difference.[127] Play disrupts any reliance on philosophical hierarchies to establish one's position, allows differences to proliferate, and retains the tension between contradictions. An insightful observation on play in the work of Derrida is offered by McGowan: "Play, then, might be characterized as what results from irresolvable contradictions; just as the distance from *différance* preserves the play of differences, so the inability to resolve these tensions generates an endless play of thought and language around various binary oppositions."[128] Moreover, Derrida understands the process of play as finite and temporal.

In comparison to the play element of *différance* in Derrida's philosophy, there is also a vast potential for play in Dōgen's philosophy. D. T. Suzuki captures the spirit of play in Zen Buddhist when he writes, "For playfulness comes out of empty nothingness, and where there is something, this cannot take place. Zen comes out of absolute nothingness and knows how to be playful."[129] To be able to play is to be free, whereas to work is to be limited and confined. The free and voluntary nature of play is a source of joy and amusement.[130] The spirit of play for Dōgen represents his transcendence of earthly dichotomies and absolute freedom. In a spirit applicable to the Zen of Dōgen, Huizinga writes, "Play lies outside the antithesis of wisdom and folly, and equally outside those of truth and falsehood, good and evil."[131] In contrast to the spirit of play in Zen, the play of Derrida is devoid of transcendence and very much involved in the dichotomies of life, although it does manifest the freedom of the writer.

Without repeating everything that was covered in chapter seven, it can be stated that Dōgen devotes attention to the temporal aspects of Buddha-nature by quoting the historical Buddha to the effect that one should watch for temporal conditions. Dōgen interprets the words of the Buddha in the following manner:

> *Should watch for* has nothing to do with a watcher and what is watched; it has no correspondence to "right" or "false" watching. It is *just seeing*. As it is just seeing it is neither the self's seeing nor any other's seeing. It is "Look! temporal conditions!" It is transcendence of conditions.[132]

Although temporal conditions are not neglected for Dōgen, they are, however, transcended because seeing refers to the intuitive grasping of Buddha-nature. In other words, temporal conditions are identical with the Buddha-nature, whereas Derrida associates *différance* with temporality. Derrida states that *différance* is an irreducible interval where time and space interconnect. Likewise, Deleuze emphasizes the temporal nature of difference by asserting that difference in-itself is already repetition.[133]

Dōgen also takes temporal conditions seriously because the Buddha-nature is impermanent: "Impermanence is itself Buddha-nature; thus both saints and ordinary men are impermanent."[134] Impermanence is an aspect of the Buddha-nature that continually emerges into being and passes out of being. This suggests that being and becoming are not separate, but are rather identical in the process of impermanence. Derrida and Deleuze agree with Dōgen's emphasis on the centrality of impermanence, which is embodied by *différance* or difference in their respective philosophies. Impermanence is multidimensional for Dōgen because it can signify the fragility and uncertainty associated with constant change, an emotional response to change, an awareness of a lack of substratum and duration in existence, and a realization that there is no substantive self or world that conceals the truth.[135] If Buddha-nature is impermanent, this means necessarily that everything is also impermanent: "Therefore, since grasses, trees, and bushes are impermanent, they are Buddha-nature. The very impermanence of man's body and mind is Buddha-nature."[136] Since nothing in the universe is static and immutable because everything is always in constant flux, this is the reason that Dōgen can refer to mountains that walk or float on the water. From Dōgen's perspective, the universe is not something fixed and immovable; it is being in time. From the perspective of Derrida, there is also constant change that he often views in terms of what he calls iteration, which is not a genus, essence, substance, or transcendental state. In order to grasp its significance, one must investigate what it does: "It dislocates, subverts, and constantly displaces the dividing-line between two terms."[137] When iteration changes something, it reveals something new or constant change. As we have previously noted for Deleuze with respect to difference, it changes to such a great extent that it does not have a stable identity and even differs from itself.

Deleuze, Dōgen and Derrida are all non-Kantian philosophers because they do not advance arguments to solve problems. And they work on the philosophical margins of their respective philosophical traditions. From a Kantian perspective, these thinkers share an antifoundationalism because Buddha-nature or emptiness cannot be construed as a firm foundation from which to construct a philosophical system, and in this sense Dōgen, Deleuze, and Derrida share a similar philosophical attitude. Since there is nothing that is ultimately and unconditionally real because everything is impermanent, these three thinkers suggest that we should focus on how things come together and are interdependent. The philosophies of Dōgen, Deleuze, and Derrida also problematize rationality by their methodological approaches. Unlike Dōgen, we can find an anti-intuitionist attitude expressed in the works of Derrida and Deleuze. Dōgen also disagrees with Derrida that knowledge amounts to asserting sentences, although he would agree with Derrida that one cannot validate a philosophical claim by encountering an object. Moreover, Dōgen tends to agree with Rorty's criticism of Derrida that "The idea that there is some neutral ground on which to mount an argument against something as big as 'logocentrism' strikes me as one more logocentric hallucination."[138] With Derrida's emphasis on contingency, play, otherness, interrelations, and difference, his work appears to deny autonomy to the subject, something that Dōgen finds absolutely essential as a prerequisite for liberation. If Dōgen's philosophy represents a nondualist perspective, Derrida and Deleuze move in the completely opposite direction by looking for fissures, breaks, cracks, tears, change, repetition, surfaces, and difference, although these three thinkers share an aversion to a representational mode of thinking.

Concluding Remarks

It is no coincidence that examples of writing an apology for nihilism or completing the unfinished agenda of humanistic atheism occurs at around the same historical time as discussions about the end of philosophy, which means the death of metaphysics. A partial message from the works of thinkers like Vattimo and Taylor is that it is not necessary to escape nihilism because it has become a relatively innocuous pattern of thought.[139] Although not all postmodern thinkers are nihilist, postmodern philosophy is characterized by an acknowledgement of its limitations and a skepticism about its potential. It is a time for thinkers to wander aimlessly, err, emphasize altarity, stress the importance of difference, communicate indirectly, and embrace irony. With respect to the topic of metaphysics, Rorty finds something ironical in the philosophy of Derrida, although he does not refer to it as such: "Derrida cannot *argue* without turning himself into a metaphysician, one more claimant to the title of the discoverer of the primal, deepest vocabulary."[140] From Derrida's perspective, we are left with only traces.

Although the trace appears for Derrida, it is not a presence, does not exist in and of itself, refers beyond itself, and functions to dislocate and displace.[141] The reason that the trace cannot become present or exist by itself is that it is always subject to effacement, which means that the trace disappears in its appearing, a feature that it shares with *différance* or the pure form of the trace. If the term Buddha-nature represents reality for Dōgen, it evokes the trace for Derrida, which suggests that Buddha-nature erases itself in its appearing and thus does not actually exist. Or due to the nature of repetition in the philosophy of Deleuze, the Buddha-nature can never become fully present.

Using notions like trace and *différance* or difference, Derrida and Deleuze seek respectively to undermine the foundations of metaphysics, which is something that is not really a problem for Dōgen. By following his path of philosophy, there is a strong suggestion in his writings that Derrida is not interested in discovering the possible limits of rationality, but he is rather concerned with those conditions that render it impossible for the exercise of reason. Or according to Deleuze, reason encounters its limits with difference, which becomes mediated by four aspects of reason: identity; analogy; opposition; and resemblance.[142] From the perspective of Deleuze, difference, an aconceptual notion, undermines the certainties traditionally associated with rationality in the West. Deleuze and Derrida agree that their respective understandings of difference eludes reason. Dōgen also finds it necessary to call attention to the limits of reason: "The Buddhist Dharma cannot be understood through rational and intellectual study."[143] Thus Derrida and Deleuze attempt to think the limits of the western philosophical tradition, while Dōgen does the same, for instance, with his reinterpretation of classical Mahāyāna texts for eastern philosophy.

By assuming the philosophical standpoint of *différance* or difference, we have seen that Derrida and Deleuze call respectively into question the presence of Being and the entire western logocentric tradition, which includes a representational type of thinking. Unlike Buddha-nature that includes both being and nonbeing, *différance* does not belong to the category of being because it does not manifest itself as present and does not exist.[144] Within the movement of *différance*, a play of traces, presence does not hold a place of privilege in Derrida's thought, whereas Deleuze argues that repetition makes it impossible for presence to assume a central position in his thought. Moreover, Deleuze argues that difference is irreducible to such concepts as identity and representation. Thus we cannot presuppose with either Deleuze or Derrida that Being becomes present. If this is the case, metaphysics is dead and that kind of philosophical speculation is at an end. Needless to say, not all contemporary philosophers agree with the conclusion that philosophy is at its end. Rosen, for instance, argues that philosophy never ends "because there is no way in which to determine conclusively which hypothesis is the best."[145]

CHAPTER 9

Signing Out

S ince I signed in while writing the first chapter, it is only appropriate that
I sign out in the final chapter. Within the context of this study of Zen
Buddhist philosophy and postmodern thinkers, it seems that the best way to
sign out is to discuss the end of philosophy because Zen, from one perspective, represents the end of philosophy as the love of wisdom and the use of
rational means to find the truth, and many postmodern thinkers share the
Zen suspicion of metaphysics and representational thinking, even though
some postmodernists might view Zen as an example of eastern logocentri-
cism. Derrida, for instance, calls metaphysics "white mythology," a kind of
Indo-European variety, because it reflects western culture and the impossibility of such an endeavor. Tragically, from the perspective of Derrida,
"white mythology" is like a metaphor that embodies its own demise:

> Metaphor, then always carries its death within itself. And this
> death, surely, is also the death of philosophy. But the genitive
> is double. It is sometimes the death of philosophy, death of a
> genre belonging to philosophy which is thought and summa-
> rized within it, recognizing and fulfilling itself within philoso-
> phy; and sometimes the death of a philosophy which does not
> see itself die and is no longer to be refound within philosophy.[1]

By affirming the death of philosophy, Derrida certainly seems to fer-
vently suggest the death of metaphysics. But if philosophy is dead, does
this mean that thinking it also dead? Derrida and other postmodernists
want to ring the death knell for representational thinking. If thinking is
dead, does this mean writing about philosophy and/or philosophical
issues is also dead? Derrida does not appear to mean that writing in general or writing in particular about philosophy is dead.

207

The process of writing is stealing and the writer is a thief for Derrida, who inverts the traditional hierarchy of speech over writing in the western philosophical tradition. If speech represents presence, immediacy, intelligibility, and possible contact with the truth, writing, a peculiar sort of secondariness, stands for the absence, lack of immediacy, unintelligibility, and estrangement from the truth.[2] Inscribing itself in the silence of space, writing is like a ghost, and can represent anything because it represents nothing in particular. This strange kind of ghost signifies forgetfulness and the subverting of spontaneous memory.[3] Writing, a dangerous and risky endeavor, is also akin to the "living-dead, a reprieved corpse, a deferred life, a semblance of breath."[4] Part of the danger associated with writing is due to its inaugural nature by which Derrida means that it does not know where it is going, but it rather wanders in its freedom in a playful way. If writing does not know where it is going, does it know where it is located? Derrida certainly thinks that he knows where it is: "It plays within the simulacrum."[5] In fact, other postmodernists agree with Derrida that we are located in the simulacrum, a copy of a copy according to Plato.

If one engages in the process of writing or comparative philosophical dialogue, it is instructive to discern where one is located. Although Heidegger would say that we are in-the-world, and whereas Dōgen and Nishitani might say that we are in emptiness, some postmodernists state unequivocally that we are situated in the simulacrum. It seems prudent at this point to grasp this situation before we attempt to review where we have been with this cross-cultural dialogue and to try to respond to the authors mentioned in the first chapter.

The Present Simulacrum

Jean Baudrillard, a postmodern cultural critic, finds himself within a simulacra, an era of simulation, which suggests for him a time in which all referentials have been liquidated. This artificial, malleable time that leans toward equivalence represents faking that which one does not possess, suggesting an absence rather than a presence and threatening the distinction between true and false, real and imaginary.[6] Within the contextual philosophical spirit of other postmodernists, Baudrillard's notion of simulation stands in direct opposition to representation, which itself originates from the principle of the equivalence of the sign and the so-called real, whereas simulation comes *"from the radical negation of the sign as value,* from the sign as the reversion and death sentence of every reference."[7]

Baudrillard asserts that there is a logic operating with the simulation, but it does not have anything to do with logical facts or reason. The logic of simulation is characterized by a preceding of the model, which implies that simulation cannot be represented. The strange logic of simulation does not have anything to do with meaning or the real. In fact, it terminates meaning,[8] and it renders the real and illusion impossible at the same time because the latter is no longer possible without the former.[9] Within such a confused context, the medium and the message also get confused because the former gets diffused, diffracted, and becomes intangible.[10] We are left with just the phantom of simulation, a manifestation of the hyper-real, a more real than real, within a context in which the real never did truly exist.[11] Living within this hyperreality devoid of linear time and dominated by cyclical reversal means that history is lost to us as a mythical referential.[12] The image created by Baudrillard is one in which difference reigns supreme within a reversible realm in which metaphysics is lost, economic exchange is annulled, and accumulation of wealth and power are terminated.

The description of the simulacrum by Baudrillard is not all that different from that described by Deleuze, who tends to view it as difference in itself, which means for him that it possesses no identity and merely appears by disguising itself. Instead of the Platonic opposition of appearance and essence, Deleuze substitutes the simulacra, demonic images devoid of resemblance that function by themselves.[13] The functioning of the simulacrum, a Dionysian machine, is simulation, a phantasm itself, that subverts the same or representative model and renders it false. By being constructed upon a difference, the simulacrum internalizes a dissimilarity, but this does not mean that it is a degraded copy because "It harbors a positive power that denies *the original and the copy, the model and the reproduction.*"[14] Such a philosophical position manifests an anti-Kantian perspective that is aconceptual and nonrepresentational.

The phantom of Nietzsche appears in Deleuze's notion of the simulacrum when the postmodernist equates it with the will to power and explicitly connects it with the eternal return. The simulacra is the will to power as simulation.[15] But it cannot be understood apart from the eternal return, an expression of chaos itself. Representing the same and the similar in a simulated form, the cyclic eternal return functions in an excentric way in relationship to a decentered center.[16] In place of the coherence of representation, the eternal return substitutes its own errant chaos and causes only phantasms to return. Writing on behalf of all human beings, Deleuze concludes that "We have become simulacra."[17]

Derrida is not as radical as Deleuze with respect to the notion of simulacra, which the former interprets as a force that continuously dislocates, displaces, and decenters. Within the context of his notion of effacing, Derrida claims that the simulacra possesses a strange essence: "For imitation affirms and sharpens its essence in effacing itself. Its essence is its nonessence."[18] Thus, there is no such thing as a perfect imitation because the tiniest difference renders the imitation absolutely distinct from the imitator.

The overall purpose behind the discussion of the simulacra among such postmodernists as Derrida, Deleuze, and Baudrillard is to undermine the Kantian conviction that metaphysics is a natural disposition of the philosophical thinker because of the very nature of reason, which possesses the ability to unify the empirical cognitions of the understanding. From the perspective of our postmodernists, it is not possible for metaphysics to extend our knowledge of reality as Kant thought possible if its propositions are synthetic and *a priori*. By adhering to the notion of the simulacra, the postmodernists also make it clear that it is impossible to cling to the Cartesian ideal of precision and certitude in thinking. Unlike Kant, the postmodernists do no think that it is possible to identify fundamental principles that are implicit in valid knowledge. Kant wanted to find invariable and unalterable truths that could not be affected by time and change. If Kant wanted to secure fixed, uniform, permanent, absolute, universal truths in his static vision of the world, the notion of the simulacra depicts an ever-changing, dynamic, pulsating, chaotic world that is always in a state of flux. Within the context of the simulacra, metaphysics and its concomitant representational thinking are dead. This static realm of the same and similar is replaced by the dynamics of the simulacra, which represents a radical form of difference. Overall, the notion of the simulacra challenges and problematizes rationality.

Past Dialogical Summary

Toward the end of the first chapter of this book, we referred to the work of Magliola and his argument that there are significant similarities between the philosophy of a postmodernist like Derrida and a Buddhist thinker like Nāgārjuna and Zen philosophers. Magliola perceives a connection between Nāgārjuna's notion of emptiness and Derrida's notion of the trace, a direct equivalence between Derrida's *différance* and emptiness, and his use of the term logocentric with Zen Buddhism represents a misunderstanding of Zen philosophy. Unable to adhere to the stress upon difference by most postmodern thinkers, Magliola appears to emphasis the similarities between Zen philosophy and Derrida. Although there are certainly many similarities between Buddhist philosophy and forms of postmodern philosophy as evident by our previous discussions, the differences are ultimately more significant. Many postmodern thinkers manifest evidence of moving in the direction of Zen, but there is always a point at which they become captives of their own radical skepticism and/or language games.

The differences between the postmodern perspective and Zen Buddhism are evident in the first chapter discussion of the gaze and a work of art. Lacan calls attention to a split between the eye itself and the gaze, Bataille grasps the eye as an erotic entity, Foucault understands the eye as an instrument of power, and Derrida claims that the gazing eye, which is devoid of essence, sees the seeing, but it does not see what is visible or nothing. These various postmodern ways of approaching the eye and gazing are very different from Dōgen's intuitive perception because the postmodernists are more concerned with the eye as a physical object or bodily organ, whereas Dōgen discusses not-seeing, a seeing without a subject or an object. Dōgen's understanding of seeing is nondual, which is lacking subject or object, or when grounded in itself manifests not-seeing for Nishitani. Instead of the emergence of truth discovered by Heidegger, the alienation between a work of art and an observer discerned by Lyotard and Lacan, the separation created by tracing in the art of drawing for Derrida, the cleaving and disfiguring of Taylor, we get an opportunity to appreciate what it would be like to view a rice cake from a nondualist position like that of Dōgen, and we surprisingly learn that it can satisfy our hunger. The nondualist perspective of Dōgen, Hakuin, and Nishitani represents a very distinct perspective from that of our postmodern thinkers.

This distinct perspective of Dōgen is evident with respect to the topic of language, even though he agrees with Derrida that words have no intrinsic denotative power, a sign possesses an alien nature, a text and language are impermanent, and language possesses no lasting structure. These points of agreement are overshadowed by Derrida's dualist view of a text, whereas Dōgen emphasizes that a text cannot be distinguished from the teacher. Nonetheless, Ch'an masters agree with the spirit of Derrida's use of naming, erasure, and repetition, an aspect of iteration that blurs, undermines, and dislocates an utterance. These features of language disrupt the mind and serve as an obstacle to rationality. Derrida also shares with the Ch'an masters an attitude toward interpersonal dialogue that understands it as a ludic activity within the context of a language game that is spontaneous and devoid of meaning, which for the postmodern philosopher represents a play of differences and a perversion that is a subversion. The Ch'an masters use language in a performative way, which like the example of the kōan makes something happen, distinguishes it from Derrida, although the postmodern thinker can appreciate the decentering function of the kōan and the openness of the Zen use of language devoid of any fixed metaphysical center. Derrida disagrees, however, with the unstated premise of the kōan that there is a deeper meaning to be discovered in the sense that a kōan points to a deeper experience of human existence. The Ch'an masters and Derrida agree, however, that silence possesses profound significance because it takes us to the limits of philosophy, liberates one from normal discourse, and avoids the danger presented by words that can lead one astray from the truth. Finally, Dōgen and Derrida agree that words cannot represent reality, but they disagree about whether or not words can produce reality. But the greatest difference between Derrida and Dōgen is that the latter understands language in a nondualistic manner.

Besides the differences witnessed with respect to language between Dōgen and the postmodernist, there are also significant distinctions to be drawn based on the problem of the body. Derrida views the body as a deprivation because the other steals it from me, whereas the body is a connection of physical forces for Levinas. Kristeva attempts to grasp the significance of the body from within the context of her theory of abjection where it experiences itself as a waste. She insightfully focuses on the borders of the body where defiling items and fluids are expelled and allow one to live. In contrast to Kristeva, Deleuze refers to the schizophrenic body that is similar to a body-sieve. Proceeding in a direction where the postmodernists would never tread, Dōgen claims that the body is both subject and object, and that the body and mind represent the entire world, which implies that we are never separated from the world. The only postmodernist in harmony with Dōgen on this point is Kristeva who agrees that it is difficult to exactly determine the boundaries of the body and the world. According to Merleau-Ponty, the body, an author of space, is our vehicle for being in the world which necessarily involves us in a definite environment, whereas Kristeva asserts that the body discovers itself as marginal due to its abject condition within space. In contrast to the condition of abjection, Levinas thinks that the position of the body is revealed by groping, and Foucault views the body within the context of power relations. Deleuze and Guattari understand the body as a complex interplay of social and symbolic forces that is devoid of ontological distinctions with all bodies functioning as causes. These diverse perspectives are distinct from the agreement of Dōgen and Merleau-Ponty who agree that the body includes time and space as it participates in the external world in such a way that the body, mind, and things of the world interpenetrate. Dōgen and Merleau-Ponty also agree that the body is dynamic, and Levinas agrees with them that there is no duality between the lived body and the physical body, a physical entity that allows us to take hold of the world. Rather than emphasizing the interrelational nature of the body, Taylor asserts that the body betrays us because of disease, and he disputes the unity perceived by Dōgen because of the internal attacks by organisms from within the body. In contrast to Taylor's vision of attacks upon the body from within it, Foucault depicts the body as subject to external danger and sees the interrelation between the body and world differently from Dōgen and Merleau-Ponty because of his political perspective that enables him to view it as a relay system for the deployment of sexuality. Deleuze and Guattari admit that the body is difficult to situate because it represents an arbitrary relationship of forces. This is emphasized even more by the body without organs, according to Deleuze and Guattari, that is a nonproductive, imageless, smooth surface, and without depth or internal organization. Such a body is antihierarchical because it is a process of intersecting forces that represent transitory, mobile, and changing spatio-temporal variables.

Some basic differences between Dōgen and the postmodernists appear when the relationship between the body and consciousness, and the body and perception are considered. Merleau-Ponty argues that the body and consciousness are interrelated because consciousness is dependent on the body and functions as a mediator of consciousness and world, and Dōgen agrees with him that consciousness is incarnate because the body participates in one's inner world. Although Lyotard agrees with Dōgen and Merleau-Ponty that consciousness is incarnate, Lyotard differs from them because he thinks that it is important to discuss gender differences that mark the body with transcendence. In contrast to Merleau-

Ponty and Lyotard, Dōgen wants to go beyond their intentional mode of thinking to non-thinking, which is more fundamental than the prereflective consciousness of Merleau-Ponty. Distinct from the position of Merleau-Ponty, Taylor thinks that the unconscious and body are structured like a language, and Kristeva, who is also influenced by Lacan, tends to agree, although she traces the trail of the signifier through the body in the form of presymbolic imagery by tracing the semiotic body, an autoerotic, preoedipal body. In contrast to Kristeva's method, Taylor traces the architecture of the body that manifests itself best when the body breaks down, an approach that presupposes that the body is structured like a communications system. For Dōgen, the body is the ground from which consciousness evolves, they penetrate each other, and are nondual, a direction to which Merleau-Ponty moves with his concept of the body but not a path followed by any postmodernists. In contrast to Dōgen, Deleuze and Guattari argue instead that the notion of grounding forms a surface for desire. Since the body presupposes a theory of perception, Merleau-Ponty and Dōgen agree that perception is embodied, whereas Kristeva stresses the abject nature of an object that stands opposed to me, disturbs me, and makes me feel uncanny. Dōgen disagrees with Kristeva when he states that the body actualizes itself and achieves a preestablished harmony.

According to Merleau-Ponty, the body unites time by dwelling within it, and Dōgen agrees with the phenomenologist, but the Zen philosopher understands the relationship between the body and time in a stronger sense by affirming that the body and mind are time. Time becomes an opportunity for creativity and transformation for Dōgen, while temporality possesses a similar ecstatic character for Merleau-Ponty. Moreover, Dōgen is sympathetic to Merleau-Ponty's position that there is no separation between oneself and others and the unity of time and being. In contrast to Dōgen and Merleau-Ponty on the subject of the encounter with other bodies, Derrida views the body in such an encounter as stolen, Foucault perceives it in terms of biopolitics, and Kristeva grasps the encounter by means of abjection. Deleuze and Guattari describe the body without organs as a surface on which intensities flow and circulate within a field of becomings and become something in this process. These bodies without organs are always dynamic, particular, and represent a field of production. The common link among postmodernists is the notion of altarity. Within the context of their consideration of time, Dōgen and Merleau-Ponty radically temporalize being, oppose a quantitative view of time, understand time as a lived reality, and propose a nondualistic equation of being, body, and time, although Merleau-Ponty disagrees with Dōgen's nondualistic assertion that things and events are time. In spite of this disagreement, Merleau-Ponty and Dōgen agree on the metaphor of bodily wholeness, whereas the more strictly postmodern thinkers view the body in such a way that it becomes a metaphor of marginality. Deleuze asserts, for instance, that the body is constituted by various desiring-machines, forming a unifying whole that represents something added to the parts.

The postmodern emphasis on marginality and lack of bodily wholeness can also be seen in their varied discussions about the self and the other. Since the self is not present as itself and cannot become present to itself, Derrida denies the privileged position of presence for the self because it occurs within a system of difference, rendering the self nothing but a trace. Likewise, the self is radically temporal for Taylor, which results in the momentary presence of the self. As a unity of identity and difference, presence and absence, the self possesses a synthetic identity. Lacking an enduring identity, the self, which is devoid of a definite presence, is disrupted and dislocated for Taylor, whereas Levinas locates the identity of the self in ipseity, a nonpresence before itself and in itself. Levinas' self is otherwise than being, which stresses its subjective nature, and it is also chosen and unique. The presence of the self is also evident in the works of Lacan and Kristeva where the self is depicted as not completely present to its own consciousness, which means that the self is alienating and alienated and possesses an illusory identity. Kristeva emphasizes that the self, which lacks a fundamental permanence, presence, or identity, is always splitting apart, resulting in a heterogenous and decentered self. In contrast to these postmodern thinkers, Dōgen indicates that a position taken by such thinkers as Lacan and Kristeva is indicative of someone superimposing psychological categories on the self, whereas Derrida and Taylor superimpose patterns of thinking that are alien to the true nature of the self. From Dōgen's perspective, the postmodernists manipulate experience, even though he agrees with the postmodernists that the self possesses no permanence or enduring presence because of its impermanent nature. Dōgen conceives of the self as concrete because it represents the immediacy of experience, but it is not something that we can possess. Due to the notion of emptiness, Nishitani rejects the postmodern distinction between categories like presense and absence. Nishitani equates the self with emptiness, and he disagrees with the postmodernists when they claim that the self cannot know itself because it cannot only know itself for Nishitani but it also knows objects in the world. According to Nishitani, self-awareness is a nexus at which the self and knowledge are emptied, although this self-awareness is a nonknowing that represents the self as nonobjective. Overall, Dōgen and Nishitani share the postmodernists' rejection of the metaphysics of presence.

The lack of presence of the self among postmodern thinkers also implies that the self lacks a center. Influenced by Derrida's deconstruction of the center, Taylor depicts the self within a context of a fluctuating network of relation, which suggests that it lacks independence and the power of knowing. Since the self is a mere transitory intersection for a plethora of relationships, its relationships undermine its autonomous nature, which results in a corelative, codependent, decentered self that is marginal and a mere trace. This marginal trace is a faceless, errant, trickster, thief, and liminal being. Agreeing in part with Taylor's conception of the self, Lacan perceives a fundamental alienation within the self that is split between the subject and ego in a psychological scenario in which the self loses its real identity in the unconscious. Kristeva explains the decentered nature of the self a bit differently than the other postmodernists because she sees rejection involved in the process of decentering and the subsequent destruction of presence. Kristeva's self is continually generated and negated by the *chora*, a repetitive process that creates discontinuities and ruptures, creating a separation of the self from objects and eventual absence of the self. In a similar fashion, Deleuze writes about a self that is always changing and fragmentary, which makes it difficult for the self to have a coherent identity. In contrast to the previous mentioned postmodernists, Levinas does not agree that the self cannot attain presence, although he does agree that the self is decentered. The self for Levinas represents one's primary identity that endures over time, but it is not completely autonomous because it is also the other. Since the self dwells with others, needs them, and realizes its identity with others, the self is constantly disrupted and decentered by the others within the context of a double movement of encountering and relating to the others.

In sharp contrast to the decentered nature of the self for the postmodernists, Nishitani thinks that the center is everywhere within the context of emptiness. Although Nishitani and Derrida agree that a true center is not a center, they disagree about whether or not this undermines the autonomy of the self. And since genuine selfhood involves restoration of an original unity for Dōgen, he is critical of Lacan and Kristeva for imposing a subjective theoretical structure on the experience of the subject that results in a false split between subject and object. Dōgen and

Nishitani agree, however, with Levinas that the self represents one's primary identity, but they do not agree that the self remains the same and that the other is responsible for decentering the self.

There is a confidence in the philosophy of Dōgen with respect to the self that is lacking in the philosophies of the postmodernists because he is convinced that *zazen* (seated meditation) authenticates the self and helps one overcome egoism. In contrast to the *zazen* advocated by Dōgen, the process of kenosis empties the self of intrinsic particularity for Taylor, and it renders the self faceless, without identity, nonpresent, acentric, and anonymous, which represents the disappearance of the self, whereas *zazen* is the realization and authentification of selfhood and disappearance of egoism. The major difference between kenosis and *zazen* is intention because Dōgen's method is intentionless in the sense that it is not thoughtout or contrived. From the perspective of Levinas, it is exposure to the other that helps the self over its egoistic tendencies by enabling us to acknowledge our resemblance to the other for whom the self is morally and ethically responsible.

Derrida disagrees with Levinas when he argues that the self and other do not represent a conceptual totality because the other, which is always located on the margin, never loses its exteriority and cannot be interiorized. For Deleuze, the other is the I as fractured, and creates a field of perception that guarantees individuation within the world. Kristeva also emphasizes the difference between the self and other especially when she stresses that the other is a stranger. Agreeing with this line of thinking, Dōgen and Nishitani think that the authentic self is a self for others within the context of a web of responsibility. In fact, Kristeva is closer to the spirit of the position of the Zen thinkers when she asserts that we are strangers within ourselves due to our divided interior natures. Derrida refines the notion of altarity when he refers to a double altarity: body and other. The latter is inscribed in the first for Derrida, whereas Dōgen playfully responds that there is no distinction in the Buddha-nature and the face of the other.

The significance of the face is an aspect of the other that is missed by Derrida and Lacan, according to Levinas for whom it is an ethical epiphany. Derrida charges that the face represents presence, whereas Nishitani equates the face with absolute nothingness, rendering the face nondual as it is for Dōgen. Since the face is grounded in emptiness and every face represents that of the Buddha, the face, for Dōgen, is really no-face. With respect to the face or no-face of the self and other, the discussion of such features as presence and absence, decentering, kenosis, and *zazen* are examples of the attempt to overcome the essentialism that is often associated with the representational mode of thinking. The post-modernists appear to suggest that the disunity of the self makes representational or any other kind of thinking that presupposes a centered, stable, or permanent self very difficult if not impossible.

However one defines the relationship between the self and other in the final analysis, the Zen philosophers and postmodernists agree that they encounter each other within the flux of temporality, although time itself is often defined differently by the various thinkers. The three ecstases of time identified by Heidegger that coexist in the present moment signify a unity of temporality, a process that is intrinsically ecstatic. There is no such unity of time for Deleuze, who replaces Heidegger's three ecstases of time with his own threefold passive syntheses of time in which an asymmetrical present is constituted by past and future. Dōgen agrees with Heidegger that we cannot be separated from time. In fact, we are nondualistically time for Dōgen, whereas Heidegger affirms that we exist in time. In contrast to the German phenomenologist, Nishitani states that we do not simply live in time, but we live time more accurately. Nonetheless, Dōgen, Nishitani, and Heidegger do agree that time is indicative of our relations with others.

Levinas also concurs that we need to include the other when considering time, which is a relational phenomenon. This emphasis by Levinas suggests necessarily that he rejects the concept of time in the philosophies of Heidegger and Dōgen because the relationship with others in their philosophies is not a face-to-face relationship. Moreover, Levinas discards the three ecstases of time identified by Heidegger because the subject becomes absorbed in the object and recovers unity, which results in the disappearance of the other. The treatment of time by Dōgen, Heidegger, and Levinas gives the distinct appearance of being a metaphysical concept for Derrida against which he counters with the notion of the trace, a simultaneous presence and absence. The trace of Derrida subverts the present and presence associated with the notion of time. From Derrida's perspective, it is impossible to have a self-identical now moment and self-contained subjectivity because the now-moment must point to other moments beyond itself in order to be itself. A similar type of subverting of time takes place in Taylor's thought with respect to the work of the eternal return that subverts the opposition between time and eternity, and since the present includes absence, it can never become fully present. With respect to the past moment, Derrida states that it cannot be conceived as itself because the past is a repetition of past presence which renders it different from any present moment, whereas the future is present in experience. In reply to Derrida and Taylor, Dōgen argues that each moment is complete in itself and cannot be subverted because each moment embodies a multitude of simultaneous perspectives. If Derrida and Taylor suggest that the impermanent nature of time is something negative, Nishitani turns its impermanence into something positive because the ever impermanent instant of time emphasizes the perpetual newness of time, which then becomes a field of limitless possibility. This also implies that time becomes a burden because it condemns us to be incessantly active.

Since time is determined by Being and it in turn is determined by time for Heidegger, the presence of time is not reducible to any present moment. In contrast to Heidegger, a different relationship between time and being is evident in Dōgen's philosophy because being and time form a union for the Zen philosopher, but neither being nor time is more fundamental. It is the now-moment (*nikon*) that represents the complete spontaneous presencing of being-time, representing a continuity of time in which past and future exist in the immediate moment. Disagreeing with the ontological stance of both Heidegger and Dōgen, Deleuze views being within the context of the simulacrum, which implies that there is no resemblance of time to ontology or space.

Dōgen and Heidegger agree that time is both temporal and spatial, and they concur that time represents a unity, which suggests that time and existence are not independent. They also agree that time is not reductionistic, nonobjective, and at the basis of all human activity. Dōgen radicalizes time by stating that everything is time, which in part means for him that space and time are inseparably interconnected and interpenetrate, a philosophical position with which Nishitani concurs. Dōgen and Heidegger also disagree about whether or not temporality is limited to human experience and the Zen master's nondualistic grasp of time. And they differ over Heidegger's stress upon the future and Dōgen's emphasis on the present moment, because the latter does not think that we can understand the future because it has not arrived. Deleuze rejects Heidegger and Dōgen when he stresses the ever-changing nature of the present and the nature of repetition, an unfolding of time itself in its pure and empty form. The present is continually being subverted by the instant, which itself constantly divides into past and future. The union of time and being for the Zen philosopher is rejected by Deleuze because he equates being with difference and Being with repetition, a philosophical scenario that is not conducive with an enduring identity. Within the context of his stance against representational thinking, Deleuze thinks that time and being are radically relative, lacking ground, without depth, devoid of identity, and free of universality.

Dōgen, Heidegger, and Nishitani are criticized by Derrida for promoting a metaphysics of presence or logocentrism because it is not possible for us to have access to such a transcendental signified due to our captivity within a field of signs. As an alternative to their concepts of time, Derrida offers the notion of *différance*, which embodies a spatiotemporal significance, although it precedes time conceived as presence. Moreover, the notion of *différance* calls the distinction between Being and beings into question. Dōgen replies to Derrida that being-time and presencing of Buddha-nature represents a leap of thinking, and the Zen philosopher concurs that Derrida appears to be engaged in an exercise of self-stultification. From the perspective of Derrida, the notion of being-time in Dōgen's philosophy appears to represent sameness, whereas the Zen master replies to such criticism by affirming that Being is impermanent, although they agree that being-time is not transcendental. Dōgen and Derrida disagree over the interconnection of space and time because for the latter space designates nothing and cannot be involved in identity, whereas Dōgen and Nishitani think that identity is necessary and inevitable because everything is empty, which implies that identity embodies a synchronic aspect (identity in the now moment) and a diachronic element (continuity over a period of time).

The emphasis on the present moment (*nikon*) by Dōgen and Nishitani is shared by Levinas, although Lyotard disagrees with Levinas on the instant and its presence. Lyotard argues that the present is something that cannot be grasped due to its paradoxical nature of being not yet and no longer present, which also makes the emphasis on the now moment by Dōgen and Nishitani unacceptable due to the paradoxical nature of the present moment. From another perspective, Levinas rejects the importance of the past and future in favor of the instant that is evanescent. This position places Levinas in conflict with Dōgen's notion of totalistic passage (*kyōryaku*) and with Deleuze's emphasis on the past. Deleuze argues that the past represents the foundation of time because it synthesizes the present and future within itself.

With respect to the experience of time, we also find different approaches for explaining it. The notion of *Ereignis*, an event of appropriation through which a person and Being reach each other, makes possible any occurrence. Although in the process of appropriating and rendering it present, Being withdraws for Heidegger. Agreeing with Heidegger that we experience neither time nor being in themselves, Dōgen states that we experience temporal existence just as it is, and we encounter a stream of ever-changing phenomena. If we do not superimpose anything upon it, we will experience an unending experience of flux and realize that nothing can be experienced independently of time or change, a line of thinking with which Derrida and Taylor concur. According to Derrida, iterability reveals, for instance, constant change and also promotes it. From another perspective, Levinas discusses the experience of time as the event of the there is (*il y a*) in which the "there is" represents a location where hypostasis is produced, which manifests an event of the present, representing a new beginning, a tearing apart, and joining together. Along similar lines of thinking, Nishitani refers to a revelation of time that is an infinite openness at the basis of an actual presence. Nishitani thinks that each instant simultaneously embodies past and future in contrast to Levinas' instant that is devoid of past and future. From a different perspective, Deleuze thinks that an event is not an occurrence in the present; it is rather past and future oriented. If one conceives of repetition as an event, it disappears even as it occurs because it totally lacks an in-itself dimension, and its vanishing tendency renders it unthinkable and incomplete. And since the notion of repetition suggests that something new can only be produced by means of repetition appearing as difference, this necessarily implies that we can not experience an event as it is or directly. Overall, the emphasis on the radical relativity of time by most postmodernists undermines any permanent personal identity. By subverting any definitive identity for a person, any opportunity to engage in representational thinking becomes extremely difficult.

In contrast to Dōgen and Heidegger, there is a tendency among some postmodernists to use provocative rhetoric with respect to the topic of death that suggests a process of deification. Heidegger's phenomenological analysis of death, which is characterized by mineness, completes the totality of the existence of *Dasein* by binding it together. Dōgen agrees with Heidegger that death is mine, if the Zen philosopher's position is understood in a nonegoistic manner. Derrida agrees with Heidegger and Dōgen that death is mine in the sense that it is irreplaceable. Unlike Heidegger and Dōgen, Derrida interprets mineness to mean the death of the other in me. Derrida disputes Heidegger's contention that

Dasein is a being-towards-the-end because he insists that one can perish, whereas Heidegger thinks that humans die but animals perish. Although Derrida does not think that a being aims at death within the context of his interpretation of Heidegger's position on death, he does agree with Heidegger about anticipating death, whereas Levinas says that we do not anticipate death because we try to postpone it by means of the Other who gives one time.

Death represents an unforeseeable character for Levinas because it is not within any encounterable horizon. In response to this position, Dōgen and Heidegger think that death is not an external power because it is co-present with life, and it is wrong to conceive of death as a termination of life because it is present in the here and now. Levinas replies to Dōgen and Heidegger that time represents an interval that separates me from my death. If death is a future event for Levinas, it is already here for Dōgen and Heidegger. In contrast to these thinkers, Derrida states that death is repetitive in the sense that its potentiality is dependent on the possibility of the absence of the repeated and manifests the potential for self-duplication. Since death repeats by redoubling itself for Derrida, it cannot be truly represented and yet is the condition for all representation.

Contrary to Heidegger's assertion that death is *Dasein's* own most potentiality-for-being, Levinas claims that it represents the impossibility of all possibilities and not the ultimate possibility of existence, whereas Heidegger and Dōgen think that Levinas is wrong to view death as an alien power. On the other hand, Derrida thinks that death is both possibility and impossibility. Derrida wants to introduce the notion of the possible into an existential analysis of death and to view it as the ultimate possibility. In contrast to Derrida, Dōgen does not think that life and death are relative to each other.

Dōgen and Heidegger suggest that we eventually encounter death, but Derrida disagrees that it is ever possible to encounter death. Again, Heidegger and Dōgen agree that it is inauthentic to view death as the terminal point of life, death is a total dynamism, which suggests that it does not impede life. This implies that death is a way to be, a way characterized by facing death and abiding in it. Derrida's approach to the subject of death means for him that death will be borderless, a neutral politics of death will be possible, and a place will be created for mourning. From the perspective of Derrida, Dōgen and Heidegger imply that death is an event that isolates an individual, whereas Derrida views death as a unifying factor. In defense of their positions, Heidegger states that *Dasein* is a being with others-unto-death, and Dōgen asserts that we must not consider death as either isolating or unifying because life and death together represent the actual appearance of truth.

Even though it is possible to find some common ground between the Zen and postmodern philosophers on such topics as language, the body, the self and other, time, and death, the sharpest distinction between them comes with the different modes of thinking that each side represents. Dōgen and the various representatives of postmodernism agree, however, about their opposition to a representational mode of thinking, agree that it is wrong to make thinking into an object for study, and agree that it is best to grasp thinking as a way or a path that one must follow, although there is considerable difference about the exact nature of this path of thinking.

Heidegger observes that what is most thought-provoking is that which one is still not thinking, and that which must be thought withdraws from us from the very beginning of the process of thinking and draws us along with it, whereas Dōgen does not think that it is possible for Buddha-nature, which is manifest, concealed, and evades the grip of knowledge, to turn away from us because it is continuously arriving. The path of thinking envisioned by Dōgen is not a matter of accumulating knowledge, but it is rather a way of unlearning that extricates one from preconceptions. Heidegger agrees with the spirit of Dōgen's path of thinking in the sense that we must learn anew the nature of thinking, but he does not think that it is possible to completely free ourselves of our preconceptions. If Heidegger wants to think that which withdraws from us and Dōgen advocates thinking the Buddha-nature, Derrida wants to think that which is prior to the ground of the unthought, which he thinks his notion of *désistance* is designed to explore by examining the structure of subjectivity within a double movement of negation. Being strongly opposed to a representational mode of thinking that is shaped by presence, Derrida wants to utilize *désistance* to see what occurs before the subject can reflect on anything. Along a similar path, Taylor wants to think the not, which involves a radical altarity, that is prior to thought itself and falls between being and nonbeing. Along with the philosophers already mentioned, Lyotard also wants to undermine representational thinking by offering a critique of rationality that subverts its effort to create unity and totalization by noting that rationality cannot think the altarity of an object because it can only think its object as represented in language. Moreover, rationality is blind to the connection between power and knowledge. Deleuze does not disagree with Lyotard about the limits of rationality, although the former wants to create ever new, singular concepts, which are paradoxically relative and absolute and composed of heterogeneous components. Like some postmodern philosophers, Deleuze wants to think difference by affirming the surface or planes as constitutions of a fluxuating series. Thus, the concepts of Deleuze are concrete, without depth, and populate a plane that continuously links them together. Deleuze's rejection of transcendence places his philosophy in opposition to Heidegger and Dōgen. If Dōgen embraces both immanence and transcendence, and if Heidegger thinks in terms of the ground of being, Deleuze wants to think difference by thinking from the surface, an aspect that now becomes primary rather than a secondary mode of focus by the philosopher.

Not only do Dōgen and Heidegger agree that thinking is a way, they also concur that before one can arrive successfully at one's destination it is necessary to cast off all prior thought and concepts in order to discover the ground of one's own self, although they differ over the direction of the way because Dōgen views the way as a radical, backward movement. Lyotard conceives of the way as a path of removal and discomfort, Taylor views it as a wandering path that leads one astray, Derrida refers to the rhythm of *désistance* that constitutes and deconstitutes us and collects and divides us, whereas Dōgen argues that everything is firmly grounded in Buddha-nature, which suggests that we wander in Buddha-nature, and we wander by means of Buddha-nature as we seek for our Buddha-nature. The path to the realization of one's Buddha-nature is connected to a call to enlightenment that is aroused by an awareness of impermanence. Dōgen and Heidegger agree that the call is unending and that the sound of the call makes no noise. Heidegger understands that the call originates with Being and that calls a person unto Being, to think, and into presence. Thus Heidegger grasps the call of Being as a call to arrival and presence, although other postmodern philosophers reject the notion of presence. Lyotard envisions the call of thinking as something sensitive and responsive, and Derrida views *désistance* as ineluctable and as something that previously happened, whereas Dōgen emphasizes presentness of the call that places his thought in sharp contrast with the emphasis on repetition by Deleuze that appears as a difference without conceptual content.

If thinking for Deleuze is a way of creating connections among a multiplicity of impersonal forces that is characterized by change, transformation, becoming, the coexistence of planes, and a movement without spatiotemporal coordinates, this ever-receding horizon in motion is very different from the non-thinking mode of Dōgen, which is object-less, subjectless, formless, and goalless. The non-thinking mode unites and sublates thinking and not-thinking. Heidegger and other postmod-ern philosophers move in a direction similar to Dōgen, but their philosophies never quite arrive at the same destination. Lyotard refers to the necessity of emptying the mind in order to think, suggesting sus-pending rules and being receptive. According to Derrida, *désistance* marks a rupture in thinking that departs from normal modes of thinking. Although this appears to take Derrida in the direction of Dōgen, the postmodernist is distinguished from the philosophy of the Zen master by his obsession with difference and his acknowledgment that *désis-tance* gives birth to insanity or the irrational, whereas Dōgen asserts that non-thinking encompasses all rationality and irrationality, sanity and insanity. Even if Taylor is correct to indicate that thinking of not is the negation implied in all thinking, the postmodern philosophers are still as a group unable to make the transition to an objectless, formless, and subjectless mode of thinking. Heidegger is the single philosopher that moves closest to the position of Dōgen by his attempt to transcend the subject-object dichotomy, although he and the other postmodernists do not arrive at a nondualistic position. If Dōgen and Heidegger move towards openness, mystery, emptiness, and unification, the postmod-ernists move toward difference in their distinct ways, although all the philosophers agree about overcoming representational thinking. The postmodern path toward difference leads them to various forms of rad-ical skepticism that includes the genealogy of Foucault, deconstruction of Derrida, schizoanalysis of Deleuze and Guattari, and the semanaly-sis of Kristeva.

The diagnostic approach of Foucault's genealogy explores patterns, traces developments, and sketches values in transition. In contrast to Hakuin, the present moment is called into question by Foucault's method by rendering its apparent truths problematic, and Foucault himself becomes a victim of the dualities in which he finds himself from the Zen perspective. Attempting to complete the work begun by Heidegger to deconstruct the presence of the present, Derrida's notion of deconstruc-tion functions in a parasitic manner that is antidialectical and subverts preexisting structures. Derrida's use of deconstruction enables him to share several common features with Zen thinkers: subordination of ratio-nality to spontaneity; criticism of subjectively based philosophy due to the impermanence of the subject; conceptual categories are impossible due to a lack of permanence; deconstruction is akin in spirit to non-thinking in Zen in the sense that they both displace human constructs; both do not attempt to deal with other things or events in an objective way; and Derrida and Dōgen are both concerned with gaps, blank spaces, and pauses. Nonetheless, Derrida's method is still dependent upon texts, an object with a subject performing the deconstruction.

Another postmodern method that tends to be destructive is the potentially revolutionary exercise of schizoanalysis by Deleuze and Guattari that they direct at capitalism and psychoanalysis in their attempt to liberate desire and to discover the nature and function of the desiring-machine in the subject and to recognize the social machines that form the context for the individual desiring-machines. Deleuze and Guattari share with Hakuin an opposition to a philosophy of subjectivity, even though the reasons are different for each party. From their unwillingness to accept anything like the possibility of the Buddha-nature, Deleuze and Guatttari are unable to liberate themselves from a dependence on categories from the perspective of Hakuin, which results in a tendency for the directness and immediacy of their experience to become obstructed. And if the method of semanalysis for Kristeva is a combination of psychoanalysis and semiology, Hakuin thinks that the concept of semiotics is inconsistent because of its claim about a lack of a teleology. Moreover, Hakuin cannot accept Kristeva's claim that symbols are restrictive except in a limited contextual sense. Overall, Hakuin's grasp of doubt as a liberating power stands in sharp contrast to the radical skepticism of the postmodern methods, which simply lead to further skepticism. In contrast to the postmodern thinkers, Hakuin views the purpose of doubt as an attempt to gain absolute certainty that is self-authenticating and self-verifiable, a position that is at odds with the skepticism of the postmodern philosophers.

There is a common link between the radical skepticism of some postmodern philosophers and the Zen use of the kōan with respect to undermining representational thinking. It is questionable, however, from Hakuin's Zen perspective whether the doubt embodied in the skepticism of some postmodern philosophers is actually liberating or whether it represents a substitution of a radical form of skepticism for the representational mode of thinking. We have called attention to the shared opposition by postmodernists and representatives of Zen philosophy to the representational mode of thinking, but the former party cannot totally free themselves from a dualistic way of thinking.

Results of Dialogue for Representational Thinking

It is evident from the results of the dialogue of this book that the Zen thinkers like Hakuin, Dōgen, and Nishitani have no intention of being captive to the representational mode of thinking, which assumes a correspondence between appearance and reality and is supported by a metaphysical edifice. Long before the advent of the philosophies of these Zen thinkers in Japan, the early Zen/Ch'an tradition rejected the representational mode of thinking as evident by the narrative of *The Platform Sūtra of the Sixth Patriarch*.

This well-known text tells the story of Hui-neng, who becomes the Sixth Patriarch after proving his preparation and worthiness by writing a poetic verse that authenticates his state of enlightenment for Hung-jen, the Fifth Patriarch and initiator of the contest. As part of the contest devised by the Fifth Patriarch to help him choose his successor, the head monk named Shen-hsiu composes a verse on a wall in the monastery at midnight in response to the challenge of the Fifth Patriarch that contains in part the following verse: "The mind is like a clear mirror."[19] The aspiring successor of the Fifth Patriarch depicts the mind as a mirror that is akin to something passive, inert, and must be continuously wiped clean of the metaphorical dust that represents the obscurities and passions aroused by desires, images, and thoughts. From his written verses, it is clear that Shen-hsiu is convinced that meditation involves purifying the mind and restoring it to its original purity. Even though the Fifth Patriarch thinks that the verses of Shen-hsiu have some utility, they are not evidence of genuine understanding or enlightenment because the verses reflect a grasp of the mind functioning in a representational manner. Due to his alleged illiterate nature, Hui-neng asks a boy to write on the south wall of the monastery the verse that he dictates to the youth. The verses recited by Hui-neng represent a rejection of the metaphor used by Shen-hsiu, that is, the mind is a mirror.

The mirror metaphor is indicative of a reflected image of consciousness and a confusing of the representation and original consciousness. Thus, the metaphor of the mirror for the mind fails to represent consciousness itself and uncritically assumes that the mind can be represented, an impossible possibility. Hui-neng, winner of the verse-writing contest, is more insightful and iconoclastic in the sense that he breaks away from the metaphor of the mirror by affirming that the mind or original consciousness cannot even be originally presented.[20] In a sense, Hui-neng receives the transmission of authority from the Fifth Patriarch because his verses represented a lucid rejection of the representational mode of thinking.

Like Hui-neng of the Ch'an/Zen tradition, many postmodernists want to reject the representational mode of thinking and discover new paradigms that are devoid of any metaphysical position and coherence theory of truth. We can find evidence of this in their grasp of perception, intention, rationality, metaphysics and opposition to any unity of thinking. This evidence will serve as further proof of their attack on the representational mode of thinking, which they share with Zen philosophy, but it will also further confirm the differences between postmodern philosophy and Zen.

If the phenomenological method, for instance, presupposes a subject who perceives an object and is able to describe that perception in an attempt to discern its structure or essence, this philosophical method suggests a metaphysical position and likely a coherence theory of truth. According to Deleuze's interpretation of his thought, Foucault gives primacy to fields of statements over the perceptual emphasis of phenomenology, and he breaks with phenomenology over the issue of intentionality because Foucault does not think that consciousness is directed towards things. Deleuze understands Foucault's major achievement to be "the conversion of phenomenology into epistemology."[21] Since there is nothing prior to or beneath it according to Foucault, everything is knowledge. Thus, if a philosopher seeks structures or essences, Foucault and other postmodernists think that this is an impossible quest.

Regardless of Foucault's criticism of intentionality for the method of phenomenology, intentionality helps to explain for Edmund Husserl how the objects of thinking are given structure. If for Husserl consciousness is always conscious of something, thinking necessarily entails an object that one thinks about and structures that which one thinks. This implies that the real is that which is intended. Unlike Foucault, Derrida attacks the notion of intentionality at both its source and *telos* or goal. Derrida argues that intention can never achieve its goal because it can never be totally fulfilled and never totally present to its object and to itself. The reason that it can never achieve its goal is because "It is divided and departed in advance, by its iterability, towards others, removed [*écartée*] in advance from itself."[22] Unable to realize its goal, intentionality is limited, moreover, in the sense of its being conscious or present to itself. Besides limitation, iteration introduces into intentionality from its inception a dehiscence, which also limits its possibilities, and a cleft.[23] In summary, iterability corrupts, contaminates parasitically, dislocates, subverts, and displaces intentionality and thus renders it impossible to realize.

Besides such philosophical issues as perception and intentionality, postmodern thinkers tend to challenge the role of reason in Enlightenment philosophy. Lyotard, for instance, makes a distinction between a rationalist and postrationalist path by drawing out their political consequences. Lyotard wants to save reason and to free it and knowledge, which is nothing more than a product to be sold, from the bondage of capitalist authorities. He wants reason to regain its practical use and to shift toward the plural, the indeterminate, the random, the irregular, and the formless in order to become more sensitive to differences and to assist us to cope with the incommensurable.[24] In sympathy with the thrust of Lyotard's leftist criticism of reason, Foucault attempts to show the power of reason to hide unreason (insanity) and to use it as a weapon in the construction of social normativity and the development of social conformity to the dominant social power. In place of reason, Deleuze and Guattari advocate desire, which is an antirational force, that can produce reality and is a life-affirming power. Kristeva undermines Kantian rationality by emphasizing abjection as a form of suffering that disturbs identity and order, which is not a suitable ground for the order of reason because it results in a marginal being outside the domain of rationality. Motivated by what he perceives to be an opacity embodied within the system of rationality, Derrida wants to investigate what is prior to reason or even thinking, and he finds that the actual possibility of reason cannot be grasped intellectually in accordance with patterns of rational necessity due to the supplemental nature of reason that suggests that the origin of reason must be nonrational, a position that does not take the "non" as a logical negation.[25] Derrida thinks that the Enlightenment conception of reason tends to be self-legitimizing because it takes a single historically and culturally specific notion of reason as its universal standard for all forms of reason, using this single standard in order to judge all competing examples of reason as unreasonable.[26] This type of exclusivistic rationalism, which tends to dominate and demand social conformity along with its concomitant metaphysical posture, is anathema to Derrida. From these sorts of thoughts about reason, one might assume that Zen philosophers and postmodernists are in general agreement about the shortcomings of reason. Although there is some truth to this, it would be a misrepresentation of Zen to draw a simplistic equivalence between the two parties because there is much more at stake in Zen than just a simple attack on the limitations of reason, which can be seen in the philosophy of Dōgen.

In his essay entitled "Kuge" in the *Shōbōgenzō*, Dōgen refers to "flowers in the sky" (*kuge*). From a rational perspective, it does not make much sense to speak of "flowers in the sky" because empirical experience, common sense, and rationality tell us that flowers do not grow in the sky, although the phrase could make sense if one speaks poetically, metaphorically, or symbolically. Yet the phrase "flowers in the sky" makes perfect sense from Dōgen's perspective, which is devoid of a rational and representational way of thinking. This is evident when Dōgen states that Buddhas and Zen adepts ride on "flowers in the sky" and equates these flowers with the worlds and teachings of the Buddhas.[27] Within the context of Japanese Buddhist culture, *kuge* refers to an eye disease, a perceptual condition that hinders one's ability to see things without obstruction or to perceive things in a state of illusion. Dōgen turns *kuge* into something positive by equating it with life, death, and nirvāna. Moreover, regardless of time and place when there is an eye there is "flowers in the eye" that are the same as "flowers in the sky." In this nonrational mode of communicating his point, Dōgen plays with the representational mode of thinking, and he wants to indirectly inform us that everything is illusory because all existence is relative or impermanent and empty of absolutes. Thus, it is not necessary to annihilate illusion because everything is illusion. Since everything is illusory and empty, illusion is identical to absolute reality. Therefore, *kuge* "actualizes itself in our eyes and vice-versa."[28] This suggests that "flowers in the sky" are not nonexistent, not existent, not void, and not substantial; they are, however, equivalent to the Buddhas of the ten directions or the totality of all things. Even though rationality is commonly associated with the representational mode of thinking, what Dōgen does with rationality is very different in its motivation and results when compared with the positions of the various postmodernists, who want to avoid anything that might be associated with metaphysics.

Having already called attention to the various attempts by postmodernists to undermine the Kantian conviction that metaphysics is a natural disposition of the philosophical thinker because of the very nature of reason and its ability to unify the empirical cognitions of understanding, postmodern thinkers want to claim that it is not possible for metaphysics to extend our knowledge of reality as Kant thought possible if its propositions are synthetic and *a priori*. By adhering to the notion of the simulacra, several postmodernists make it clear that it is impossible to cling to the Cartesian ideal of precision and certitude in thinking. And unlike Kant, many of the postmodernists do not think that it is possible to identity fundamental principles that are implicit in valid knowledge. Kant wanted to find invariable and unalterable truths that could not be affected by time and change, but this is too static for postmodern thinkers. If Kant wanted to secure fixed, uniform, permanent, absolute, universal truths in his static vision of the world, the notion of the simulacra depicts an ever-changing, dynamic, pulsating, chaotic world that is always in a state of flux. Within the context of the simulacra, metaphysics and its concomitant representational thinking are dead. This static realm of the same and similar is replaced by the dynamic of the simulacra, which represents a radical form of difference. It is ironical that Zen philosophy finds a way to embrace the static and dynamic, the permanent and relative, sameness and difference without being grounded in a metaphysical position and avoiding the representational mode of thinking.

We have also called attention to the different attempts by postmodern philosophers to undermine the unity of thought, whereas the process of thinking for Kant presupposes a unity for each individual act of analysis, which he refers to as the synthetic unity of apperception. According to Kant, thinking unifies itself at each stage because it represents a synthetic unity of various objects of thought that cannot appear unless they are thought, whereas many postmodern philosophers embrace disunity and skepticism. As a representative of Zen philosophy, Dōgen offers certainty, realization and authentification, for instance, of selfhood by means of *zazen*. Correct thinking for Dōgen represents an unlearning that frees one from erroneous preconceptions that may have been gained by a representational type of thinking. Rather than undermining any unity of thinking, the non-thinking of Dōgen is objectless, formless, and goalless, which is certainly not true of the modes of thinking of any of the postmodern philosophers, although a philosopher like Heidegger in his later works makes an attempt to move in the direction of nondual thinking. The non-thinking advocated by Dōgen unites and sublates thinking and not-thinking rather than undermining and dividing like many of the postmodernists, and it encompasses rationality and irrationality without leading to the radical skepticism of the postmodern philosophers and their failure to extricate themselves from the subject/object dichotomy that is typical of Enlightenment philosophy. Thus, for all the apparent similarities between Zen philosophy and postmodern philosophy, they are actually very different.

Zen Through the Prism of Postmodern Philosophy

As previously mentioned in the first chapter of this book, a secondary intention of this work is to review and respond to the recent contributions of Magliola, Loy, Dilworth, and Glass to the discussion of comparative philosophy as their works pertain to the subject of this book. Since I have already responded to Magliola in the first chapter and earlier in the final chapter of this work, I will concentrate the subsequent discussion on the other three figures by beginning with Glass.

Newman Robert Glass attempts to reread the Buddhist notion of emptiness through a philosophy of desire, which suggests viewing it as an affective state that is "constructed through the maintenance of 'positive desire.'"[29] Such a position presents some serious problems in general for Buddhist philosophy and Dōgen in particular. Glass thinks that emptiness needs to be approached in terms of affect, emotion, force, or desire, and it should not be approached in terms of thinking or object because such an approach misses the point. Glass claims to find hints of such a reading within the specific context of the Tathāgatagarbha literature of Mahāyāna Buddhism, a body of works that contain an emptiness of what he calls essence. This third kind of emptiness (essence) is to be distinguished from alternative readings referred to as the working of presence and difference, which are all capable of grounding thinking and behavior. These classifications of emptiness are dependent on two different readings of codependent arising: affirmation, presence, or positive codependent arising and its opposite form of negation, difference, or negative codependent arising. This distinction means that there are two types of Buddhism: a Buddhism of presence (codependent arising) and a Buddhism of difference (dependent arising). If the Buddhist tradition itself offers two possible readings of emptiness, Glass appears to suggest that it is reasonable to offer a third reading, although he never really justifies this third alternative except to claim that it represents a superior way to understand enlightenment in Dōgen. He does inform his reader, however, that his third reading of emptiness accepts dependent arising, but it does not view it as primary to an interpretation of emptiness. In addition to claiming that Buddhist literature itself justifies a third reading of emptiness, Glass uses Nāgārjuna's distinction between two types of truth: conventional (*samvṛtti-satya*) and ultimate (*paramartha-satya*). In the former type of truth he places emptiness as dependent co-arising and in the category of ultimate truth is emptiness as Buddha-nature, which he equates with essence.[30]

Admitting that he wants to retrieve the real truth about the nature of emptiness, Glass equates emptiness with nothingness: "The un-thought, the not-a-thought that is a condition of thought, can be seen as a 'nothing' or 'emptiness.'"[31] Numerous scholars of Mahāyāna Buddhism testify to the erroneous nature of this interpretation.[32]

From the perspective of his so-called subtraction/essence reading of Mahāyāna Buddhism, Glass attempts to reinterpret the philosophy of Dōgen, which he claims is a more legitimate reading of the Zen master and superior to either a positive or negative dependent co-arising reading. This approach gets the author into some serious interpretative problems with respect to the philosophy of Dōgen that tend to misinterpret or misrepresent his position. Glass claims, for instance, that Dōgen distinguishes between two aspects or two types of *zazen* (seated meditation): a general *zazen* and another based on the transmission of the Buddhas and patriarchs.[33] The quotation that Glass uses to support his interpretation does not help him make an unequivocal case. Moreover, his interpretation of *zazen* is diametrically opposed to that of Dōgen who makes no such distinction with *zazen*. As we have already noted, Dōgen grasps *zazen* in a nondualistic manner by not drawing a distinction between *zazen* and enlightenment. A good example of Glass' misreading of Dōgen is evident by the following statement: "All monks may do zazen, but not all zazen is the transmission of the Law. The zazen of the beginner may not be the same as the zazen of the Zen Master."[34] This type of interpretation ignores Dōgen's emphatic assertion that one becomes enlightened the very first time that one begins to practice meditation. Glass also misinterprets Dōgen's notion of "dropping off body and mind" when he claims that it represents a shift not merely from thinking to non-thinking, but it manifests a change "from the realm of thought to the realm of the unsense, essence: dropping off mind (thinking) *and* body (sense)."[35] This rereading of an important notion in Dōgen is interpreted as a movement from the field of sense to a field of essence, a movement that would be unrecognizable to Dōgen because emptiness is devoid of essence for him. Moreover, from a phenomenological perspective, David Shaner interprets "casting off" as not denunciation or negative positing of body and mind:

"Dōgen makes it clear that the act of neutralization (casting off) elimi-
nates any conception of a static, permanent 'mind' or fixed Buddha."[36] By
casting off body and mind, all relative thinking and common opinions are
suspended for the individual, an implication of Dōgen's philosophy that
might not be evident when reading it through the philosophy of Deleuze.

By rereading Dōgen through the postmodern perspective of
Deleuze, the result is a distortion of his philosophy and a transformation
of his language into Deleuzean jargon. Glass views, for instance, the
movement from what he calls the field of sense to that of essence as a
movement from defiled desire to an intense plateau of undefiled desire.
Even though any language possesses inherent limitations attempting to
capture the fundamental message of Dōgen, such use of Deleuzean language by Glass distorts the philosophical position of the Zen master.
Glass is correct to indicate that using such Deleuzean language requires a
rereading of Dōgen's metaphors of enlightenment. The basic problem
with such an approach is that the philosophy of Dōgen becomes transformed into something that it is not or was ever intended to be. A good
example of such a distortion is the claim by Glass that emptiness is not an
achieved state of non-thinking but is rather an achieved state of desire.
This is certainly true of Deleuze, but it is a completely erroneous interpretation of Dōgen despite Glass' claim that desire becomes totally transformed into something intense that burns off karmic defilements.[37] If
Glass believes that the codependent arising and the dependent arising
readings of Buddhism fail because neither can adequately account for
enlightenment in Dōgen's thought, he is mistaken to think that Deleuzean
desire is a better alternative because it does not adhere to the nondualistic stance of Dōgen's philosophy.

Rather than attempting to grasp Buddhism through the postmodern
philosophy of Deleuze like Glass, the approach of Loy is very much the
exact opposite because he begins by supporting the fundamental claim
of Mahāyāna Buddhism that *saṃsāra* is nirvāna, and he sets forth to
indicate problems with dualistic categories and philosophies. A fundamental problem with dualistic categories "is that they are part of a conceptual grid which we normally but unconsciously superimpose upon
our immediate experience and which deludes us by distorting that experience."[38] Dualistic thinking includes, moreover, any conceptual label-
ing, which would certainly include Deleuze's notion of philosophy as the
creation of concepts. Hence Loy advises us that one should not even
name the nondual whole.

From the nondual perspective of Mahāyāna Buddhism, Loy criticizes Derrida's notion of deconstruction because it is incomplete and not radical enough due to the fact that it cannot deconstruct itself. Derrida's method thus "misses the possibility for a new, nonconceptual 'opening' to something very different."[39] In his optimistic assessment of the possibilities of deconstruction, Loy thinks that it could lead to a transformation of our normal way of experiencing the world. The basic problem with Derrida's use of the method from Loy's viewpoint is that Derrida is unaware that to deconstruct one term (e.g., a transcendental signified) necessarily involves the transformation of the other, which only leads to a temporary and inconclusive result. The shortcoming of Derrida's method and its failure from the nondualist viewpoint is made clear by Loy: "Derrida's single-deconstruction leads to the 'temporary' reversal of their hierarchy, and/or to a discontinuous, irruptive 'liberation' from reference grounded in the search for unattainable origins, into the dissemination of a free-floating meaning beyond any conceptual clôture. For the nondualist, this can be only the illusion of liberation, while remaining trapped in a textual 'bad infinity' that tends to become increasingly ludic."[40] Derrida would agree with Loy about the temporary and ludic aspects of deconstruction because he refers himself to the necessity of deconstructing texts again and again and to its playful nature, and I think that Derrida would agree about the illusory nature of liberation, although he would completely disagree that there is a possibility to attain anything permanent, a possibility that seems to be implied by Loy's comments. From a nonpostmodern or postmodern viewpoint, a basic problem with Loy's approach is that he assumes that all nondualistic positions are the same. By assuming that the nondualism of Mahāyāna Buddhism is the best paradigm of nondualism, Loy does not pay much attention to differences in the positions of nondualists. In the second part of his interesting book, Loy, for instance, deals with conflicting ontological claims of nondualists. According to Loy, such differences do not negate the core theory constructed in the first part of his book. Why is this the case? Loy answers that "these ontological differences arise not from different experiences but from emphasizing different aspects of the same nondual experience."[41] This quotation is very instructive because it informs us that, within the fundamental hermeneutical presuppositions of his position, Loy assumes that all nondualistic experiences are the same. The validity of this basic assumption is never proven by him in part because it represents a controlling hermeneutical principle that falsely allows him to incorporate different, although similar positions, into his overarching purpose. If Loy is correct about the unity of all nondualist positions, why did philosophical arguments and disagreements occur between, for instance, Advaita Vedāntist and Buddhist? Thus it appears that Loy's position lacks any historical context and fails to reflect the philosophical debates between nondualist. Again, Loy focuses on sameness to the detriment and neglect of difference, which tends to obscure possible differences between nondualistic positions. Therefore, Loy gives the impression of being a captive of his own hermeneutical presuppositions and hierarchy, making his work a candidate for a necessary deconstruction.

An equally ambitious work like that of Loy is the contribution to comparative philosophy by Dilworth and his encyclopedic approach to the subject. Dilworth attempts to construct an all-encompassing typology that not only includes Zen philosophy but also some of the postmodernists that have been considered in this study. There are four major parts of Dilworth's typology: reality, method, principle, and perspective. By reality, Dilworth means the ontological focus of a philosopher, which can be existential, substrative, noumenal, or essential. The existential focus gives priority to historical data and human actions and affairs. The substrative approach finds the surface of life too deceptive and attempts to delve into a more basic and invisible level of human existence, whereas the noumenal focus perceives a reality that transcends appearances and points to a supersensible and eternally perfect sphere or action. The final ontological focus is the essential in which ideal, enduring aspects form gradated patterns, functions, and values that can be realized within nature and human experience.[42] With respect to method, Dilworth divides these into four possibilities: agonistic or paradoxical, logistic or computational (reduces complex units to simples), dialectical or sublational, and synoptic or problematic, which converts a problem into an analysis of generic and specific, relevant and irrelevant features.[43] Dilworth identifies the four principles as either creative, elemental or simple, comprehensive, or reflective. The creative emphasizes the new replacing the old, whereas the simple principle reflects sameness, identity, homogeneity or parity, which can involve the recycling or repetition of the same nature, essence or element. This occurs when a philosopher uses an ideal set, parity, or multiplicity of forms that stresses the perfect form of the whole and attributes its parts their assigned places. The final principle is reflexive, which can be described as "Aristotle's principle of the essential variety of goods and functions, or as the principle of self-sufficiency, autonomy, and self-completion of a specific nature or of a thing's intrinsic form or function."[44] The final typological category used by Dilworth is perspective by which he means the authorizing voice of a text that can assume four possible forms: personal, objective, diaphanic (or voice of religion), disciplinary (or voice of a first person plural of an ideal community).[45]

Dilworth's work is impressive in its cross-cultural scope and its intellectual courage. Like most typolgies it helps us to understand a particular philosopher, but it also opens itself to criticism of being hierarchical, static, and nonhistorical. It also gives rise to specific problems of classification concerning aspects of the thought of particular philosophers. Dilworth typologizes Derrida, Deleuze, and Foucault in the following way with respect to reality: Derrida is substrative; Deleuze and Foucault are classified as existential. In terms of method, all three philosophers are agnostic, whereas Derrida's principle is creative, and the other two thinkers are called elemental, and all three share an objective perspective. Even if we assume for the sake of argument that Dilworth's typology accurately reflects the work of these philosophers, it still misses the obvious political thrust and agenda of these three philosophers. And by missing the leftist political aspects of their philosophies, this serious omission reflects a shortcoming of Dilworth's typology.

Although one can argue for or against particular classifications, I am more concerned with how these postmodern philosophers compare with Dilworth's characterization of Zen philosophy. Acknowledging some overlap with the existential ontological focus of Zen, Deleuze, and Foucault, Dilworth classifies the methods of all four philosophies as agonistic. The major difference between Zen and the postmodern philosophers are in the areas of perspective, which for Zen is diaphanic or governed by the theme of the immanence of the absolute in which one awakens to one's original nature. Dilworth unequivocally states the diaphanic element of Buddhism is the notion of *śūnyatā* (emptiness) that "is an elemental principle of absolute identity, sameness, and synchronity."[46] From what we have previously seen with respect to the notion of Buddha-nature in the philosophy of Dōgen, Dilworth's characterization of emptiness as representing sameness and synchronity, implying the neglect or total absence of difference and diachronity, and being something static does not accurately reflect the case for the Zen philosopher. Moreover, the static, hierarchical, conservative, and timeless characteristics of Dilworth's typology invites the ire and criticism of postmodern philosophers because it reflects the product of a representational mode of thinking that is common for those influenced by Enlightenment philosophy and the order promised by such a philosophy.

The End of a Conclusion

As we witnessed in the previous chapter, a number of postmodernists embrace some of the ideas of Nietzsche and especially the Dionysian spirit of his work. Just as Nietzsche refers to overcoming metaphysics as a liberating event, several postmodernists concur with the German philosopher and add that the overcoming of traditional metaphysics marks the end of philosophy. Since verifying the end of philosophy is apparently impossible to determine because of our impermanent status and inability to ascertain which philosophical position is superior, it is best to discern the postmodern proclamation about the end of philosophy as a prophetic announcement that is an attempt to exercise a performative utterance, an attempt to make it happen.

In place of metaphysics some postmodern philosophers offer a philosophy of difference. If we take into consideration the philosophical positions of Derrida and Deleuze and their distinctive calls for a philosophy of difference, such a philosophy is intended to dislocate, subvert, undermine, and disrupt philosophical hierarchies and the notion of presence associated with metaphysics. Such a philosophy is a challenge to representational modes of thinking with its emphasis on unity or identity. And Deleuze and Derrida agree that difference is not a notion that establishes an ultimate entity or state. If Heidegger's philosophy represents an attempt to retrieve Being, the work of postmodernists like Derrida and Deleuze is an effort to retrieve and think difference. Deleuze claims, for instance, that difference disappears in thought when it is subordinated to the identity of a concept.

Without reiterating the differences and common features between Dōgen, Deleuze and Derrida, we have suggested that the Zen master finds a philosophical way to discuss both identity and difference without neglecting the flux of temporality. Dōgen's notion of Buddha-nature both embodies and transcends Derrida's notion of *différance* and the difference of Deleuze. It is impossible to subvert Buddha-nature with the neologism of *différance* that subverts every realm or with the Deleuzean difference that undermines representational thinking. Since Buddha-nature corresponds to no particular thing or quality in the world, this suggests that it represents the epitome of difference. In contrast to the postmodern philosophers, Dōgen finds another way to discuss and attend to difference without neglecting or rejecting sameness or forgetting about the process of becoming.

Dōgen and Nishitani also reject the nihilism embraced by some postmodernists. For Deleuze, nihilism is the *ratio cognoscendi* of the will to power, which is a will to nothingness that reveals all past and present values and transports us beyond suffering and the interiority associated with meditation.[47] The threat of nihilism is too destructive for Dōgen and Nishitani because complete nihilism is self-destructive in two senses: "Completion means that nihilism defeats itself so that the final act of the negative will to power is to extinguish itself; also, the completion of nihilism is the end of 'man' as a constructed interiority—it is the suicide of the 'last man.'"[48] Nihilism is completed by the eternal return by negating the reactive forces within the eternal return.[49] If we take Deleuze as representative of the postmodern position, his pessimistic philosophy stands in sharp contrast to the more hopeful Zen Buddhist perspective. But this statement must not be accepted as a definitive conclusion because strictly speaking there is no conclusion.

Due to the absence of an end, a definite conclusion is impossible. The most that we can affirm is that a conclusion is inconclusive, and yet we must come to some sort of end. I tend to agree with Taylor who thinks that one must end where one finds oneself.[50] It has not been the intention of this dialogue between representatives of the Zen philosophical tradition and postmodern thought to arrive at a final solution to any philosophical problems. The inconclusive end of this intercultural dialogue terminates with an interlude that anticipates a continuation of the dialogue at a future date. Unable to come to final conclusions or a definitive end, it seems advisable to simply sign out.

Notes

Chapter 1. Signing In

1. Jacques Derrida, *Signéponge/Signsponge*, trans. Richard Rand (New York: Columbia University Press, 1984), p. 56.

2. Ibid., p. 56.

3. Idem, *Limited Inc.*, trans. Samuel Weber (Evanston, IL: Northwestern University Press, 1988), p. 20.

4. Idem, *Signéponge*, p. 54.

5. Jean-Paul Sartre, *Being and Nothingness: An Essay in Phenomenological Ontology*, trans. Hazel E. Barnes (New York: Philosophical Library, 1956), pp. 258, 262.

6. Ibid., p. 410.

7. Idem, *Genet: Actor and Martyr*, trans. Bernard Frechtman (New York: George Braziller, 1963).

8. Jacques Lacan, *The Four Fundamental Concepts of Psycho-Analysis*, ed. Jacques-Alain Miller and trans. Alan Sheridan (New York, London: W. W. Norton & Company, 1981), p. 84.

9. Ibid., p. 84.

10. Ibid., p. 182.

11. Ibid., p. 182.

12. Michel Foucault, *Discipline and Punishment: The Birth of the Prison*, trans. Alan Sheridan (New York: Pantheon Books, 1977), p. 201.

13. Idem, *The Birth of the Clinic: An Archaeology of Medical Perception*. trans. A. M. Sheridan Smith (New York: Vintage/Random House, 1975), p. XIV.

14. Idem, *Madness and Civilization: A History of Insanity in the Age of Reason* (New York: Random House, 1973), p. 108.

15. Jacques Derrida, *Given Time 1: Counterfeit Money*, trans. Peggy Kamuf (Chicago and London: University of Chicago Press, 1992), p. 163.

16. Idem, *Memoirs of the Blind: The Self-Portrait and Other Ruins*, trans. Pascale-Anne Brault and Michael Naas (Chicago and London: University of Chicago Press, 1993), p. 106.

17. Ibid., p. 68.

18. Ibid., p. 126.

19. Dōgen Zenji, *Shōbōgenzō (The Eye and Treasury of the True Law)* 4 Vols., trans. Kōsen Nishiyama (Tokyo: Nakayama Shobo, 1986), I: 105. Heinrich Dumoulin refers to Dōgen's *Shōbōgenzō* as "a literary work of exceptional quality and unique importance (p. 72)" in *Zen Buddhism: A History Volume 1, India and China*, trans. James W. Heisig and Paul Knitter (New York: Macmillan Publishing Company, 1988). And Carl Bielefeldt calls this text a "masterwork" and "remarkable" (p. 46) in *Dōgen's Manuals of Zen Meditation* (Berkeley: University of California Press, 1988). David Putney discusses textual problems and changes in Dōgen's philosophy in "Some Problems in Interpretation: The Early and Late Writings of Dōgen," *Philosophy East and West*, Vol. 46, No. 4 (1996): 497–531.

20. Ibid., II: 96.

21. Hakuin, *The Zen Master Hakuin: Selected Writings*, trans. Philip B. Yampolsky (New York and London: Columbia University Press, 1971), p. 36.

22. Dōgen, III: 134.

23. Ibid., I: 11.

24. Dōgen, II: 79. In fact, Dōgen recommends opening the eyes during meditation in order to overcome drowsiness and to enhance the power of concentration, according to Bielefeldt, p. 113.

25. Dōgen, *Shōbōgenzō*, I: 118.

26. Ibid., II: 138.

27. Ibid., II: 111.

28. Ibid., II: 117.

29. Keiji Nishitani, *Religion and Nothingness*, trans. Jan Van Bragt (Berkeley: University of California Press, 1982), p. 152.

30. Dōgen, IV: 75.

31. Shigenori Nagatomo, "An Analysis of Dōgen's 'Casting Off Body and Mind,'" *International Philosophical Quarterly*, Vol. XXVII, No. 3 (1987), pp. 229, 232.

32. Nishitani, p. 153.

33. Lacan, p. 89.

34. Martin Heidegger, *Holzwege* (Frankfurt: Vittorio Klostermann, 1963), p. 7.

35. Ibid., p. 17.

36. Ibid., pp. 25, 28.

37. Lacan, p. 108.

38. Jean-François Lyotard, *Toward the Postmodern*, eds. Robert Harvey and Marks Roberts (New Jersey, London: Humanities Press, 1993), p. 5.

39. Ibid., p. 174.

40. Jacques Derrida, *Blind*, pp. 53, 55.

41. Ibid., p. 54.

42. Mark C. Taylor, *Disfiguring: Art, Architecture, Religion* (Chicago and London: University of Chicago Press, 1992), p. 7.

43. Ibid., p. 9.

44. Ibid., p. 278.

45. Dōgen, I: 87.

46. Ibid., I: 87.

47. Ibid., I: 87.

48. Ibid., I: 87.

49. Ibid., I: 89.

50. D. T. Suzuki, *Essays in Zen Buddhism*, First Series (London: Rider and Company, 1949; reprint New York: Grove Press, Inc., 1961); *Essays in Zen Buddhism*, Second Series, ed. Christmas Humphreys (New York: Samuel Weiser Inc., 1953, 1971); *Essays in Zen Buddhism*, Third Series, ed. Christmas Humphreys (New York: Samuel Weiser Inc., 1953, 1971).

51. Hu Shih, "Ch'an (Zen) Buddhism in China Its History and Method," *Philosophy East and West*, Vol. 3, No. 1 (1953): 3–24.

52. Idem, *Essays*, First Series, pp. 229–30; 261.

53. Idem, *Essays*, Second Series, p. 24.

54. Idem, *Essays*, First Series, p. 268.

55. Bernard Faure, *Chan Insights and Oversights: An Epistemological Critique of the Chan Tradition* (Princeton: Princeton University Press, 1993), p. 4.

56. Ibid., p. 53.

57. Ibid., pp. 53, 55, 57.

58. Ibid., p. 61.

59. Ibid., pp. 64–114.

60. Hseuh-li Cheng, *Exploring Zen* (New York: Peter Lang, 1991), p. 124.

61. Ibid., p. 126; Although Suzuki stresses the superior nature of sudden enlightenment, Bernard Faure indicates that the distinction between sudden and gradual enlightenment in the southern and northern schools is due to a question of style—of rhetoric as well as practice—because both were sudden and both were to some degree gradual in *The Rhetoric of Immediacy: A Cultural Critique of Chan/Zen Buddhism* (Princeton: Princeton University Press, 1991).

62. Calvin O. Schrag, *The Resources of Rationality: A Response to the Postmodern Challenge* (Bloomington and Indianapolis: Indiana University Press, 1992), p. 14.

63. John McGowan, *Postmodernism and Its Critics* (Ithaca and London: Cornell University Press, 1991), pp. 1, 13.

64. Martin Heidegger, *Nietzsche Volume IV: Nihilism*, trans. Frank A. Capuzzi and ed. David Farrell Krell (San Francisco: Harper & Row, p. 28.

65. Mark C. Taylor, *Nots* (Chicago and London: University of Chicago Press, 1993), p. 61.

66. Fredric Jameson, *Postmodernism, or The Cultural Logic of Late Capitalism* (Durham, N. C: Duke University Press, 1991), p. 309.

67. Ibid., p. ix.

68. Jean-François Lyotard, *The Postmodern Condition: A Report on Knowledge*, trans. Geoff Bennington and Brian Massumi, Theory and History of Literature, Vol. 10 (Minneapolis: University of Minnesota Press, 1984), p. 5.

69. John Keane, "The Modern Democratic Revolution: Reflections on Lyotard's The Postmodern Condition," in *Judging Lyotard*, ed. Andrew Benjamin (London and New York: Routledge, 1992), p. 90.

70. Jean-François Lyotard, *The Inhuman: Reflections on Time*, trans. Geoffrey Bennington and Rachel Bowlby (Cambridge: Polity Press, 1991), p. 24.

71. Ibid., p. 25.

72. Richard Beardsworth, "On the Critical 'Post': Lyotard's Agitated Judgement," in *Judging Lyotard*, ed. Andrew Benjamin (London and New York: Routledge, 1992), p. 55.

73. Keane, p. 91.

74. Lyotard, *Inhuman*, p. 26.

75. Ibid., p. 28.

76. Christopher Norris, *What's Wrong with Postmodernism: Critical Theory and the Ends of Philosophy* (Baltimore, MD: Johns Hopkins University Press, 1990), p. 30.

77. Jameson, p. 313.

78. Ibid., p. 315.

79. Gilles Deleuze and Claire Parnet, *Dialogues*, trans. Hugh Tomlinson and Barbara Habberjam (New York: Columbia University Press, 1987), p. 2.

80. Julia Kristeva, "Postmodernism?," *Bucknell Review*, Vol. 25, No. 11 (1980), p. 137.

81. Deleuze, p. 69.

82. Andreas Huyssen, "Mapping the Postmodern," *New German Critique,"* Vol. 33 (1984), p. 8.

83. Taylor, *Disfiguring*, p. 317.

84. Deleuze, p. 38.

85. Jameson, p. 382.

86. Schrag, p. 47.

87. Ibid., p. 47.

88. Hakuin, p. 121.

89. Robert R. Magliola, *Derrida on the Mend* (West Lafayette, IN: Purdue University Press, 1984), pp. 87–89.

90. Ibid., p. 97.

91. D. T. Suzuki, *Studies in the Lankavatara Sutra* (London: Routledge & Kegan Paul Ltd., 1930; reprint 1968), pp. 44–65.

92. David W. Chappell, "The Teachings of the Fourth Ch'an Patriarch Tao-hsin (580–651)," in *Early Ch'an in China and Tibet*, eds. Whalen Lai and Lewis R. Lancaster, Berkeley Buddhist Studies Series (Berkeley: Asian Humanities Press, 1983), p. 85. Chappell's position is confirmed by John R. McRae, *The Northern School and the Formation of Early Ch'an Buddhism*, Kuroda Institute Studies in East Asian Buddhism 3 (Honolulu: University of Hawaii Press, 1986), pp. 90–91; it is also confirmed by Heinrich Dumoulin, *Zen Buddhism: A History Volume 1 Indian and China*, trans. James W. Heisig and Paul Knitter (New York: Macmillan Publishing Company, 1988), pp. 109–110.

93. Philip Yampolsky, "New Japanese Studies in Early Ch'an History," in *Early Ch'an in China and Tibet*, eds. Whalen Lai and Lewis R. Lancaster, Berkeley Buddhist Studies Series (Berkeley: Asian Humanities Press, 1983), p. 3.

94. Robert E. Buswell, Jr., *The Formation of Ch'an Ideology in China and Korea: The Vajrasamādhi-Sūtra, A Buddhist Aprocryphon* (Princeton: Princeton University Press, 1989), p. 148.

Chapter 2. Language, Disruption, and Play

1. Martin Heidegger, *On the Way to Language*, trans. Peter D. Hertz (New York: Harper & Row, 1971), pp. 73–75.

2. Ibid., p. 124.

3. Ibid., p. 126.

4. Ibid., p. 135.

5. Idem, *Identity and Difference*, p. 38.

6. Idem, *Holzwege* (Frankfurt: Vittorio Klostermann, 1963), p. 286.

7. Idem, *Vorträge und Aufsätze* (Tübingen: Verlag Günther Neske Pfullin-gen, 1959), p. 148.

8. Idem, *Basic Concepts*, trans. Gary E. Aylesworth (Bloomington and Indianapolis: Indiana University Press, 1993), p. 54.

9. Idem, *An Introduction to Metaphysics*, trans. Ralph Manheim (New Haven and London: Yale University Press, 1964), p. 171.

10. Ibid., p. 171.

11. Idem, "Holderin and the Essence of Poetry," trans. Douglas Scott in *Existence and Being*, ed. Werner Brock (Chicago: Regnery, 1949), p. 297.

12. Richard Rorty, *Essays on Heidegger and Others, Philosophical Papers Volume 2* (Cambridge: Cambridge University Press, 1991), p. 52.

13. Rodolphe Gasché, *The Tain of the Mirror: Derrida and the Philosophy of Reflection* (Cambridge and London: Harvard University Press, 1986), p. 143.

14. Rorty, p. 125. Rodolphe Gasché defends Derrida against the criticism of Rorty by claiming that Rorty does not notice that Derrida's infrastructures are conditions of impossibility, and Rorty's negative appraisal of them is based on his analysis of them as enabling functions (p. 4) in *Inventions of Difference: On Jacques Derrida* (Cambridge: Harvard University Press, 1994).

15. Candrakīrti, *Lucid Exposition of the Middle Way: The Essential Chapters from the Prasannapadā of Candrakīrti*, trans. Mervyn Sprung (London and Henley: Routledge & Kegan Paul, 1979), 364–65.

16. Richard H. Robinson, *Early Mādhyamika in India and China* (Madison, Milwaukee, and London: University of Wisconsin Press, 1967), p. 49.

17. Chang Chung-yuan, "Ch'an Teachings of Yun-men School," *Chinese Culture*, Vol. V, No. 4 (1964), p. 30.

18. Thomas and J. C. Cleary, trans. *The Blue Cliff Record* (Boulder, CO: Prajñā Press, 1978), p. 81.

19. William F. Powell, trans., *The Record of Tung-shan* (Honolulu: University of Hawaii Press, 1986), p. 58.

20. Ruth Fuller Sasaki, trans. *The Recorded Sayings of Ch'an Master Lin-chi Hui-chao of Chen Prefecture* (Kyoto: The Institute for Zen Studies, 1975), p. 59.

21. *The Record of Tung-shan*, p. 29.

22. Dōgen, II: 60.

23. Faure, *Chan Insights*, p. 29.

24. Dale S. Wright, "The Discourse of Awakening:Rhetorical Practice in Classical Ch'an Buddhism," *Journal of the American Academy of Religion*, Vol. LXI, No. 1 (1993), pp. 37–38.

25. Ibid., p. 37.

26. See Robert E. Buswell, Jr., "Ch'an Hermeneutics: A Korean View," in *Buddhist Hermeneutics*, ed. Donald S. Lopez, Jr. (Honolulu: University of Hawaii Press, 1988), pp. 231–256.

27. Dōgen, III: 80.

28. Ibid., III: 82.

29. Ibid., II: 170.

30. Ibid., II: 164.

31. Ibid., III: 81.

32. Ibid., III: 81.

33. Jacques Derrida, *Of Grammatology*, trans. Gayatri Chakravorty Spivak (Baltimore and London: Johns Hopkins University Press, 1976), pp. 216–17.

34. *Blue Cliff Record*, p. 406.

35. Dōgen, *A Primer of Soto Zen: A Translation of Dōgen's Shōbōgenzō Zuimonki*, trans. Reihō Masunaga (Honolulu: East-West Center Press, 1971), p. 9.

36. Wright, p. 32.

37. *Recorded Sayings of Ch'an Master Lin-chi*, p. 47.

38. Ibid., p. 48.

39. *The Blue Cliff Record*, p. 66.

40. Jacques Derrida, *Margins of Philosophy*, trans. Alan Bass (Chicago: University of Chicago Press, 1986), p. 96.

41. *The Blue Cliff Record*, p. 353.

42. Ibid., p. 636.

43. *The Recorded Sayings of Ch'an Master Lin-chi*, p. 4.

44. *The Blue Cliff Record*, p. 18.

45. Jacques Derrida, *Writing and Difference*, trans. Alan Bass (Chicago: University of Chicago Press, 1978), p. 296.

46. *The Blue Cliff Record*, p. 362.

47. Jacques Derrida, *Limited Inc.*, trans. Samuel Weber (Evanston, IL: Northwestern University Press, 1988), p. 92.

48. Ibid., p. 59.

49. *The Recorded Sayings of Ch'an Master Lin-chi*, pp. 43–44.

50. Ibid., p. 2.

51. Zenkei Shibayama, *Comments on the Mumonkan*, trans. Sumiko Kudo (New York: Harper & Row, 1974), p. 148.

52. Bavo Lievens, trans. *The Recorded Sayings of Ma-tsu*, trans. Julian F. Pas, Studies in Asian Thought and Religion Volume 6 (Lewiston/Queenston: Edwin Mellen Press, 1987), pp. 99–100.

53. Ibid., p. 94.

54. Ibid., p. 101.

55. Derrida, *Writing and Difference*, p. 292.

56. Idem, *Of Grammatology*, p. 62.

57. Ibid., p. 65.

58. Idem, *Cinders*, trans. Ned Lukacker (Lincoln and London: University of Nebraska Press, 1991), p. 39.

59. Idem, *Speech and Phenomena and Other Essays on Husserl's Theory of Signs*, trans. David B. Allison (Evanston, IL: Northwestern University Press, 1973), p. 156.

60. *The Record of Tung-shan*, p. 52.

61. Ibid., p. 55.

62. *The Blue Cliff Record*, p. 578.

63. Ibid., p. 434.

64. Ibid., p. 514.

65. *The Recorded Sayings of Ma-tsu*, p. 107.

66. Derrida, *Writing and Difference*, p. 260.

67. *The Blue Cliff Record*, p. 525.

68. Thomas P. Kasulis, "The Origins of the Question: Four Traditional Japanese Philosophers of Language," in *Culture and Modernity: East-West*

Philosophic Perspectives, ed. Eliot Deutsch (Honolulu: University of Hawaii Press, 1991), p. 221.

69. Dōgen, *Shōbōgenzō*, II: 40.

70. J. L. Austin, *How To Do Things with Words* (Cambridge: Harvard University Press, 1967), p. 5.

71. Ibid., p. 34.

72. Ibid., pp. 34–36.

73. Derrida, *Limited Inc.*, p. 14.

74. Ibid., p. 18.

75. Ibid., p. 93.

76. *The Record of Tung-shan*, p. 25.

77. *The Recorded Sayings of Ch'an Master Lin-chi*, p. 60.

78. Ibid. p. 53.

79. *The Blue Cliff Record*, p. 123.

80. Ibid., p. 125.

81. Ibid., p. 125.

82. Wright, p. 30.

83. Heinrich Dumoulin, *Zen Enlightenment: Origins and Meaning*, trans. John C. Maraldo (New York: Weatherhill, 1979), p. 62.

84. Chang Chung-yuan, trans. *Original Teachings of Ch'an Buddhism: Selected from the Transmission of the Lamp* (New York: Pantheon Books, 1969), p. 132.

85. R. H. Blyth, *Zen and Zen Classics Volume Three* (Tokyo: The Hokuseido Press, 1970; reprint 1972), p. 154.

86. Heinrich Dumoulin, *A History of Zen Buddhism*, trans. Paul Peachey (New York: Pantheon Books, 1963), p. 101.

87. Peter D. Hershock, *Liberating Intimacy: Enlightenment and Social Virtuosity in Ch'an Buddhism* (Albany, NY: State University of New York Press, 1996), p. 81.

88. Bernard Faure, "Fair and Unfair Language Games in Chan/Zen," in *Mysticism and Language*, ed. Steven T. Katz (New York, Oxford: Oxford University Press, 1992), p. 160.

89. Ibid., pp. 173–74.

90. Idem, *Chan Insights*, pp. 212–14.

91. Ibid., p. 213.

92. Chung-ying Cheng, "On Zen (Ch'an) Language and Zen Paradoxes," *Journal of Chinese Philosophy*, Vol. 1, No. 1 (1973), p. 93.

93. Steven Heine, *Dōgen and the Kōan Tradition: A Tale of Two Shōbōgenzō Texts* (Albany, NY: State University of New York Press, 1994), p. 203.

94. Ibid., p. 205.

95. Derrida, *Writing and Difference*, p. 279.

96. *The Blue Cliff Record*, p. 424.

97. Chang, *Original Teachings*, p. 197.

98. Ibid., p. 147. Dumoulin, writes that "Silence is the stillness that grounds the enlightened mind, whose natural ability to 'shine' is revealed in silence" (p. 256) in *Zen Buddhism*, I. For a discussion of the silence of the Buddha and its Mādhyamika interpretation see Gadjin M. Nagao, *Mādhyamika and Yogācāra: A Study of Mahāyāna Philosophies*, ed. and trans. L. S. Kawamura (Albany, NY: State University of New York Press, 1991), pp. 35–49.

99. Wright, p. 31.

100. Edmond Jabès, *The Book of Questions, Vol. II*, trans. Rosmarie Waldrop (Middletown, CT: Wesleyan University Press, 1991), p. 195.

101. Idem, *The Book of Shares*, trans. Rosmarie Waldrop (Chicago and London: University of Chicago Press), p. 9.

102. Ibid., p. 3.

103. Derrida, *Of Grammatology*, p. 68.

104. Derrida, *Psyché*, p. 547.

105. Dōgen, *Shōbōgenzō*, I: 130–31.

106. Dale S. Wright, "Rethinking Transcendence: The Role of Language in Zen Experience," *Philosophy East and West*, Vol. 42, No. 1 (1992), p. 126.

107. *Mumonkan*, p. 72.

108. Derrida, *Signéponge*, pp. 14, 16.

109. Ibid., p. 14.

110. Idem, *Of Grammatology*, p. 245.

111. Charles Taylor, *Philosophical Arguments* (Cambridge: Harvard University Press, 1995), p. 16.

112. Hee-Jin Kim, "'The Reason of Words and Letters': Dōgen and Kōan Language," in *Dōgen Studies*, ed. William R. LaFleur (Honolulu: University of Hawaii Press, 1985), p. 59. In this essay Kim shows how Dōgen transforms language in terms of lexical components, semantic reconstruction through syntactic change, explication of semantic attributes, reflexive self-causative utterances, upgrading ordinary notions and use of neglected metaphors, use of homophonous expressions, and reinterpretation based on the principle of absolute emptiness.

113. Faure, *Chan Insights*, p. 241.

114. Derrida, *Writing and Difference*, p. 178.

115. *The Blue Cliff Record*, p. 548.

Chapter 3. Ways of Thinking

1. *Mumonkan*, p. 311.

2. Martin Heidegger, *What Is Called Thinking?*, trans. Fred D. Wieck and J. Glenn Gray (New York: Harper & Row, 1968), p. 12.

3. Idem, *Der Satz vom Grund*, Fourth Edition (Pfullingen: Verlag Günther Neske, 1971), p. 159.

4. Jean-François Lyotard, *Peregrinations: Law, Form, Event* (New York: Columbia University Press, 1988), pp. 6–7.

5. Gilles Deleuze and Félix Guattari, *What Is Philosophy?*, trans. Hugh Tomlinson and Graham Burchell (New York: Columbia University Press, 1994), p. 140.

6. Heidegger, *What Is Called Thinking?*, p. 4.

7. Ibid., p. 3.

8. Ibid., p. 4.

9. Dōgen, *A Primer of Soto Zen*, p. 65.

10. Martin Heidegger, *Being and Time*, trans. John Macquarrie & Edward Robinson (New York: Harper & Row, 1962), p. 191.

11. Idem, *What Is Called Thinking?*, p. 7. It is precisely statements like this that cause Stanley Rosen to call Heidegger a bad poet and to state that "Whereas I deplore Heidegger's own attempt to develop a 'new' or 'poetic' thinking about Being, I judge it to be a defective version of Platonism, namely, the attempt to elicit the senses of Being in myths, poetic dramas, and even in simple accounts of how philosophy emerges from everyday life'" in *The Question of Being: A Reversal of Heidegger* (New Haven and London: Yale University Press, 1993), p. 43. On the other hand, John D. Caputo proposes to demythologize Heidegger's metanarrative of Being by means of a deconstructive process that includes an operation of denazification and puts Heidegger's philosophy in the service of others in *Demythologizing Heidegger* (Bloomington: Indiana University Press, 1993).

12. Norman Waddell & Abe Masao, trans. "Shobogenzo Buddha-nature I," *The Eastern Buddhist*, Vol. 8, No. 2 (1975), p. 105.

13. Mark C. Taylor, *Nots* (Chicago and London: University of Chicago Press, 1993), p. 1. From the perspective of Deleuze, Taylor starts a dialectical negation that cannot be ended. Deleuze advocates a nondialectical conception of negation that is both more simple and absolute because it negates and attacks everything negated with unrestrained force and represents the extreme of nihilism, points made lucid by Michael Hardt, *Gilles Deleuze: An Apprecenticeship in Philosophy* (Minneapolis, London: University of Minnesota Press, 1993), p. xii.

14. Martin Heidegger, "Letter on Humanism," trans. Frank A. Capuzzi in *Basic Writings*, ed. David Farrell Krell (New York: Harper & Row, 1977), p. 238. An important scholarly discussion on the nature of thinking in the philosophy of Heidegger is provided by Reiner Schürmann, *Heidegger on Being and Acting: From Principles to Anarchy*, trans. Christine-Marie Gros (Bloomington: Indiana University Press, 1987).

15. Jacques Derrida, *Psyché: Inventions de l'autre* (Paris: Galilée, 1987), p. 601.

16. Friedrich Wilhelm Nietzsche, *Complete Works* (New York: Russell & Russell, 1964), 13: 14.

17. Ibid., 11: 36.

18. Lyotard, *Postmodern Condition*, p. 82.

19. Idem, *The Differend: Phrases in Dispute*, trans. Georges Van Der Abbeele, Theory and History of Literature, Volume 46 (Minneapolis: University of Minnesota Press, 1988), p. 13.

20. See for instance the following works by Michel Foucault, *The History of Sexuality. Volume I: An Introduction*, trans. Robert Hurley (New York: Vintage/Random House, 1980); *Power/Knowledge: Selected Interviews and Other Writings 1972–1977*, ed. Colin Gordon, Leo Marshall, John Mepham, Kate Soper (New York: Pantheon Books, 1980); "The Subject and Power," in *Michel Foucualt: Beyond Structuralism and Hermeneutics*, ed. Hubert L. Dreyfus and Paul Rabinow, Second Edition (Chicago: University of Chicago Press, 1983).

21. See Richard Rorty, *Philosophy and the Mirror of Nature* (Princeton: Princeton University Press, 1979). A very critical critique of Rorty is offered by Stanley Rosen who accuses Rorty of lacking a genuine philosophical argument, of offering an ideology or propaganda, being a Platonist, of not being able to tell the difference between a human being and a machine, replacing the transcendental ego with an intersubjectivity that originates with linguistic history, and accuses Rorty of finally arriving at psychologism or historicism "because he belongs to that school of neo-Kantians that cannot justify synthesis" (p. 184) in *The Ancients and the Moderns: Rethinking Modernity* (New Haven and London: Yale University Press, 1989).

22. Deleuze and Guattari, *What Is Philosophy?*, p. 5.

23. Ibid., pp. 19–20.

24. Immanuel Kant, *Critique of Pure Reason*, trans. Norman Kemp Smith (London: Macmillan & Company, Ltd., 1964), p. 65.

25. Deleuze and Guattari, *What Is Philosophy?*, pp. 16, 21.

26. Ibid., p. 36.

27. Heidegger, *What Is Called Thinking?*, p. 9.

28. Ibid., p. 9.

29. Ibid., p. 18.

30. Idem, "Letter on Humanism," p. 193.

31. Vincent Vycinas, *Earth and Gods: An Introduction to the Philosophy of Martin Heidegger* (The Hague: Martinus Nijhoff, 1961), p. 80.

32. Norman Waddell and Masao Abe, trans. "'One Bright Pearl': Dogen's Shobogenzo Ikka Myoju," *The Eastern Buddhist*, Vol. 4, No. 2 (1971), p. 113.

33. Heidegger, *What Is Called Thinking?*, p. 21.

34. Lyotard, *Peregrinations*, pp. 8–9.

35. Dōgen, *Primer*, p. 40.

36. Ibid., p. 51.

37. Dōgen, "Buddha-nature I," p. 105.

38. Norman Waddell and Masao Abe, trans. "Shobogenzo Buddha-nature II," *The Eastern Buddhist*, Vol. 9, No. 1 (1976), p. 94.

39. Heidegger, *What Is Called Thinking?*, pp. 168–69.

40. Ibid., p. 170.

41. William J. Richardson, S. J., *Heidegger: Through Phenomenology to Thought* (The Hague: Martinus Nijhoff, 1963), p. 598.

42. Dōgen, *Primer*, p. 29.

43. Norman Waddell and Masao Abe, trans. "Dogen's Fukanzazengi and Shobogenzo Zazengi,"*The Eastern Buddhist*, Vol. 6, No. 2 (October 1973), p. 122.

44. Norman Waddell and Masao Abe, trans. "Shobogenzo Genjokoan," *The Eastern Buddhist*, Vol. 5, No. 1 (October 1972), p. 122. Steven Heine objects to Kasulis' translation of *datsuraku* as molting because it does not capture the appropriate sense of effortlessness and spontaneity (p. 56) in "Dōgen Casts Off 'What': An Analysis of *Shinjin Datsuraku*," *Journal of the International Association of Buddhist Studies*, Vol. 9, No. 1 (1986). Shigenori Nagatomo views the activity of casting off body and mind as an attunement in which the action aspect is somatic in character in contrast to the intellectual judgment in which the action aspect of the judgment is *cogito* allegedly divorced from the body in "An Analysis of Dōgen's 'Casting Off Body and Mind,'" *International Philosophical Quarterly*, Vol. XXVII, No. 3 (1987): 227–42.

45. Lyotard, *Peregrinations*, p. 20.

46. Idem, *The Inhuman: Reflections on Time*, trans. Geoffrey Bennington and Rachel Bowlby (Cambridge: Polity Press, 1991), p. 20.

47. Mark C. Taylor, *Erring: A Postmodern A/theology* (Chicago and London: University of Chicago Press, 1984.

48. Ibid., p. 150.

49. Jacques Derrida, *Psyché: Inventions de l'autre* (Paris: Galilée, 1987), p. 627.

50. Deleuze and Guattari, *What Is Philosophy?*, p. 59.

51. Ibid., p. 38.

52. T. P. Kasulis, *Zen Action/Zen Person* (Honolulu: University Press of Hawaii, 1981), p. 64.

53. Gilles Deleuze, *Difference and Repetition*, trans. Paul Patton (New York: Columbia University Press, 1994), p. 15. Todd May argues that Deleuze is not a thinker who thinks that difference is to be privileged over unity. May tries to make the case that Deleuze is not a coherent thinker of difference in "Difference and Unity in Gilles Deleuze," in *Gilles Deleuze and the Theater of Philosophy*, eds. Constantin V. Boundas and Dorothea Olkowski (New York, London: Routledge, 1994), pp. 33–50.

54. Deleuze, *Difference and Repetition*, p. 27.

55. Heidegger, *What Is Called Thinking?*, p. 118.

56. Hee-Jin Kim, *Dogen Kigen—Mystical Realist* (Tucson, AZ: The University of Arizona Press, 1975), p. 27.

57. Norman Waddell and Masao Abe, trans. "Shobogenzo Buddha-nature III," *The Eastern Buddhist*, Vol. 9, No. 2 (1976), p. 86.

58. Heidegger, *What Is Called Thinking?*, p. 124.

59. Dōgen, *Primer*, p. 103.

60. Norman Waddell and Masao Abe, trans. "Dogen's Bendowa," *The Eastern Buddhist*, Vol. 4, No. 1 (1971), p. 137.

61. Dōgen, "Buddha-nature I," p. 112.

62. Ibid., p. 111.

63. Lyotard, *Peregrinations*, p. 9.

64. Derrida, *Psyché*, p. 597.

65. Deleuze, *Difference and Repetition*, p. 37.

66. Ibid., p. 41.

67. Richardson, p. 506.

68. Martin Heidegger, *Discourse on Thinking*, trans. John M. Anderson and E. Hans Freund (New York: Harper & Row, 1966), p. 68.

69. Richardson, p. 603.

70. Dōgen, Genjokoan," p. 135.

71. Dōgen, *Primer*, p. 28.

72. Dōgen, "Buddha-nature I," p. 105.

73. Lyotard, *Peregrinations*, p. 32.

74. Idem, *The Inhuman*, p. 156.

75. Idem, *Peregrinations*, p. 7.

76. Deleuze and Guattari, *What Is Philosophy?*, p. 50.

77. Heidegger, *Discourse on Thinking*, p. 64.

78. Ibid., p. 66.

79. Ibid., p. 61. For a comparative essay that elucidates this subject, see Reiner Schürmann, "Heidegger and Meister Eckhart on Releasement," *Research in Phenomenology*, III 1973): 95–119.

80. Dōgen, "Genjokoan," p. 134.

81. Heidegger, *Discourse on Thinking*, p. 82.

82. Masao Abe, "Dōgen on Buddha Nature," *The Eastern Buddhist*, Vol. 10, No. 1 (1971), p. 45.

83. Kim, p. 78.

84. Heidegger, *Discourse on Thinking*, p. 74.

85. Ibid., p. 81.

86. Ibid., p. 84.

87. Derrida, *Psyché*, p. 622.

88. Deleuze and Guattari, *What Is Philosophy?*, p. 151.

89. Ibid., p. 156.

90. Ibid., p. 158.

91. Gilles Deleuze, *Nietzsche and Philosophy*, trans. Hugh Tomlinson (New York: Columbia University Press, 1983), p. 108.

92. Heidegger, *Holzwege*, p. 325. My translation of this passage.

93. Derrida, *Writing and Difference*, p. 141.

94. Dōgen, "Fukanzazengi," p. 123; "Zazengi," p. 128.

95. Dōgen, *Shōbōgenzō*, II: 80.

96. Heidegger, *Der Satz vom Grund*, p. 86.

97. John Steffney, Transmetaphysical Thinking in Heidegger and Zen Buddhism," *Philosophy East and West*, Vol. XXVII, No. 3 (1977), pp. 323–35.

98. Dōgen, *Shōbōgenzō*, I: 10.

99. Ibid., I: 116.

100. Lyotard, *The Inhuman*, p. 19.

101. Derrida, *Psyché*, p. 620.

102. Taylor, *Nots*, p. 25.

103. Deleuze and Guattari, *What Is Philosophy?*, p. 59.

104. Rosen, *The Ancients and the Moderns*, p. 168.

105. John Steffney, "Transmetaphysical Thinking in Heidegger and Zen Buddhism," *Philosophy East and West*, Vol. XXVII, No. 3 (1977), pp. 323–35.

106. Heidegger, *Discourse on Thinking*, p. 67.

107. Richardson, p. 113.

108. Martin Heidegger, *Kant and the Problem of Metaphysics*, trans. James S. Churchill (Bloomington: Indiana University Press, 1965), p. 128.

109. Dōgen, *Primer*, p. 93.

110. Kim, p. 77.

111. Abe, "Dōgen on Buddha Nature," p. 45.

112. Heidegger, *Discourse on Thinking*, p. 84.

113. Idem, "Letter on Humanism," p. 202.

114. Idem, *Discourse on Thinking*, p. 79.

115. John Sallis, *Echoes After Heidegger* (Bloomington and Indianapolis: Indiana University Press, 1990), p. 35.

116. A. C. Graham, *Unreason Within Reason: Essays on the Outskirts of Rationality* (La Salle, IL: Open Court, 1992), p. 14–15.

117. Deleuze, *Difference and Repetition*, p. 43.

Chapter 4. Radical Skepticism and Doubt

1. Friedrich Nietzsche, *Thus Spoke Zarathustra: A Book for Everyone and No One*, trans. R. J. Hollingdale (London: Penguin Books, 1969), p. 102.

2. Idem, *The Will To Power*, trans. Walter Kaufman and R. J. Hollingdale (New York: Random House, 1967), p. 301.

3. Idem, *Basic Writings of Nietzsche*, ed. and trans. Walter Kaufman (New York: Modern Library, 1968), pp. 319–20.

4. Idem, *Will To Power*, p. 505.

5. Hakuin, p. 118.

6. Ibid., p. 118.

7. Kasulis, *Zen Action*, p. 115.

8. Hakuin, p. 134.

9. Ibid., p. 146.

10. Kasulis, *Zen Action*, p. 113.

11. Hakuin, p. 164.

12. Kasulis, *Zen Action*, p. 115.

13. Hakuin, p. 166.

14. Ibid., p. 144.

15. Ibid., p. 135.

16. Ibid., p. 135.

17. Michel Foucault, "Nietzsche, Freud, Marx," in *Nietzsche*, Proceedings of the Seventh International Philosophical Colloquium of the Cahiers de Royaumont, 4–8 July (Paris: Editions de Minuit, 1967), p. 189.

18. Idem, *The Order of Things: An Archaeology of the Human Sciences*, trans. Alan Sheridan Smith (New York: Random House, 1973), p. 9.

19. Arnold I. Davidson, "Archaeology, Genealogy, Ethics," in *Foucault: A Critical Reader*, ed. David Couzens Hoy (London: Basil Blackwell, 1986), p. 227.

20. Friedrich Nietzsche, *The Use and Abuse of History*, trans. Adrian Collins (New York: Macmillan Publishing Company, 1957), p. 22.

21. Ibid., p. 12.

22. Foucault, *Power/Knowledge*, p. 52.

23. Ibid., p. 50.

24. Idem, *Language, Counter-Memory, Practice: Selected Essays and Interviews*, ed. Donald F. Bouchard and trans. Donald F. Bouchard and Sherry Simon (Ithaca, NY: Cornell University Press, 1977), p. 230.

25. Idem, *The History of Sexuality I*, pp. 5–6.

26. Idem, "Nietzsche, Genealogy, History," in *Language, Counter-Memory, Practice: Selected Essays and Interviews*, ed. Donald F. Bouchard and trans. Donald F. Bouchard and Sherry Simon (Ithaca, NY: Cornell University Press, 1977), p. 153.

27. Ibid., pp. 152–57.

28. Robert C. Neville, *Reconstruction of Thinking* (Albany, NY: State University of New York Press, 1981), p. 12.

29. Richard Rorty, "Foucault and Epistemology," in *Foucault: A Critical Reader*, ed. David Couzens Hoy (London: Basil Blackwell, 1986), p. 43.

30. Foucault, "Nietzsche, Freud, Marx," p. 140.

31. Derrida, *Psyché*, p. 390.

32. Heidegger, *Being and Time*, p. 49.

33. Idem, "The Question Concerning Technology," in *Basic Writings*, ed. David Farrell Krell (New York: Harper & Row, 1977), p. 180.

34. Derrida, *Margins of Philosophy*, p. 131.

35. Rodolphe Gasché, *The Tain of the Mirror: Derrida and the Philosophy of Reflection* (Cambridge, London: Harvard University Press, 1986), p. 120

36. Derrida, *Limited Inc.*, p. 147. John D. Caputo argues that deconstruction is motivated by a religious or prophetic aspiration, a movement of transcendence, that suggests excess and a passion for transgression of the horizons of that which is possible in *The Prayers and Tears of Jacques Derrida: Religion without Religion* (Bloomington: Indiana University Press, 1997).

37. Idem, *Psyché*, p. 391.

38. Ibid., pp. 387–88.

39. Ibid., p. 391.

40. Ibid., p. 392.

41. Idem, *Limited Inc.*, p. 141.

42. Idem, *Of Grammatology*, p. 24; *Positions*, trans. Alan Bass (Chicago: University of Chicago Press, 1981), p. 41.

43. Calvin O. Schrag, *The Resources of Rationality: A Response to the Postmodern Challenge* (Bloomington, Indianapolis: Indiana University Press, 1992), p. 87.

44. Hilary Putnam, *Renewing Philosophy* (Cambridge, London: Harvard University Press, 1993), p. 140.

45. Ibid., p. 124.

46. Charles Taylor, *Sources of the Self: The Making of the Modern Identity* (Cambridge: Harvard University Press, 1989), p. 489.

47. Rorty, *Philosophical Papers II*, p. 100.

48. David Loy, *Nonduality: A Study in Comparative Philosophy* (New Haven and London: Yale University Press, 1988), p. 249.

49. Derrida, *Psyché*, p. 391.

50. Idem, *Given Time I: Counterfeit Money*, trans. Peggy Kamuf (Chicago and London: University of Chicago Press, 1992), p. 9.

51. Ibid., p. 12.

52. Ibid., p. 14.

53. Idem, *Of Spirit: Heidegger and the Question*, trans. Geoffrey Bennington and Rachel Bowlby (Chicago and London: University of Chicago Press, 1989), p. 26.

54. Ibid., p. 40.

55. Ibid., p. 62.

56. Ibid., p. 84.

57. Masanobu Takahashi, *The Essence of Dōgen*, trans. Yuzoru Nobuoka (London: Kegan Paul International, 1983), p. 62.

58. Richard B. Pilgrim, "Intervals (*Ma*) in Space and Time: Foundations for a Religio-Aesthetic Paradigm in Japan," *History of Religions*, Vol. 25, No. 3 (1986), pp. 255–62.

59. Taylor, *Philosophical Arguments*, pp. 9, 77.

60. Gilles Deleuze and Félix Guattari, *Anti-Oedipus: Capitalism and Schizophrenia*, trans. Robert Hurley, Mark Seem, and Helen R. Lane (Minneapolis: University of Minnesota Press, 1983), p. 2.

61. Ibid., p. 74.

62. Ibid., pp. 81–82.

63. Ibid., p. 311.

64. Ibid., p. 322.

65. Ibid., p. 340.

66. Ibid., p. 77.

67. Hakuin, p. 47.

68. Deleuze, *Dialogues*, p. 92.

69. Deleuze and Guattari, *Anti-Oedipus*, p. 11.

70. Ibid., p. 9.

71. Jacques Lacan, *Écrits: A Selection*, trans. Alan Sheridan (New York, London: W. W. Norton and Company, 1977), p. 94/2.

72. Ibid., p. 98/5.

73. Kelly Oliver, *Reading Kristeva: Unraveling the Double-bind* (Bloomington and Indianapolis: Indiana University Press, 1993), p. 18.

74. Kristeva, *Revolution in Poetic Language*, p. 74.

75. Idem, "Semiotics: A Critical Science and/or a Critique of Science," trans. Seán Hand in *The Kristeva Reader*, ed. Toril Moi (New York: Columbia University Press, 1986), p. 77.

76. Ibid., p. 78.

77. Ibid., pp. 78–80.

78. Ibid., p. 79.

79. Idem, "From Symbol to Sign," trans. Seán Hand in *The Kristeva Reader*, ed. Toril Moi (New York: Columbia University Press, 1986), p. 70; see also my book entitled *The Theology and Philosophy of Eliade: A Search for the Centre* (London: Macmillan, 1992) for a comparison of Mircea Eliade and Kristeva on this issue (pp. 84–88) and (pp. 68–77) for a comparison of Kristeva, Eliade and Habermas on the nature of dialogue.

80. Kristeva, "From Sign to Symbol," p. 70.

81. Ibid., pp. 71–72.

82. Hakuin, pp. 35–38.

83. Dumoulin, *Zen Buddhism I*, p. 246.

84. See essay by Chung-ying Cheng for a more detailed discussion of the

nature of paradoxes in Zen that is entitled "On Zen (Ch'an) Language and Zen Paradoxes," *Journal of Chinese Philosophy*, Vol. I, No. 1 (1973): 77–102.

85. Hakuin, p. 166.

86. Hakuin, "Talks by Hakuin Introductory to Lecture on the Records of Old Sokkō (*Sokkō-roku kaien fusetsu*)," trans. Norman Waddell, *The Eastern Buddhist*, Vol. 19, No. 2 (1986), p. 81.

Chapter 5. The Body

1. Hee-Jin Kim, *Dōgen Kigen*, p. 128.

2. Maurice Merleau-Ponty, *Phenomenology of Perception*, trans. Colin Smith (London: Routledge and Kegan Paul, 1962), p. 236.

3. Alphonso Lingis, *Foreign Bodies* (New York, London: Routledge, 1994), p. 4.

4. Derrida, *Writing and Difference*, p. 180.

5. Emmanuel Levinas, *Totality and Infinity: An Essay on Exteriority*, trans. Alphonso Lingis, Eighth Printing (Pittsburgh: Duquesne University Press, 1990), p. 164.

6. Gilles Deleuze, *The Logic of Sense*, trans. Mark Lester and ed. Constantin V. Boundas (New York: Columbia University Press, 1990), p. 5.

7. Julia Kristeva, *Powers of Horror: An Essay on Abjection*, trans. Leon S. Roudiez (New York: Columbia University Press, 1982), p. 3.

8. Francis Dojun Cook, trans. "Hotsu Mujō," in *How To Raise An Ox* (Los Angeles, CA: Center Publications, 1978), p. 120.

9. Ibid., p. 121.

10. Deleuze, *Logic*, p. 87.

11. Merleau-Ponty, *Phenomenology of Perception*, p. 82. Jean-Paul Sartre disagrees with Merleau-Ponty that one's body is for the person an object within the world (p. 303) in *Being and Nothingness*.

12. Lingis, p. 14.

13. Merleau-Ponty, *Phenomenology of Perception*, p. 82.

14. Kristeva, *Powers of Horror*, p. 25.

15. Levinas, p. 168.

16. Foucault, *The History of Sexuality*, pp. 44–45.

17. Deleuze and Guattari, *Anti-Oedipus*, pp. 8–9.

18. Ibid., p. 85.

19. Norman Waddell and Masao Abe, trans. "One Bright Pearl: Dōgen's Shōbōgenzō Ikka Myōju," *The Eastern Buddhist*, Vol. 4, No. 2 (1971). p. 113.

20. Merleau-Ponty, *Phenomenology of Perception*, p. 205.

21. Gary Brent Madison, *The Phenomenology of Merleau-Ponty* (Athens, OH: Ohio University Press, 1981), p. 30.

22. Taylor, *Nots*, p. 215.

23. Ibid., p. 216.

24. Levinas, p. 165.

25. Ronald Bogue, *Deleuze and Guattari* (London and New York: Routledge, 1989), pp. 91–92.

26. Deleuze and Guattari, *Anti-Oedipus*, p. 326.

27. Ibid., p. 42.

28. Foucault, *The History of Sexuality*, pp. 106–07.

29. Ibid., p. 139.

30. Ibid., p. 139.

31. For a discussion of this period of Japanese history and the Sōtō sect, see William M. Bodiford, *Sōtō Zen in Medieval Japan*, Studies in East Asian Buddhism 8 (Honolulu: University of Hawaii Press, 1993).

32. Norman Waddell and Masao Abe, trans. "Dōgen's Shōbōgenzō Zenki 'Total Dynamic Working and Shōji, Birth and Death'," *The Eastern Buddhist* Vol. 5, No. 1 (1972), p. 75.

33. Taylor, *Nots*, p. 239.

34. Deleuze and Guattari, *Anti-Oedipus*, p. 12.

35. Levinas, p. 165. Sartre agrees with Merleau-Ponty and Levinas that there is an ambiguous aspect to the body because "In one sense the body is what I immediately am. In another sense I am separated from it by the infinite density of the world; it is given to me by a reflux of the world toward my facticity, and the condition of this reflux of the world toward my facticity is a perpetual surpassing" (p. 326) in *Being and Nothingness*.

36. Levinas, p. 166.

37. Merleau-Ponty, *Phenomenology of Perception*, p. 167.

38. For a more complete discussion of the notion of element, see Madison, *Phenomenology*, pp. 176–77, and Remy C. Kwant, *From Phenomenology to Metaphysics: An Inquiry into the Last Period of Merleau-Ponty's Philosophical Life* (Pittsburgh, PA: Duquesne University Press, 1966), pp. 62–63.

39. Maurice Merleau-Ponty, *The Visible and the Invisible*, trans. Alphonso Lingis (Evanston, IL: Northwestern University Press, 1968), p. 136. Three articles that discuss Merleau-Ponty's notion of flesh at length are: Raymond J. Devettere, "The Human Body as Philosophical Paradigm in Whitehead and Merleau-Ponty," *Philosophy Today* 20 (1976): 317–26; Atherton C. Lowry, "The Invisible World of Merleau-Ponty," *Philosophy Today* 23 (1979): 294–303; François H. Lapointe, "The Evolution of Merleau-Ponty's Concept of the Body," *Dialogos* (1974): 139–51.

40. Merleau-Ponty, *Phenomenology of Perception*, p. 403. James F. Sheridan, Jr. notes the danger of this type of approach to the problem of consciousness in *Once More from the Middle: A Philosophical Anthropology* (Athens, OH: Ohio University Press, 1973) when he writes, "The temptation to found the con-

scious upon the pre-conscious, the deliberate upon the pre-predicative always leads us to run the risk of committing the error of making the indefinite fundamental and our formulation of the relation between indefiniteness and definiteness as the articulation of experience or as a development from the implicit to the explicit suffers from that temptation" (p. 12).

41. Merleau-Ponty, *Phenomenology of Perception*, p. 297.

42. Madison, *Phenomenology*, p. 55. Sartre agrees that "my body is a conscious structure of my consciousness" (329) in *Being and Nothingness*.

43. Lyotard, *The Inhuman*, p. 16.

44. Ibid., p. 23.

45. Waddell and Abe, trans. "Dōgen's Fukanzazengi," p. 123. For a comparison of Martin Heidegger and Dōgen on thinking, see my article entitled, "The Leap of Thinking: A Comparison of Heidegger and the Zen Master Dōgen," *Philosophy Today* 25 (1981): 55–62.

46. Taylor, *Nots*, p. 220.

47. Julia Kristeva, *Desire in Language: A Semiotic Approach to Literature and Art*, trans. Thomas Gora, Alice Jardine, and Leon S. Roudiez (New York: Columbia University Press, 1980), p. 285.

48. Taylor, *Nots*, p. 221.

49. Ibid., p. 231.

50. Merleau-Ponty, *Phenomenology of Perception*, pp. 138–39.

51. See John D. Glenn, Jr., "Merleau-Ponty and the Cogito," *Philosophy Today* 23 (1979): 310–20.

52. Norman Waddell and Masao Abe, trans. "Dōgen's Bendōwa," *The Eastern Buddhist* Vol. 4, No. 1 (1971), pp. 146–47.

53. Deleuze and Guattari, *Anti-Oedipus*, p. 11.

54. Deleuze, *Difference and Repetition*, p. 274.

55. Ibid., p. 275.

56. Merleau-Ponty, *Phenomenology of Perception*, p. 235.

57. Norman Waddell and Masao Abe, trans. "Shōbōgenzō Genjokōan," *The Eastern Buddhist* Vol. 5, No. 2 (1972), p. 134.

58. Merleau-Ponty, *Phenomenology of Perception*, p. 203.

59. Dōgen, *Buddha-nature I*, p. 103.

60. Merleau-Ponty, *Phenomenology of Perception*, p. 130.

61. Samuel B. Mallin, *Merleau-Ponty's Philosophy* (New Haven: Yale University Press, 1979), p. 113.

62. Ibid., pp. 20–21.

63. Merleau-Ponty, *The Visible and the Invisible*, p. 9.

64. Lapointe, "Evolution," p. 148.

65. Kristeva, *Powers of Horror*, p. 1.

66. Ibid., p. 4.

67. Norman Waddell and Masao Abe, trans. "The King of Samdhis

Samadhi: Dōgen's Shōbōgenzō Sammi O Zammai," *The Eastern Buddhist*, Vol. 7, No. 1 (1974), p. 121.

68. See T. P. Kasulis, *Zen Action/Zen Person*, who notes that the term "molting" is to be preferred because it is a recurrent event (p. 91). Steven Heine criticizes Kasulis' translation of *shinjin datsuraku* (molting of body-mind) because his rendering of the terms gives a false impression that it is a natural event. Heine explains, "As zazen, *datsuraku* requires determination, resolution, and utmost concentration. It is not an automatic act or an involuntary response to stimuli, but lies at the very ground of decision-making. Thus, molting probably does not capture the appropriate sense of effortlessness or spontaneity" (p. 5). Masao Abe stress that casting off of body-mind signifies the rejection of "all possible idealization, conceptualization, and objectification" (p. 23). And it demonstrates that practice and the attainment of enlightenment are a single dynamic unity in which "the horizontal dimension (practice) and the vertical dimension (attainment) are inseparably united" (p. 25) in *A Study of Dōgen: His Philosophy and Religion*. ed. Steven Heine (Albany, NY: State University of New York Press, 1992).

69. Dōgen, "Bendōwa," p. 134.

70. Dōgen, *Shōbōgenzō* I: 19.

71. See Remy C. Kwant, *The Phenomenological Philosophy of Merleau-Ponty* (Pittsburgh, PA: Duquesne University Press, 1963), pp;. 96–111.

72. Dōgen, *Buddha-nature II*, p. 98. The key to understanding Dōgen's concept of Buddha-nature lies in his notion of *gūjin* (thoroughness), according to Masanobu Takahashi, in *The Essence of Dōgen*, trans. Yuzuru Nobuoka (London: Kegan Paul International, 1983).

73. Deleuze and Guattari, *Anti-Oedipus*, p. 13.

74. Merleau-Ponty, *Phenomenology of Perception*, p. 153.

75. Ibid., p. 240.

76. Richard M. Zaner, *The Problem of Embodiment: Some Contributions to a Phenomenology of the Body* (The Hague: Martinus Nijhoff, 1964), p. 181.

77. N. A. Waddell, trans., "Being Time: Dōgen's Shōbōgenzō Uji," *The Eastern Buddhist*, Vol. 12, No. 1 (1979), p. 118.

78. Ibid., p. 121.

79. Ibid., p. 118.

80. Ibid., p. 123.

81. Kim, *Dōgen Kigen*, p. 117.

82. Merleau-Ponty, *Phenomenology of Perception*, pp. 239–40.

83. Dōgen, "Genjokōan," p. 136. See also Hee-Jin Kim, "Existence/Time as the Way of Ascesis: An Analysis of the Basic Structure of Dōgen's Thought," *The Eastern Buddhist*, Vol. 11, No. 2 (1978): 43–73.

84. Dōgen, "Genjokōan," p. 136.

85. Kim, "Existence/Time," p. 64.

86. Merleau-Ponty, *Phenomenology of Perception*, p. 354.

87. Kasulis, *Zen Action*, p. 91.

88. Dōgen, "Being Time," p. 119.

89. Ibid., p. 116.

90. Abe, "Dōgen on Buddha Nature," p. 69.

91. Kim, "Existence/Time," p. 52.

92. Taylor, *Nots*, p. 218.

93. Ibid., p. 253. Along similar lines of thought, Sartre emphasizes the not: "To have a body is to be the foundation of one's own nothingness and not to be the foundation of one's being; I am my body to the extent that I am; I am not my body to the extent that I am not when I am" (p. 326) in *Being and Nothingness*.

94. Sartre shares Taylor's emphasis on altarity, although the former tends to stress the contingent nature of the body of the other. Sartre elaborates, "The body of the Other is given to me as the pure in-itself of his being-an-in-itself among in-itselfs and one which I surpass toward my possibilities. This body of the Other is revealed therefore with two equally contingent characteristics: it is here and could be elsewhere. . . ." (p. 343) in *Being and Nothingness*.

95. Dōgen, "Being Time," pp. 120, 126.

96. Deleuze and Guattari, *Anti-Oedipus*, p. 329.

97. Richard Zaner, "The Alternating Reed: Embodiment as Problematic Unity," in *Theology and Body*, ed. John Y. Fenton (Philadelphia: Westminster Press, 1974), p. 61.

98. Ibid., p. 62.

99. Merleau-Ponty, *Phenomenology of Perception*, p. 164.

100. Lingis, p. 53.

101. Madison, *Phenomenology*, p. 70.

Chapter 6. The Self and Other

1. Immanuel Kant, *Critique of Pure Reason*, trans. Norman Kemp Smith (London: Macmillan & Company, Ltd. New York: St. Martin's Press, 1964), pp. 152–53.

2. Ibid., p. 168.

3. S. Körner. *Kant* (Baltimore: Penguin Books, 1955), p. 67.

4. Kant, p. 136.

5. G. W. F. Hegel, *The Phenomenology of Mind*, trans. J. B. Baillie. Second Edition (London: George Allen & Unwin Ltd., New York: Humanities Press, Inc., 1966), p. 86.

6. Soren Kierkegaard, *The Sickness Unto Death: A Christian Psychological Exposition for Upbuilding and Awakening*, ed. and trans. Howard V. Hong and Edna H. Hong (Princeton: Princeton University Press, 1980), p. 13.

7. Ibid., p. 19.

8. Idem, *The Concept of Anxiety: A Simple Psychologically Orienting Deliberation on the Dogmatic Issue of Hereditary Sin*, ed. and trans. Reidar Thomte (Princeton: Princeton University Press, 1980), p. 61.

9. Idem, *Sickness Unto Death*, pp. 33–34.

10. Ibid., p. 36.

11. Friedrich Nietzsche, *Human, All Too Human: A Book for Free Spirits*, trans. R. J. Hollingdale (Cambridge: Cambridge University Press, 1986), p. 112.

12. Idem, *The Portable Nietzsche*, ed. and trans. Walter Kaufmann (New York: The Viking Press, 1954), p. 580.

13. Idem, *Thus Spoke Zarathustra*, p. 43.

14. Idem, *The Will To Power*, trans. Walter Kaufmann and R. J. Hollingdale (New York: Random House, 1967), pp. 55, 399.

15. Idem, *Thus Spoke Zarathustra*, p. 41.

16. Ibid., p. 109.

17. Jean-Paul Sartre, *Being and Nothingness: An Essay in Phenomenological Ontology*, trans. Hazel E. Barnes (New York:), pp. 73–74.

18. Ibid., p. 103.

19. Heidegger, *Basic Concepts*, p. 97.

20. Idem, *Holzwege*, p. 277.

21. Derrida, *Speech and Phenomena*, p. 147. Stanley Rosen sees something ironical in Derrida's philosophy because Rosen thinks that the supresession of presence by absence is another form of presence in *Ancients and the Moderns*, p. 1.

22. Derrida, *Psyché*, p. 168.

23. Idem, *Writing and Difference*, p. 230. In an interview, Derrida clarifies his position by stating that "the self does not exist, it is not present to itself before that which engages it in this way and which is not it. There is not a constituted subject that engages itself at a given moment in writing for some reason or another. It is given by writing, by the other . . . (p. 347)" in *Points . . . Interviews 1974–1994*, ed. Elisabeth Weber and trans. Peggy Kamuf and others (Stanford: Stanford University Press, 1995), p. 347.

24. Taylor, *Erring*, p. 42.

25. Ibid., p. 43.

26. Ibid, pp. 49–50.

27. Ibid., p. 51.

28. Emmanuel Levinas, *Otherwise Than Being or Beyond Essence*, trans. Alphonso Lingis (The Hague, Boston, London: Martinus Nijhoff Publishers, 1981), p. 127.

29. Jacques Lacan, *The Seminar of Jacques Lacan, Book II: The Ego in Freud's Theory and in the Technique of Psychoanalysis 1954–1955*, trans. Sylvana Tomaselli (New York, London: W. W. Norton & Company, 1988), p. 178.

30. Idem, *Écrits*, p. 99.
31. Kristeva, *Polylogue*, pp. 78, 96.
32. Idem, *Revolution in Poetic Language*, pp. 46–47.
33. Deleuze, *Difference and Repetition*, p. 257.
34. Dōgen, *Shōbōgenzō*, I:2.
35. Ibid., I: 47.
36. Nishitani, p. 151.
37. Deleuze, *Difference and Repetition*, p. 278.
38. Nishitani, p. 152.
39. Ibid., p. 154.
40. Masao Abe, "Nishitani's Challenge to Western Philosophy and Theology," in *The Religious Philosophy of Nishitani Keiji: Encounter with Emptiness*, ed. Taitetsu Unno (Berkeley: Asian Humanities Press, 1989), pp. 20, 31.
41. Ibid., p. 156.
42. Keiji Nishitani, "The Problem of Anjin in Zen," trans. Mark L. Blum, *The Eastern Buddhist*, Vol. XXIX, No. 1 (1996), p. 6
43. Kasulis, *Zen Action*, p. 102.
44. Francis H. Cook, "Enlightenment in Dōgen's Zen," *Journal of the International Association of Buddhist Studies*, Vol. 6, No. 1 (1983), p. 20.
45. Derrida, *Writing and Difference*, p. 279.
46. Taylor, *Erring*, p. 136.
47. Ibid., p. 20.
48. Ibid., p. 160.
49. Ibid., p. 138.
50. Ibid., p. 139.
51. Lacan, *Seminar II*, p. 44.
52. Ibid., p. 178.
53. Kristeva, *Polylogue*, p. 71.
54. Idem, *Revolution in Poetic Language*, pp. 28, 182.
55. Ibid., p. 26.
56. Ibid., p. 26.
57. Emmanuel Levinas, *Time and the Other*, trans. Richard A. Cohen (Pittsburgh: Duquesne University Press, 1987), p. 53.
58. Idem, *Existence and Existents*, trans. Alphonso Lingis (Dordrecht, Boston, London: Lluwer Academic Publishers, 1988), p. 88.
59. Ibid, p. 47.
60. Idem, *Time and the Other*, p. 36.
61. Idem, *Otherwise Than Being*, p. 114.
62. Nishitani, *Religion and Nothingness*, p. 146.
63. Ibid., p. 158.
64. Ibid., p. 263.
65. Francis H. Cook, "Dōgen's View of Authentic Selfhood and its Socio-

ethical Implications," in *Dōgen Studies*, ed. William R. LaFleur (Honolulu: University of Hawaii Press, 1985), p. 137.

66. Nishitani, *Religion and Nothingness*, p. 252.
67. Lacan, *Écrits*, p. 101.
68. Dōgen, *Shōbōgenzō*, I: 124.
69. Idem, "The King of Samadhis Samadhi," p. 121.
70. Idem, "Bendōwa," p. 134.
71. Taylor, *Erring*, p. 142.
72. Dōgen, *Primer*, p. 103.
73. Taylor, *Erring*, p. 147.
74. Dōgen, *Shōbōgenzō*, IV: 126.
75. Idem, "Fukanzazengi," pp. 123, 128.
76. Idem, *Buddha-nature III*, p. 72.
77. Idem, *Shōbōgenzō*, II: 123.
78. Dōgen, *Primer*, p. 94.
79. Idem, *Shōbōgenzō*, IV: 49.
80. Levinas, *Otherwise Than Being*, p. 158.
81. Idem, *Collected Philosophical Papers*, trans. Alphonso Lingis, Phaenomenological 100 (Dordrecht, Boston, Lancaster: Martinus Nijhoff Publishers, 1987), p. 97.
82. Idem, *Otherwise Than Being*, p. 114.
83. Ibid., p. 117.
84. Idem, *Entre Nous: On Thinking-of-the-Other*, trans. Michael B. Smith and Barbara Harshau (New York: Columbia University Press, 1998), p. 6.
85. Ibid., p. 10.
86. Derrida, *Psyché*, p. 174.
87. Ibid., p. 186.
88. Ibid., p. 560.
89. Julia Kristeva, *Strangers to Ourselves*, trans. Leon S. Roudiez (New York: Columbia University Press, 1991), p. 13.
90. Ibid., p. 42.
91. Deleuze, *Difference and Repetition*, p. 281.
92. Dōgen, *Shōbōgenzō*, III: 127.
93. Ibid., p. 127.
94. Idem, *Shōbōgenzō*, I: 12, 45–46, 103, 105.
95. Idem, *Shōbōgenzō*, II: 176.
96. Nishitani, *Religion and Nothingness*, p. 149.
97. Nishitani, "Problem of Anjin," p. 12.
98. Masao Abe, "Will, Śūnyatā, and History," in *The Religious Philosophy of Nishitani Keiji: Encounter with Emptiness*, ed. Taitetsu Unno (Berkeley: Asian Humanities Press, 1989), p. 287.
99. Lacan, *Four Fundamental Concepts*, p. 214.

100. Kristeva, *Strangers to Ourselves*, p. 103.
101. Levinas, *Otherwise Than Being*, p. 150.
102. Lacan, *Four Fundamental Concepts*, p. 130.
103. Idem, "Wholly Otherwise," trans. Simon Critchley, in *Re-Reading Levinas*, ed. Robert Bernasconi and Simon Critchley (Bloomington and Indianapolis: Indiana University Press, 1991), p. 5.
104. Dōgen, *Shōbōgenzō*, IV: 125.
105. Nishitani, *Religion and Nothingness*, p. 265.
106. Kristeva, *Strangers to Ourselves*, p. 13.
107. Levinas, *Time and the Other*, p. 86.
108. Lacan, *Four Fundamental Concepts*, pp. 29–30.
109. Mark C. Taylor, *Tears* (Albany, NY: State University of New York Press, 1990), p. 95.
110. Kristeva, *Strangers to Ourselves*, pp. 8, 10.
111. Levinas, *Collected Philosophical Papers*, p. 54.
112. Derrida, *Writing and Difference*, p. 114.
113. Ibid., p. 126.
114. Lacan, *Four Fundamental Concepts*, p. 131.
115. Derrida, *Writing and Difference*, p. 124.
116. Dōgen, *Shōbōgenzō*, IV: 139.
117. Ibid., IV: 140.
118. Kristeva, *Strangers to Ourselves*, p. 182.
119. Levinas, *Totality and Infinity*, p. 207.
120. Idem, *Collected Philosophical Papers*, p. 103.
121. Derrida, *Writing and Difference*, p. 101.
122. Levinas, "Wholly Otherwise," p. 5.
123. Kristeva, *Strangers to Ourselves*, pp. 3–4.
124. Nishitani, *Religion and Nothingness*, p. 71.
125. Dōgen, *Shōbōgenzō*, II: 138.
126. Kasulis, *Zen Action*, p. 132.
127. Toshihiko Izutsu, "The Structure of Selfhood in Zen Buddhism," *Eranos-Jahrbuch*, Vol. XXXVIII, 1969 (Zürich: Rhein-Verlag, 1972), p. 115.
128. Richard Rorty, *Contingency, Irony, and Solidarity* (Cambridge: Cambridge University Press, 1989), p. 40.

Chapter 7. Time and Death

1. Kant, pp. 74–75.
2. Ibid., p. 75.
3. Ibid., p. 78.
4. Ibid., p. 79.

5. Hegel, p. 800.

6. Idem, *Philosophy of Nature*, trans. M. J. Petry (New York: Humanities Press, 1970), pp. 229–30.

7. Ibid., p. 233.

8. Idem, *Phenomenology of Mind*, p. 800.

9. Nietzsche, *Thus Spoke Zarathustra*, p. 178.

10. Idem, *The Gay Science* in *The Portable Nietzsche*, pp. 101–02.

11. Robert John Ackermann, *Nietzsche: A Frenzied Look* (Amherst: University of Massachusetts Press, 1990), p. 56.

12. Nietzsche, *Will To Power*, sec. 55.

13. Ibid., sec. 462.

14. Edmund Husserl, *The Phenomenology of Internal Time Consciousness*, ed. Martin Heidegger and trans. James S. Churchill (Bloomington and London: Indiana University Press, 1966), pp. 46–47.

15. Ibid., p. 23.

16. Ibid., pp. 84–85.

17. Idem, *Cartesian Meditations: An Introduction to Phenomenology*, trans. Dorion Cairns (The Hague: Martinus Nijhoff, 1969), pp. 75–76.

18. Merleau-Ponty, *Phenomenology of Perception*, p. 410.

19. Ibid., p. 415.

20. Ibid., p. 424.

21. Ibid., p. 427.

22. Ibid., pp. 420–21.

23. Ibid., p. 420.

24. Nāgārjuna, *A Translation of His Mūlamadhyamakakārika*, trans. Kenneth K. Inada (Tokyo: The Hokuseido Press, 1970), 19.1–4.

25. Frederick J. Streng, *Emptiness: A Study in Religious Meaning* (Nashville, NY: Abingdon Press, 1957), p. 50.

26. Nāgārjuna, 19.5.

27. Lyotard, *Inhuman*, p. 59.

28. Richardson, note 175, p. 87.

29. Martin Heidegger, *Sein und Zeit*, (Tübingen: Max Niemeyer Verlag, 1972), p. 325.

30. Ibid., p. 326.

31. Ibid., p. 329.

32. Otto Pöggeler, *Martin Heidegger's Path of Thinking*, trans. Daniel Magurshak and Sigmund Barber (Atlantic Highlands, NJ: Humanities Press International, Inc., 1990), p. 170.

33. Martin Heidegger, *On Time and Being*, trans. Joan Stambaugh (New York: Harper & Row, 1972), p. 12.

34. Ibid., p. 14.

35. Dōgen, *Shōbōgenzō*, I: 69.

36. Nishitani, *Religion and Nothingness*, p. 159.
37. Levinas, *Existence and Existents*, p. 93.
38. Idem, *Totality and Infinity*, p. 284.
39. Idem, *Time and the Other*, p. 41.
40. Idem, *Totality and Infinity*, p. 41.
41. Derrida, *Of Grammatology*, p. 65.
42. Idem, *Speech and Phenomena*, p. 156.
43. Ibid., p. 82.
44. Taylor, *Erring*, p. 114.
45. Ibid., *Erring*, p. 50; *Tears*, p. 5.
46. Derrida, *Speech and Phenomena*, p. 152.
47. Idem, *Writing and Difference*, p. 95.
48. Nishitani, *Religion and Nothingness*, p. 220.
49. Ibid., p. 221. Thomas P. Kasulis draws an interesting parallel between Nishitani's theory of history and that of western Enlightenment philosophy: "In both cases, values are inherent in the universe itself without having to be put there by either God of the human will" (p. 272). The major difference between them is that the Western view is based on reason, whereas the Buddhist position is based on intuition, a contemplative recognition of the equality in all things in "Whence and Whither: Philosophical Reflections on Nishitani's View of History," in *The Religious Philosophy of Nishitani Keiji: Encounter with Emptiness*, ed. Taitetsu Unno (Berkeley: Asian Humanities Press, 1989).
50. Deleuze, *Difference and Repetition*, p. 79.
51. Ibid., p. 81.
52. Ibid., pp. 81–82.
53. Ibid., p. 94.
54. Heidegger, *On Time and Being*, p. 3.
55. Ibid., p. 3.
56. Ibid., p. 6.
57. Steven Heine, *Existential and Ontological Dimensions of Time in Heidegger and Dōgen* (Albany, NY: State University of New York Press, 1985.
58. Deleuze, *The Logic of Sense*, pp. 162–63.
59. Ibid., p. 165.
60. Dōgen, *Shōbōgenzō*, I: 42. David Edward Shaner makes an insightful comment about *uji*: "Since time itself is time, authentication of things-as-experienced occurs at the same time there is cultivation" (p. 149) in *The Bodymind Experience in Japanese Buddhism: A Phenomenological Perspective of Kūkai and Dōgen* (Albany, NY: State University of New York Press, 1985).
61. Steven Heine, *A Dream Within a Dream: Studies in Japanese Thought* (New York: Peter Lang, 1991), p. 27.
62. Deleuze, *Difference and Repetition*, p. 202.
63. Joan Stambaugh, *Impermanence Is Buddha-nature: Dōgen's Understanding of Temporality* (Honolulu: University of Hawaii Press, 1992), p. 99.

64. Derrida, *Margins of Philosophy*, pp. 54–55.
65. Dōgen, *Shōbōgenzō*, I: 71.
66. Faure, *Chan Insights*, p. 187.
67. Deleuze, *Difference and Repetition*, p. 67.
68. Dōgen, *Shōbōgenzō*, I: 13.
69. Ibid., *Shōbōgenzō*, I: 68.
70. Heine, *Existential and Ontological Dimensions of Time*, p. 61.
71. Faure, *Chan Insights*, p. 188.
72. Ibid., p. 188.
73. Nishitani, pp. 175–76. Nishitani denies a simply cyclical Buddhist concept of time: "But in Buddhism, time is circular, because all its time systems are simultaneous; and, as a continuum of individual 'nows' wherein the systems are simultaneous, it is *rectilinear* as well. Time is at once circular and rectilinear" (p. 216).
74. Faure, *Chan Insights*, p. 189.
75. Nishitani, *Religion and Nothingness*, p. 197.
76. Ibid., p. 222.
77. Derrida, *Of Grammatology*, pp. 49–50.
78. Idem, *Speech and Phenomena*, p. 136.
79. Idem, *Margins of Philosophy*, p. 13.
80. This possibility was suggested to me by David Wood, *The Deconstruction of Time* (Atlantic Highlands, NJ: Humanities Press International, Inc., 1989), p. 274.
81. Dōgen, *Shōbōgenzō*, I: 70.
82. Derrida, *Speech and Phenomena*, p. 153.
83. Idem, *Positions*, p. 81.
84. Levinas, *Existence and Existents*, p. 76.
85. Ibid., p. 78.
86. Ibid., p. 78.
87. Lyotard, *The Inhuman*, p. 59.
88. Heidegger, *Time and Being*, p. 19.
89. Idem, *Identity and Difference*, trans. Joan Stambaugh (New York, Evanston, and London: Harper & Row, 1969), p. 37.
90. Idem, *Time and Being*, p. 21.
91. J. L. Mehta, *The Philosophy of Martin Heidegger* (Varanasi: Banaras Hindu University Press, 1967), p. 486.
92. Dōgen, *Shōbōgenzō*, I: 82.
93. Deleuze, *Difference and Repetition*, p. 220.
94. Ibid., p. 90.
95. Ibid., p. 15.
96. Derrida, *Limited*, p. 102.
97. Levinas, *Time and the Other*, pp. 46–48.
98. Ibid., p. 51.
99. Nishitani, *Religion and Nothingness*, p. 224.

100. Ibid., p. 271.

101. Jabès, *Book of Questions*, II: 129.

102. Idem, *Book of Shares*, p. 72; a similar citation is made in the *Book of Questions*: "Death lets us see the world as it was or will be" (II: 308).

103. Maurice Blanchot, *The Gaze of Orpheus and Other Literary Essays*, trans. Lydia Davis (Barrytown, N. Y: Station Hill Press, 1981), p. 43. Blanchot differentiates between death and dying. With respect to dying, Caputo explains that "Blanchot means to point a silent finger at the weakness, the fragility of the self, the inertia . . . , being cut off from the busy flow of the word, the disaster, the impotent, impoverished weakness from which any work of art, would issue (p. 85)," in *Prayers and Tears*.

104. Georges Bataille, *Death and Sensuality: A Study of Eroticism and the Taboo* (New York: Walker and Company, 1962), p. 24.

105. Deleuze, *Difference and Repetition*, p. 113.

106. Jean Baudrillard, *Symbolic Exchange and Death*, trans. Iain Hamilton Grant (London: Sage Publication, 1993), p. 159.

107. Jabès, *Book of Questions*, II: 226.

108. Derrida, *Writing and Difference*, p. 246. *Circumfession: Fifty-nine Periods and Periphrases* in *Jacques Derrida* by Geoffrey Bennington and Jacques Derrida (Chicago: University of Chicago Press, 1993), 206. Maurice Blanchot, *The Writing of the Disaster*, trans. Ann Smock (Lincoln and London: University of Nebraska Press, 1988), p. 91.

109. Taylor, *Erring*, p. 23.

110. Idem, *Hiding* (Chicago: University of Chicago Press, 1997), p. 233.

111. Jacques Derrida, *Aporias*, trans. Thomas Dutoit (Stanford: Stanford University Press, 1993), p. 74.

112. Heidegger, *Being and Time*, p. 303.

113. Ibid., p. 281.

114. Dōgen, *Shōbōgenzō*, I: 81.

115. Derrida, *Aporias*, p. 76.

116. Idem, *Of Grammatology*, p. 184.

117. Idem, *Aporias*, p. 40.

118. Heidegger, *Vorträge und Aufsätze*, p. 177.

119. Derrida, *Points*, p. 321.

120. Levinas, *Totality and Infinity*, p. 234.

121. Deleuze, *Difference and Repetition*, p. 259.

122. Dōgen, *Shōbōgenzō*, I: 21.

123. Idem, *Primer*, p. 67.

124. Idem, *Shōbōgenzō*, I: 15.

125. Idem, *Shōji*, p. 79.

126. W. R. LaFleur, "Death and Japanese Thought: The Truth and Beauty of Impermanence," in *Death and Eastern Thought: Understanding Death in*

Eastern Religions and Philosophies, ed, Frederick H. Holck (Nashville, TN: Abington Press, 1974), pp. 238–39.

127. Levinas, *Totality and Infinity*, p. 235.

128. Ibid., p. 72.

129. Derrida, *Of Grammatology*, p. 292.

130. Idem, *Writing and Difference*, p. 299.

131. Idem, *Aporias*, p. 66.

132. Dōgen, *Shōbōgenzō*, I: 82.

133. Heidegger, *Being and Time*, p. 299.

134. Dōgen, *Shōji*, p. 79.

135. Kim, *Dōgen Kigen*, p. 226.

136. Heidegger, *Being and Time*, p. 310.

137. Levinas, *Totality and Infinity*, p. 235.

138. Dōgen, *Shōbōgenzō*, I: 21.

139. Derrida, *Aporias*, p. 70.

140. Ibid., p. 77.

141. Dōgen, *Shōbōgenzō*, I: 2, 16.

142. Derrida, *Writing and Difference*, p. 203.

143. Idem, *Glas*, trans. John P. Leavey, Jr. and Richard Rand (Lincoln and London: University of Nebraska Press, 1986), p. 118.

144. Idem, *Aporias*, p. 76.

145. Dōgen, *Zenki*, p. 74.

146. Idem, *Shōji*, p. 79.

147. Derrida, *Aporias*, p. 55.

148. Idem, *Of Grammatology*, p. 69.

149. Levinas, *Time and the Other*, p. 74.

150. Dōgen, *Shōbōgenzō*, I: 81.

151. Heidegger *Vorträge und Aufsätze*, p. 177.

152. Richard Rorty, *Consequences of Pragmatism (Essays: 1972–1980)* (Minneapolis, MN: University of Minnesota Press, 1982; reprint 1994).

153. Robert Nozick, *Philosophical Explanations* (Cambridge: Harvard University Press, 1981), p. 69.

154. Kasulis, *Zen Action*, p. 82.

155. Edith Wyschogrod, *Saints and Postmodernism: Revisioning Moral Philosophy* (Chicago and London: University of Chicago Press, 1990), p. 234.

Chapter 8. Nihilism and Metaphysics

1. Nietzsche, *Will To Power*, pp. 4, 7.

2. Martin Heidegger, *Nietzsche Volume I: The Will to Power as Art*, trans. David Farrell Krell (New York: Harper & Row, 1979), p. 26.

3. Nietzsche, *Complete Works*, 13: 11.

4. Idem, *Will To Power*, p. 9.

5. Ibid., p. 14.

6. Martin Heidegger, *Nietzsche Volume III: The Will to Power as Knowledge and as Metaphysics*, trans. Joan Stambaugh, David Farrell Krell, Frank A. Capuzzi (San Francisco: Harper & Row, 1987), p. 204.

7. Nietzsche, *Will To Power*, p. 15.

8. Ibid., pp. 17–18.

9. Martin Heidegger, *Nietzsche Volume IV: Nihilism*, trans. Frank A. Capuzz and ed. David Farrell Krell (San Francisco: Harper & Row, 1982), p. 55.

10. Nietzsche, *Complete Works*, 12.9.

11. Rosen, *Question of Being*, p. 247.

12. Nietzsche, *Will To Power*, p. 12.

13. Ibid., p. 36.

14. Martin Heidegger, *Nietzsche Volume Two: The Eternal Recurrence of the Same*, trans. David Farrell Krell (San Francisco: Harper & Row, 1984), pp. 156, 172.

15. Nietzsche, *Complete Works*, 12.17.

16. Idem, *Will To Power*, pp. 25–26.

17. Ibid., pp. 26–27.

18. Jameson, p. 382.

19. Nietzsche, *Will To Power*, p. 23.

20. Hilary Putnam, *Renewing Philosophy* (Cambridge: Harvard University Press, 1992), p. 72. Putnam views deconstruction as moving from relativism to nihilism. Charles Taylor find's Foucault's position contradictory and incoherent in *Philosophical Papers 2*, p. 167.

21. Nietzsche, *Will To Power*, p. 18.

22. Gianni Vattimo, *The End of Modernity: Nihilism and Hermeneutics in Postmodern Culture*, trans. Jon R. Snyder (Baltimore: Johns Hopkins University Press, 1991), p. 40.

23. For a discussion of *Gestell*, see Heidegger's work *Vorträge und Aufsätze* (p. 27), who claims that the ordinary meaning of the word is tool or instrument (*Gerät*). *Gestell* is also called a skeleton (*Knochengeripple*).

24. Vattimo, p. 41.

25. Ibid., p. 41.

26. Taylor, *Erring*, p. 33.

27. Ibid., p. 23.

28. Ibid., p. 73.

29. Ibid., p. 114.

30. Ibid., pp. 160–61.

31. Ibid., p. 161.

32. Kristeva, *Desire in Language*, p. 78.

33. Ibid., p. 79.

34. Jean Baudrillard, *Simulacra and Simulation*, trans. Sheila Faria Glaser (Ann Arbor: University of Michigan Press, 1994), p. 161.

35. Ibid., p. 163.

36. Idem, *The Illusion of the End*, trans. Chris Turner (Stanford: Stanford University Press, 1994), p. 27.

37. Nietzsche, *Will To Power*, p. 18.

38. David J. Kalupahana, *A History of Buddhist Philosophy: Continuities and Discontinuities* (Honolulu: University of Hawaii Press, 1992), p. 53.

39. Gadjin Nagao, *The Foundational Standpoint of Mādhyamika Philosophy*, trans. John P. Keenan (Albany, NY: State University of New York Press, 1989), p. 6. C. W. Huntington, Jr., *The Emptiness of Emptiness: An Introduction to Early Indian Mādhyamika* (Honolulu: University of Hawaii Press, 1989), p. 18.

40. Nāgārjuna, *A Translation of His Mūlamadhyamakakārika*, trans. Kenneth K. Inada (Tokyo: The Hokuseido Press, 1970), 7.30.

41. Candrakīrti, *Mūlamdhyamakakārikas de Nāgārjuna avec la Prasannapadā Commentaire de Candrakīrti*, ed. La Vallée Poussin, Bibliotheca Buddhica IV (Osnabrück: Biblio Verlag, 1970), p. 329. 10–18.

42. Huntington, p. 132.

43. Nishitani, *Religion and Nothingness*, p. 47.

44. Ibid., p. 234.

45. Ibid., p. 47.

46. Ibid., p. 52.

47. Nishitani Keiji, *The Self-Overcoming of Nihilism*, trans. Graham Parkes (Albany, NY: State University of New York Press, 1990), p. 175.

48. Ibid., p. 177.

49. Idem, *Religion and Nothingness*, p. 54.

50. Ibid., p. 97. For a discussion of Nishitani's response to the challenge of nihilism, see Stephen H. Phillips, "Nishitani's Buddhist Response to 'Nihilism,'" *Journal of the American Academy of Religion*, Vol. LV, No. 1 (1987): 75–104.

51. Nishitani, *Religion and Nothingness*, p. 97.

52. Ibid., p. 105.

53. Abe, "Will, Śūnyatā, and History," p. 302.

54. Nishitani, *Religion and Nothingness*, p. 123.

55. Fred Dallmayr, *The Other Heidegger* (Ithaca and London: Cornell University Press, 1993), p. 211.

56. Nishitani, *Religion and Nothingness*, p. 129.

57. Heidegger, *Basic Concepts*, pp. 46, 61.

58. Ibid., p. 45.

59. Nietzsche, *Human, All Too Human*, p. 23.

60. Heidegger, *Nietzsche*, IV: 4. John D. Caputo reviews Heidegger's critique of metaphysics (pp. 47–96), and he claims that Heidegger shares with mystics a

rejection of metaphysics (p. 218) in *The Mystical Element in Heidegger's Thought* (Athens, Ohio: Ohio University Press, 1978). In another work, Caputo proposes "a rewriting of Heidegger from Derrida's standpoint, which results in a rewriting of Derrida from Heidegger's standpoint, a kind of double repetition, a productive double cross . . . (p. 155)" in *Radical Hermeneutics: Repetition, Deconstruction, and the Hermeneutic Project* (Bloomington: Indiana University Press, 1987).

61. Rosen, *Question of Being*, p. 217.

62. Heidegger, *Time and Being*, p. 24.

63. Idem, "Letter on Humanism," p. 202.

64. Ibid., p. 242.

65. Rosen, *Question of Being*, p. 97. Within the context of discussing presence and absence, Rosen draws a distinction between existence and being by asserting that the former is narrower in meaning than being: "Whatever exists, is, but not everything that is, exists" (p. 115)."

66. Richardson observes that *Überwindung* "suggests that, since the drag towards dis-arrangement continues in beings, it must be mastered continually, not conquered once and for all and then put aside, as *Überwindung* might suggest," note 10, p. 519.

67. Heidegger, *Vorträge und Aufsätze*, p. 72.

68. Joseph J. Kockelmans, *On the Truth of Being: Reflections on Heidegger's Later Philosophy* (Bloomington: Indiana University Press, 1984), p. 276.

69. Heidegger, *Vortäge und Aufsätze*, p. 83.

70. Idem, *Holzwege*, p. 91f.

71. Dominique Janicaud and Jean-François Mattéi, *Heidegger from Metaphysics to Thought*, trans. Michael Gendre (Albany, NY: State University of New York Press, 1995), p. 29.

72. Idem, *Der Satz vom Grund*, p. 90f.

73. Ibid., p. 93.

74. Sallis, *Echoes*, p. 34. Caputo claims that the thrust of Heidegger's philosophy results in essential thinking that reproduces the complete logic of traditional essentialism on a higher level by maintaining "the distinction between the pure inside of human beings—where there is truth, clearing, Being, language, world—and the impure, contaminated outside—where there are only organic functions and enviornment, brute stupidity, mute silence, in a word (or two), '(mere) life'" (p. 125) in *Demythologizing Heidegger*.

75. Sallis, *Echoes.*, p. 28.

76. Schrag, *Resources of Rationality*, p. 31.

77. Gasché, *Inventions*, p. 59.

78. Jürgen Habermas, *Postmetaphysical Thinking: Philosophical Essays*, trans. William Mark Hohengarten (Cambridge, London: MIT Press, 1992), p. 34.

79. Ibid., p. 34. For a defense of Derrida from the criticism of Habermas, see Christopher Norris, *What's Wrong with Postmodernism.*

80. Rosen, *Ancients and Moderns*, p. 167.

81. Gilles Deleuze and Félix Guattari, *A Thousand Plateaus: Capitalism and Schizophrenia*, trans. Brian Massumi (Minneapolis: University of Minnesota Press, 1988), p. 16.

82. Michel Foucault, "Nietzsche, Genealogy, History," in *Language, Counter-Memory, Practice: Selected Essays and Interviews*, ed. Donald F. Bouchard and trans. Donald F. Bouchard and Sherry Simon (Ithaca: Cornell University Press, 1977), p. 153. The postmodern writer Jean Baudrillard confesses: "For a time I believed in Foucauldian genealogy, but the order of simulation is antinomical to genealogy," (p. 73) in *Forget Foucault* (New York: Semiotext(le), 1987).

83. Ibid., pp. 152–57.

84. Jacques Derrida, *Dissemination*, trans. Barbara Johnson (Chicago: University of Chicago Press, 1981), 6.

85. Derrida, *Margins of Philosophy*, pp. 258, 261.

86. Rorty, *Philosophy and the Mirror of Nature*, p. 12.

87. Derrida, *Of Grammatology*, p. 12.

88. Rorty, *Philosophical Papers 2*, p. 13.

89. Paul Ricoeur, *The Rule of Metaphor: Multi-disciplinary Studies of the Creation of Meaning in Language*, trans. Robert Czerny (Toronto: University of Toronto Press, 1977; reprint 1991), p. 284.

90. Derrida, *Positions*, p. 17.

91. Idem, *Of Grammatology*, p. 91.

92. Faure, *Chan Insights*, pp. 223–24.

93. Some recent investigations into the historical development of the notion of Buddha-nature are the following works: Paul J. Griffiths, *On Being Buddha: The Classical Doctrine of Buddhahood* (Albany, NY: State University of New York Press, 1994); Sallie B. King, *Buddha-nature* (Albany, NY: State University of New York Press, 1991); S. K. Hookam, *The Buddha Within: Tathagatagarbha Doctrine According to the Shentong Interpretation of the Ratnagotravibhaga* (Albany, NY: State University of New York Press, 1991).

94. Dōgen, *Shōbōgenzō*, IV: 121.

95. Ibid., IV: 121.

96. Ibid., IV: 123.

97. Derrida, *Speech and Phenomena*, p. 134.

98. Ibid., p. 130.

99. Deleuze, *Difference and Repetition*, p. 234.

100. Dōgen, *Shōbōgenzō*, IV: 133–34.

101. Derrida, *Margins of Philosophy*, p. 4.

102. Deleuze, *Difference and Repetition*, p. 182.

103. Ibid., p. 56.

104. Dōgen, "Buddha-nature I," p. 100.

105. Kim, *Dōgen Kigen*, p. 164.

106. Hardt, p. 5.

107. Derrida, *Of Grammatology*, p. 62.

108. Ibid., p. 47.

109. Deleuze, *Difference and Repetition*, p. 262.

110. Heidegger, *Being and Time*, p. 22.

111. Masao Abe, *A Study of Dōgen: His Philosophy and Religion*, ed. Steven Heine (Albany, NY: State University of New York Press, 1992), p. 56.

112. Dōgen, "Buddha-nature III," p. 75.

113. Abe, "Dōgen on Buddha Nature," p. 51.

114. Deleuze, *Difference and Repetition*, p. 266.

115. Heidegger, *Being and Time*, p. 170.

116. Dōgen, *Shōbōgenzō*, I: 81–82.

117. Dōgen, "Buddha-nature I," pp. 101–02.

118. Abe, "Dōgen on Buddha Nature," p. 45.

119. Derrida, *Speech and Phenomena*, p. 153.

120. Kim, *Dōgen Kigen*, p. 169.

121. Derrida, *Speech and Phenomena*, p. 134.

122. Dōgen, "Buddha-nature I," p. 94.

123. Deleuze, *Difference and Repetition*, p. 235.

124. Dōgen, *Shōbōgenzō*, IV: 125.

125. Derrida, *Speech and Phenomena*, p. 141; *Positions*, p. 27.

126. Christopher Johnson, *System and Writing in the Philosophy of Jacques Derrida* (Cambridge: Cambridge University Press, 1993), pp. 109–110.

127. Derrida, *Writing and Difference*, p. 292.

128. McGowan, p. 106. From a more critical perspective, McGowan thinks that the notion of play in Derrida's philosophy is ultimately tragic. Play also registers a protest against a certain order without being able to effect the transformation of that order. McGowan critically observes that "Only in annihilation could we experience the liberation that play appears to promise. To desire play is to desire the impossible (p. 119)."

129. Daisetz T. Suzuki, *Sengai: The Zen Master* (Greenwich, CT: New York Graphic Society Ltd., 1971), p. 7.

130. Roger Caillois, *Man, Play and Games*, trans. Meyer Barash (New York: The Free Press, 1961), p. 6.

131. John Huizinga, *Homo Ludens: A Study of the Play Element in Culture* (London: Routledge & Kegan Paul Ltd., 1950; reprint Boston: Beacon Press, 1955), p. 6.

132. Dōgen, "Buddha-nature I," p. 103.

133. Deleuze, *Difference and Repetition*, p. 129.

134. Dōgen, *Shōbōgenzō*, IV: 128.

135. Heine, *A Dream Within a Dream*, p. 117.

136. Dōgen, *Shōbōgenzō*, IV: 128.

137. Derrida, *Limited Inc.*, p. 102. Leonard Lawlor claims that Derrida's notion of difference is a dialectical notion of temporality (p. 107) in *Imagination and Chance: The Difference between the Thought of Ricoeur and Derrida* (Albany, NY: State University of New York Press, 1992), but this interpretation is contradicted by Derrida's explicit criticism of the Hegelian notion of *Aufhebung*.

138. Rorty, *Philosophical Papers 2*, p. 121.

139. A similar observation is made about nihilism in the twentieth century by Karen L. Carr: "Nihilism, the bane of the nineteenth century, is fast becoming the banality of the late twentieth century" (p. 140) in *The Banalization of Nihilism: Twentieth-century Responses to Meaninglessness* (Albany, NY: State University of New York Press, 1992).

140. Rorty, *Philosophical Papers 2*, p. 101.

141. Derrida, *Speech and Phenomena*, p. 156; *Of Grammatology*, p. 167.

142. Deleuze, *Difference and Repetition*, p. 29.

143. Dōgen, *Shōbōgenzō*, III: 129; In the same vain, Dōgen writes, "The words of Shakyamuni are beyond rational comprehension" (III: 157).

144. Derrida, *Speech and Phenomena*, p. 134.

145. Rosen *Question of Being*, p. 178.

Chapter 9. Signing Out

1. Derrida, *Margins of Philosophy*, p. 271.

2. Idem, *Of Grammatology*, p. 35; *Dissemination*, p. 137.

3. Idem, *Of Grammatology*, p. 37.

4. Idem, *Dissemination*, p. 143.

5. Ibid., p. 105.

6. Baudrillard, *Simulacra and Simulation*, p. 3.

7. Ibid., p. 6.

8. Idem, *Forget Foucault* (New York: Semiotext(e), 1987), p. 82.

9. Idem, *Simulacra and Simulation*, p. 82.

10. Ibid., p. 30.

11. Idem, *Fatal Strategies*, trans. Philip Beitchman and W. G. J. Niesluchowski (New York: Semiotext(e), 1990), p. 108.

12. Idem, *Simulacra and Simulation*, p. 43; *Symbolic Exchange*, p. 2.

13. Deleuze, *Difference and Repetition*, pp. 127–28.

14. Idem, *Logic of Sense*, p. 262.

15. Ibid., p. 301.

16. Ibid., pp. 264–65.

17. Ibid., p. 257.

18. Derrida, *Dissemination*, p. 139.

19. Philip B. Yampolsky, trans. *The Platform Sutra of the Sixth Patriarch* (New York and London: Columbia University Press, 1967), p. 130.

20. Ibid., pp. 130–33.

21. Gilles Deleuze, *Foucault*, trans. Seán Hand (Minneapolis: University of Minnesota Press, 1988), p. 109.

22. Derrida, *Limited Inc*, p. 56.

23. Ibid., p. 105.

24. Lyotard and Thébaud, p. 86.

25. Derrida, *Of Grammatology*, p. 259.

26. Idem, *Margins of Philosophy*, p. 213.

27. Dōgen, *Shōbōgenzō*, I: 48.

28. Ibid., I: 51.

29. Newman Robert Glass, *Working Emptiness: Toward a Third Reading of Emptiness in Buddhism and Postmodern Thought* (Atlanta, GA: Scholars Press, 1995), p. 2.

30. Ibid., p. 3.

31. Ibid., p. 6.

32. See Streng, pp. 59, 78. J. W. de Jong (pp. 59–67) criticizes Streng for not relying more on Buddhist commentaries on the philosophy of Nāgārjuna, which is reflected in the inadequacy of his analysis of the relationship between reason, intuition, and wisdom in *Buddhist Studies*, ed. Gregory Schopen (Berkeley: Asian Humanities Press, 1979). In contrast to scholars like Glass, Richard Robinson responds (p. 43) that emptiness "has no status as an entity nor as the property of an existent or an inexistent" in *Early Mādhyamika in India and China* (Madison, Milwaukee, and London: University of Wisconsin Press, 1967). And T. R. V. Murti states that emptiness is not a mere nothing (p. 234) in *The Central Philosophy of Buddhism: A Study of the Mādhyamika System*, Second Edition (London: George Allen and Unwin Ltd., 1968). Other important contributions to the discussion of emptiness are located in the following works: André Bareau, "L'Absolu dans le Bouddhisme," *Entretiens* 1955, Publications de l'Institut français d'indologie N 4 (Pondichéry: Institut français d'indologie, 1956): 37–43; André Bareau, Walther Schubring, und Christoph von Fürer-Haimendorf, *Die Religionen Indiens III: Buddhismus, Jinismus, Primitivvölker* (Stuttgart: W. Kohlhammer Verlag, 1964), pp. 153–62; Th. Stcherbatsky, *The Conception of Buddhist Nirvāna* (Leningrad: Academy of Sciences, 1927; reprint, The Hague: Mouton & Company, 1965); Edward Conze, *Buddhist Thought in India* (London: George Allen & Unwin Ltd., 1962). A good historical survey of the problem is provided by Guy Richard Welbon, *The Buddhist Nirvāna and Its Western Interpreters* (Chicago and London: University of Chicago Press, 1968).

33. Glass, p. 71.

34. Ibid., p. 71.

35. Ibid., p. 98.

36. Shaner, p. 139.

37. Glass, p. 96.

38. Loy, p. 21.

39. Ibid., p. 12.

40. Ibid., p. 249.

41. Ibid., p. 185.

42. David A. Dilworth, *Philosophy in World Perspective: A Comparative Hermeneutic of the Major Theories* (New Haven and London: Yale University Press, 1989), pp. 28–29.

43. Ibid., pp. 29–30.

44. Ibid., p. 31.

45. Ibid., p. 28.

46. Ibid., p. 147.

47. Deleuze, *Nietzsche and Philosophy*, p. 172.

48. Hardt, *Gilles Deleuze*, p. 51.

49. Deleuze, *Nietzsche and Philosophy*, p. 70.

50. Taylor, *Erring*, p. 183.

Bibliography

Abe, Masao. "Dōgen on the Buddha Nature." *The Eastern Buddhist.* Vol. 10, No. 1 (1971): 28–71.

———. "Nishitani's Challenge to Western Philosophy and Theology." In *The Religious Philosophy of Nishitani Keiji: Encounter with Emptiness.* Edited by Taitetsu Unno. Berkeley: Asian Humanities Press, 1989, pp. 13–45.

———. *A Study of Dōgen: His Philosophy and Religion.* Edited by Steven Heine. Albany, NY: State University of New York Press, 1992.

———. "Will, Sunyata, and History." In *The Religious Philosophy of Nishitani Keiji: Encounter with Emptiness.* Edited by Taitetsu Unno. Berkeley: Asian Humanities Press, 1989, pp. 279–304.

Ackerman, Robert John. *Nietzsche: A Frenzied Look.* Amherst: University of Massachusetts Press, 1990.

Austin, J. C. *How to do Things with Words.* Cambridge: Harvard University Press, 1967.

Bareau, Andre. "L' Absolu dans le Bouddhisme." *Entretiens.* 1955. Publications de L' Institut Francais d' indologie, N 4. Pondichery: Institut Francais d' indologie, 1956, pp. 37–43.

Bareau, Andre, Schubring, Walther, and Furer-Haimendorf, Christoph von. *Die Religionen Indiens III: Buddhismus, Jinismus, Primitivvolken.* Stuttgart: W. Kohlhammer Verlag, 1964.

Bataille, Georges. *The Absence of Myth.* Translated by Michael Richardson. London and New York: Verso, 1994.

———. *The Accursed Share.* Volume II. Translated by Robert Hurley. New York: Zone Books, 1991.

———. *The Accursed Share.* Volume III. Translated by Robert Hurley. New York: Zone Books, 1991.

———. *Death and Sensuality: A Study of Eroticism and the Taboo.* New York: Walker and Company, 1962.

281

——. *The Tears of Eros*. Translated by Peter Connor. San Francisco: City Light Books, 1990.

——. *Visions of Excess Selected Writings, 1927–1939*. Translated by Allan Stoekl. Theory and History of Literature, Vol. 14. Minneapolis: University of Minnesota Press, 1991.

Baudrillard, Jean. *The Illusion of the End*. Translated by Chris Turner. Stanford: Stanford University Press, 1994.

——. *Fatal Strategies*. Translated by Phillip Beitchman and W. G. J. Niesluchowski. New York: Semiotext(e), 1990.

——. *Forget Foucault*. New York: Semiotext(e), 1987.

——. *Seduction*. Translated by Brian Singer. New York: St. Martin's Press, 1990.

——. *Simulacra and Simulation*. Translated by Sheila Faria Glaser. Ann Arbor: University of Michigan Press, 1994.

——. *Symbolic Exchange and Death*. Translated by Iain Hamilton Grant. London: Sage Publications, 1993.

Beardsworth, Richard. "On the Critical 'Post': Lyotard's Agitated Judgement." In *Judging Lyotard*. Edited by Andrew Benjamin. London and New York: Routledge, 1992, pp. 43–80.

Bielefeldt, Carl. *Dōgen's Manuals of Zen Meditation*. Berkeley: University of California Press, 1988.

Blanchot, Maurice. *The Gaze of Orpheus and Other Literary Essays*. Translated by Lydia Davis. Barrytown, NY: Station Hill Press, 1981.

——. *The Space of Literature*. Translated by Ann Smock. Lincoln and London: University of Nebraska Press, 1982.

——. *The Step Not Beyond*. Translated by Lycette Nelson. Albany, NY: State University of New York Press, 1992.

——. *The Writing of the Disaster*. Translated by Ann Smock. Lincoln and London: University of Nebraska Press, 1988.

Blyth, R. H. *Zen and Zen Classics, Volume III*. Tokyo: The Hokuseido Press, 1970: reprint 1972.

Bodiford, William M. *Sōtō Zen in Medieval Japan*. Studies is East Asian Buddhism 8. Honolulu: University of Hawaii Press, 1993.

Bogue, Ronald. *Deleuze and Guattari*. London and New York: Routledge, 1989.

Buswell, Robert E., Jr. "Ch'an Hermeneutics: A Korean View." In *Buddhist Hermeneutics*. Edited by Donald S. Lopez, Jr. Honolulu: University of Hawaii Press, 1988, pp. 231–256.

——. *The Formation of Ch'an Ideology in China and Korea: The Vajnasamādhi-Sūtra, A Buddhist Aprocryphon*. Princeton: Princeton University Press, 1989.

Butler, Judith P. *Subjects of Desire: Hegelian Reflections in Twentieth-Century France*. New York: Columbia University Press, 1987.

Caillois, Roger. *Man, Play, and Games.* Translated by Meger Barash. New York: The Free Press, 1961.

Candrakīrti. *Lucid Exposition of the Middle Way: The Essential Chapters from the Prasannapadā of Candrakīrti.* Translated by Mervyn Sprung. London and Henley: Routledge and Kegan Paul, 1979.

———. *Mūlamadhyama kakārikas de Nāgārjuna avec la Prasannapadā Commentaire de Candrakīrti.* Edited by La Vallee Poussin. Bibliotheca Buddhica IV. Osnabruek: Biblio Verlag, 1970.

Caputo, John D. *Demythologizing Heidegger.* Bloomington: Indiana University Press, 1993.

———. *The Mystical Element in Heidegger's Thought.* Athens, OH: Ohio University Press, 1978.

———. *The Prayers and Tears of Jacques Derrida: Religion without Religion.* Bloomington: Indiana University Press, 1997.

———. *Radical Hermeneutics: Repetition, Deconstruction, and the Hermeneutic Project.* Bloomington: Indiana University Press, 1987.

Carr, Karen L. *The Banalization of Nihilism: Twentieth-Century Responses to Meaninglessness.* Albany, NY: State University of New York Press, 1992.

Chang, Chung-Yuan. "Ch'an Master Niu-t'ou Fa-Yung and His Teachings on Prajñāparamita." *Chinese Culture.* Vol. VII, No. 1 (1967): 32–50.

———. "Ch'an Teachings of Fa-Yen School." *Chinese Culture.* Vol. VI, No. 3 (1965): 55–80.

———. "Ch'an Teachings of Kuei-Yang School." *Chinese Culture.* Vol. VII, No. 4 (1966): 12–53.

———. "Ch'an Teachings of Yun-men School." *Chinese Culture.* Vol. V, No. 4 (1964): 14–35.

———, Translator. *Original Teachings of Ch'an Buddhism: Selected From the Transmission of the Lamp.* New York: Pantheon Books, 1969.

Chappell, David C. "The Teachings of the Fourth Ch'an Patriarch Tao-hsin (580–651)." In *Early Ch'an in China and Tibet.* Edited by Whaler Lai and Lewis R. Lancaster. Berkeley: Asian Humanities Press, 1983, pp. 89–129.

Cheng, Chung-Ying. "On Zen (Ch'an) Language and Zen Paradoxes." *Journal of Chinese Philosophy.* Vol. I, No. 1 (1973): 77–102

Cheng, Hseuh-Li. *Exploring Zen.* New York: Peter Lang, 1991.

Cleary, Thomas and J.C. Cleary, Translators. *The Blue Cliff Record.* Boulder, CO: Prajna Press, 1978.

Conze, Edward. *Buddhist Thought in India.* London: George Allen and Unwin Ltd., 1962.

Cook, Francis Dojun, Translator. *How to Raise an Ox.* Los Angeles: Center Publications, 1978.

————. "Dōgen's View of Authentic Selfhood and its Socio-ethical Implications." in *Dōgen Studies*. Edited by William R. LaFleur. Honolulu: University of Hawaii Press, 1985, pp. 131–149.

————. "Enlightenment in Dōgen's Zen." *Journal of the International Association of Buddhist Studies*. Vol. VI, No. 1 (1983): 7–30.

Coward, Harold. "A Hindu Response to Derrida's View of Negative Theology." In *Derrida and Negative Theology*. Edited by Harold Coward and Toby Foshay. Albany, NY: State University of New York Press, 1992, pp. 199–226.

Coward, Harold and Foshay, Toby, Editors. *Derrida and Negative Theology*. Albany, NY: State University of New York Press, 1992.

Dallmayr, Fred. *The Other Heidegger.* Ithaca and London: Cornell University Press, 1993.

Davidson, Arnold I. "Archaeology, Genealogy, Ethics." in *Foucault: A Critical Reader.* Edited by David Couzens Hoy. Oxford: Basil Blackwell, 1986: reprint 1992.

Deleuze, Gilles and Parnet, Claire. *Dialogues*. Translated by Hugh Tomlinson and Barbara Habberjam. New York: Columbia University Press, 1987.

————. *Difference and Repetition*. Translated by Paul Patton. New York: Columbia University Press, 1994.

————. *Foucualt*. Translated by Sean Hand. Minneapolis: University of Minnesota Press, 1988.

————. *The Logic of Sense*. Translated by Mark Lester. Edited by Constantin V. Boundas. New York: Columbia University Press, 1990.

————. *Nietzsche and Philosophy*. Translated by Hugh Tomlinson. New York: Columbia University Press, 1983.

Deleuze, Gilles and Guattari, Félix. *Anti-Oedipus: Capitalism and Schizophrenia*. Translated by Robert Hurley, Mark Seem, and Helen R. Lane. Minneapolis: University of Minnesota Press, 1983.

————. *A Thousand Plateaus: Capitalism and Schizophrenia*. Translated by Brian Massumi. Minneapolis: University of Minnesota Press, 1988.

————. *What is Philosophy?* Translated by Hugh Tomlinson and Graham Bouchell. New York: Columbia University Press, 1994.

Deleuze, Gilles and Parnet, Claire. *Dialogues*. Translated by Hugh Tomlinson and Barbara Habberjam. New York: Columbia University Press, 1987.

Derrida, Jacques. *Aporias*. Translated by Thomas Dutoit. Stanford: Stanford University Press, 1993.

————. *Cinders*. Translated by Ned Lukacker. Lincoln and London: University of Nebraska Press, 1991.

————. *Circumfession: Fifty-nine Periods and Periphrases* In *Jacques Derrida* By Geoffrey Bennington and Jacques Derrida. Chicago: University of Chicago Press, 1993.

——— . *Dissemination.* Translated by Barbara Johnson. Chicago: University of Chicago Press, 1981.

——— . *D'un ton apocalyptique: Adopté naguère en philosophie.* Paris: Éditions Galilée, 1983.

——— . *The Gift of Death.* Translated by David Wills. Chicago and London: University of Chicago Press, 1992.

——— . *Given Time I: Counterfeit Money.* Translated by Peggy Kamuf. Chicago and London: University of Chicago Press, 1992.

——— . *Glas.* Translated by John P. Leavey, Jr. and Richard Rand. Lincoln and London: University of Nebraska Press, 1986.

——— . "Introduction: Desistance." in *Typography: Mimesis, Philosophy, Politics.* by Philippe Lacoue-Labarthe. Edited by Christopher Fynsk. Cambridge and London: Harvard University Press, 1989, pp 1–42.

——— . *Limited Incorporated.* Translated by Samuel Welsen. Evanston, Illinois: Northwestern University Press, 1988.

——— . "Living On: Borderlines." Translated by James Hulbert. In *Deconstruction and Criticism.* Edited by Harold Bloom et.al. New York: Seabury Press, 1975, pp. 75–176.

——— . *Margins of Philosophy.* Translated by Alan Bass. Chicago: University of Chicago Press, 1986.

——— . *Memoirs of the Blind: The Self-Portrait and Other Ruins.* Translated by Pascale-Anne Brault and Michael Naas. Chicago and London: University of Chicago Press, 1993.

——— . *Of Grammatology.* Translated by Gayatri Chakravarty Spivak. Baltimore and London: Johns Hopkins University Press, 1976.

——— . *Of Spirit: Heidegger and the Question.* Translated by Geoffrey Bennington and Rachel Bowlby. Chicago and London: University of Chicago Press, 1989.

——— . *On the Name.* Edited by Thomas Dutoit. Stanford: Stanford University Press, 1995.

——— . *Points . . . Interviews 1974–1994.* Edited by Elisabeth Weber and Translated by Peggy Kamuf and others. Stanford: Stanford University Press, 1995.

——— . *Positions.* Translated by Alan Bass. Chicago: University of Chicago Press, 1981.

——— . *The Post Card: From Socrates to Freud and Beyond.* Translated by Alan Bass. Chicago and London: University of Chicago Press, 1987.

——— . "Post-Scriptum: Aporias, Ways and Voices." Translated by John P. Leavey, Jr. In *Derrida and Negative Theology.* Edited by Harold Coward and Toby Foshay. Albany, NY: State University of New York Press, 1992, pp. 283–323

——— . "The Principle of Reason: The University in the Eyes of Its Pupils." *Diacritics* Vol. 13 (1983): 3–20.

——. *Psyché: Inventions de l'autre*. Paris: Galilée.

——. "The Question of Style." In *The New Nietzsche: Contemporary Styles of Interpretation*. Edited by David B. Allison. Cambridge: MIT Press, 1985, pp. 176–189.

——. *Signéponge/Signsponge*. Translated by Richard Rand. New York: Columbia University Press, 1984.

——. *Speech and Phenomena And Other Essays on Husserl's Theory of Signs*. Translated by David B. Allison. Evanston: Northwestern University Press, 1973.

——. *Spurs*. Translated by Barbara Harlow. Chicago and London: University of Chicago Press, 1979.

——. *Writing and Difference*. Translated by Alan Bass. Chicago: University of Chicago Press, 1978.

Devettere, Raymond J. "The Human Body as Philosophical Paradigm in Whitehead and Merleau-Ponty." *Philosophy Today 20* (1976): 317–326.

Dilworth, David A. *Philosophy in World Perspective: A Comparative Hermeneutic of the Major Theories*. New Haven and London: Yale University Press, 1989.

Dōgen. "Being Time: Dōgen's Shōbōgenzō Uji." Translated by N. A. Waddell. *The Eastern Buddhist*. Vol. XII, No. 1 (1979): 114–29.

——. "Dōgen's Bendōwa." Translated by Norman A. Waddell and Masao Abe. *The Eastern Buddhist*. Vo. IV, No. 1 (1971): 124–33.

——. "Dōgen's Fukanzazengi and Shōbōgenzō Zazengi." Translated by Norman Waddell and Masao Abe. *The Eastern Buddhist*. Vol. VI, No. 2 (1973): 115–28.

——. "Dōgen's Shōbōgenzō Zenki 'Total Dynamic Working and Shoji, Birth and Death.'" Translated by Norman Waddell and Masao Abe. *The Eastern Buddhist*. Vol. V, No. 1 (1972): 70–80.

——. "The King of Samdhis Samadhi: Dōgen's Shōbōgenzō Sammi O Zammai." Translated by Norman Waddell and Masao Abe. *The Eastern Buddhist*. Vol. VII, No. 1 (1974): 118–23.

——. "One Bright Pearl: Dōgen's Shōbōgenzō Ikka Myōju." Translated by Normal Waddell and Masao Abe. *The Eastern Buddhist*. Vol. IV, No. 2 (1971): 108–18.

——. *A Primer of Sōtō Zen: A Translation of Dōgen's Shōbōgenzō Zuimonki*. Translated by Reiho Masunaga. Honolulu: East-West Center Press, 1971.

——. *Shōbōgenzō: The Eye and Treasury of the True Law*. Four Volumes. Translated by Kosen Nishiyama and John Stevens. Tokyo: Nakayama Shobo, 1975–1977, 1983, 1986.

——. "Shōbōgenzō Buddha-Nature I." Translated by Norman Waddell and Masao Abe. *The Eastern Buddhist*. Vol. VIII, No. 2 (1975): 94–112

——. "Shōbōgenzō Buddha-Nature II." Translated by Norman Waddell and Masao Abe. *The Eastern Buddhist*. Vol. IX, No. 1 (1976): 87–105.

——. "Shōbōgenzō Buddha-Nature III." Translated by Norman Waddell and Masao Abe. *The Eastern Buddhist*. Vol. IX, No. 2 (1976): 71–87.

——. "Shōbōgenzō Genjokōan." Translated by Norman Waddell and Masao Abe. *The Eastern Buddhist*. Vol. V, No. 1 (1972): 129–40.

Dumoulin, Heinrich. *A History of Zen Buddhism*. Translated by Paul Peachy. New York: Pantheon Books, 1963.

——. *Zen Buddhism: A History. Volume I: India and China*. Translated by James W. Heisig and Paul Knitter. New York: Macmillan Publishing Company, 1988.

——. *Zen Buddhism: A History. Volume II: Japan*. Translated by James W. Heisig and Paul Knitter. New York: Macmillan Publishing Company, 1990.

——. *Zen Enlightenment: Origins and Meaning*. Translated by John C. Maraldo. New York: Weatherhill, 1979.

Dupré, Louis. *Passage to Modernity: An Essay in the Hermeneutics of Nature and Culture*. New Haven and London: Yale University Press, 1993.

Faure, Bernard. *Chan Insights and Oversights: An Epistemological Critique of the Chan Tradition*. Princeton: Princeton University Press, 1993.

——. "Fair and Unfair Language Games in Chan/ Zen." In *Mysticism and Language*. Edited by Steven T. Katz. New York and Oxford: Oxford University Press, 1992, pp. 158–180.

——. *The Rhetoric of Immediacy: A Cultural Critique of Chan/ Zen Buddhism*. Princeton: Princeton University Press, 1991.

Foucault, Michel. *The Archaeology of Knowledge and the Discourse on Language*. Translated by A. M. Sheridan Smith. New York: Pantheon Books, 1972.

——. *The Birth of the Clinic: An Archaeology of Medical Perception*. Translated by A.M. Sheridan Smith. New York: Vintage/ Random House, 1975.

——. *The Care of the Self: The History of Sexuality*. Vol. III. Translated by Robert Hurley. New York: Vintage Books, 1988.

——. *Discipline and Punish: The Birth of the Prison*. Translated by Alan Sheridan. New York: Pantheon Books, 1977.

——. *Madness and Civilization: A History of Insanity in the Age of Reason*. New York: Random House, 1973.

——. *The History of Sexuality. Volume I: An Introduction*. Translated by Robert Hurley. New York: Vintage/ Random House, 1980.

——. "Nietzsche, Freud, Marx." In *Nietzsche, Proceedings of the Seventh International Philosophical Colloquium of the Cahiens de Royamont*, 4–8 July 1964. Paris: Éditions de Minuit, 1967, pp. 183–200.

———. "Nietzsche, Genealogy, History." In *Language, Counter-Memory, Practice: Selected Essays and Interviews*. Edited by Donald F. Bouchard. Translated by Donald F. Bouchard and Sherry Simon. Ithaca, NY: Cornell University Press, 1977, pp. 137–164.

———. *The Order of Things: An Archaeology of the Human Sciences*. Translated by Alan Sheridan Smith. New York: Random House, 1973.

———. *Power/Knowledge: Selected Interviews and Other Writings 1972–1977*. Edited by Colin Gordon. Translated by Colin Gordon, Leo Marshall, John Mepham, Kate Soper. New York: Pantheon Books, 1980.

———. "The Subject of Power." In *Michel Foucault: Beyond Structuralism and Hermeneutics*. Edited by Hurbert L. Dreyfus and Paul Rabinow. Second Edition. Chicago: University of Chicago Press, 1983.

———. *The Use of Pleasure: Volume II of The History of Sexuality*. Translated by Robert Hurley. New York: Vintage Books, 1986.

Gasché, Rodolphe. *Inventions of Difference: On Jacques Derrida*. Cambridge: Harvard University Press, 1994.

———. *The Tain of the Mirror: Derrida and the Philosophy of Reflection*. Cambridge and London: Harvard University Press, 1986.

Gilkey, Langdon. "Nishitani Keiji's *Religion and Nothingness*." In *The Religious Philosophy of Nishitani Keiji:Encounter with Emptiness*. Edited by Taitetsu Unno. Berkeley: Asian Humanities Press, 1989, pp. 49–69.

Glass, Newman Robert. *Working Emptiness: Toward a Third Reading of Emptiness in Buddhism and Post Modern Thought*. Atlanta, Georgia: Scholars Press, 1995.

Glenn, John D., Jr. "Merleau-Ponty and the Cogito." *Philosophy Today*. Vol. 23 (1979): 310–320.

Graham, A. C. *Unreason Within Reason: Essays on the Outskirts of Rationality*. La Salle, Illinois: Open Court, 1992.

Griffiths, Paul J. *On Being Buddha: The Classical Doctrine of Buddhahood*. Albany, NY: State University of New York Press, 1994.

Habermas, Jurgen. *Der Philosophische Diskurs der Moderne*. Zwölf Vorlesungen Frankfurt am Main: Suhrkamp Verlag, 1985.

———. *Postmetaphysical Thinking: Philosophical Essays*. Translated by William Mark Hohengarten. Cambridge and London: MIT Press, 1992.

———. *The Theory of Communicative Action, Volume I: Reason and the Rationalization of Society*. Translated by Thomas McCarthy. Boston: Beacon Press, 1984.

———. *The Theory of Communicative Action, Volume II: Life World and System: A Critique of Functional Reason*. Translated by Thomas McCarthy. Boston: Beacon Press, 1987.

Hakuin. "Talks by Hakuin Introductory To Lectures on the Records of Old Sōkō (Sokkō-roko Kaieu Fusetso)." Translated by Norman Waddell. *The*

Eastern Buddhist. Vol. XVIII, No. 2. New Series (1985)): 79–82; Vol. XIX, No. 2 (Fall 1986): 75–84; Vol. XX, No. 2 (Fall 1987): 89–99; Vol. XXI, No. 2 (Spring 1988): 101–111; Vol. XXII, No. 2 (Fall 1989): 85–104; Vol. XXIII, No. 1 (Spring 1990): 114–137.

———. *The Zen Master Hakuin: Selected Writings.* Translated by Philip B. Yampolsky. New York and London: Columbia University Press, 1971.

Hardt, Michael. *Gilles Deleuze: An Apprenticeship in Philosophy.* Minneapolis and London: University of Minnesota Press, 1993.

Hegel, G. W .F. *The Phenomenology of Mind.* Translated by J. B. Baillie. Second Edition. London: George Allen and Unwin Ltd., New York: Humanities Press, Inc., 1966.

———. *Philosophy of Nature.* Translated by M. J. Petry. New York: Humanities Press, 1970.

Heidegger, Martin. *Basic Concepts.* Translated by Gary E. Aylesworth. Bloomington and Indianapolis: Indiana University Press, 1993.

———. *Being and Time.* Translated by John Macquarrie and Edward Robinson. New York: Harper and Row, 1962.

———. *Discourse on Thinking.* Translated by John M. Anderson and E. Hans Freund. New York: Harper and Row, 1966.

———. *Holzwege.* Frankfurt: Vittorio Klostermann, 1963.

———. *Identity and Difference.* Translated by Joan Stambaugh. New York, Evanston, and London: Harper and Row, 1969.

———. *An Introduction to Metaphysics.* Translated by Ralph Manheim. New Haven and London: Yale University Press, 1964.

———. *Kant and the Problem of Metaphysics.* Translated by James S. Churchill. Bloomington: Indiana University Press, 1965

———. "Letter on Humanism." In *Basic Writings.* Edited by David Farrell Krell. Translated by Frank A. Capuzzi. New York: Harper and Row, 1977, pp. 193–242.

———. *On the Way to Language.* Translated by Peter D. Hertz. New York: Harper and Row, 1971.

———. *On Time and Being.* Translated by Joan Stambaugh. New York: Harper and Row, 1982

———. *Nietzsche Volume I: The Will to Power as Art.* Translated by David Farrel Krell. New York: Harper and Row, 1979.

———. *Nietzsche Volume II: The Eternal Recurrence of the Same.* Translated by David Farrel Krell. San Francisco: Harper and Row, 1984.

———. *Nietzsche Volume III: The WIll to Power as Knowledge and as Metaphysics.* Translated by Joan Stambaugh, David Farrel Krell, Frank A. Capuzzi. San Francisco: Harper and Row, 1987.

———. *Nietzsche Volume IV: Nihilism.* Edited by David Farrel Krell. Translated by Frank A. Capuzzi. San Francisco: Harper and Row, 1982.

———. "The Question Concerning Technology." In *Basic Writings*. Edited by David Farrel Krell. New York: Harper and Row, 1977, pp. 189–242

———. *Der Satz vom Grund*. Fourth Edition. Pfullingen: Verlag Günther Neske, 1971.

———. *Sein and Zeit*. Tübingen: Max Niemeyer Verlag, 1972.

———. *Vorträge and Aufsätze*. Tübingen: Verlag Günther Neske Pfullingen, 1959.

———. *What is Called Thinking?* Translated by Fred W. Wiecke and J. Glenn Gray. New York: Harper and Row, 1968.

———. *Zur Sache des Denkens*. Tübingen: Max Niemeyer Verlag, 1969.

Heine, Steven. *Dōgen and the Kōan Tradition: A Tale of Two Shobogenzo Texts*. Albany, NY: State University of New York Press, 1994

———. "Dōgen Casts off 'What': An Analysis of *Shinjin Datsuraku*." *Journal of the International Association of Buddhist Studies*. Vol. IX, No. 1 (1986): 53–70.

———. *A Dream Within a Dream: Studies in Japanese Thought*. New York: Peter Lang, 1991.

———. *Existential and Ontological Dimensions of Time in Heidegger and Dōgen*. Albany, NY: State University of New York Press, 1985.

Hershock, Peter D. *Liberating Intimacy: Enlightenment and Social Virtuosity in Ch'an Buddhism*. Albany, NY: State University of New York Press, 1996.

Hookham, S. K. *The Buddha Within: Tathagatagarbha Doctrine According to the Shentong Interpretation of the Ratnagotravibhaga*. Albany, NY: State University of New York Press, 1991.

Hu, Shih. "Ch'an (Zen) Buddhism in China: Its History and Method." *Philosophy East and West*. Vol. 3, No. 1 (1953): 3–24.

Huizinga, John. *Homo Ludens: A Study of the Play Element in Culture*. London: Routledge and Kegan Paul Ltd., 1950: Reprint Boston: Beacon Press, 1955.

Huntington, Jr., C. W. *The Emptiness of Emptiness: An Introduction to Early Indian Mādhyamika*. Honolulu: University of Hawaii Press, 1989.

Husserl, Edmund. *Cartesian Meditations: An Introduction to Phenomenology*. Translated by Dorion Cairns. The Hague: Martinus Nijhoff, 1969.

———. *Ideas: General Introduction to Pure Phenomenology*. Translated by W. R. Boyce Gibson. London: George Allen and Unwin Ltd. and New York: The Macmillan Company, 1958.

———. *The Phenomenology of Internal Time Consciousness*. Edited by Martin Heidegger. Translated by James S. Churchill. Bloomington and London: Indiana University Press, 1966.

Huyssen, Andreas. "Mapping the Postmodern." *New German Critique*. Vo. XXXIII (1984): 5–52.

———. "The Search for Tradition: Avant Garde and Postmodernism in the 1970s." *New German Critique.* Vol. XXII (1981): 23–40.

Izutsu, Toshihiko. "The Structure of Selfhood in Zen Buddhism." *Eranos-Jahrbuch.* Vol. XXXVIII, 1969. Zurich: Rheina-Verlag, 1972, pp. 95–150.

Jabès, Edmond. *The Book of Dialogue.* Translated by Rosmarie Waldrop. Middletown, Connecticut: Wesleyan University Press, 1987.

———. *The Book of Questions Volume I.* (Three volumes in one). Translated by Rosmarie Waldrop. Middletown, CT: Wesleyan University Press, 1991.

———. *The Book of Questions Volume II.* (Four volumes in one). Translated by Rosmarie Waldrop. Middletown, CT: Wesleyan University Press, 1991.

———. *The Book of Shares.* Translated by Rosmarie Waldrop. Chicago and London: University of Chicago Press, 1989.

Janicaud, Dominique and Mattéi, Jean-François. *Heidegger From Metaphysics to Thought.* Translated by Michael Gendre. Albany, NY: State University of New York Press, 1995.

Jay, Martin. "In the Empire of the Gaze: Foucault and the Denigration of Vision in Twentieth-Century French Thought." In *Foucault: A Critical Reader.* Edited by David Couzens Hoy. Oxford: Basil Blackwell, 1986; Reprint 1992, pp. 175–204.

Johnson, Christopher. *System and Writing in the Philosophy of Jacques Derrida.* Cambridge: Cambridge University Press, 1993.

Jong, J. W., De. *Buddhist Studies.* Edited by Gregory Schopen. Berkeley: Asian Humanities Press, 1979.

Kalupahana, David J. *A History of Buddhist Philosophy: Continuities and Discontinuities.* Honolulu: University of Hawaii Press, 1992.

Kant, Immanuel. *Critique of Pure Reason.* Translated by Norman Kemp Smith. London: Macmillan and Company, Ltd. and New York: St Martin's Press, 1964.

Kasulis,Thomas P. "The Origins of the Question: Four Traditional Japanese Philosophies of Language." In *Culture and Modernity: East-West Philosophic Perspectives.* Edited by Eliot Deutsch. Honolulu: University of Hawaii Press, 1991, pp. 213–222.

———. "Whence and Whither: Philosophical Reflections on Nishitani's View of History." In *The Religious Philosophy of Nishitani Keiji: Encounter with Emptiness.* Edited by Taitetsu Unno. Berkeley: Asian Humanities Press, 1989.

———. *Zen Action/ Zen Person.* Honolulu: University Press of Hawaii, 1981.

Kaufman, Walter. Editor and Translator. *Basic Writings of Nietzsche.* New York: Modern Library, 1968.

———. Editor and Translator. *The Portable Nietzsche.* New York: The Viking Press, 1954.

Keane, John. "The Modern Democratic Revolution: Reflections on Lyotard's *The Postmodern Condition*." In *Judging Lyotard*. Edited by Andrew Benjamin. London and New York: Routledge, 1992, pp. 81–98.

Kierkegaard, Søren. *The Concept of Anxiety: A Simple Psychologically Orientating Deliberation on the Dogmatic Issue of Heredity Sin*. Edited and Translated by Reidar Thomte. Princeton: Princeton University Press, 1980.

———. *The Sickness Unto Death: A Christian Psychological Exposition for Upbuilding and Awakening*. Edited and Translated by Howard V. Hong and Edna H. Hong. Princeton: Princeton University Press, 1980.

Kim, Hee-Jin. *Dōgen Kigen, Mystical Realist*. Tucson, AZ: The University of Arizona Press, 1975.

———. "Existence/ Time as the Way of Ascesis: An Analysis of the Basic Structure of Dōgen's Thought." *The Eastern Buddhist*. Vol. XI, No. 2 (1978): 43–73.

———. "The Reason of Words and Letters: Dōgen and Kōan Language." In *Dōgen Studies*. Edited by William R. LaFleur. Honolulu: University of Hawaii Press, 1985, pp. 54–82.

King, Sallie B. *Buddha Nature*. Albany, NY: State University of New York Press, 1991.

Kockelmans, Joseph J. *On the Truth of Being: Reflections on Heidegger's Later Philosophy*. Bloomington: Indiana University Press, 1984.

Körner, S. *Kant*. Baltimore: Penguin Books, 1955.

Kristeva, Julia. *Desire in Language: A Semiotic Approach to Literature. and Art*. Translated by Thomas Gora, Alice Jardine, and Leon S. Roudiez. New York: Columbia University Press, 1980.

———. "From Symbol to Sign." Translated by Seán Hand. In *The Kristeva Reader*. Edited by Toril Moi. New York: Columbia University Press, 1986, pp. 62–73.

———. *The Kristeva Reader*. Edited by Toril Moi. New York: Columbia University Press, 1986.

———. *Language-The Unknown: An Initiation into Linguistics*. Translated by Anne M. Menke. New York: Columbia University Press, 1989.

———. *Polylogue*. Paris: Éditions du Seuil, 1977.

———. "Postmodernism?" *Bucknell Review*. Vol. XXV, No. 1 (1980): 136–41.

———. *Powers of Horror: An Essay on Abjection*. Translated by Leon S. Roudiez. New York: Columbia University Press, 1982.

———. *Revolution in Poetic Language*. Translated by Margaret Waller. New York: Columbia University Press, 1984.

———. "Semiotics: A Critical Science and/ or a Critique of Science." In *The Kristeva Reader*. Edited by Toril Moi. New York: Columbia University Press, 1986.

————. *Strangers to Ourselves*. Translated by Leon S. Roudiez. New York: Columbia University Press, 1991.

————. *Tales of Love*. Translated by Leon S. Roudiez. New York: Columbia University Press, 1987.

Kwant, Remy C. *From Phenomenology to Metaphysics: An Inquiry into the Last Period of Merleau-Ponty's Philosophical Life*. Pittsburgh, PA: Duquesne University Press, 1966.

————. *The Phenomenological Philosophy of Merleau-Ponty*. Pittsburgh, PA: Duquesne University Press, 1963.

Lacan, Jacques. *Ecrits: A Selection*. Translated by Alan Sheridan. New York and London: W. W. Norton and Company, 1977.

————. *The Four Fundamental Concepts of Psycho-Analysis*. Edited by Jacques-Alain Miller. Translated by Alan Sheridan. New York and London: W. W. Norton and Company, 1981.

————. *The Seminar of Jacques Lacan Book I: Freud's Papers on Technique 1953–1954*. Edited by Jacques-Alain Miller. Translated by John Forrester. New York and London: W. W. Norton and Company, 1988.

————. *The Seminar of Jacques Lacan Book II: The Ego in Freud's Theory and in the Technique of Psychoanalysis 1954–1955*. Edited by Jacques-Alain Miller. Translated by Sylvana Tomaselli. New York and London: W. W. Norton and Company, 1988.

————. *Speech and Language in Psychoanalysis*. Translated by Anthony Wilden. Baltimore and London: Johns Hopkins University Press, 1991.

LaFleur, W.R. "Death and Japanese Thought: The Truth and Beauty of Impermanence." In *Death and Eastern Thought: Understanding Death in Eastern Religions and Philosophies*. Edited by Frederick H. Holck. Nashville, TN: Abingdon Press, 1974, pp. 226–256.

Lapointe, Francois H. "The Evolution of Merleau-Ponty's Concept of the Body." *Dialogos* (1974): 139–151.

Law, Bimala Churn. *A History of Pali Literature*. Vol. I. Varanasi: Bhantiya, 1933.

Lawlor, Leonard. *Imagination and Chance: The Difference Between the Thought of Ricoeur and Derrida*. Albany, NY: State University of New York Press, 1992.

Lee, Jonathan Scott. *Jacques Lacan*. Amherst: University of Massachusetts Press, 1990.

Levinas, Emmanuel. *Collected Philosophical Papers*. Translated by Alphonso Lingis. Phaenomenologica 100. Dordrecht/ Boston/ Lancaster: Martinus Nijhoff Publishers, 1987.

————. *Entre Nous: On Thinking-of-the-Other*. Translated by Michael B. Smith and Barbara Harshau. New York: Columbia University Press, 1998.

————. *Existence and Existents*. Translated by Alphonso Lingis. Dordrecht, Boston, London: Kluwer Academic Publishers, 1988.

————. *Otherwise Than Being or Beyond Essence*. Translated by Alphonso Lingis. The Hague, Boston, London: Martinus Nijhoff Publishers, 1981.

————. "The Trace of the Other." Translated by Alphonso Lingis. In *Deconstruction in Context: Literature and Philosophy*. Edited by Mark C. Taylor. Chicago and London: University of Chicago Press, 1986, pp. 345–359.

————. *Time and the Other*. Translated by Richard A. Cohen. Pittsburgh: Duquesne University Press, 1987.

————. *Totality and Infinity: An Essay on Exteriority*. Translated by Alphonso Lingis. Eighth Printing. Pittsburgh: Duquesne University Press, 1990.

————. "Wholly Otherwise." Translated by Simon Critchley. In *Re-Reading Levinas*. Edited by Robert Bernascori and Simon Critchley. Bloomington and Indianapolis: Indiana University Press, 1991, pp. 3–10.

Lievens, Bavo, Translator. "The Recorded Sayings of Ma-tsu." Translated by Julian F. Pas. *Studies in Asian Thought and Religion Volume VI*. Lewiston and Queenston: Edwin Mellen Press, 1987.

Lingis, Alphonso. *Foreign Bodies*. New York and London: Routledge, 1994.

Lowry, Atherton C. "The Invisible World of Merleau-Ponty." *Philosophy Today*. Vol. XXIII (1979): 294–303.

Loy, David. *Nonduality: A Study in Comparative Philosophy*. New Haven and London: Yale University Press, 1988.

Lyotard, Jean-François. *The Difference: Phrases in Dispute*. Translated by Georges van den Abbeele. Theory and History of Literature Vol. 46. Minneapolis: University of Minnesota Press, 1988.

————. *The Inhuman: Reflections on Time*. Translated by Geoffry Bennington and Rachel Bowlby. Cambridge: Polity Press, 1991.

————. *Instructions Paierres*. Paris: Gallilee, 1977.

————. *Peregrinations: Law, Form, Event*. New York: Columbia University Press, 1988.

————. *The Postmodern Condition: A Report on Knowledge*. Translated by Geoffry Bennington and Brian Massumi. Theory and History of Literature Vol. 10. Minneapolis: University of Minnesota Press, 1984.

————. *Toward the Postmodern*. Edited by Robert Harvey and Mark S. Roberts. New Jersey, London: Humanities Press, 1993.

————. "Response a la Question: Qu'est-ce que la postmoderne?" *Critique* Number 419 (1982): 357–367.

Lyotard, Jean-François and Thébaud, Jean-Loup. *Just Gaming*. Translated by Wlad Godzick. Theory and History of Literature Vol. 20. Minneapolis: University of Minnesota Press, 1985.

Madison, Gary Brent. *The Phenomenology of Merleau-Ponty*. Athens, OH: Ohio University Press, 1981.

Magliola, Robert R. *Derrida on the Mend*. West Lafayette, IN: Purdue University Press, 1984.

Mallin, Samuel B. *Merleau-Ponty's Philosophy*. New Haven: Yale University Press, 1979.

Marion, Jean-Luc. *God Without Being*. Translated by Thomas A. Carlson. Chicago and London: University of Chicago Press, 1995.

Masunaga, Reiho, Translator. *A Primer of Sōtō Zen: A Translation of Dōgen's Shōbōgenzō Zuimanki*. Honolulu: East-West Center Press, 1971.

May, Todd. "Difference and Unity in Gilles Deleuze." In *Gilles Deleuze and the Theater of Philosophy*. Edited by Constantin V. Boundas and Dorothea Olkowski. New York and London: Routledge, 1994, pp. 33–50.

McGowan, John. *Postmodernism and Its Critics*. Ithaca and London: Cornell University Press, 1991.

McRae, John R. *The Northern School and the Formation of Early Ch'an Buddhism*. Kuroda Institute Studies in East Asia Buddhism 3. Honolulu: University of Hawaii Press, 1986.

Mehta, J. L. *The Philosophy of Martin Heidegger*. Varanasi: Banaras Hindu University Press, 1967.

Merleau-Ponty, Maurice, *Phenomenology of Perception*. Translated by Colin Smith. London: Routledge and Kegan Paul, 1962.

———. *The Visible and the Invisible*. Translated by Alphonso Lingis. Evanston, Illinois: Northwestern University Press, 1968.

Murti, T. R. V. *The Central Philosophy of Buddhism: A Study of the Mādhyamika System*. Second Edition. London: George Allen and Unwin Ltd., 1968.

Nagao, Gadjin M. *The Foundational Standpoint of Mādhyamika Philosophy*. Translated by John P. Keenan. Albany, NY: State University of New York Press, 1989.

———. *Mādhyamika and Yogacara: A Study of Mahāyāna Philosophies*. Edited and translated by L. S. Kawamura. Albany, NY: State University of New York Press, 1991

Nāgārjuna. *The Philosophy of the Middle Way: Mūlamadhyamakakārikā*. Translated by David J. Kalupahana. Albany, NY: State University of New York Press, 1986.

———. *A Translation of His Mūlamadhyamakakārikā*. Translated by Kenneth K. Inada. Tokyo: The Hokuseido Press, 1970.

Nagatomo, Shigenori. "An Analysis of Dōgen's 'Casting Off Body and Mind.'" *International Philosophical Quarterly*. Vol. XXVII, No. 3 (1987): 227–242.

Neville Robert C. *Reconstruction of Thinking*. Albany, NY: State University of New York Press, 1981.

Nietzsche, Friedrich. *Complete Works. 12 Volumes*. Edited by Oscar Levy. New York: Russell and Russell, 1964.

———. *Human, All too Human: A Book for Free Spirits*. Translated by R. J. Hollingdale. Cambridge: Cambridge University Press, 1986.

296 *Bibliography*

———. *Thus Spoke Zarathustra: A Book for Everyone and No One.* Translated by R. J. Hollingdale. London: Penguin Books, 1969.

———. *The Use and Abuse of History.* Translated by Adrian Collins. New York: Macmillan Publishing Company, 1957.

———. *The Will to Power.* Translated by Walter Kaufmann and R. J. Hollingdale. New York: Random House, 1967.

Nishitani, Keiji. "The Problem of Anjin in Zen." Translated by Mark L. Blum. In *The Eastern Buddhist.* Vol. XXIX, No. 1 (1996): 3–32.

———. *Religion and Nothingness.* Translated by Jan van Bragt. Berkeley: University of California Press, 1982.

———. *The Self-Overcoming of Nihilism.* Translated by Graham Parkes. Albany, NY: State University of New York Press, 1990.

Norris, Christopher. *What's Wrong with Postmodernism: Critical Theory and the Ends of Philosophy.* Baltimore, MD: Johns Hopkins University Press, 1990.

Nozick, Robert. *The Examined Life: Philosophical Meditations.* New York: Simon and Schuster, 1989.

———. *The Nature of Rationality.* Princeton: Princeton University Press, 1993.

———. *Philosophical Explanations.* Cambridge: Harvard University Press, 1981.

Oliver, Kelly. *Reading Kristeva: Unraveling the Double-bind.* Bloomington and Indianapolis: Indiana University Press, 1993.

Olson, Carl. "Beatings, Shouts and Finger Raising: A Study of Zen Languages." *Journal of Religious Studies.* Vol. X, No. 2 (1983): 45–50.

———. "The Existential Doubt of Tillich and the Great Doubt of Hakuin." *Buddhist-Christian Studies* Vol. IX (1989): 5–12.

———. "The Human Body as a Boundary Symbol: A Comparison of Merleau-Ponty and Dōgen." *Philosophy East and West.* Vol. XXXVI, No. 2 (April 1986): 107–120

———. "The Leap of Thinking: A Comparison of Heidegger and the Zen Master Dōgen." *Philosophy Today.* Vol. 25 (1981): 55–62.

Phillips, Stephen H. "Nishitani's Buddhist Response to 'Nihilism.'" *Journal of the American Academy of Religion.* Vol. LV, No. 1 (1987): 75–104.

Pilgrim, Richard B. "Intervals (Ma) in Space and Time: Foundations For a Religio-Aesthetic Paradigm in Japan." *History of Religions.* Vol. XXV, No. 3 (1986): 255–277.

Pöggeler, Otto. *Martin Heidegger's Path of Thinking.* Translated by Daniel Magurshak and Sigmund Barber. Atlantic Highlands, NJ: Humanities Press International, Inc., 1990.

Powell, William F. *The Record of Tung-Shan.* Honolulu: University of Hawaii Press, 1986.

Putnam, Hilary. *Renewing Philosophy.* Cambridge and London: Harvard University Press, 1993.

Putney, David. " Some Problems in Interpretation: The Early and Late Writings of Dōgen." *Philosophy East and West.* Vol. 46, No. 4 (October 1996): 497–531.

Rapaport, Hermann. *Heidegger and Derrida: Reflections on Time and Language.* Lincoln and London: University of Nebraska Press, 1991.

Richardson, S. J. William J. *Heidegger: Through Phenomenology to Thought.* The Hague: Martinus Nijhoff, 1963.

Ricoeur, Paul. *Oneself as Another.* Translated by Kathleen Blamey. Chicago and London: University of Chicago Press, 1992.

————. *The Rule of Metaphor: Multi-disciplinary Studies of the Creation of Meaning in Language.* Translated by Robert Czerny. Toronto: University of Toronto Press, 1977: Reprint 1991.

Robinson, Richard. *Early Mādhyamika in India and China.* Madison, Milwaukee, and London: University of Wisconsin Press, 1967.

Rorty, Richard. *Consequences of Pragmatism (Essays: 1972–1980).* Minneapolis, Minnesota: University of Minnesota Press, 1882; reprint 1994.

————. *Contingency, Irony, and Solidarity.* Cambridge: Cambridge University Press, 1989.

————. *Essays on Heidegger and Others, Philosophical Papers.* Vol. II. Cambridge: Cambridge University Press, 1991.

————. "Foucault and Epistemology." In *Foucault: A Critical Reader.* Edited by David Couzens Hoy. London: Basil Blackwell, 1986, pp. 41–49.

————. *Objectivity, Relativism, and Truth, Philosophical Papers.* Vol. I. Cambridge. Cambridge University Press, 1991.

————. *Philosophy and the Mirror of Nature.* Princeton: Princeton University Press, 1979.

Rosen, Stanley. *The Ancients and the Moderns: Rethinking Modernity.* New Haven and London: Yale University Press, 1989.

————. *The Question of Being: A Reversal of Heidegger.* New Haven and London: Yale University Press, 1993.

Sallis, John. *Echoes After Heidegger.* Bloomington and Indianapolis: Indiana University Press, 1990.

Sartre, Jean-Paul. *Being and Nothingness: An Essay in Phenomenological Ontology.* Translated by Hazel E. Barnes. New York: Philosophical Library, 1956.

————. *Genet: Action and Martyr.* Translated by Bernard Frechtman. New York: George Braziller, 1963.

Sasaki, Ruth Fuller, Translator. *The Recorded Sayings of Ch'an Master Lin-chi Hui-chao of Chen Prefecture.* Kyoto: The Institute for Zen Studies, 1975.

Schrag, Calvin O. *The Resources of Rationality: A Response to the Postmodern Challenge.* Bloomington and Indianapolis: Indiana University Press, 1992.

Schürmann, Reiner. "Heidegger and Meister Eckhart on Releasement." *Research in Phenomenology*, III (1973): 95–119.

———. *Heidegger on Being and Acting: From Principles to Anarchy*. Translated by Christine-Marie Gros. Bloomington: Indiana University Press, 1987.

Shaner, David Edward. *The Bodymind Experience in Japanese Buddhism: A Phenomenological Perspective of Kukai and Dōgen*. Albany, NY: State University of New York Press, 1985.

Sheridan, James F., Jr. *Once More From the Middle: A Philosophical Anthropology*. Athens, OH: Ohio University Press, 1973.

Shibayama, Zenkei. *Comments on the Mumonkan*. Translated by Sumiko Kudo. New York: Harper and Row, 1974.

Stambaugh, Joan. *Impermanence Is Buddha-nature: Dōgen's Understanding of Temporality*. Honolulu: University of Hawaii Press, 1992.

Stcherbatsky, Th. *The Conception of Buddhist Nirvana*. Leningrad: Academy of Sciences, 1927; Reprint, The Hague: Mouton and Company, 1965.

Steffrey, John. "Transmetaphysical Thinking in Heidegger and Zen Buddhism." *Philosophy East and West*. Vol. XXVII, No. 3 (1977): 323–325.

Streng, Frederick J. *Emptiness: A Study in Religious Meaning*. Nashville and New York: Abingdon Press, 1957.

Suzuki, D. T. *Essays in Zen Buddhism First Series*. London: Rider and Company, 1949; Reprint New York: Grove Press, Inc., 1961.

———. *Essays in Zen Buddhism Second Series*. Edited by Christmas Humphreys. New York: Samuel Weiser, Inc,. 1953, 1971.

———. *Essays in Zen Buddhism Third Series*. Edited by Christmas Humphreys. New York: Samuel Weiser, Inc., 1953, 1971.

———. *Sengai: The Zen Master*. Greenwich, CT: New York Graphic Society Ltd., 1971.

———. *Studies in the Lankavatara Sutra*. London: Routledge and Kegan Paul Ltd., 1930; Reprint 1968.

Takahashi, Masanobu. *The Essence of Dōgen*. Translated by Yuzuru Nobuoka. London: Kegan Paul International, 1983.

Taylor, Charles. *Philosophical Arguments*. Cambridge: Harvard University Press, 1995.

———. *Philosophy and the Human Sciences*: Philosophical Papers II. Cambridge: Cambridge University Press, 1985; Reprint 1993.

———. *Sources of the Self: The Making of the Modern Identity*. Cambridge: Harvard University Press, 1989

Taylor, Mark C. *Deconstructing Theology*. New York: Crossroad Publishing Company and Scholars Press, 1982.

———. *Disfiguring: Art, Architecture, Religion*. Chicago and London: University of Chicago Press, 1992.

———. *Hiding*. Chicago: University of Chicago Press, 1997.

———. "No Not No." In *Derrida and Negative Theology*. Edited by Harold Coward and Toby Foshay. Albany, NY: State University of New York Press, 1992, pp. 167–198.

———. *Nots*. Chicago and London: University of Chicago Press, 1993.

Unno, Taitetsu. *The Religious Philosophy of Nishitani Keiji*. Berkeley: Asian Humanities Press, 1989.

Vattimo, Gianni. *The End of Modernity: Nihilism and Hermeneutics in Post-modern Culture*. Translated by Jon R. Snyder. Baltimore: Johns Hopkins University Press, 1991.

Vycinas, Vincent. *Earth and Gods: An Introduction to the Philosophy of Martin Heidegger*. The Hague: Martinus Nijhoff, 1961.

Welbon, Guy Richard. *The Buddhist Nirvana and Its Western Interpreters*. Chicago and London: University of Chicago Press, 1968.

Wood, David. *The Deconstruction of Time*. Atlantic Highlands, NJ: Humanities Press International, Inc., 1989.

———. *Philosophy at the Limit: Problems of Modern European Thought*. Scranton: Unwin Hyman, 1990.

Wright, Dale S. "The Discourse of Awakening: Rhetorical Practice in Classical Ch'an Buddhism." *Journal of the American Academy of Religion*. Vol. LXI, No. 1 (1993): 23–40.

———. "Doctrine and the Concept of Truth in Dōgen's *Shōbōgenzō*." *Journal of the American Academy of Religion*. Vol. LIV, No. 2 (1986): 257–277.

———. "Rethinking Transcendence: The Role of Language in Zen Experience." *Philosophy East and West*. Vol. 42, No. 1 (1992): 113–138.

Wyschograd, Edith. *Saints and Postmodernism: Revisioning Moral Philosophy*. Chicago and London: University of Chicago Press, 1990.

Yampolsky, Philip. "New Japanese Studies in Early Ch'an History." In *Early Ch'an in China and Tibet*. Edited by Whalen Lai and Lewis R. Lancaster. Berkeley Buddhist Studies Series. Berkeley: Asian Humanities Press, 1983, pp. 1–11.

———. Translator. *The Platform Sutra of the Sixth Patriarch*. New York and London: Columbia University Press, 1967.

Zaner, Richard. "The Alternating Reed: Embodiment as Problematic." In *Theology and Body*. Edited by John Y. Fenton. Philadelphia: Westminster Press, 1974.

———. *The Problem of Embodiment: Some Contributions to a Phenomenology of the Body*. The Hague: Martinus Nijhoff, 1964.

Index

301

Printed in the United States
1219900004BA/13-33